# When the
# Tempest Gathers

*Give us Men!*
*Men who, when the tempest gathers,*
*Grasp the standard of their fathers*
*In the thickest fight; [...]*

Josiah Gilbert Holland

# When the Tempest Gathers

From Mogadishu to the Fight Against ISIS, a Marine Special Operations Commander at War

Andrew Milburn

Pen & Sword
**MILITARY**

First published in Great Britain in 2020 by
Pen & Sword Military
An imprint of
Pen & Sword Books Ltd
Yorkshire – Philadelphia

ISBN 978 1 52675 055 6

A CIP catalogue record for this book is
available from the British Library.

Typeset by Mac Style
Printed and bound in the UK by TJ International Ltd,
Padstow, Cornwall.

Pen & Sword Books Limited incorporates the imprints of Atlas,
Archaeology, Aviation, Discovery, Family History, Fiction, History,
Maritime, Military, Military Classics, Politics, Select, Transport,
True Crime, Air World, Frontline Publishing, Leo Cooper, Remember
When, Seaforth Publishing, The Praetorian Press, Wharncliffe
Local History, Wharncliffe Transport, Wharncliffe True Crime
and White Owl.

For a complete list of Pen & Sword titles please contact

PEN & SWORD BOOKS LIMITED
47 Church Street, Barnsley, South Yorkshire, S70 2AS, England
E-mail: enquiries@pen-and-sword.co.uk
Website: www.pen-and-sword.co.uk

Or

PEN AND SWORD BOOKS
1950 Lawrence Rd, Havertown, PA 19083, USA
E-mail: Uspen-and-sword@casematepublishers.com
Website: www.penandswordbooks.com

# Contents

# Acknowledgements

I wouldn't be in a position to make acknowledgments at all, were it not for the help of several people:

Worth Parker took great pains to go through several drafts with me, giving up his weekends to do so. Worth is one of those rare individuals who excels in every one of his life's roles: Marine officer, endurance runner, writer, husband and father, and combines formidable talent with unstinting generosity. I am proud to count him as a friend.

I first met Anne Garrels, long-time NPR correspondent famous for her clear-eyed reporting of the Iraq war, in Fallujah some 15 years ago where, true to form, she was very much at the sharp end. Anne offered to read an early (very rough) draft of the manuscript, and returned it to me with invaluable feedback. Her enthusiastic support meant more to me at the time than she probably realizes.

Bing West has been a mentor since the early days of the Marine advisor mission described in this book. From the time that I first mentioned my plans to write a book, he has provided unfailing encouragement, persuading me to persevere at a time when, battered by rejection, I might otherwise have given up.

Ben Connable, former Marine officer and senior political analyst at the Rand Corporation, also read an early draft of the book, and provided the type of input that made me wish that I had thought of it myself. It was Ben who persuaded me to include some of the more difficult aspects of my story – and I am very grateful to him for doing so.

I am delighted to have this book published by Pen & Sword, whose team – Chris Evans, (Senior Editor in the US), Amy Jordan and Tara Moran – have helped me considerably with their patience, professionalism and wise counsel.

To thank my wife Jess for her support, would be quite inadequate. In all her roles, she has always been an inspiration to me, and continues to make an immeasurable contribution to my life and work.

My children, Siobhan, Marcus and Sophia have spent much of their lives without a father, but have flourished nevertheless (perhaps because of that fact). I hope that this story will, in some small way, atone for my frequent absence. I promise now to do better.

And lastly, an acknowledgement of the debt that I owe to the men and women with whom I have served. They are quite simply the reason why I remained a Marine as long as I did.

# Foreword

This is simply the finest war memoir to emerge from the past two decades of constant fighting. Andy Milburn was in the thick of the action from Somalia to Colombia to Ethiopia to Liberia to Iraq to Libya, then back to Iraq and on to Afghanistan. Along the way, he commanded a Marine platoon, a company, a battalion, a regiment and a Special Operations Joint Task Force. And at various ranks he led teams advising – that is, fighting alongside – Iraqi, Kurdish and Afghan regular and commando units.

There are no boring interludes in this book. The action is non-stop, as Milburn plunges into one chaotic battle after another. He has a novelist's sense of pace and immediacy, literally dragging the reader along with him from one danger-filled scene to another. As the chapters unfold, the reader begins to understand the internal rhythms of battlefields, how to sense peril, evaluate the enemy, lead the troops, cajole allies, accommodate higher headquarters and accomplish the mission.

Milburn has a keen eye and writes in vivid detail. His exceptional skill is telling each story of battle and then knitting them into a coherent whole. By the end of the book, the reader understands what happened on the ground in the wars against terrorists over the past twenty years. He brings the reader on the victorious march to Baghdad in 2003, then returns to the grinding street-by-street battle for Fallujah. After that, it's off to the Syrian border, then back to street fighting in Mosul. The reader comes to understand the deep sectarian divide between the Sunnis and Shiites, and the malignant influence of Al Qaeda.

Milburn accomplishes this task without ever writing a dry or boring sentence. His story is that of a combat leader who accomplished each task at hand with the American and foreign soldiers under his influence, if not his direct command. He is forever getting into trouble, by nature enthusiastic and risk-taking. Fortunately for him and for his readers, the Marine Corps fosters and promotes mavericks who get results, even when they disobey the rules. In the Marines, rules are more like guide posts than walls. You can ignore them, and if you succeed, you will be commended. If you fail, well, then you should have followed the guidelines. In Milburn's case, he slid off from a stateside unit to go to war, he posed as a British citizen to rescue two

American families and he frequently had radio communication 'failures' to call fire upon the enemy when higher headquarters was unwilling to do so.

This is a factual book about a remarkable career, written neither in anger nor in zest. The action itself carries the reader along. What emerges is a portrait of how infantry forces – Marines, Special Forces from many countries, Iraqi and Afghan soldiers – fight a modern war against Islamic zealots determined to resurrect a mythical medieval caliphate. On the battlefield, there is no compromise position or political settlement. The reader marvels at how Milburn and thousands like him maintain such steel tenacity year after year, deployment after deployment, loss after loss. The personal toll is great and Milburn doesn't gloss over the pain of divorce and the tragedy on the home front.

He has written a rousing tale that is a lasting testimonial to those on the frontlines for the past twenty years. At the same time, his memoir implicitly raises the question: what were we as a nation doing? What was the strategy? What was gained at a cost of three to four trillion dollars and the deaths of seven thousand young soldiers?

Toward the end of the book, Milburn wrote:

> A profession that commits them to being instruments, but not architects, of national policy. That is the lot that they have chosen. 'Their's not to reason why; their's but to do and die': in the words of Victorian poet, Lord Alfred Tennyson. ... I was troubled by a darker concern: that all the pride and optimism and sense of purpose was so easily squandered by the careless ministrations of those in power..., so many young men and women who had drawn their first breath as Marines on this same parade deck, had drawn their last in places with no significance, and for a cause without rationale. There is a difference between the well-intended but glib *thank you for your service* and the deeper sense of responsibility to ensure that their blood is shed for a coherent cause.

What are we readers to make of that indictment from a stalwart professional warrior? Our policymakers and generals invaded Afghanistan in 2001 in order to destroy the Al Qaeda force that murdered three thousand civilians at the World Trade Center. Yet our military command allowed Al Qaeda to escape into Pakistan. President George W. Bush then changed the mission; the US would remain in Afghanistan to transform a 9th Century impoverished tribal society into a flourishing democracy. If our intelligence agencies knew that was futile, they did not speak up.

Two years later, we invaded Iraq in order to prevent the Saddam regime from employing weapons of mass destruction against us and other Western countries. The United Nations agreed with that invasion. There were no weapons of mass destruction. But President Bush decided our military had to stay because we owed the Iraqis a freedom under a liberal democracy.

To great fanfare, our top military command changed the mission: 'Soldiers and Marines are expected to be nation-builders as well as warriors.' No military order has been more conceited and bombastic. Throughout Milburn's book that encompasses seventeen years of battlefield deployments, the reader encounters not one case of our soldiers building a democratic nation in Afghanistan or Iraq.

In 2019, we have thousands of soldiers in Iraq to combat the Islamist terrorists. But even more, they are trying to advise and stay close to the Iraqi army in order to lessen the influence of an Iran that has more political influence in Iraq than do we. What sort of nation-building was that? Our generals blame our politicians. In fact, though, our generals failed because they set our troops upon an impossible task. The same is true in Afghanistan, where thousands of American soldiers are still fighting. Our generals now admit the war cannot be won in that remote land-locked country of contentious tribes. We remain only to insure 'a decent interval' before leaving. We seek only to avoid a global humiliation like leaving Saigon in 1975 on helicopters from the roof of the American embassy. Thus it is not possible to congratulate our military high command upon their leadership over the past two decades. Yet our senior generals are feted; there has been no reckoning and no learning from two decades of strategic failure at the top. That bothers Milburn, and rightly so. Strategic ineptitude does not, however, permeate his fine book. It lurks only between the lines.

The reader watches with fascination as our troops at the tactical level adapt and become sharper and more lethal, deployment after deployment. Small unit leadership, remarkable initiative, courage and camaraderie suffuse this memoir. The reader finishes the book understanding why our military is the finest fighting force in the world. Our military is comprised solely of volunteers who know what they are signing up for, are equipped with excellent technologies and share an ethos of task accomplishment. Milburn doesn't list these characteristics; instead, he lets the reader feel them, story after story, chapter after chapter.

*Bing West, a former assistant secretary of defense and combat Marine, has written ten books about America's wars in Vietnam, Iraq and Afghanistan.*

# Introduction

'Why do you want to go back?' The question came during a casual conversation with a middle-aged American couple sitting next to me on the plane to Frankfurt. They were en route to a vacation in Europe, I was on my way to Fallujah.

I wasn't sure how to answer. I had already conceded that it was no longer easy to explain why the US military was in Iraq. The surge of patriotism that followed 9/11 carried us into the war almost without question; but now, eighteen months later, with casualties mounting, it was hard to see an end to it; and the American public appeared to have lost interest. And yet, hard though it might be for me to explain, I did want to go back. But how to articulate that without sounding glib, or blood thirsty, or simple-minded?

I told them that I enjoy being around like-minded people dedicated to a common purpose, and with whom I share a reciprocal bond forged by shared experience and a sense of mutual obligation. That our common purpose may serve no clearly articulated cause was not the point. As an officer, my responsibility was to accomplish the mission and take care of my Marines. In that order. Strategic goals were not my concern.

At the time, it seemed like a good answer; but the question has remained in the back of my mind during the ensuing years of war. During that time, it has seldom been easy to discern a link between military efforts and any coherent overarching strategy. Nor, with the exception of a few brief flurries, has there been real Congressional scrutiny into the conduct of America's wars. Of course, for such a debate to happen, there would have to be a level of public interest fueled by a sense that the American public has something at stake.

Perhaps that is what is missing. A very small percentage of Americans serve in today's military, so it should be no surprise that they feel little personal investment in the wars currently fought on their behalf. Without that sense of investment there is nothing to drive media attention or Congressional action: 'America is not at war; the Marine Corps is at war; America is at the Mall' was an oft-repeated refrain by graffiti artists from Al Qaim to Camp Fallujah. Hence, perhaps, the curiosity of my fellow passengers, who told me they didn't know anyone in the military.

In writing this book it isn't my intention to protest or bring about change – even if I had a remote possibility of doing so. I don't aim to galvanize Congress to provide closer oversight of the nation's wars (although I agree that such an outcome would certainly be desirable), or to reinstitute the draft ("God forbid" is how I and, I suspect, most of my peers would react to such a proposal), though I do fear that the absence of public debate may be an inevitable consequence of having an all-volunteer force.

This is simply the story of what it is like at the sharp end, told from one Marine's perspective. It's a perspective that varies widely in context, from the experiences of a raw second lieutenant leading Marines through the streets of Mogadishu, to those of a task force commander directing special operations forces in a complex fight against a formidable foe. In that sense it offers at least some variety and, I hope, a sense of progression.

Although I am the one telling the story, it is intended to be as much about those with whom I served as it is about me. Because I am a Marine – and without, I hope, appearing parochial – much of this story is about Marines, who in a sense belong to a world of their own. With its emphasis on ritual, tradition, obedience and hierarchy, the Marine Corps is a culture far removed from the society that it protects. Its rites of passage purposely sever those ties, and by an almost Pavlovian process of indoctrination transform civilians into novitiates, and then fully fledged members of a fraternal order. And it works. Marines enjoy belonging to a profession whose demands most Americans would avoid. There is something enduringly familiar about their collective personality that I have always found comforting. The Marines who landed with me in Mogadishu were much the same as those who marched on Baghdad, captured Fallujah, and subsequently took the fight to ISIS in Northern Iraq: upbeat, funny, brave, gracious, savvy and profane. And devoted to one another to an extent that often surprises outsiders.

It is this aspect of the culture that motivates its members far more than lofty concepts of duty or country: they do what they do for each other. It is the camaraderie engendered by shared hardship for a common cause that helps offset the trauma of combat, and the frustrations, discomfort, frequent boredom, and modest pay that define military service.

Marines mourn the loss of comrades with the intensity of a family member. But they accept that the possibility of death is an implicit clause in the contract which – as they remind each other frequently – no one forced them to sign. They express this through dark humor and a wry acceptance of the way things are. It's not a culture that encourages hand-wringing or self-pity.

In this regard, Marine Corps culture is not dissimilar to the special operations community, to which I have belonged for the last ten years. It is perhaps because America's warriors belong to this distinct and peculiar world that they are able to make sense of sacrifice: the loss of life, the years spent away from loved ones, and the toll, physical and emotional, wrought by war. Their culture offers an antidote to bitterness and despair. Which is why the removal from that culture, and the transition to civilian life can be for many veterans so traumatic an experience.

While I recognize that it may appear unhealthy for a democracy to rely on a small warrior caste to fight its wars, I wonder if the peculiar demands of these wars don't require a level of adaptability and expertise and resilience that only such a group can provide. As this story relates, the counter-insurgency in Anbar Province, and the special operations fight against ISIS were both campaigns that required organizations able to learn, adapt and innovate in the face of chaos. Those aren't everyman qualities.

Unfortunately, tactical and even operational success is rapidly squandered by strategic misdirection. This leads to another aspect of the story: the role of the military leader in making sense of the mission. Since their subordinates have a cultural tendency towards obedience which – at times – can lead to self-sacrifice, should leaders not shield them from those demands that appear truly senseless? As Marines we are taught that the mission comes first, the men second; but it's not always so clear cut. At what point do indecipherable or unobtainable goals shift the leaders' responsibility back to the led?

I don't suggest that there is an absolute answer to this question; but it's one that I have had cause to ponder, and would imagine that others have done the same. I'm also aware that I probably haven't always struck the right balance in this regard. Nor have I always tackled the challenges of homecoming with the same resolve that I have faced deployments. And in so far as this story is a memoir, I have made every effort to describe things as they were, rather than how I may have wanted them to be. I was fortunate during my career that a combination of tolerant seniors and circumstance allowed me to learn from my mistakes along the way.

That's my belated answer to the question I was asked on the plane those many years ago; and it's the story that I want to tell here. I hope that it will resonate with those who already have an interest in the military; and for those who don't, I hope that it will at least intrigue, and provide some insight into what it's like to fight America's wars.

# Prologue

## Bashiqa Ridge, Iraq, May 2016

Below me, the lights of Mosul glimmered with deceptive tranquility. I had been up on the front line several times, but still found it surreal to look down on the city that was our ultimate objective. It seemed so close, so reachable, strangely benign, as though you could just get in a car and drive there, merging with the glimmer of headlights that I could see moving along the city's streets. There was nothing to suggest that this was a city in the grip of medieval savagery and under siege.

We were overlooking the very heart of the Islamic State's Caliphate, a beacon to young disaffected Muslims from across the diaspora, which is why ISIS would counter with fanatical determination any encroachment across the berm that separated our world from theirs. And it was the reason why we were here now: a small group of Americans, Kurds, and Sunni tribal fighters, about to prod the hornets' nest.

Despite the cold, which had us shivering in the pre-dawn darkness, I was only half-conscious when Griff's nudge jolted me awake. Lean, dark and wiry, Griff was hunched forward, his elbows on the sandbagged rim of the trench, binoculars pressed against his face.

'Here they come.' He was whispering though the ISIS-held village was a good 300 meters way.

I followed his outstretched finger and, in the gloaming, could just make out movement by the berm that marked the end of Peshmerga territory and the beginning of no man's land. I offset my gaze, and the movement became a column of figures, weapons at the ready, snaking furtively through the wet knee-high grass. I was as excited as though I was among them preparing to attack the village now emerging from the gloom as the horizon lightened. And, in a very real sense Griff and I and the other twelve Americans standing on the observation post that morning were all with the men crouching by the berm. We had worked hard together to get here, and there was much at stake.

I'd had to negotiate with officials in the Turkish Army, Iraqi security forces and the Kurdish Peshmerga to allow us to recruit and train a group of local fighters to conduct a raid into ISIS-held territory. Because this group, which we dubbed the Ninewah Strike Force or NSF, comprised Sunni Arabs, their willingness to fight Daesh would, we hoped, spark an awakening among their co-religionists in Mosul. But it also meant that the Kurds, who had for centuries been at loggerheads with their Arab neighbors, were likely to view our efforts with some suspicion; and it had taken much delicate negotiation to get to this point.

And then I had to persuade my own chain of command to accept the risks involved. Failure would hand the Islamic State a moral victory and undermine our efforts to recruit other tribes. Failure would convince my superiors that the risk calculus for special operations around Mosul was too high. And failure would be catastrophic for the men now in front of us, whose cheerful courage had earned our admiration and respect. It was much harder to watch them go into harm's way than if we had been physically with them.

The lead soldiers had taken up position lying against the berm, a chest-high dirt embankment that marked the front line. With only their heads exposed, they peered towards the village now clearly visible in the monochrome twilight: a cluster of concrete buildings and dirt streets. A radio near me spluttered with guttural Arabic, shockingly loud:

'He wants to know if he can push forward', the interpreter, a chubby middle-aged man, told Mike the team leader.

'Yes – go.' Mike's eager schoolboy features were now furrowed with concentration. The interpreter translated in a stage whisper, and the radio crackled a brief acknowledgement.

I peered at the man at the head of the column – a stocky figure, the only one not wearing a helmet, his huge gun-fighter moustache now clearly visible through my binoculars. His name was Ibrahim, but the Americans referred to him as Pipe Hitter because of his flamboyant tough-guy style. He had rallied a small group of his subordinate leaders, and was talking to them in an animated manner, gesticulating towards the village, then back to each one of them in turn.

'Hurry up, dammit!' Griff's defining characteristic was calm, but I could hear the excitement in his voice.

The horizon was glowing, imparting enough light for us to see clearly the column of men crouched in the grass, their breath misting the air around them as they peered intently ahead. Pipe Hitter tapped the shoulders of the first two men in column, and then, with a push, sent them forward. They scrambled across the berm, and took up position on the other side, scanning the village with their rifles. Next came Pipe Hitter himself, walking upright and at a stately pace, then the rest of the column in twos and threes, scurrying over the earthen bank and into a loose arrow-head formation in the long grass beyond.

It was hard to watch. The village was only some 200 meters from the berm, and the ground in between, though covered in knee-high grass, was mostly flat. We had planned for Ibrahim and his men to close this distance while it was still dark; but a series of hitches had delayed their step-off until just before dawn. And despite our constant emphasis on dispersion, the men moving into danger were bunched tightly together, driven by an instinct that we all recognized but learned to guard against.

The group made short work of the crossing, and in just a few minutes the entire column was in no man's land, snaking its way towards the buildings. Pipe Hitter paused again on the very edge of the town, where the grass gave way to hardscrabble dirt, just a few yards from the nearest buildings. Another quick huddle, and then they were streaming into the town, hunched double in the familiar instinctive posture that men adopt in the face of fire. Within seconds they had all disappeared, with the exception of a group of four or five who remained crouched in the grass. We waited. There were a few terse reports on the radio, and then the crack of shots, sharp in the cold air – three or four – then silence again.

'Shooting at shadows ... or a negligent discharge,' someone conjectured.

He was probably right, because there were no more shots, and the radio remained silent. The sun was above the horizon now, bringing into vivid color the verdant grassland around us and warming the back of my neck. Peering through binoculars at the village in front of us, still cast in shadow, I could make out black shapes flitting between buildings and hoped that they were our men.

An eternity of waiting, and then Pipe Hitter's voice crackled over the radio. The interpreter turned from the handset grinning:

'The town is clear – no Daesh,' he announced, using the colloquial Iraqi term for the Islamic State.

We exchanged expressions of relief, although all were aware that danger still lay ahead. A Peshmerga soldier arrived bearing a tray of steaming glasses. I took one and sipped it gingerly. The tea was sickly sweet, and so hot it burned my tongue, but I was grateful for the comforting reminder of domesticity, an echo from childhood. Tea is the universal panacea for so many cultures; it just makes things seem better. I wondered if the ISIS fighters opposite us were also drinking tea.

A radio crackled. 'Aircraft on the way,' announced the team's forward air controller. This was good news because, lacking permission to move side by side with our protégés, aircraft and unmanned drones gave us our most effective ability to support them. We had one of our own drones aloft now – relaying video to a small laptop-like device over which an operator crouched intently. With well-practiced movements on this console he was guiding the drone beyond the town, above the undulating grassland that stretched towards the outskirts of Mosul.

But it was Griff who with naked eye picked up the brief flash of reflected sunlight from a windshield. There it was again, and another: several vehicles approaching along parallel tracks from the direction of Mosul, still perhaps 4 or 5 kilometers away. Those with eyes on the approaching threat guided the others, voices taut with excitement. The drone operator had picked them up too, and was calling out landmarks.

'Tracking four vehicles.' 'Lead one just disappeared behind that ridge, two fingers to the left of the water tower.'

'I've got another – over there to the left, about three clicks out.'

So intent were we on the approaching vehicles that we might have missed the tell-tale plumes of smoke that arched up from a ridgeline beyond the town. The Islamic State has no shortage of skilled rocketeers, and, as we were to find out, had pin-pointed our location.

Fortunately, we had with us that morning a keen-eyed administration clerk. I had brought along Corporal Adams, as part of my effort to give Marines with the least glamorous jobs a sense of involvement in the mission.

'Chief, check out that smoke,' Adams said, addressing the team's chief petty officer.

Joe glanced in the direction of Adam's outstretched finger, and bellowed a warning, pulling Adams to the ground with him. The rest of us dived for what cover we could find – behind the wall of sandbags or under vehicles. I found myself heading for the same shallow scrape as Griff, and we huddled together, our hands on the back of our heads, willing ourselves into the ground.

The first rocket landed behind us – perhaps 50 meters away – with an explosion that was muffled by the soft soil, but close enough that the blast tugged at my sleeves and left my ears ringing. Then I heard the next rocket whistling downwards, right above us – and everything jumped into sharp focus. I felt the wet sand against my face, the curve of my helmet pushing into the back of my cupped hands – and then a thud as the rocket hit the ground meters away. Then silence, except for a dull thumping that was my heart moving into fifth gear.

'Must be a dud,' someone said eventually.

Griff and I disentangled ourselves and brushed off the sand, joking weakly.

'Air on station.' The forward air controller was squinting skywards, radio handset clamped to his ear. This meant that there were aircraft overhead, awaiting our direction to drop bombs.

And just in time. We could see vehicles and columns of figures moving through the grass from the direction of Mosul, all converging on the town. Clearly Daesh was determined to take it back.

In the euphoria that follows a period of sustained tension, the NSF had failed to post lookouts on the far side of the town, and didn't see the Daesh fighters closing in on them. Nor were they manning the one radio that provided our only link. We could see them gathered in clusters, smoking and chatting in the open spaces between buildings, quite at home.

'Jesus!' exclaimed Mike pointing. A group of Ibrahim's men had commandeered bicycles and were circling each other playfully in the center of town. Although alarmed, I was not really surprised. Iraqi soldiers, or *jundi* as we called them, often display an uncanny ability to detach themselves from their immediate surroundings. I once saw a *jundi* pause during a fire fight in Fallujah to feed a caged canary. The unsuspecting NSF were in a precarious position. The Daesh infantry was still beyond the range of our organic weapons, and aircraft alone were unlikely to reverse their advance.

There was a crackle of gunfire and Pipe Hitter's men scattered in all directions, scurrying for the cover of buildings. Then the hollow *thunk* of mortars being fired from the Peshmerga positions behind us.

Two jets were now circling out of sight far overhead, awaiting our instructions to guide them on to a target; but the mortars prevented us from doing so since we couldn't risk directing an aircraft under the arc of their explosive projectiles.

We were trying to get the attention of the Peshmerga mortar crews, yelling and flapping our arms, when there was a bone-shuddering blast from the ridgeline a couple of hundred meters behind our position.

A cloud of smoke and dust dispersed to reveal a tank, poised on the ridgeline, its dark silhouette barely visible against the backdrop of green hills beyond. Before the echo of the first shot had died away, there was another shattering boom. The noise of a tank gun has to be heard to be believed, but it wasn't the noise that bothered us, it was the risk to our incoming aircraft.

In this situation, we might be willing to take that risk, but the US general who controlled all fires from his headquarters in Erbil, the Kurdish city 50 miles to our south-east would hold back all aircraft until the firing stopped.

The tanks belonged to a Turkish task force that had pushed across the border several months previously, uninvited by the Iraqis, and it was not going to be easy to stop them. Because of political sensitivities, US personnel were forbidden from dealing with the Turks, and though I had met a couple of their officers, I had no means of getting hold of them now.

I glanced at the air controller who was brandishing his handset at the tank in a gesture of frustration.

'I'm heading over to talk to them,' I shouted, and took off running towards the Turkish position, careful to offset my approach from their line of fire. A cluster of Turks standing behind the tank saw me coming – one of them peeled away and dived into a nearby bunker. He reappeared with their commander in tow, a shaven-headed giant of a man wearing a one-piece olive-green boiler suit. I jumped into their gun pit, and he smiled disarmingly, displaying a row of gold teeth, and extended a huge hand. I was struck by his resemblance to Odd Job, the villain in the Bond movie *Goldfinger* (in times of stress my mind has a tendency to spark random thoughts).

'Welcome,' he said, as though really glad to see me.

'Hello,' I replied, and then – because I was aware that I didn't have much time – 'we need you to stop shooting please, we have aircraft overhead.'

'But we are killing terrorists.' He was still beaming, but spoke as though explaining an obvious fact to a rather slow child.

'Well so are we,' I countered absurdly, adding, 'and I think that we can kill more with our planes, but not if you are shooting at the same time.'

After a few minutes of negotiation, Odd Job agreed to cease fire and, turning down the offer of tea, I ran back towards our position. As I did so, a column of smoke billowed up towards the sky from the direction of the town, followed immediately by the pummeling crump of an explosion that shook the ground under my feet.

I was unable to see how close the base of the plume was to Pipe Hitter and his men, but could tell that the group of Americans had seen something to alarm them. There was a rush to grab helmets, and the muzzles of our three heavy-caliber machine guns swiveled in unison towards a target beyond my line of sight. As I started to run, they opened fire in a hammering flurry of dust and smoke.

*Part I*

# Baptism

*When first under fire and wishful to duck,*
*Don't look or take heed of the man that is struck,*
*Be thankful you're livin' and trust to your luck,*
*And march to your front like a soldier.*

Rudyard Kipling

# Chapter 1

By the time I took command of a special operations task force and turned to the task of expelling the Islamic State from Iraq, I felt well prepared for the mission, completely at home. It hadn't always been that way of course, and to explain how I got to this point, I have to explain where I came from and what happened along the way.

I find it hard to remember now why I joined the Marine Corps. Not that I spend much time dwelling on this question since, after almost thirty-two years, it's rather a moot point. But occasionally someone will ask, and when they do, I have to pause to think. Not patriotism, certainly, since I had never even visited the United States prior to enlisting. Nor did I really know much about the Corps, aside from what I had read in the memoirs and novels of former Marines; *Fields of Fire* by Jim Webb, and *Goodbye Darkness* by William Manchester being two that I enjoyed in particular. And having grown up the UK, I had little sense of the almost mystical status that the Marine Corps enjoys in American lore. Later – once I had been steeped in the Corps' pervasive culture – it would be the camaraderie engendered by shared experience that kept me in. But before I joined, I had no way of knowing how important to me this would become.

The truth was that I enlisted almost on a whim, driven by the desire to do something completely different from what I had experienced up to that point in life. And the final clincher was a chance encounter with three Marine security guards in the US Embassy in Islamabad in early 1987. What I was doing in Islamabad I'll get to in a moment; but first a little about me, without which the reader will be puzzled by references to my British background.

I was born in Hong Kong, the son of a British father and American mother who met in New York during the Second World War. My father was at the time an officer in the British merchant navy (merchant marine to the American reader) serving aboard the Queen Mary, a giant ocean liner converted to troop ship that carried thousands of GIs at a time across the Atlantic. The prospect of being able to remove, with just one torpedo, an entire Allied division, made the Queen Mary a much sought-after prize among U-boat commanders. And for the ship's crew, each safe crossing must have seemed to reduce the chances of making the next. My father was the ship's navigator, responsible for plotting a course that would take her through this gauntlet back to Southampton.

With all this to ponder, I am sure that he was looking for distraction when, one afternoon in September 1942, he stopped by the officers' club in Manhattan for a drink. There he met my mother who was working for *Time Life* magazine, and they subsequently saw each other every time his ship docked in New York (although he was never able to give her advance warning of their dates).

My mother subsequently joined the Red Cross and served with the 1st Marine Division in the Far East during the closing months of the war. Her only contact with my father for four years was by letter – until, by the same medium, my father proposed. They married in London in 1949 and moved to Hong Kong, then a British colony, where they remained until his retirement in the early 1970s.

I arrived late in my parents' life, eleven years after my youngest sibling Cindy. My mother never admitted that I wasn't planned, although she did concede that it was quite unusual back then for a 47-year-old woman to have a baby. Planned or not, I couldn't have hoped for a better start in life than the one they gave me. They spared no expense on my education, sending me to an English boarding school and then to St Paul's School in London, where I would have won the class prize for most unpromising student had there been one. I studied philosophy – not, as it happens, a common choice among Marine infantry officers – at University College, London; and then law at Westminster University (also the Alma Mater of one Mohammed Emwazi, better known as Jihadi John).

As for what I was doing in Islamabad – that is a story worth telling since it involves an unusual trip across Iran at the height of that country's war with Iraq, when it was very much closed to Westerners. I was at the time half way through law school and, having failed an exam, was compelled to take a seven-month sabbatical prior to retaking it. My girlfriend at the time was in Australia, and, rather than kick my heels in London, I decided that I would visit her, planning to make as much of the journey as was possible by land. This is where I became a little too ambitious.

Through an improbable chain of connections between University College London and the Iranian Embassy in London (whose vice consul was, like me, a UCL philosophy graduate), I obtained an Iranian visa and set off by bus across Europe and Turkey to the Iranian border. There I waited three days, during which time I was questioned by the Iranian border guards and witnessed them catch and then summarily execute three drug smugglers. By then it was too late to turn back, so I boarded the bus for Tehran.

Youthful optimism is a strong antidote to the prospect of danger. And to discomfort, which is fortunate because I wouldn't want to repeat now that ride in the back of a wheezing bus packed to capacity with people and livestock. Nor, for that matter, that entire trip across Iran, during which I experienced an Iraqi air raid (deep irony) while in Isfahan, was interrogated by the Revolutionary Guard in Tehran, arrested and detained overnight in Shiraz, and chased by a crowd in Zahedan, before making it across the border to Pakistan.

There my troubles weren't over. I arrived in Quetta during mass rioting against the Pakistani authorities whose reaction was to shoot scores of people in the street before imposing a curfew. The riot started as an argument between Pathans and Baluchis over bus seats – a story that anyone who is familiar with this part of the country will find unsurprising. When it ended a few days later, I traveled by train to Islamabad, an interminable journey interrupted at frequent intervals by Pakistani soldiers on the search for troublesome Baluchis.

It was at the US Embassy in Islamabad, where I had gone to retrieve my passport, that I found myself sharing a table with three Marine security guards. Cropped haired, fit-looking and boisterous, they regaled me with stories of travel and adventure. Later I attended a party at their residence, which they referred to as the Marine House, a plush three-story building with bar, gym and swimming pool. *This is the life*, I thought. *Why not take a four-year sabbatical to see the world before settling down to a career as a barrister?* Ten months later, after completing Law School, I visited the US Marine recruiter in London (there was one then), and enlisted. I'm sure that he is still telling the story.

My parents were understandably disappointed that I had enlisted in the Marine Corps thus squandering years of expensive education. My argument that a Law Degree guaranteed me the rank of 'Private First Class out of Boot Camp' did little to comfort them.

Beyond basic entry requirements, the Marine Corps cares little for civilian education but, contrary perhaps to popular opinion, does demand among its leaders the ability to think critically. In this regard, my parents' money was not wasted, and though I have struggled at times to learn the lessons that life has thrown at me, I was at least mentally prepared to do so. I retain two other characteristics that I can only attribute to a British education: a love for argument – or debate as I prefer to call it – and a tendency to remember random passages from literature, word for word. During the course of my career I have learned to keep this last trait to myself.

The Marine Corps Recruit Depot at Parris Island was my first introduction to the United States, and to say that it was a culture shock would be an understatement. It was as though everyone spoke a completely different language. During an initial medical examination, I described my alcohol intake as being 'one to two pints a day' – pints being the customary British measurement for beer. Thinking that I meant hard liquor, the doctor detoured me to a bench reserved for medical rejects. I was able to resolve this misunderstanding (by no means my last with the Corps), only to face again the prospect of my career ending before it had begun when I failed the medical examination due to an old rugby injury that prevented my leg from bending to the required angle. I was saved by an administrative oversight – no one could find the line of accounting to purchase a plane ticket back to the UK, and so I continued on my path to becoming a US Marine. My leg still doesn't bend and has caused me to fail every physical examination since, but in every case someone has determined that it would cost the Corps more to discharge me than to keep me on active duty.

Marine recruit training in the 1980s was quite a raw experience, especially for those unfortunate enough to be assigned to the infamous 'thumping' 3rd Battalion, located in a remote corner of the Marine Corps Recruit Depot at Parris Island. As the nickname might suggest, corporal punishment was not uncommon in 3rd Battalion back then. I still have a scar on the bridge of my nose as result of having it rubbed against the metal frame of a bunk bed in an effort to teach me a lesson about rifle cleanliness. As a 24-year-old British law school graduate, I was not the typical recruit – a fact that was a source of both irritation and amusement to my drill instructors. For my part, I could understand, on average, only about a third of what they said which caused them some disgruntlement. It took me some time to realize that the phrase 'Where's milburnat?' referred to me (my expensive education not having prepared me to deal with sentences that ended in prepositions).

But I adapted and by the final phase was even beginning to enjoy myself – Boot Camp was not very different from British boarding school.

As part of the hard bargain that I drove with my recruiter, I had insisted on going into the infantry and the Marine Corps kept its word. After Boot Camp, I attended the school of infantry at Camp Geiger, Camp Lejeune where I trained to be an anti-tank gunner, learning how to shoot the Dragon missile system, an absurdly cumbersome and ineffective weapon, now thankfully obsolete.

Two years later, having reached the dizzy heights of corporal and discarded my plans to practice law, I reported to Officer Candidate School in Quantico, beginning the fourteen-month rite of passage to become a Marine infantry officer.

Saddam Hussein invaded Kuwait while my cohort of lieutenants were mid-way through our training, and we all assumed that we were bound for war. Alas, it was not to be – at least not then. Instead we found ourselves assigned to a casualty replacement company in California where we watched the four-day war on television. We were disconsolate, thinking that we had missed our only chance to practice for real the skills that we had just spent over a year learning.

# Chapter 2

In April 1991, I flew to Okinawa with two other lieutenants fresh from the Infantry Officers' Course to join my battalion. Our welcome was less than enthusiastic. Second Battalion, Ninth Marines (2/9) had been the wallflower of the Desert Storm: the only infantry battalion not to participate in Saddam's defeat, sitting out the war instead on Okinawa where it spent a full year instead of its scheduled six-month deployment.

Unable to train, because all ammunition had been shipped to Saudi Arabia, morale was at rock bottom by the time we arrived. The battalion had watched the homecomings and victory parades on television, and had just learned that they were to be extended on the Rock, as Okinawa was not-so-affectionately known, for another two months. The timing couldn't have been worse for a group of fledgling infantry officers, eager to practice what they'd learned, and who found themselves instead dealing with a scale of disciplinary infraction that would have brought disrepute to an entire division. Cheap alcohol fueled the general sense of malaise. Every night the camp was the scene of fights that started between individuals, and rapidly escalated into wide-ranging brawls between platoons, companies and – on one memorable occasion the night before our departure – entire battalions. It was quite a welcome to the Fleet Marine Force.

Nevertheless, I was excited to be there, and from the time I met my first platoon, always a momentous occasion for a new platoon commander, I knew that I had chosen the right profession. I had always found the interplay of infantry tactics absorbing – but now discovered too that I enjoyed leading Marines: teaching, coaching, mentoring and helping solve their problems (some of which defied description). And with the help of Sergeant Robertson, my stalwart (and sober) platoon sergeant, I worked hard to shape my forty-two Marines into a cohesive unit. It wasn't easy – there were few real training opportunities and the Marines were, not surprisingly dispirited. It was a rare weekend that didn't see several of them delivered to camp by the Shore Patrol, comatose from alcohol; and a week or so after taking command, I had to deal with an attempted suicide.

In August 1991, 2/9 returned to the United States and things began to improve. Most of the Marines departed, having reached their end of service, and an equal proportion of the officers moved on to assignments elsewhere in the corps. There was an influx of new company commanders, freshly graduated from the Marine Corps' Amphibious Warfare School and eager to take command – a stark contrast to the old crew who were, to say the least, uninspiring.

The battalion changed hands and the new commander, though somewhat aloof, was competent and engaged. Most exciting of all, we learned that 2/9 was destined to deploy to the Western Pacific as part of the 15th Marine Expeditionary Unit. A MEU comprises an infantry battalion, aviation squadron and logistic element under a single headquarters commanded by a colonel; some 2,000 Marines in all. The unit deploys aboard ships to form an Amphibious Readiness Group, designed to respond at short notice to crises around the globe; a prospect far more interesting than sitting on Okinawa for six months.

For me there was more good news. I was to take command of the battalion's mortar platoon, a coveted assignment among lieutenants, and although I had some doubts about the battalion commander's wisdom in choosing me, I resolved to justify his blind faith.

At such times a platoon commander's success or failure can hinge upon the caliber of his platoon sergeant. I couldn't have been luckier with mine: Gunnery Sergeant Robin White was a stocky Hoosier who exuded leadership and competence. This was his second tour as platoon sergeant for a mortar platoon, and if he was disappointed to be getting a second lieutenant as platoon commander he never showed it.

The 81mm mortar platoon is called the battalion commander's hip-pocket artillery, for its ability to provide responsive fires in support of battalion operations. The platoon is about twice the size of a rifle platoon, and more complex in the way it operates. To command it effectively, I would have to master the science of gunnery, a skill that most infantrymen understand at only the basic level. Gunny White, an artilleryman, spent hours teaching me the black art of his trade, from the calculations required to turn map locations into firing data, to the small muscle adjustments of the mortar sight to make the shell go where needed. I didn't always get it right. On one occasion, when firing a new type of ammunition, one of our guns dropped a round only 50 meters from the battalion field headquarters. It was an incident that could have cost me my job – but, after I had explained to the battalion commander what had happened, he decided to keep me in command. It made me all the more determined to prove him right.

Another incident also threatened to end my career, though I would have regarded this a small price to pay for what I gained in return. In August of that year I became a father for the first time when my daughter Kaela was born. I had met her mother Nancy in Atlanta while attending the infantry officer mortar leaders' course in nearby Fort Benning – and it was a shock to learn that she was pregnant. Although Nancy and I would never be more than friends, I was determined to be part of Kaela's life.

She was born during the battalion's final pre-deployment exercise, and, to my everlasting regret, I missed her birth. I flew to Atlanta as soon as the exercise was over, and was thrilled to hold the little squalling bundle in my arms. I spent only two days with her before rushing back to Camp Pendleton to rejoin my platoon as we prepared to board ship. Looking back, that was the first of many times when an off-kilter sense of what was important would cause me to place work above family; and I regret every time that I have done so.

When I took Kaela's birth certificate to the battalion adjutant for entry in my records, he peered at me over his glasses.

'You're not married?'

'No, I'm not.'

'No plans to get married?'

'None.'

'Well, the command is going to take a dim view of this. I would guess that your career is over.'

He made this prediction in good faith. The battalion commander was adamant about maintaining a high moral tone in the battalion. He required, for instance, all Marines to sign a contract prior to deployment committing them to remain sober (the contract included a detailed definition of intoxication) and to avoid the company of prostitutes (no definition provided). The contract stirred up a heated debate throughout the battalion; but, to my surprise, no one refused to sign it. Several months later while on Shore Patrol in Pattaya Beach Thailand, it occurred to me that this was because the Marines had simply resolved to pay it no heed.

The adjutant's warning deflated me; I couldn't imagine not being a Marine. I needn't have worried: if the battalion commander did find out about Kaela, he must have decided that it would be better to deploy with a morally corrupt mortar platoon commander than to have to train a new one.

One night over a beer, Gunny White toasted my luck: 'That's great news, sir – congratulations. But I've got to ask you something.' He lent forward and looked me in the eye. 'The CO doesn't strike me as being a very forgiving guy, but he's letting you run rampant. Do you have dirt on him?'

My new platoon had a well-deserved reputation, as mortar platoons often do, as the bad boys of the battalion.

'Many of them appear to have lost sight of the fact that they are Marines,' the battalion commander commented, after breaking the news to me that the platoon was now mine to fix. My company commander was more direct. 'They've gone completely fucking feral,' he said, before listing the milestones on their road to perdition.

'Drugs cases, UA, – you name it. Every Friday, there's a line of mortarmen outside my office. Last month, we had to evacuate several of them from the field with injuries. Turns out they were jamming C-4 into bottles and then throwing them into the fire – some kind of game, I guess. Beer bottles, by the way, and a fucking camp fire in the field, which shows you how serious they are about training. The platoon commander was away for that one, so I relieved the platoon sergeant. Two weeks ago on a company hike, they started a fight with Heavy Guns platoon. I tell you, it's keeping me awake at night.'

Normally an easygoing man, my company commander was now clearly incensed, and I had the impression that he wasn't exaggerating the insomnia part.

'If they were good at their job, that would be some consolation – but they just failed the division's combat readiness evaluation,' he continued. The CRE was the Marine Corps' benchmark for assessing whether a unit was ready to deploy. Failing it was a significant de-merit, word of which would have traveled fast throughout the division.

'You've got six months to get them in shape and re-take it,' he finished. He didn't have to add an 'or' to this statement. Failing the CRE again would put the platoon in an unheard-of category of incompetence. It wasn't a prospect that I wanted to think about.

Turning a unit around is a challenge that appeals to most idealistic platoon commanders, but it's always a tougher task than it first might appear. Once bad behavior becomes embedded in a unit's culture, it's very difficult to change.

I had a rapid introduction to the scale of the problem. Drugs of all types were a scourge in Pendleton, and my platoon was deeply immersed in the shadowy world of on-base distribution – or so I was informed in a meeting with agents from the Naval Criminal Investigative Service. One day, soon after taking command, while conducting a routine barracks inspection, I used a broom handle to prod at the loose ceiling tiles of a barracks room, and a large stash of drugs cascaded out. This was pure chance, but won me undeserved kudos with the platoon's NCOs.

On another occasion, the military police were called out when one of my Marines pulled a gun during a fight at the Enlisted Club. At any given time, I had several Marines awaiting disciplinary proceedings.

Gunny White and I figured out that the root of the problem was a cabal of old-timers: Marines, many of whom were NCOs, nearing the end of their first enlistment. The only way to fix this problem, we decided, was to wage a counter-insurgency campaign: systemically targeting the bad-actors, firing some, paring away others to billets outside the battalion; while giving those we judged reconcilable offers they couldn't refuse. And in their place we promoted good Marines into positions of responsibility.

Corporal Dropic was a case in point. Cocky and outspoken, Dropic was the type of Marine who makes a point of questioning everything, coming close at times to insubordination but never quite crossing the line. I had tasked every Marine in the platoon with writing an autobiography; Dropic's was particularly well-written, and his aptitude scores were higher than those of most officers. He was one of those charismatic, strong characters that gather others around him – for better or for worse. Corporal Dropic, I decided, would play a key role in turning the platoon around.

As would Sergeant Clack. There have been Sergeant Clacks in the Corps since the first group of Marines gathered in Tun Tavern to pound beers and gripe about the British. Built like a tank, with a pugnacious face and thinning blond hair, Clack demanded Marine-like behavior from his subordinates and wouldn't tolerate those who failed to toe the line. 'You're fucking up my Marine Corps,' he would announce as a prelude to offering to help the culprit mend his ways.

With Clack and Dropic, and a crew of new NCOs on side, we re-directed the platoon's boisterous energy into a punishing program of hikes and PT. Every Friday, the platoon donned flak jackets and played combat soccer, a cross between rugby and Gaelic football, in which there were very few rules – until my company commander, alarmed by the resulting stream of casualties, ordered me to stop.

During one particularly tough night hike at Twenty-Nine Palms the platoon's grumbling came close to mutiny. At the conclusion of a rest break, the Marines ignored cries to saddle-up and remained seated.

'Never seen anything like it,' Gunny White fumed. 'Fuckers are refusing to move.' But after he and Clack had a quiet word with them, they changed their minds – and that night became embedded in platoon lore.

Anthropologist Clifford Geertz defined culture as being 'the stories we tell ourselves about ourselves.' Before long, the Mortar Platoon never tired of telling stories about themselves, and gradually developed into a cohesive team as they rode out, and even began to relish the hard training. There is no simplistic moral to this story; I am not suggesting that tough training cures all ills – I've seen plenty of examples where an uncompromising style of leadership has back-fired, causing more problems than it solves. I walked a fine line between challenging the platoon and simply alienating them, and without the balanced support of Gunny White, Clack, Dropic and the squad leaders, would have failed. Now, twenty-eight years later, two-thirds of the platoon are still in contact, and continue to regale each other with stories on Facebook.

The platoon was scheduled to re-take the division combat readiness evaluation one month prior to our deployment date. We practiced all the drills over and over, by day and night until all of us were thoroughly sick of them; but we passed the CRE with flying colors. It was late on Friday night by the time we returned from the field and finished cleaning our weapons. I was walking out to my car in the parking lot when a barracks window flew open behind me.

'Sir, sir, – just like Lazarus,' a voice hollered, anonymous in the dark. 'Like Lazarus from the fucking grave!' I couldn't have put it better.

# Chapter 3

While we readied for deployment, a tragedy was unfolding in Somalia due to all the usual causes; civil war, overpopulation, and misuse of land and rivers. The images on television were harrowing: stick figures, crying babies with distended bellies, flies cramming into their eyes and mouths. Media attention and public opinion combined in a mounting call for intervention.

This would be just fine with the Marines of 2/9's mortar platoon. Nothing stokes excitement in a Marine infantry unit like the prospect of action. I was no different; but also had my own idealistic reasons for wanting to be involved. The Cold War was over, and if the United States with all its resources couldn't be a force for good, I reasoned, then what was the point in having so powerful a military. I hadn't yet learned the fickle relationship between politics, national interest and public opinion.

In October 1992, we embarked aboard the USS *Tripoli*, an amphibious assault ship equipped with a large flat deck for launching helicopters, and a hull that acted as a floating dock for landing craft. The *Tripoli* had carried Marines to Vietnam, at which time she was the pride of the navy's amphibious fleet. But to the Marines of Weapons Company 2/9 she was an aging, rusty scow with a permanent list to starboard and a propensity to break down as soon as she was out of sight of land (a tendency that increased in frequency, the closer she came to the equator). Nevertheless, she was an impressive sight as she pulled gamely away from the peer thronged with families, and swung beneath the Coronado Bridge, her complement of sailors and Marines manning the rail in lines of white and khaki.

We were in mid-Pacific when President Bush made the decision to send US forces into Somalia. And somewhere in the Pentagon, at echelons beyond reason as Marines are fond of saying, someone decided that 15th MEU would spearhead this commitment. On ship, there was a flurry of activity as orders were issued, maps studied, weapons test-fired, gear checked and re-checked. In early hours of December 9 1992, the mortar platoon lay sprawled on the ship's hangar deck amidst piles of equipment, awaiting our turn to go ashore by helicopter. It's one of the Corps' inviolate traditions that all hands must be ready and waiting hours before any scheduled event, and this one was no exception. The ship's crew entertained the waiting Marines by playing music over the intercom system. It was a limited repertoire, and the fourth re-play of Tom Petty's *'Waiting is the Hardest Part'* was no longer amusing.

Confusion reigned from the start. Our helicopter started to descend far short of the point that I had indicated to the pilot on the map; the intercom connection on my helmet wasn't working, and I couldn't understand the crew chief's shouted explanation. By then it was too late, the Sea Stallion was shuddering downwards, the noise of its engines rising in pitch. As the ramp lowered against a backdrop of scrubland and billowing dust, my platoon suffered its first casualty: a Marine lost his balance under the weight of a rucksack bulging with mortar rounds and broke his leg. He remained on the helicopter, never getting the chance to set foot in Somalia.

We struggled off the ramp, collapsing into a loose semicircle as the giant bird rose behind us and clattered over our heads, pelting us with grit as it did so. I registered low sand dunes, the ocean shimmering to our right, the sprawl of a shanty town to our front, and the fetid stench of raw sewage. Beyond the shanty town I could make out docks and a breakwater stretching out to sea; the port, which was where we were supposed to be. Then Corporal Reddick was yelling: 'Sir – Technicals!'

We knew all about 'Technicals' from intelligence briefs and television. They were civilian pick-up trucks mounted with machine guns, used by Somalia's warlords as makeshift fighting vehicles. Their frequent appearance in news reports on television had come to symbolize the whole sorry mess that Somalia had become. Reddick's warning was the equivalent to someone yelling 'Shark!' to a group of swimmers who had just seen *Jaws*.

I turned as two jeeps mounted with machine guns rode into the base of our semicircle and came to a halt. Marines shimmied behind their packs, pointing their weapons at this sudden threat.

'Don't shoot!' I shouted, and was instantly grateful that I had – they were Pakistani soldiers from the UN contingent.

I was happy to accept their offer of help, and we used the jeeps to ferry our mortars and ammunition to our intended location near the port. There we set up our guns, under the gaze of a curious crowd who gathered to watch this strange ritual; and waited. Later that afternoon, when it became apparent that the MEU's landing was unopposed and thus had no need for mortar support, we received a fresh mission.

'Head to the port Redman,' the battalion operations officer told me over the radio. Lance Corporal Wayne Ponkilla, my radio operator and a full-blooded Navajo had chosen our platoon's call sign. When I demurred on the grounds that some might find it offensive, he pointed at his pouch of chewing tobacco, a popular brand that bore the same name.

The operations officer continued. 'Conduct relief in place with Fox Company, and start running security patrols to prevent anyone interfering with the off-load of relief supplies.' The last part of this order, its intent, was the most important.

We struggled the few hundred meters to the port, linked up with Fox Company, and happily dumped our mortars. That night, we slept in a festering warehouse beside the docks, listening to the crackle of gunfire outside the port gates as the local warlords continued to fight among themselves. The warehouse stank abominably and swarmed with rats, but I drifted off to sleep feeling strangely content; this was what Marines were supposed to do.

The platoon had been assigned a sector of the city that was to prove to be the most volatile – since it lay across the 'Green Line', a road that delineated the boundary between the city's two most powerful and antagonistic warlords: Mohammed Farah Aidid and Ali Mahdi Muhammad. Our patch also included the Hotel Olympic, scene several months later of the infamous 'Blackhawk Down' confrontation in which eighteen American soldiers lost their lives and another seventy were wounded.

Sometime in the next day or so, the *Jack Lummus*, a giant US Navy cargo ship was due to dock at the port. If all went well, this would be the vanguard of a renewed relief effort to the country's stricken hinterland.

Most of Mogadishu was controlled by Aidid, and his militia, the self-proclaimed Somali Liberation Army or SLA. However, the district immediately around the port belonged to Ali Mahdi, the nominal President of Somalia and Aidid's arch-rival. The SLA surrounded this enclave – which was known, incongruously, as Bermuda – cutting its inhabitants off from the city's markets and sources of water. In an effort to help this population, we distributed supplies which we had appropriated from cargo being offloaded at the docks, and with a group of volunteer medics we set up makeshift aid stations during our patrols through the area.

Despite these efforts, or perhaps because of them, someone started to shoot at us within days of arrival. At first we thought these incidents were the result of crossfire between the warring clans but it soon became evident that we were being targeted. Bob Simon and his team from CBS News captured on film one fusillade of hostile fire that had me and two other

Marines pinned to a roof top during a tense stand-off. Bob was engaging company, and his team became good friends with the platoon, allowing them to call home on their satellite phones – and, unbeknownst to me at the time – supplying them with bottles of whiskey. They were part of a widening group of journalists who began to gather at the port to cover the fighting along the Green Line, as the novelty of the relief effort wore off. I was soon to have every reason to be grateful for their presence.

In the days before our arrival, several ships trying to dock at the port were driven away by heavy machine-gun fire. According to our new-found friends in Bermuda, the culprits were SLA fighters who had set up position in the Parliament building atop the hill overlooking the port.

The building was only about a mile away as the crow flies, but at least twice that distance by road – outside the usual radius of our security patrols. Nevertheless, it was obviously key terrain and I wanted to ensure that the SLA didn't feel comfortable enough to return. The *Jack Lummus* had arrived by then and lay tethered to the dock, her superstructure towering over the surrounding warehouses, a tempting target for any Kat-crazed teenager eager to impress his buddies.

So ten days after we landed, I led a reinforced patrol out of the gates of the port, bound for the Parliament building.

# Chapter 4

'Every Marine is a rifleman.' The Marine Corps makes this pithy catchphrase a reality by devoting two weeks of Boot Camp to teaching recruits how to shoot.

The fundamentals of marksmanship are taught in the same way that everything is taught at Boot Camp, through mind-numbing repetition, until every aspect of shooting becomes instinctive: rifle butt pulled firmly into

## MOGADISHU

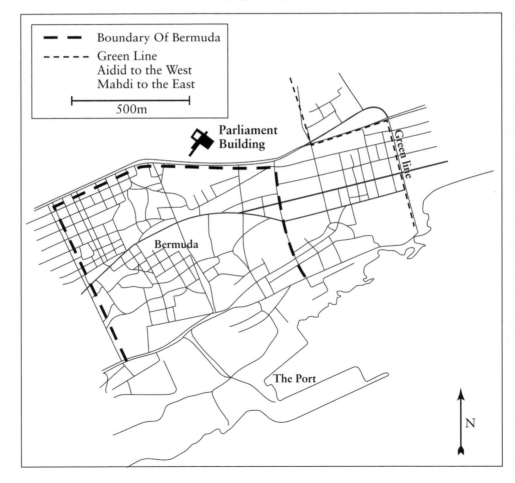

shoulder, a gentle squeeze to take up the slack in the trigger, a deep breath – half exhaled – and your whole world becomes the tip of your front sight, a black column against the blurry smudge of the target. You don't look at the target or you'll upset the delicate alignment between your front and rear sights. So you learn to focus instead on the blade of your front sight tip. And this works to your benefit in more ways than one. When you are aiming at a human being for the first time, it helps not to be reminded of that fact in the second before pulling the trigger.

When that moment comes, the hours of tedious conditioning serve their purpose: pounding heart, tunnel vision, shaking hands, shallow breathing all succumb to muscle memory. And instinct plays a role. A primordial corner of our subconscious primes us to act aggressively in the face of danger; to kill or be killed. The knowledge that another human being threatens your survival will override, in an instant, years of parental guidance, education, religious observance and all the social trappings of civilized society. Adrenalin and training fuse into a potent mix. Shooting someone becomes shockingly easy.

And this instinct is by no means the exclusive preserve of the psychopath or the hyper-violent – I have seen it activated in the most mild-mannered and level-headed people. We have all types in the Marine Corps; not everyone is naturally aggressive, and very few are born warriors. But when the time comes, Marines tend to respond with remarkable uniformity – and without hesitation.

If you are in charge, it's more difficult – because then it's in your hands to decide when to shoot. That's a much tougher task to train for.

Before there was a war, before it became the norm to make split-second decisions based on interpretations of imminent threat and hostile intent; before deadly encounters became commonplace; the decision to open fire, to cross the line from peace to combat, from everyday commonplace soldiering to the use of lethal force, was a momentous one. And despite all my training, I didn't really believe that I would ever be called upon to make that decision. Until, on an otherwise relatively quiet day, I had to.

It was as pleasant a day as you could expect in Mogadishu, marred only by intermittent gunfire none of which sounded close, and the omnipresent stench that characterized the city: a putrid mix of human waste and decay which, had there been no breeze, would have had some of us gagging.

Without a word being spoken, there was a perceptible change in mood as we left behind us the narrow streets and bustling crowds around the port, and streamed with well-practiced ease onto the road leading to the

Parliament building, scanning the derelict buildings on either side with eyes aching from the glare of the sun.

You could never relax in this part of town. The road along which we walked, a wide boulevard fringed on either side by ornate Italian architecture ravaged by years of conflict, was the Green Line, the disputed boundary between Aidid and Mahdi. In a city teeming with life, it was empty and still – redolent with menace.

As we neared a wide intersection at the top of the hill, the point man paused to wave up the two Marines whose job it was to provide flank security. Then came the sharp report of several gun shots close by, followed by a series of cracks overhead. Recalling his time as a young rifleman in Burma during the Second World War, George MacDonald Fraser wrote that when you are inexperienced, and you want to know how scared you have a right to be, look at the men around you. But if they are equally inexperienced and you happen to be a young platoon commander, they are going to be looking at you. And so it was now. I was keenly aware of everyone's eyes on me as I glanced up and down the staggered files to make sure no one was hurt. I was suddenly very aware of my surroundings as though someone had twisted a dial bringing them into sharp focus.

Lance Corporal Ponkilla crouched beside me, fumbling to unclip the radio handset from his H-harness.

'Were those aimed at us, sir?'

'I don't think so,' I said, trying to sound reassuring. 'Probably some of Aidid's yahoos high on Kat just popping caps for fun.' Kat was the local drug of choice; Somalis chewed it for its immediate simulative effect, and you could predict the city's cycle of violence by the schedule of Kat distribution. I had barely finished speaking when there was another volley of shots, like a string of firecrackers, accompanied by spurts of dust in the road a few steps away from where we crouched.

I reached for the radio handset, ignoring Ponkilla's pointed stare.

'Redman main, Redman six.'

The response crackled back: 'Gotcha six, go ahead'

I recognized Gunny White's voice.

'We are on route green, half a klick north of CP 5 – taking ineffective fire. Move the QRF to the gate and stand-by.'

The Quick Reaction Force, somewhat grandiosely titled, consisted of ten Marines mounted on two open-back Humvees, which was the best that we could muster. Even with this start, it would take them at least twenty minutes to navigate the crowded streets to our position.

It's hard to tell where shots are coming from at the best of times; even more difficult when you are surrounded by buildings that magnify and echo their sound. Nevertheless, Marines always think that they know, and now there was a chorus of suggestions that covered every direction of the compass.

'Reddick, see where those came from?' I called to the point man.

Corporal Reddick, stocky, blond and quietly dependable, was squatting on his haunches, pressed against the side of the last building before the intersection. He pointed with a knife-hand chopping motion.

'From over there, I think, sir – from the direction of the Parliament building but I can't see shit from here.'

The Parliament building lay just beyond the intersection but obscured from our view by the buildings against which we now crouched.

'Well get to where you can see.'

Without reply, Reddick peered around the corner, and instantly sprang back as another burst of firing rent the air, followed by the whine of a ricochet.

'Incoming has the right of way,' chortled Sergeant Clack.

'Whaddya have, Reddick?'

'Yep, those came from the Parliament building. Saw movement on the second deck.'

Across the street, Sergeant Clack disengaged his bulky frame from the doorway where he had taken refuge, and jogged over to me bent double. His broad face was flushed, and sweat dripped from his chin as he squatted against the wall beside me.

'What now Boss?'

What now indeed. There was no telling how many of them there were in the Parliament building, and to get to them we would have to cross an open area. If we were operating against a declared hostile force in a combat situation, and if I had additional firepower and more Marines, this would be a simple tactical problem: suppress the threat (blast the front of the Parliament building with every available weapon); obscure the enemy's view (toss smoke grenades up–wind and wait for the smoke to gather mass); then send one squad into the building to gain a foothold. As it was, I had a pitifully small force with which to clear so large a building.

And this was a humanitarian mission; we weren't supposed to be shooting. We were just a few blocks away from where eighteen US soldiers would be killed, but that was nine months away and beyond my frame of reference.

Aside from our own QRF, we had no reinforcements at hand. The range on my radio allowed me to speak only to platoon headquarters in the port over a mile away. Any requests for support would have to be relayed through them, and were unlikely to be met because there wasn't much available. The battalion, in its entirety, was on its way inland as the spearhead for a humanitarian convoy, leaving a skeleton crew to man the radios back at the airfield (this was in the early days of Operation Restore Hope, before it became a massive military operation).

Even if I could get hold of someone in authority, I would probably be told to withdraw to the port. This wasn't our fight and there was no sense looking for trouble. I was still stinging from a rebuke a few days previously, after one of my patrols had disarmed a gunman.

'You aren't here to take these people's weapons, lieutenant,' the battalion operations officer, a major, admonished me over the radio. 'You'd better find whoever it was and give him back his damn weapon.' I was incredulous. *How the fuck was I going to do that?*

'Sir, we've been shot at more than once. And this yahoo just walked right into the flank of my patrol waving a gun. We had to take it.'

'Listen to me, lieutenant,' the major's voice took on an edge. 'You had better pull your head out of your ass, and rein in your platoon. Do you understand me?'

'Got it, Gunslinger,' I said, my face burning. We were on the battalion's tactical net; everyone had heard.

'Water off a duck's back,' Gunny White had advised me, but the incident still weighed on me.

Withdrawal now was an option – but to my mind, not a good one. This wasn't simply a question of hubris. Our patrols had come under fire with increasing frequency; to turn tail now would send the wrong message, and likely put future patrols at greater risk. No, I had to deal with this situation aggressively, but without getting any of my Marines killed.

Sergeant Clack fished a wad of tobacco out of his lower lip and flicked into onto the ground without breaking eye contact.

'We're going to clear the Parliament building,' I said, as evenly as I could.

Clack's eyebrows went up, and he eased his helmet back off his forehead. It was a familiar gesture, one that I knew presaged a respectful but persistent analysis of my thought process, so I went on.

'If we head back, these guys will get the message that we're intimidated. I'll have Gunny reinforce the QRF and move them up here now. They'll be in position to blast anyone who takes a shot at us as we move into the building.'

I was interrupted by Reddick.

'They're leaving – four … no five … dudes running out the side of the building. All armed. Lost 'em – they ran down a side street.'

This was an opportunity I couldn't squander. I grabbed the handset 'Redman three, move the QRF up to CP-5 now, and standby once there. I'm taking the patrol into the Parliament Building'.

'Roger, Redman six – got it'. Gunny White's mid-Western drawl was strangely reassuring.

Clack cupped his hand and hollered 'Umberger, Martinez – guns up!'

Both Marines lumbered up panting, each cradling a machine gun, their eyes fixed intently on Clack. They were a study in contrasts. Umberger built like a line-backer, fair-skinned with earnest all-American features carried the heavier M-60 machine gun. Martinez, stocky and deeply tanned, his braces exposed in a trademark impish grin, held the lightweight squad automatic weapon.

Clack pointed up the road towards the intersection. 'Flank security, either side of this road – cover the intersection. Stay under cover but don't lose sight of us. Go!'

'Aye aye, sergeant.' It was funny how Boot Camp mannerisms returned in times of stress.

Umberger took off across the road at a flat sprint. Martinez jogged up beside Reddick, placed his weapon on the ground and lay behind it, squinting through the sights. Clack turned to me.

'Boss, you wanna wait for the QRF?'

'No – stack the patrol. We're going to rush across.'

There was no way of knowing for certain, but I felt confident that the immediate threat was gone. It didn't feel reckless. The opposition was feisty, but not crafty enough, I thought, to leave a stay-behind ambush.

Clack looked back and pumped his fist in the air again: 'Team leaders up'. Three Marines leapt from their positions in the column and ran to our position, dropping into a squat around me.

'We're going to clear the Parliament building as planned. Only difference is that the intersection is now a danger area – flank security is already out. When I give the word, we cross in pairs. Sergeant Clack's got traffic control. Reddick – you and me are going to move up now, and will be first across.

'Once we're in the building – same drill as always. We've done this a hundred times, nothing's different now. Questions?'

Reddick and Cardona shook their heads, Dropic grinned and gave me the thumbs-up.

'OK – Two minutes to brief your Marines. Go to it.'

# Chapter 5

We rushed headlong across the intersection: Reddick, Ponkilla and I, zigzagging across the open ground, then up the marble steps, through the cavernous doorway, sprinting for cover behind the nearest pillars. We crouched a few feet apart panting like dogs, peering into the gloom. Once my eyes adjusted, I could see that we were alone in the giant chamber. With its vaulted dome and ornate pillars, it looked like a place of worship, except for the rubble and trash strewn across the tiled expanse.

The clatter of feet behind us was our signal to move. We stood and began walking towards the center of the chamber, rifles raised, the crunch of broken glass beneath our boots. I glanced behind me as the next two Marines ran through the door and then moved in opposite directions, hugging the wall. By the time that we reached the foot of the palatial staircase at the back of the chamber, the entire patrol had entered the building, fanning out behind us.

'Reddick – get your team upstairs and clear.'

There wasn't much of a second floor, just a walkway that lined the interior wall of the chamber, leading to a balcony that overlooked the front of the building. Reddick's team glided up the staircase, rifles swiveling. I followed them as they jogged along the walkway and through the open door of the balcony.

'Clear!' Reddick reappeared and gave me the thumbs-up. 'There's a shit-load of shell casings out there though.'

I followed him onto the balcony. It was about the length of a tennis court, but thinner, and was paved with white marble that reflected the harsh glare of the mid-day sun. Beyond the chest-high balustrade lay the intersection, then the red tiled roofs of Bermuda falling away to the Indian Ocean, a vast expanse of sparkling cobalt. It was an incredibly peaceful scene; no sound but the wind, and for a moment I could imagine I was somewhere completely different.

Strewn across the paving stones were scores of brass casings, gleaming gold. Reddick picked one up and displayed it between thumb and forefinger.

'AK-47.' The totemic weapon of our enemies.

I leaned on the balustrade and looked down towards the port.

'They had a good view of our approach from here, until we started to get close to the cover of those buildings – that's when they started shooting. Get the M-60 up here in case they show up again.'

Clack lumbered onto the balcony. 'Hey Boss, the QRF's at CP-5, Ponkilla just got the call'. He looked at the shell casings. 'Fuckers.'

'They most certainly are that.'

'Someone's gonna get hurt' He spit a quid of brown Copenhagen juice into the brass.

'Yep, and they'll probably keep playing this game with us every time we come up here until someone does.'

'Well, not much happening up here now. You wanna start back, Boss?'

Clack paused to scowl at a short, skinny Marine who had just walked onto the balcony, festooned with belts of machine-gun ammunition.

'Goddammit Neal – you're not Pancho-fucking-Villa, you'd better square away that ammo or I'll wrap it round your neck.'

'Aye aye, sergeant,' Neal twanged. Every platoon has at least one Neal: 100 per cent deep-boondock rural without a trace of pretense. Neal shed his ammunition, and laid the belts carefully on the balustrade before helping Umberger manhandle the machine gun into place.

'Check out this view, Sergeant Clack.'

He walked over and leant against the balustrade beside me. 'With a little work, this would be a nice place to spend a vacation.'

'I'm not seeing it, sir.'

I paused for thought, and came to a decision.

'Get the team leaders up, I have an idea.'

'Oooh shit.'

Clack yelled for the team leaders, and we met them at the foot of the stairs.

'As soon as we're gone, they're going to come right back and reoccupy this building,' I began, 'so, we're going to make them think we're gone, and then catch them in the open.'

'How's that, sir?' Clack asked.

'We send the bulk of the patrol back to the port, leaving a stay-behind element. We have the QRF on standby.'

'What'll we do when they show up?' *Good question, Reddick.*

'We'll take their weapons. Look – we've got the drop on them now. We need to make them understand that we're not going to take anymore shit.' *That sounded good at least.*

'What if they won't let us?'

'Listen – if any of you have a better idea, I'm all ears'.

They looked at me but said nothing. Dropic was grinning again. He and Cardona, side by side – were good friends but had nothing in common aside from being Grunt NCOs. Dropic was well over 6ft tall and looked like Clark Kent – down to the GI-issue black-framed glasses that he insisted on wearing. In a platoon that broiled with sardonic humor, he was a stand-out comedian. Cardona, slightly built and intensely serious was quiet by the standards of Marine infantrymen. True to form he said nothing now, just looked at me and nodded.

'It's worth a shot, sir.'

Clack tilted his helmet back. His head was so big that he could never find one that fit him comfortably. 'Who's staying back?'

'I'll take Reddick's squad with the 60.' Six Marines in a mortar squad, plus me made seven.

Dropic's grin disappeared; he scowled at Reddick.

'Seven dudes is pretty thin,' Clack said. 'We don't know how many they have, and it's going to take a while for the QRF to get here.'

'Anymore and they'll probably twig that we didn't all leave.' I sounded more confident than I felt. 'We'll be fine.'

'Owwwwkaaay, sir. But I'm going to leave you St Almand anyway – he's pretty handy.'

Clack gripped Dropic and Cardona's shoulders, pulling himself to his feet.

'C'mon ladies, get' em lined up ready to go. Dropic, your squad is on point. Cardona, no need to put flank security out as we leave, Reddick will have us covered from the second deck. We're moving in five minutes. Leatherdale!'

A tall rangy youth emerged from the gloom carrying a radio. 'Sergeant?'

'Get a comm check with Gunny White, and Ponkilla.'

Clack turned to me.

'Good hunting, sir – see you back at the barn.'

I watched from the second-floor balcony as they left, streaming across the intersection and down a side street (not the one we used to arrive, Clack was too good to make that mistake). I could just make out the port, the dun-brown roofs of the warehouses merging in a haze with the water beyond. It seemed a long way away, and I wondered if I had made the right call.

There were five of us on the balcony. Umberger and Neal were setting up the machine gun; Ponkilla sat on the ground by the radio, absent-mindedly tapping the handset against his flak jacket; Reddick, who had returned after positioning the other three Marines downstairs, was standing a few feet back from the balustrade, peering down into the intersection. I was looking through binoculars at the bridge of the *Jack Lummus* thinking how easy it would be to sweep it clean with one burst from a machine gun.

'Sir!'

Neal was pointing across the intersection. Below us a vehicle had swung into view from one of the side streets, and was heading towards us. It was a pick-up truck, its bed packed to capacity with armed men, and above their heads poked the muzzle of a heavy machine gun. There were about ten of them crammed into the vehicle: some sitting astride the sides of the truck-bed, others hanging onto the gun pintle, swaying to and fro as the vehicle lurched over potholes. Following the vehicle, spread in a line across the intersection, was a larger group of fighters. They were dressed like a garage sale, a mix of military surplus and beachwear, but there was no mistaking the weapons they carried or the bandoliers on their chest. They were militiamen, probably from the SLA, Aidid's men. Neal turned around to gape at me, while Umberger crouched with his back to the balustrade, clutching the M-60 to his chest, barrel upwards. *They hadn't set it up.*

'Joogso!' Stop! I yelled – and then, hoping that my pronunciation was intelligible: 'Dig Burundi,' Drop your guns.

Time stopped for a second, maybe a millisecond – then everything happened at once. The men on foot scattered, scurrying for cover on either side of the intersection. The vehicle spun into a U-turn, shedding its load of gunmen, who scrambled in all directions, some running for the steps of our building. Neal was yelling unintelligibly; Umberger had thrown the machine gun onto the balustrade and was fumbling with the charging handle. I whipped my rifle up to cover the gun in the back of the truck – the most dangerous threat – and, with my thumb, clicked the safety catch off. The vehicle stopped, its tailgate now facing towards us. Over my sights I watched as a tall skinny Somali in a lurid floral shirt seized the handle of the mounted gun and swung the barrel in an arc towards us.

Without conscious thought my finger took up the slack and then squeezed the trigger, one, two, three shots, my sights blurred with concentration and sweat, I heard shouting from downstairs – St Almand I think – and then there was a single burst of automatic fire to my left. I was dimly aware of scattered shots in return, and the crack of rounds flying overhead. Floral shirt was lying on the bed of the vehicle and the figure in the passenger seat was slumped on the dashboard. The driver gunned the engine, and the truck lurched forward then shot across the intersection and down a side street. Below us, I could see fighters running across the intersection away from our building.

'Cease fire!' *We didn't need to be shooting people in the back.*

'Shit!'

Umberger slammed the feed tray shut, the gun had jammed after a single burst; he cleared it in seconds but too late to rejoin the fray. There followed a few stunned moments as we caught our breath. Neal was leaning over the balustrade, talking to St Almand below, but there was a loud thudding in my ears and I couldn't hear what they were saying. My mouth was bone dry.

'Anyone hurt, Reddick?'

'No sir, we're all good. Got a couple of them though by the looks of things.'

'Damn straight we did, corporal,' Neal interjected, dancing from foot to foot as he changed the magazines in his weapon. I grabbed the handset from Ponkilla, but before I could speak into it Reddick tugged my sleeve.

'Listen!'

From across the intersection came the loud hum of many voices raised in anger. I couldn't tell for sure, but the noise seemed to be coming from the street down which the truck had disappeared.

'Holy Shit!' said Neal. I pressed the button on the handset, noticing that my hands were shaking. 'Redman three, Redman six.'

'Gotcha six – send it.'

'We need pick up from the Parliament building, time now,' I paused. 'Approach with caution – hostiles and a Technical in the vicinity.'

'Roger,' Gunny drawled. 'Oscar Mike – ETA one zero mikes.'

*Ten minutes – an eternity.* I acknowledged and handed the headset back to Ponkilla, who was grinning uncharacteristically.

'Sounds as though they're pissed,' Neal said, taking his forward hand off his rifle to jab towards the intersection.

'Thank you, Neal.'

The hum of voices rose to a clamor and took on a rhythm in which one or two individual voices could be heard above the others – yelling commands, or perhaps exhorting the others to take action – like an angry Baptist revival. Our small group was silent. Umberger had the machine gun up now and was leaning against the balustrade alongside Neal, their weapons pointed in the direction of the noise, while Ponkilla squatted with the handset pressed against his ear.

I ran through a quick assessment of our situation. We were definitely outnumbered and outgunned; the only advantage we had was that we were in a commanding position, there was only one entrance to the building, and the mob, which is what it sounded like, would have to cross the intersection to get at us. But we could only hold them off for so long and they would be between us and the QRF.

'Hey Gunny,' I said, dropping all radio protocol, 'how far out are you?'

'About 5 mikes.'

'OK, as you cross the intersection, leave one truck in place to cover the west side, we've got an unknown group of hostiles there, and it sounds as though they may be planning to attack.'

'Roger, sir – got it'. Imperturbable. That was Gunny White.

I took a deep breath. It would do no good to blame myself now. I had to get everyone out of here.

'Umberger, Neal – if that crowd starts around the corner, be prepared to fire warning shots in front of them. Don't aim directly at them right off the bat.'

Their response was drowned by the whir of white noise from loud speakers followed by a long, drawn-out wail. It was the afternoon call for prayer. The mournful keening, harsh but melodic, echoed across the roof tops below us and eddied back and forth across the city, one voice picking up as another died. It sounded as though a hundred Imams were competing for the Friday faithful – at least all those not too high on Kat or busy shooting one another.

The voices waivered to an end and the sound of the invisible crowd returned.

'Keep your eyes outboard,' I snapped at Neal who was staring over his shoulder at me again, sweat dripping off his chin, as if to confirm that I was hearing the same thing.

# Chapter 6

'The QRF's here!' I looked in the direction of Reddick's outstretched finger as the radio crackled.

Gunny White's voice crackled over the radio: 'Got a visual on your pos.'

'OK, Gunny, here's the plan. Send one vehicle across the intersection when I give you the word. We'll jump in and haul-ass back.'

I peered over the balustrade. Where the road from the port met the intersection I could make out the tan hood of a Humvee. It edged forward until we could see the driver, hunched over the steering wheel, and then a flash of goggles as the gunner swiveled his machine gun to cover the intersection, now deserted except for whirligig spirals of dust and garbage whipped up by the wind.

I turned; the Marines around me were silent, motionless, their eyes fixed on that Humvee.

'OK fellas, down the stairs. Umberger and Neal, you bring up the rear.'

As I reached the foot of the stairs Ponkilla called from behind: 'They're ready Boss.'

We stacked on either side of the entrance. I peered out and waved at the Humvee; the driver waved back. I could recognize him even at that distance; after more than a year together, we all knew each other well. It was Webster, an earnest Mid-Westerner older than his years, who wanted to be a Baptist preacher when his enlistment ended.

I took the handset: 'OK – go!'

A second later the Humvee raced across the intersection, screeching to a halt amidst a cloud of dust. Before it had stopped, the Marines were stampeding down the steps and clamoring over the tailgate in a headlong rush. Those on board grabbed straps, blouses, anything they could, hauling their comrades over the transom in a blur of limbs. I put one foot on the tailgate, pulled on outstretched hands, and tumbled on top of Ponkilla, jarring my jaw against the radio.

'All aboard!' someone yelled, and with a loud growl of diesels we were moving – clinging for dear life as we careered across the intersection.

There was a scatter of shots but nothing that sounded close. I pulled myself into a sitting position in the truck bed – the benches were all manned by Marines facing outboard – and peered over the tailgate, but could see nothing but the diminishing bulk of the Parliament building through a rooster tail of dust.

Back at the port we decanted the vehicles amidst much backslapping and excited chatter, effervescent with relief. Gunny White was standing by the tailgate as I jumped down, he gripped my hand and grinned, but his tone was serious.

'Sir, I called the incident in. The assistant operations officer is expecting you on the net.' I nodded and followed him to our makeshift command post in the warehouse.

'Andy, Mike here.' The assistant operations officer was a fellow lieutenant, a friend of mine.

'Listen, we need your report about what happened, because MEF Forward is spinning up.'

The headquarters for 1st Marine Expeditionary Force (I MEF) was scheduled to deploy from Camp Pendleton to Mogadishu in the next few days, and a small advance element, referred to as MEF Forward, was already at the airfield. Somehow – I never found out the details – they had already received an intelligence report that several militiamen belonging to Farah Aidid had been killed in a clash with US Marines.

'Some colonel wants to initiate an investigation right away. And the thing is, we haven't been able to get hold of the battalion commander to tell him what happened.' Both the battalion and Marine Expeditionary Unit commanders were with the bulk of the battalion on a relief mission to Baledogle, far inland.

'OK, I'll write a statement now.'

'You're gonna need witnesses.' Mike added, assuming the role of my legal advisor. 'It'll help if you can find someone who's not one of your Marines.'

*Not much chance of that*, I thought as I pulled a pen and notebook from my rucksack. Before I had begun to write, the warehouse door opened and in walked First Lieutenant Jack Rassmussen who commanded the company of military police stationed at the port. Jack mixed Marine officer with back-woods trapper; never without a hefty dip of Copenhagen in his lip and a funny story. Now though, he was stony faced.

'Am I under arrest, Ras?'

'Well, no Andy – at least not yet,' Ras gestured helplessly. 'I'm under orders to have you escorted to the airfield.'

I shrugged. 'OK, but you know I'm happy to go anyway.'

'I know you are bro'. It's just ... orders.' He shrugged.

'Sir, the Marines on patrol with you have been told to write statements,' Gunny White added.

Ras nodded and rested his hand on my shoulder.

'Andy, later today I'm gonna have to send some of my guys with yours back to where it happened. To get the spent casings, take photos, that sort of thing. We'll probably have to take the weapons off everyone who fired.'

'OK, do whatever you need to.' I got to my feet and picked up my rifle. 'Let's go.'

An hour later, I was at the airfield, sitting outside the large tent that functioned as the MEF headquarters, waiting – for what I wasn't sure. I wasn't exactly under arrest but a dour looking colonel had told me not to go anywhere. MEF Forward was still in the process of setting up, and a stream of people passed me as I waited on my campstool, mostly staff officers going about their tasks. No one spoke to me. It was as though my new-found status as war crime suspect might be contagious, which left me plenty of time to think.

I was certain that the decision to open fire had been the right one, the gun swiveling towards us signaled both hostile intent and imminent threat. But I was still shadowed by self-doubt. I had chosen to place my Marines in that situation – and maybe that alone made me culpable. Maybe I'd been too aggressive, too impetuous in a situation that demanded maturity.

On the other hand, I reminded myself, our mission was to provide security in the area around the port, enabling relief supplies to be off-loaded and transported inland. We couldn't do that by sitting in the port itself. In order to secure an area you had to get out and control its environs, dominate the key terrain; that was a fundamental tenet of infantry tactics.

The shadows lengthened, and a fiery-red sun sloped towards the Indian Ocean; while in my mind prosecution and defense sparred with equal determination.

As dusk settled over the airport, a tall, lugubrious lieutenant colonel appeared to question me.

'I'm with the MEF,' he announced, and read me my rights in a flat monotone.

'OK – now tell me what happened, in your own words.'

I wanted to ask him whose words he thought I might use if not my own, but thought better of it. I started to recount the day's events, but as I began, a military policeman hurried through the opening in the concertina wire surrounding the tent, and tugged my inquisitor's sleeve. There followed a hushed conversation, the lieutenant colonel rose and followed the MP through the wire into the shadows beyond. I waited.

When he reappeared – it seemed hours later, but probably wasn't more than ten minutes or so – he was clutching a brown envelope.

'You're free to go, lieutenant. We've got evidence that you acted in self-defense.' He reached out his hand, and it took me a moment to realize that he was offering to shake mine.

'We've got photos of the whole thing,' he explained. He didn't offer to show them to me, but I was happy to take his word for it.

I did get to see them later; they had been taken by an AP photographer and showed in neat sequence of six frames the gunner in the back of the technical swinging the machine gun around in a blurred arc towards our position on the roof. And that wasn't all. On closer inspection, I saw that there were several gunmen in the undergrowth surrounding the building, also pointing their weapons towards us. St Almand, who had been on the ground floor, told me later that he had seen the same thing, and shouted a warning which I failed to hear. We had acted just in time

When I returned to the port, accompanied by the same MPs who had escorted me there, Gunny White explained that the AP photographer trailed the patrol from the port and had started to return with Sergeant Clack's group when he realized that some of us were still in the Parliament building, and decided to join us. He was just preparing to cross the intersection from the far side when the incident happened. He'd developed the photographs in a makeshift darkroom in our warehouse, and upon hearing of my situation and realizing that he had evidence of my innocence, he gave the photos to the MPs.

Every member of the patrol had been questioned, and every one of them had a slightly different recollection of events. It was my first experience of the distorting effect that floods of adrenalin have on perception and memory.

It was never clear to me who at the MEF ordered the investigation. When informed of the incident, the MEF Commanding General Lieutenant, General Johnston, had simply asked 'What does the lieutenant say happened?' Sometimes a casual comment from a general officer will lead his staff to unintended consequences in their efforts to discern his intent. The MEU Commander, Colonel Greg Newbold wrote me a personal note commending the platoon for their performance throughout our time in Mogadishu. It was gesture typical of his style of command. Ten years later he would resign as Director of Operations for the Joint Staff after criticizing Secretary Rumsfeld's plans for the invasion of Iraq.

Karl Maier was a journalist covering the operation in Somalia for the UK's *Independent* newspaper. Writing about our brush with Aidid's militia, he commented:

> A decision on how to react to a challenge from one of the warring factions often had to be made in a split second by an officer in his mid-20s who was never sure if his superiors would support the action.

It was an early lesson for me of a phenomenon that became commonplace later in my career: the high level of scrutiny given to tactical decisions made in the heat of the moment; and the narrow margin in such cases between censure and approbation. Years later, on the tarmac of Tripoli airport and on the outskirts of Mosul, I would walk again this same fine line.

We remained in the port until early February when another infantry battalion arrived from Camp Pendleton to replace us. We continued to run patrols, but though we were sometimes caught in the crossfire between the SLA and Mahdi's militia, no one shot at us intentionally again. The locals warmed to us, and every patrol pulled a crowd of noisy children in its wake. They seemed to have an instinct for sensing trouble, and would melt away abruptly seconds before an outbreak of fighting – as though responding to a signal that only they could hear. We learned to pay attention to them, and on more than one occasion a patrol changed course based on their warnings.

The presence of danger was not enough to distract the mortar platoon from their fondness for high jinx. Late at night on Christmas Eve, Gunny White and I were woken by Reddick.

'Sir, Bradley's fallen in the shit pit and wigged out.'

Translation: Lance Corporal Bradley had fallen into the communal latrine and was evidently upset. I could hear a commotion, the sound of raised voices interspersed by shrieks, as I fumbled for my boots and flashlight, and followed Reddick and Gunny White towards the platoon's berthing area in the derelict warehouse that we called home.

This area, now bathed in silver moonlight from the gaping roof, was the scene from a horror movie. The Marines, in various states of undress, were standing in a loose circle jabbering excitedly, while in their midst, blundering between the camp beds with arms outstretched, was a hideous apparition covered head to toe in slime that reflected a dull brown from the light of several flashlights. As we watched, the figure hollered something incomprehensible and lunged at the nearest Marines, who darted away, leaping camp beds in their haste and squealing like frightened school girls.

'It's the ghost of Christmas Present,' someone shouted.

I gestured to Gunny White: 'All yours.' I knew better than to plunge into this fracas.

Gunny White yelled at the apparition to stand still and, with the help of the squad leaders, restored order. Two Marines were detailed to take Bradley outside and sluice him clean with buckets of water, while Gunny White took the squad leaders aside. He returned to our sleeping area some time later and placed by my camp bed three bottles of whiskey, nearly empty.

'Those are the culprits.'

'Where the hell did they get those?'

Alcohol was off limits to all US personnel in Somalia.

'Marines will find a way,' Gunny said sagely – though I suspected that he knew.

I sat up. 'Gunny, we're the only unit running patrols around here – everyday, live ammunition, getting shot at. We can't afford to have our guys getting drunk.'

Gunny lay on his camp bed, and sighed.

'You're right. They'll suffer for it in the morning and I guarantee it won't happen again.' He raised himself on one elbow and looked at me.

'What's that Kipling quote you were fond of throwing at me back in Pendleton.'

'We aren't no thin red heroes, nor we aren't no blackguards too; but single men in barracks most remarkable like you; and if sometimes our conduct isn't all your fancy paints; why, single men in barracks don't grow into plaster saints.'

'That's it. Well they're no plaster saints either.' Gunny yawned and lay back, closing his eyes. 'Good night sir.'

The next morning's patrol brief had the air of a funeral wake; but by the time we left the gates the Marines were as alert as always. I never brought up the incident again, and there were no repetitions.

The fighting between the SLA and Mahdi's militia continued intermittently, occasionally erupting into lengthy battles. I was manning an observation post with Dropic's squad during the most memorable of these; it was New Year's Eve, and both sides were evidently trying to outdo each other in their eagerness to see out the old year. We lay on our rooftop and watched the show: streams of red tracer snaking back and forth across the Green Line, the flash and crump of mortars, and dark shapes flitting between shadows in the street below.

In early January, we searched the building that housed Radio Mogadishu, the city's only working station. Intelligence reports indicated that the SLA was stockpiling weapons in the compound that surrounded the building, and we had orders to confiscate them. Sure enough, we found several dozen German G-3s, a weapon far superior to the AK-47, still in their original packing cases. For reasons that were not clearly explained, I was instructed to turn these over to one of the local sub-clan leaders. We did so, but only after removing the firing pins, rendering them inoperable.

As the battalion re-embarked on ship, I remained ashore for two weeks as a liaison to a newly arrived Pakistani Brigade, part of the United Nations task force. Two months after we left, the SLA ambushed a company from this brigade as they searched the Radio Mogadishu compound, killing twenty-three and wounding sixty. It was the beginning of a cycle of clashes between UN forces and the SLA that led to the debacle of Task Force Ranger in October, the subsequent withdrawal from Somalia of US forces, and the collapse of the UN mission.

*Part II*

# The Harshest School

*We should remember that one man is much the same as another, and that he is best who is trained in the harshest school.*

THUCYDIDES

(Quote displayed on the walls of Marine Officer Candidate School)

# Chapter 7

After Somalia, my experience of the 1990s was, as for many in the military, one of some frustration, with little prospect of action to break the repetitive cycle of training on a tight budget.

Upon my battalion's return from Somalia, I turned over command of the platoon and spent a few months at the MEF's Special Operations Training Group as I awaited the results of a board to decide my future. Because I had been commissioned from the ranks, I fell into a category of officers who, after their initial three-year term of service, had to compete for a regular commission in order to remain in the Marine Corps. In the early 1990s, the Corps had more junior officers than it needed, and the selection rate was habitually below the 20 per cent mark – so I was on tenterhooks. I had recently married and we were expecting a child; but what really concerned me was the prospect of no longer being a Marine.

SOTG, as it was known, was responsible for conducting the training that enabled MEUs to be designated special-operations capable. My boss there was a lieutenant colonel who had just been removed from his position as a MEU operations officer after philandering his way across the Pacific at great government expense. In search of new opportunities for plunder, he wasn't the slightest bit interested in me; so I took the opportunity to undergo the full gamut of courses that SOTG offered – shooting, explosives, reconnaissance and surveillance – all wonderfully distracting activities for a young lieutenant uncertain about his future. One course, however – SERE school – was singularly unpleasant. SERE stands for Survival Evasion Resistance Escape – which pretty much sums up the school's purpose: how to avoid capture, and if caught, how to resist giving up information that might help the enemy. It's a short course, only two weeks, and would hardly be worth a mention were it not for its use of interrogation technique, namely waterboarding, that was to excite much controversy in the post 9/11 era.

The interrogation part occurs during the resistance phase when students are imprisoned in a mock prison camp (which seems very real at the time), deprived of sleep and food and generally treated roughly. No one envies the student who holds the highest rank during this phase, because the prison guards focus much of their attention on him. In my class, the senior prisoner, a navy pilot, abdicated his responsibilities at the beginning of the phase, whereupon the prison authorities bestowed on me this unwanted honor. I emerged at the end of the course several pounds lighter, with a number of fresh bruises and a determination never to be taken prisoner. At the beginning of the course the school's director warned us that his instructors were told to treat us 'in the brutal manner that you can expect your enemies to behave.' In light of this statement, I always considered one of the subsequent defenses of enhanced interrogation – that we use it on our own personnel at SERE school – to be somewhat ironic.

In the fall of 1993, Headquarters Marine Corps informed me that I could remain a Marine until, as is customary for officers, such time as I was passed over twice for promotion.

'Whenever the Marine Corps gives you good news, you'd better brace yourself,' I remember one of my drill instructors saying. ('Brace yourself' is the bowdlerized version of what he actually said, but the meaning is the same). Sure enough, within a week I received orders for the Marine Corps Recruit Depot at San Diego. *Ah well*, I thought at the time, *beggars can't be choosers.*

My tour at MCRD San Diego turned out to be like an extended version of SERE school: overall not an enjoyable experience, but one that left me with some valuable lessons.

While there, I took command of a company after its previous leadership had been relieved and a number of drill instructors court-martialed for the abuse of recruits. When I use the term, abuse, I don't just mean violations of the recruit training SOP, but sadistic, morally bereft behavior that ranged from swindling recruits financially, to making them undergo humiliating, homo-erotic rituals. My mandate was simple: to get the ship back on course – but this was a task that was to prove easier said than done. I had a company staff that was inexperienced, and at times appeared to be intimidated by an unhealthy, almost feral ethos that held sway among the drill instructors. I learned some hard lessons, and it took a full year before the company was back on track.

It needn't have taken that long. If I had understood the keystone of that company's culture – the extraordinary influence wielded by senior drill instructors – I would have simply promised each of them that if anything happened in their platoons, they would lose their jobs. Instead I wasted time trying to stem the flow of abuse by going after culprits as incidents came to light. Incidentally, senior drill instructors are fairly junior NCOs, sergeants and staff sergeants, which goes to show that even in a hierarchical organization like the Marine Corps, real power is often linked to personality (good and bad) rather than rank.

I was very much under the spotlight during this period, and came close to being relieved myself – a prospect that filled me with greater dread than any of my subsequent experiences in combat.

My tour at the Depot had an amusing sequel. Disillusioned by my experiences there, I decided to leave the Marine Corps. I submitted an application to the Drug Enforcement Administration, as part of which I was asked to list any use of illegal drugs. My trip across Iran and South East Asia had included an illicit excursion across the border from Thailand into Burma with a group of three Swedish mercenaries whose intention was to assist the Karen National Liberation Army in their rebellion against the Burmese government. I wasn't going to join them in this venture, but was intrigued by the Karen people, and decided to stay with them for several days before returning to Thailand. In the village where I was staying, there was an evening ritual which involved everyone gathering together in a communal hut to share stories – and smoke opium. Not wanting to offend my hosts, I did the same. I dutifully listed this incident on my DEA application (although whether this practice was illegal in that part of Burma, I couldn't say). Not surprisingly, the DEA decided that they could continue without me; and so, by a strange trick of fate, the decision to smoke opium saved my Marine Corps career.

In 1998, I joined 3rd Battalion, 4th Marines (3/4) where I was to spend four years as company commander and operations officer – one of the happiest periods of my career. The battalion was stationed at the Marine Corps Base in Twenty-Nine Palms California which encompasses a vast swath of the Mojave Desert. It's a desolate place, referred to by Marines, with pithy lack of affection, as 'The Stumps.' It even smells bad: thanks to a hopelessly inefficient waste treatment facility the stench of sewage hangs over the base like a rancid pall. We didn't know it then, but it was the perfect place to prepare for Iraq.

It wasn't the perfect place for my wife Madolyn, and the move sounded the death-knell for our marriage, but we parted amicably. It had been crumbling for some time in any case, and I think that we had only remained together for the sake of our daughter Siobhan. Parting with Siobhan was unutterably painful, as any father separated from his children by divorce knows. In the years to come, with deployments and moves across the Marine

Corps, I never saw as much of Siobhan as I wanted to – and it is a credit to her understanding that we are so close today.

A Marine infantry company comprises roughly 160 Marines, divided into a headquarters section, three platoons and a weapons platoon. The platoons, each of which is commanded by a lieutenant, are the company's maneuver elements, designed – in the words of the infantry manual – to locate, close with and destroy the enemy. The weapons platoon is home to the company's fire support: machine guns, mortars and anti-tank rockets, which are used to pin the enemy down, enabling the platoons to close on his position.

Company command is the single most important milestone for an infantry officer. It's the first time that he commands a self-contained unit, the first time that he is in charge of other officers and the last time that he will be close enough to his Marines to know all their names. It's a make or break assignment. For the next ten years or so, the first thing that any selection board will look at is how he performed while in company command.

It's been twenty years now since I took command of Company L (called Lima Company) 3rd Battalion, 4th Marines – but I still remember the joy of commanding that particular group of Marines, in that place, at that time. We have a saying in the Marine Corps that it's better to have to rein in subordinates than prod them to action, and the lieutenants of Lima Company were chomping at the bit. Ford Philips my XO, Scott Huesing, Eddie Correa, Jim Williamson, Marcus Tessier and Philip Waggoner were all thoroughbreds, driven with an energy that permeated the entire company. I had a strong company staff and rock-solid non-commissioned officers; it was as though fate had deliberately handed me the antithesis to my experience at the recruit depot. And the Marines were Marines – a joy to work with.

There can be few better locations in which to command an infantry company than the desert. In a two-year cycle, Marine infantry units will typically spend a month at Twenty-Nine Palms, during which time all hands count the days until they can return to civilization. Third Battalion, Fourth Marines was one of four battalions belonging to the 7th Marine Regiment, for whom Twenty-Nine Palms was their permanent home, its savage austerity a badge of honor.

With no one for miles around, we could use live ammunition for our training, which injected an air of realism. The sound of bullets cracking overhead never fails to get the adrenalin pumping, even if you know that they aren't aimed at you; and for officers and NCOs, charged with ensuring that the angle between lethal impact and charging infantrymen never violated the margin of safety, it could be a nerve-racking business. We loved it.

I even came to enjoy Twenty-Nine Palms. I liked waking up in the field to the blue-gray light of dawn, before the sun turned the desert into an inferno, and listening to the sounds of the company coming to life. You could look to the horizon on all sides without sight of another human being; just rolling breakers of sand, lava rock, and salt lakes, dry since pre-historic times; with the sky a brightly hued mosaic of red and gold as the sun rose. The nights were glorious too: the stars etched brilliantly against the velvet-black of the sky, the cool breeze soothing sun-parched skin, and then a moon that bathed the landscape yellow; bright as day.

But no one becomes accustomed to the heat of day in summer, when the sun becomes a searing, malevolent presence, sapping the body of energy and making the lightest task an effort. Burdened as we were with body armor, weapons and ammunition, nerves spooled by the proximity of live rounds, it made training all the more challenging.

Cross-desert marches, or hikes as they are misleadingly called in the Marine Corps, were a regular part of training. I suspect any infantryman who claims to enjoy hikes to be lying; but they are a time-honored method to build endurance and unit cohesion. 'March or Die' is the 7th Marine Regiment's motto; and march we did: across the rock-strewn desert floor and up the steep hills that ring the base like brooding sentinels. The memory of those hikes stays with me: plodding along drenched in sweat, gritty with layers of sand, lashed by a hot wind, with nothing to divert the mind but the file of helmets, packs and weapons ahead, blurred by clouds of dust.

Then, every hour, the blessed relief of a short break. For officers, a time to check on their Marines, while corpsmen examined blisters and the Marines joked, bitched, and berated each other in language so profane that it was close to art.

The town of Twenty-Nine Palms is relatively cosmopolitan now, but back then offered little to do. On Fridays, most single Marines, officer and enlisted, headed for greener pastures: San Diego or Los Angeles, returning to the high desert on Sunday afternoon to prepare for the week ahead.

It was during one of these weekend sojourns that I met my wife-to-be Jessica. I was in a small bar in downtown Carlsbad, just south of Camp Pendleton, when I saw a girl chatting to my friends at the bar. She had long dark hair that tumbled down her back in ringlets and a beautiful smile. I was entranced.

'What's her name?' I asked a friend, trying to figure out how to approach her.

'Jessica,' he replied.

I walked up to the group at the bar, fixed my eyes on her and blurted out. 'Jessica.' That was it; not an impressive opening gambit. I still squirm at the memory, but in my defense, living in a place like Twenty-Nine Palms can cause your social skills to atrophy.

Jessica agreed to go out with me the following night – I think more out of curiosity about my British accent than anything else. That date went well enough, though in the course of our conversation she accused me of faking my accent (later, after I took her to England and introduced her to my family, she still claimed that I had gone to the trouble of setting up an elaborate ruse). She was studying to be an occupational therapist and lived in nearby Vista with her mother, who was first generation Italian, and her brother, a former Marine. She loved dogs and the theater. I was smitten.

Our next date was a disaster. I invited her to Twenty-Nine Palms (my first mistake), and took her to a bar called the Stumps (my second) where we watched a series of drunken lance corporals sing karaoke. I decided that we needed a change of venue so took her to the Joshua Tree Saloon (third mistake), a pub whose clientele reminded Jessica of the bar scene in Star Wars. I said goodbye later that night, convinced that I wouldn't see her again. Despite this inauspicious start, it was the beginning of a relationship that would survive frequent separation and some hard times during the years to come.

After a year, I turned Lima Company over to the capable hands of a good friend, Brandon McGowan, and took command of the battalion's weapons company. Weapons Company comprises the battalion's 81mm mortar platoon, heavy machine guns platoon and anti-tank platoon – filling the same function for the battalion as weapons platoon does for the company.

Again, I had a superb stable of lieutenants, all hand-picked from across the battalion: Ford Philips, who followed me from Lima, Brian Coyne, Brandon Graham and Jerry Willingham. They generally made my life easy, although I was alternately amused and irritated by the antics of the mortar platoon who seemed intent on carrying on the bad-boy tradition.

On one occasion I was summoned to explain to the base commanding general why the platoon had dropped their shorts and mooned him during an inter-unit basketball tournament. He had been in civilian clothes at the time (they claimed not to have recognized him), and had remonstrated with them for not wearing their shirts, whereupon they decided to display much more. Almost *verklempt* with anger, he wanted to know how I managed to command so ill-disciplined a group of Marines. I couldn't answer his question, and he dismissed me with the threat of relief should it happen again. Years later, as a senior civilian official in the Pentagon, the same general was himself relieved of his duties for the improper use of government funds. There's a moral in that story somewhere.

In addition to leading the company, the weapons company commander is the battalion's fire support coordinator – responsible for orchestrating in concert the employment of artillery, aviation and mortars in support of the battalion's maneuver, without hurting the wrong people. And again, Twenty-Nine Palms was the perfect place to practice this skill.

In the summer of 2000, I turned over Weapons Company to become the battalion operations officer. Lieutenant Colonel Blake Crowe had just taken over the battalion and my first task was to put together a two-year training schedule which would cover his time in command. I heard that the Marine Corps Warfighting Laboratory was planning to conduct a battalion-sized urban combat exercise, and, always on the lookout for something to break routine, asked Crowe if we could volunteer 3/4 to be the exercise force. He agreed.

Our battleground was a disused air force base in Victorville, California, an area as large as a small town. We used chalk ammunition to add realism, and the lab brought in experts from the UK and Israel to evaluate us.

Every morning, I had to come up with a plan to conduct an attack into a particular part of the city based on the scenario given me by the exercise control cell. Playing the opposition was the battalion's Lima Company, led by Captain Martin Wetterauer, a hatchet-faced Cajun with a reputation for tactical competence; and though we were friends that wasn't going to blunt Martin's determination to win. He had an all-important advantage on his side: his team was in the defense, hunkered down in buildings waiting for us to come to them. You can't conceal the movement of an entire battalion through a built-up area, and he would always be able to locate us.

But we had an advantage on our side too. Commanding Kilo Company was Chris Nicewarner, a tough Arizonan with the uncontrived stance and slow drawl of a western gunfighter. Chris was quite simply the quintessential Marine infantry officer: a skilled tactician who cared deeply for his Marines and believed in his profession the way that a Jesuit believes in Catholicism. Chris was the reason why Kilo Company was invariably the battalion's main effort and why we could give Wetterauer a run for his money.

Nevertheless, in Victorville we learned one of the fundamental lessons of urban warfare: dislodging a determined enemy is a costly business, no matter how much firepower you have on your side. By the end of the exercise, I doubt that there was a battalion in the Marine Corps better prepared for urban combat. But I hoped that we would never have to use what we had learned.

# Chapter 8

The battalion was mid-way through a six-month deployment to the Far East, when Al Qaeda attacked the World Trade Center. We had just completed a month of mountain warfare training in Korea, and I was in a restaurant in Seoul with a group of officers from the battalion when the unforgettable images appeared on the television above the bar.

Without sound or context, the terrible clear shots looked to us like scenes from a movie: the underside of a silver jetliner against a brilliant blue sky as it sailed into the flank of a majestic skyscraper; the slow-motion collapse of the second tower leaving in its place a phantom shape sculpted in smoke. Subtitles appeared, shattering our illusions; and then a breathless military policeman ordered us back to base.

It has since become axiomatic to say that things were never the same after 9/11, but for those in the military the contrast was particularly stark. Until that point, our lives had been a predictable cycle of training and peacetime deployments. The attack on the World Trade Center brought to an end the certainty of routine and rendered our future a void.

I stayed up that night watching the news, sickened and angry but unable to turn it off. Nor did I feel like joining my friends in the hotel bar where they had gathered after our return from downtown. The bellicose talk, at first cathartic, had become repetitive, a hollow reminder of our helplessness. Our nation was under attack, and we whose mission it was to defend her were on the other side of the world drinking beer.

I called Jessica, wanting distraction from the ghastly repetitive scenes on television. It was still morning in California, and she had woken up to the news.

'What happens now?' she asked. She had been crying.

'I wish that I knew,' I admitted, aware that my wooden answer offered no solace. 'Something I hope.'

Two months later, US forces invaded Afghanistan, among them Marines from two shipborne expeditionary units. The battalion was in Okinawa at the time, and we followed the news hungrily, with emotions that swung between pride and envy. The campaign to overthrow the Taliban seemed to have been a resounding success – and, glumly, we assumed that the war was done.

If this desire to go to war seems distasteful, I offer context. Our professional lives were focused on preparing ourselves and our Marines for combat; now we sought validation. The attack on our country demanded retribution, and we believed it our duty to exact this toll. Many Americans appeared to expect the same: 'When are you guys going to get over there and kick ass?' an airport security officer asked me as we arrived back in California.

'I thought that all you Marines were in Afghanistan,' one of Jessica's friends offered unhelpfully.

By the time that the battalion returned home in March 2002, collective mourning had given way to a surge of patriotism. Members of the military were applauded in public places, people gave up their first-class seats on planes, bought us drinks and offered free tickets to sporting events. Many of us, myself included, felt chagrined to be riding the wave of popular sentiment without paying our dues.

We soon glimpsed the opportunity to do so. The battalion returned from post-deployment leave to rumors that an invasion of Iraq was in the offing. A week or two later, 7th Marine Regiment confirmed these rumors with the order to prepare for war; though no one knew yet when this might be.

That summer, training picked up in earnest. As operations officer, I was working long days to help orchestrate the countless tasks that go into preparing a unit for war: ordering intelligence briefings on the Iraqi army, working with the logistics officer to develop plans for getting the battalion to Kuwait by aircraft, and coordinating training exercises.

Although not unexpected, I was bitterly disappointed to receive orders sending me to Quantico.

'That's it for us, bro'.' Chris Nicewarner commiserated. He too was leaving the battalion. 'We'll be watching the war on CNN and drowning our sorrows.'

In late summer 2002, I transferred to a unit called the Coalition and Special Warfare Center or CSW; and, as I kicked my heels in Quantico and the drumbeat to war grew louder, it appeared as though Chris's prediction would prove correct.

CSW consisted of three majors, whose task it was to put together training missions in South America and Eastern Europe. I questioned the value of this assignment in light of current events, making myself a thorough nuisance. When I reached out directly to the 7th Marines' commanding officer, Colonel Stephen Hummer, to solicit a billet on his staff, my chain of command had had enough. I was called in for a tongue-lashing by my boss, a rotund colonel who having just finished commanding a helicopter squadron, was biding his time until retirement and saw the impending war as a nuisance. He was one of those forcedly hearty officers who mistakes platitudes and false bonhomie for leadership, for which reason we called him Jolly Roger.

'You need to settle down or he's really going to screw you over,' predicted Brian Fitzgibbons. Brian had been one of my instructors at the Marine Infantry Officer Course, and was now a colleague and close friend. I would normally follow his advice, but was frustrated by our inactivity and Jolly Roger's intransigence. Brian's prediction proved correct: Jolly Roger made comments on my performance evaluation that threatened to scupper my chances for promotion. I wasn't to discover this until several months later, but even if I had known, would have considered it worth the cost of going to war.

In October, Congress voted to authorize the use of military force against Iraq. I was interested to read that this resolution wasn't based solely on the threat from weapons of mass destruction, but cited also Saddam's 'brutal repression of Iraq's civilian population.'

*Why not?* I thought. The Responsibility to Protect, a doctrine that holds the international community responsible to protect all citizens of the world, had not yet been endorsed by the UN but had a wide body of support among its members. The Canadian government had championed the doctrine in a 2001 proposal to the UN, arguing that if a government fails to meet its obligation to protect its own citizens, then it forfeits the sanctity afforded by the international community to the sovereignty of states. Not yet a legal justification perhaps, but certainly a moral one; and one that made sense to me.

That Christmas, while on leave in the UK, I found myself defending the argument for invading Iraq. President Bush had just announced the deployment of US troops to Kuwait, sparking heated debate among my British friends, most of whom were opposed to the war.

I conceded that UN Resolution 1441 probably did not offer sufficient legal grounds for going to war, but argued that there was no body of international law that made invasion, strictly speaking, illegal. Opposition to the war, I said, was based on an outmoded view of state sovereignty dating back to the Treaty of Westphalia in 1648, and no longer made sense in the twenty-first century.

On the other hand, I argued, invasion could be justified morally according to the theory of Just War: the ethical doctrine, dating back to Roman times and adopted by Christian theologians, that establishes moral parameters for the use of military force. According to this theory, war is justified if its purpose is to redress a wrong (Saddam's repression of his own people) with the intention of establishing a peace preferable to the current status quo. This sounded convincing after several pints of beer in the pub, but my argument was flawed. War unleashes a chain of events so complex that no one can predict their outcome.

# Chapter 9

'Andy, you need to get back here ASAP.' Fitz's voice over the phone was uncharacteristically serious.

'Why what's up?' I stood up, pointing at the phone and making a face at my 9 -year-old daughter Siobhan. I was on leave in San Clemente California, and we were eating lunch at a restaurant on the pier.

'Your orders just arrived – you're going to war, bro'.'

It was early March 2003, and I had given up hope of getting assigned to 7th Marines, already in Kuwait.

'What do they say?'

'They say to get your ass over there so that they can kick this thing off.'

'Seriously, Fitz.'

I was wary; Fitz enjoyed practical jokes, and I could imagine him covering the phone and grinning at Tony Marro, the third major in our troika.

'Major Andrew R. Milburn, you are directed to report to 1st Marine Division for duty with 7th Marine Regiment for a period of 189 days,' Fitz read. 'Do you want me to go on?'

That sounded real. I stifled a celebratory yell.

'But you've got to check in with 1st Marine Division Rear in Camp Pendleton for pre-deployment training.'

I groaned; the war was expected to begin any day. Pre-deployment training would mean at least a week. I leaned over the side of the pier. It was a cool misty southern California day; several surfers were riding the rolling breakers below, while gulls wheeled and dived amongst them.

'Listen Fitz, I'm just outside Pendleton now. Doesn't make sense for me to head back to Quantico. I'll just check in here tomorrow.'

'OK bro', sounds good. You're a lucky mofo and I'm happy for you, but Tony says that you are a conniving bastard,' Fitz chuckled. 'And Jolly Roger's going to lose his mind.'

'He'll get over it. I'll ask Frank to smooth things over.'

Frank Topley was the long-suffering lieutenant colonel in charge of us three majors. I hung up the phone and dialed Frank's number but there was no answer. *I'll call him later,* I thought and rejoined my daughter, my mind humming with anticipation.

The next day I reported to 1st Marine Division headquarters on Camp Pendleton where a sympathetic gunnery sergeant rushed me from the rifle range to the gas chamber to the supply warehouse in a single day, which may be a record. Then, after an interminable ride on a military-chartered airplane – stopping, it seemed, at every conceivable destination in between – I hitched a ride to the desert encampment near the Iraqi border that was 7th Marines' temporary home.

'Good luck, sir,' said the Marine truck driver from whom I had cadged a ride. 'Don't worry – this war will be a short one.' I wondered what information he had to suggest that, as I jumped down from the cab, retrieved my rucksack and looked around.

I seemed to have arrived in the middle of a sandstorm which, I would discover, was a regular late-afternoon event in this part of the world. Through billowing swirls of dust I could make out the blurred outline of large tents: row upon row stretching for hundreds of yards on all sides, and beyond them the featureless gray desert rising to merge in a dusky haze with a horizon tinged orange by the dying sun.

It was my first experience of the desert that extends from Kuwait across the lower two-thirds of Iraq. It was nothing like the rolling dunes depicted in the movies; more like a giant building site: hard scrabble dirt covered by a layer of powder that rose in choking clouds at the least movement.

I stopped two Marines striding past, their faces obscured by goggles and neckerchiefs, and asked them for directions.

'Seventh Marines headquarters is over there, about 200 yards or so,' said one, pointing. 'Welcome to the asshole of the world, sir,' he added. 'I think they stuck the grunts out here to get us good and pissed off for the war.'

'Iraq's gotta be better than this,' agreed the other Marine. Little did he know.

'Welcome aboard, Andy – glad you made it.' Lieutenant Colonel Nick Vuckovich, the operations officer for 7th Marines, met me in the headquarters tent a few minutes after my arrival. Nick was stocky and had Slavic features under a mop of jet black hair. His warm welcome was, I would learn, typical of the man; and I had immediate reason to be grateful.

'Listen Andy, we received word from Headquarters Marine Corps that you are UA.' UA stood for unauthorized absence, the Marine Corps' equivalent of AWOL.

'What?'

By the time the words were out of my mouth, I guessed what had happened.

'Apparently your command in Quantico reported you missing.' Nick was grinning now. 'Fortunately, the officer at headquarters who received the report guessed what happened and called us. We confirmed that you checked in on Pendleton. Anyway, now you're here I wouldn't worry. I doubt CSW will pursue this; it doesn't make sense to charge you for going to war.'

I thought of Jolly Roger and wasn't so sure. Still, I had only myself to blame.

'OK, let's meet the fellas, then get to work.' Nick slapped my back. 'You might end up wishing that you'd gone to the brig instead.' Over the course of subsequent weeks I would be grateful time and again for Nick's steady hand and enlightened leadership. It came as no surprise to me to discover later that while we were still Iraq he took the time write to my parents back in England giving them glowing reports of my performance. A real leader without trace of pretense or ego, that was Nick.

Later that evening, Nick gathered his team together in a corner of the operations tent. Raising his voice just enough to be heard above the hum of a generator, he addressed the assembled group – some ten or so officers – in even, measured tones, looking intently around the circle of faces.

'Fellas, at this stage of the game, you don't need a bunch of direction from me; but I want to share a few words of advice before we kick this thing off. None of us knows how long this war will last, so make sure that you pace yourselves. Lives really will depend on the decisions that you make, and you won't realize how much tiredness has affected your judgment until it's too late. This isn't a training exercise and you can't just power through without sleep.'

On the eve of battle, the first thing that Nick had to tell us was to get some rest. At the time, it wasn't the advice that I expected to hear, but in the years since have been reminded often of its wisdom. The kind of bone-deep tiredness wrought by prolonged stress and lack of sleep doesn't simply sap your ability to make sound decisions, it alters the filter through which you see the world. I have seen exhausted commanders, myself included, driven by a sense of responsibility, and perhaps the Marine tendency towards masochism, do things that they would never contemplate when rested. This same ethos infuses the staff and subordinate commanders with the result that those who should be getting the most sleep, end up with the least.

'Second,' Nick continued, 'as long as you understand the commander's intent, and make decisions according to that, I will back you 100 per cent.'

This was the Marine Corps creed of war fighting distilled to a single phrase. The only aspect of combat that is thoroughly predictable is its unpredictability. The enemy and circumstance combine to frustrate the simplest of plans, interfering with the normal rules of cause and effect. And the further you are away from the action, the longer it takes to find out what's happening, to make informed decisions and to transmit those decisions to your subordinates.

Marine Corps doctrine is based on an understanding of this phenomenon, which Clausewitz referred to as friction. The only practical way to deal with friction is to empower subordinates to make decisions based on their understanding of the mission, and their interpretation of what is happening in front of them. It's a philosophy of command that requires a high degree of trust, a question of character more than education or training. This may be why some commanders appear to find it impossible to practice.

Nick went on to discuss the division of labor between each member of his team.

'Andy and John, in addition to your duties as the future ops cell, you are going to be my eyes and ears forward – the directed telescope thing. You need to get with Gunner Eby, who has the same task, and sort out how to do that.'

Major John Schaar, an old friend from Twenty-Nine Palms, was a tank officer by trade, but also an expert in fire support – the science of integrating everything that goes boom to support the infantry in the attack. John was my opposite in almost every respect: tall and blond, and meticulous in his attention to detail. Despite our contrasts – or maybe because of them – we got along famously, never allowing our frequent arguments to degenerate into rancor. Now he and I exchanged grins, elated not to be tethered to headquarters during the upcoming fight.

Chief Warrant Officer Jeff Eby, the Regimental Gunner, or Weapons Officer as was the official title, was bantam-weight and grizzled, with a face like an angry troll. If Marine Infantry were a religious order – and the analogy isn't a bad one – gunners would be the high priests, guardians of the sacred rites; and Jeff had, through a genuine love for his profession, earned his place among the most exalted. Despite his appearance, he was among the most generous and patient of men. Now he winced, clapping his forehead in mock dismay. 'So I've got two majors to babysit – thanks Nick.'

Vuckovich looked around the circle of faces. 'Any questions, fellas?'

There were none.

'Well I've got one for you.'

Nick pointed at Lieutenant Colonel Andrew Balding, a reservist on temporary loan to the regiment, who had the incongruously debonair nickname Blade.

'Why hasn't someone policed up Blade? Those shorts are affecting morale.'

The lower half of Blade's ponderous bulk was squeezed into a pair of tiny khaki shorts; a garment that had, much to our chagrin, become his trademark off-duty attire. Blade looked crestfallen but everyone else roared, happy for an excuse to undercut the tension.

A Marine regiment comprises four infantry battalions but when the regiment goes to war it is augmented with artillery, tank, mechanized and support units to form a Regimental Combat Team or RCT. Seventh Marines, now designated RCT-7, was assigned its own camp located a few miles from the Kuwaiti border, and as rumors spread that the invasion would take place in a matter of days, the place was abuzz with anticipation. Squads of Marines practiced drills across the hardpacked sand, officers gathered for meetings, and a continuous stream of trucks delivered a mountain of supplies.

This was to be a mechanized war, with the infantry being carried on armored personnel carriers and trucks, and the camp was a vast parking lot with row upon row of vehicles. There were sleek Abrams tanks, 7-ton trucks, every variant of the ubiquitous Humvee, high-speed light armored vehicles of the type known by Marines as LAVs, and row upon row of bulbous amphibious assault vehicles, the trademark carrier of Marine infantry since the 1960s. These lumbering, top heavy thinly armored museum pieces were referred to as amtracs or simply tracks – terms that I will use from here on.

A few days after my arrival, Colonel Hummer summoned together the officers of RCT-7 for a brief on the plan of the attack. We crammed together in the operations tent, sitting shoulder to shoulder on metal chairs facing a large map on the wall.

The regiment's intelligence officer, Major Ron Spears, began the brief with an overview of the Iraqi order of battle: the location and size of the enemy units arrayed against us.

The Iraqi Army 3rd Corps, made up of three divisions, an estimated 30,000 soldiers, had the mission of defending southern Iraq, he said, pointing to a map where red rectangles depicted the location of enemy units. Spears didn't rate 3rd Corps highly but warned against assuming that they would simply give up.

'This isn't like the Gulf War when they were stuck on a limb in Kuwait. Now there're fighting on their home turf.'

Saddam had reserved his best troops, the Republican Guard, to defend the area around Baghdad. Spears used a pointer to trace the line of the Euphrates River that ran north-west to south-east across the map.

'The Euphrates is key terrain for several reasons. First, it's a significant natural barrier, and we can expect the Iraqis to blow the bridges if they can, blocking our advance on Baghdad. Second, once we cross the Euphrates we are going to be facing Saddam's varsity team, the Republican Guard with the nation's capital at their backs. Third, if he hasn't already done so, this is where Saddam is likely to make the decision to use chemical weapons.'

The threat of chemical weapons was the reason why all US troops wore MOPP suits. MOPP stands for Mission Oriented Protective Posture; an acronym as absurdly cumbersome as the suits themselves. The charcoal-lined overgarments trapped body heat, and were only mission oriented if the mission didn't require any physical activity. The boots, resembling rubber car mats with strings attached, had to be wrapped around your real boots and tied off. They made us walk like cartoon characters and were constantly unraveling.

'Do you think that Saddam's going to pull the trigger on using chem?' someone asked.

'Oh yes,' Ron replied cheerfully. 'We're gonna get slimed. It's just a question of when. Could be as soon as we cross the border, or maybe when we reach Baghdad.'

Nick Vuckovich took the pointer from Ron and launched into his brief without preamble.

'OK fellas, there's been one significant change since the last time you heard this. As you know, the army's 4th Infantry Division was supposed to attack through Turkey, making this a two-front war. Well, the Turks shut that down, so it's not going to happen.'

Turning to face the map he talked through the opening moves for the invasion.

'So now everyone's coming from the south out of Kuwait. Furthest west, the army's 5th Corps is going to cross the border and head for Baghdad from across the desert. To their right, 1st Marine Division will destroy the Iraqi 3rd Armor Corps and attack towards Baghdad along two parallel routes. On the division's far left flank, Task Force Tarawa and RCT-1 attack to seize a bridgehead across the Euphrates at Nasiriyah. To our immediate left RCT-5 attacks to seize the Rumaila oilfields. To our right, the Brits will seize the port of Um Qasr and then attack to secure Basrah.'

Baghdad was the ultimate goal, its seizure represented 'cutting off the head of the snake', a phrase that had been used to the point of cliché over the preceding months. If one of the two routes to the capital was blocked, then the division would funnel its main effort up the other. Speed was imperative. We were not only racing against the enemy, but also against any attempt by the international community to negotiate a peace short of US victory.

Nick was skimming through the missions of higher and adjacent units; most of his audience could have recited them in their sleep. He then came to ours:

RCT-7 will attack to destroy the enemy's 51st Mechanized Division south of Basrah to enable the subsequent push towards Baghdad.

He went on to outline the tasks for each subordinate unit, emphasizing in each case the intent of their mission as a guide for action should their specified tasks become irrelevant. When Nick was done, Colonel Hummer stood up and spoke briefly. He told everyone to expect friction. Things would not go according to plan: the enemy, weather, poor communications and chance would conspire to derail the plan that had just been briefed. But, he emphasized, we had trained together for months as a team and knew what needed to be done. He ended by wishing everyone luck. John and I exchanged glances: *This certainly sounded like the final brief.* Then the chaplain rose to give a prayer. *Yep, that settles it.*

# Chapter 10

A day later Vuckovich called us together to pass the word: we would cross the line of departure on March 21, two days hence. As the others trooped out of the tent, Nick pulled Jeff Eby and me aside. 'I want you to go with the PsyOp guys tomorrow on their mission.'

Attached to us was an Army Psychological Operations unit who had been ordered up to the border on the eve of the attack in an effort to induce the Iraqi front-line units to surrender. For this purpose, they had giant speakers mounted on the back of their Humvee, which – their captain had assured me – could put out more decibels than a rock concert.

'No problem, sir – what's up?'

'Well, all the intel folks at Division think that the Iraqis are ready to pack it in, like they did back in the First Gulf War. They just need a push and someone to tell them how to do it without getting shot.'

I had heard the same, and it made sense. If I was an Iraqi commander no matter how patriotic, I would be considering my options. They had outdated equipment, poor logistics support and a chain of command that displayed psychosis and denial in equal measure. And they faced annihilation at the hands of a vastly superior force backed by a staggering array of fire power. Earlier that day, a British officer had told me that the UK contingent had a plan to lob illumination rounds at thirty second intervals over the Iraqi positions all night, followed by a broadcast, delivered by an Iraqi defector, informing them that they had an hour to surrender or the next shells would be high explosives.

'So, this PsyOp mission has a real chance of succeeding.' Nick looked almost disappointed at the prospect. 'I don't want anything to screw it up, and I want to make sure that we are prepared to respond if the Iraqis react favorably.'

The next night, Jeff and I sat in our Humvee, shivering in the cold. We could just make out the border, an earth berm topped by concertina wire about 200 yards or so in front of our vehicle.

We heard the door slam on the PsyOp vehicle parked next to us, and the PsyOp team leader, a captain, wandered over.

'Ten mikes,' he said. I grunted acknowledgement, and Jeff asked, 'what exactly are you broadcasting?'

'The usual stuff: your situation is hopeless, give yourselves up or you'll all be killed.'

'Who checks this stuff?'

Jeff's question made sense. Our landing in Mogadishu had been preceded by a barrage of leaflets explaining that US troops saw Somalis as being their friends. We learned later that the term used for friend on the leaflet, was actually Somali for slave.

'All these messages are put together by native Arabic speakers, and are approved at the highest level,' the captain sniffed.

A few minutes later, I watched as his team, in a state of barely suppressed excitement, fiddled with the sound equipment. There was a squawk, a crackle of static and then a booming voice, guttural and harsh. Even forewarned, its loudness took me by surprise; if the Iraqis were, as reported, only a few hundred yards away, they would hear certainly hear it. The message, delivered in a hectoring monotone, lasted several minutes, followed by a pause – during which we scanned the berm for signs of movement – before starting again.

After about ten minutes, I walked over to where Jeff had parked our Humvee. In between broadcasts there had been no sign of life, aside from the sound of baying dogs, and I wondered if anyone was there to listen. Suddenly there came a hollow *thunking* sound from the direction of the border. Jeff vaulted out of the vehicle and we both threw ourselves flat, yelling in unison: 'Mortars!'

After long moments of tense silence they landed: loud crumps and flashes of light in the darkness to our left.

Before the echoes had died away, there was another series of *thunks*. Jeff started to count out loud, and I instantly wished he wouldn't. A mortar's time of flight averages between thirty and forty seconds – an eternity when you are on the receiving end. This time, the rounds landed to our right, on the far side of the PsyOp vehicle, four explosions in quick succession that shook the hard ground beneath me. We had been bracketed, meaning that the enemy had our range and direction and, unless we were lucky, could now drop the next volley on our heads. I ran over to the PsyOp vehicle, Jeff bumping after me in the Humvee.

'Move now – follow us!'

They needed no urging. The PsyOp Humvee lurched into a tight U-turn and followed us as we gathered speed back the way we had come. We careened across the desert, bumping over ruts and potholes in a desperate effort to put distance between us and the next volley of mortars. I peered through my night vision goggles trying to spot the Kuwaiti border post that we had passed through earlier.

Suddenly streaks of red light floated lazily towards us, cracking over our heads.

'Tracers.' My warning was unnecessary, Jeff had already braked.

I could just make out a cluster of buildings a couple hundred meters in front of us.

'That came from the border post.'

Jeff cupped his hand and yelled to the soldiers who had parked alongside us.

'I thought that you fellas left someone with the Kuwaitis.'

'We did,' said the captain.

He reached for the radio but was interrupted by the hammering of distant guns. More tracer whipped over our heads. Without discussion, we bailed out of the vehicles and lay on the ground. There was a burst of answering fire from the direction of the border, and the red streams intersected above us.

The Iraqis picked up the exchange with short bursts while the Kuwaitis continued to cut loose with abandon, eliciting a stream of invective from Jeff who appeared as upset by their lack of fire discipline as he was about our predicament. 'And I bet we gave them the fucking ammo,' he added. After a while he fell silent, and we lay on our backs watching the light show.

Eventually the Kuwaitis ran out of ammunition or just got bored, and the firing came to a stop. We re-mounted our vehicles and approached the border station cautiously. We found the soldier we'd left there earlier on the roof with a cluster of Kuwaitis who were chattering loudly with excitement, gathered around the still smoking guns. The soldier was almost in tears. 'I tried to stop them, but they wouldn't listen.' Jeff patted his shoulder and scowled at the Border Guard commander who shrugged unrepentantly.

We raised 7th Marines on the radio.

'What the fuck is going on up there.' Nick asked. It wasn't like him to break radio protocol. 'You weren't supposed to start the war early.'

'The Iraqis didn't appreciate our message, fired a few mortar rounds, and the Kuwaitis went apeshit,' I explained, wondering if I had lost his confidence already.

'Well, there's a platoon of tanks and a section of Cobras en route now.' Nick said. The Kuwaitis continued to jabber happily, smoking and peering over the balustrade at the Iraqi border, now dark and silent.

A few minutes later the tanks came clanking up the road behind the border station, four low-slung shapes glinting dully by the light of a yellow moon that had begun to edge above the horizon. I raised them on the Humvee radio to pass on our location.

'Everything's quiet now,' I added.

'Roger,' acknowledged the platoon commander, 'We're going to push up to the border and take a look through our thermals.'

Back on the roof, I watched as the tanks left the road and crawled past our position in a loose diamond formation. They had almost reached the berm when two helicopters clattered overhead, close enough for us to make out their skids and thin, menacing fuselages: Cobra gunships. A second later, there was a whoosh as one of them fired a missile – point blank into the rear of one of the tanks.

It took us a couple of seconds to register what had happened, then we were running down the stairs. Jeff jumped in the Humvee and I grabbed the radio. It was still on the tank platoon's frequency and the net was alive with excited chatter. I switched to 7th Marines net and got the watch officer on line.

'Ripper main – we've just seen a Cobra fire up an Abrams – I repeat they hit a US tank with a hellfire. We are moving now to assist. Get word to Division.' We had no other means of contacting the Cobras, which were now circling above us. I hoped that they weren't lining up for another shot.

Jeff drove us pell-mell towards the stricken tank. As we neared, we saw figures clambering out of the smoking hull, aided by the crew of another tank that had pulled alongside.

It turned out that the crew was mostly unharmed, with the exception of the tank commander, a lieutenant, who received some shrapnel in one eye, and was evacuated by Humvee for treatment. The Abrams tank has a very distinctive shape, and since the platoon was clearly on the Kuwaiti side of the border, I wondered what had prompted the Cobra pilot to consider it a target. Friction, perhaps, rearing its head before the war had even begun.

Shortly before dawn, the first US vehicles crossed into Iraq, beginning a chain of events that even now has yet to run its course. Jeff and I drove back to find our place in the long column of vehicles waiting their turn to pass through the breach site, while the horizon behind us rumbled like a bass drum as US artillery and planes pounded Iraqi positions.

In the gray light of early dawn, we rolled through the Safwan border crossing, deserted except for a single stray dog running back and forth alongside the column barking furiously – as though a harbinger of things to come.

The official First Marine Division history devotes an uncharacteristically amusing paragraph to our escapade on the border that night, attributing to me a fate-tempting statement that does sound like something I might have said:

'I wonder why we haven't seen any indirect fires from these guys yet.' Milburn wondered aloud. There were apparently a few Iraqis who agreed and were not convinced by the PsyOp's message, because he had no sooner said the words out loud than the Iraqis obliged the PsyOp's team by lobbing mortar rounds at them. US Army Sergeant Thomas Stiffey, the team chief, was not amused. From that point on, Sergeant Stiffey was leery of traveling anywhere with Major Milburn. Smart man.

Years later, I ran into the commander of the PsyOp team in Hawaii. While reminiscing about that night's events he told me that all the messages broadcast by his team, indeed by all PsyOp teams during the invasion, were recorded in a dialect unintelligible to Iraqis. It was a symbol of greater misunderstandings to come.

# Chapter 11

For most of RCT-7, the next day was just one long slow drive along dirt roads, with little to see aside from mile upon mile of scrubby desert. Occasionally we would come across small groups of civilians by the side of the road, waving white flags or staring at us blankly, but for the most part the population appeared to have locked themselves behind closed doors.

Our sense of anticlimax was heightened by transmissions over the radio which made it sound as though the forward battalions were fighting a massive battle with Iraqi tanks:

'Six T-72s approaching from West, grid: 347215, time now – moving to engage.'

'Destroyed four enemy tanks, expended all ammo.'

FIRST MARINE DIVISION'S ADVANCE ON BAGHDAD – 2003

Every request for supporting fire sounded urgent, making it difficult for the regiment to prioritize.

Despite the dramatic reports, there were surprisingly few prisoners – or enemy casualties for that matter. Several weeks later, a senior intelligence officer assigned to the division told me that the soldiers of the Iraqi 51st Mechanized Division had fled in our path, leaving in their wake a trail of abandoned vehicles, equipment and even uniforms. What had sounded on the radio like a furious tank battle had been an expensive target-shooting exercise.

The RCT seized its objectives south of Basrah and then advanced north-west along a four-lane highway named Route One, the southernmost of the division's two avenues of advance towards Baghdad. On the evening of the second day, the regiment's headquarters set up tents in a dust bowl just north-west of a town called Jalibah, which was little more than a collection of squat concrete huts.

The next morning, John and I boarded one of the venerable CH-46 helicopters assigned to the regiment for what should have been a short flight to division headquarters where we were to plan the next phase of the operation. The 46, or Frog as it was known, had been a Marine workhorse since Vietnam, and this particular one looked as though it had participated in that conflict.

We donned headsets and buckled ourselves into the web seats, giving the crew chief a thumbs-up as the ramp came up and the gunner cocked his weapon. The Frog shuddered into the air, and the pilot set course north towards the Euphrates River, skimming so low that he had to vault the occasional power line. Through the porthole opposite me I could see a landscape dotted with palm groves and crisscrossed by canals. It was agricultural land, as fertile as it gets in southern Iraq – green swathes of cultivated field that contrasted with the arid desert in between.

'Hey gents,' the pilot's voice cut in loudly over my headphones. 'Just got a change of mission – it's a CASEVAC,' a casualty evacuation, 'about 15 mikes from here, some place called Nasiriyah.' I remembered Nasiriyah from the briefs. RCT-1, reinforced by a composite unit from 2nd Marine Division called Task Force Tarawa, was tasked with seizing the town's two bridges across the Euphrates, opening the second route to Baghdad.

'Just got word that it's a hot LZ,' the pilot added.

Which meant that someone on the ground wanted to do us harm and would have every chance of doing so. The Frog would have to slow to a hover before landing, offering its long flanks and paper thin fuselage to anyone waiting for a shot.

John rolled his eyes at me, and I shrugged; *no use thinking about it now, we were committed.* The crew chief tapped my knee and pushed the talk button on his microphone.

'Gonna need you two to de-plane to provide security. Stay near the ramp and make sure that you keep an eye on me so you know when to board again.' I nodded and ratcheted the charging handle on my weapon, sending a round into the chamber, John did the same.

'Ten WIA,' the co-pilot announced. 'Going to need a hand carrying them. We're five mikes out.' Then, a moment later: 'Holy shit, look at that'.

I learned forward and looked through the front canopy. A giant pall of smoke marked where we were heading.

'Tracers three o'clock,' the co-pilot announced. The door gunners crouched behind the pintles of their guns, swinging the muzzles back and forth, but hadn't seen where the firing originated.

'One minute.'

Yellow smoke wisped past the portholes. I unfastened the seatbelt, tore off my headphones and reached for my helmet as the Frog's nose lifted, the whump of its blades took on a deeper pitch and we dropped with the feeling of an elevator cut free from its cable.

The wheels touched earth with a jolt then lifted again slightly, the floor swaying like the carriage on a high-speed train. We stood and staggered towards the rear of the aircraft where the lowering ramp exposed a widening circle of light.

The crew chief, his face veiled behind an opaque green visor, slapped me on the shoulder as I passed and leaned to yell something in my ear, but his words were drowned by the sound of the engines. I followed John headlong down the ramp. Shapes emerged from the smog, half running, carrying stretchers. One of them shouted to us:

'There's more that way.' He jerked a thumb over his shoulder. Running blindly through the pall of smoke and dust, we came across a makeshift aid station. There were bodies on the ground, some cocooned in ponchos, others lying on stretchers.

'This one's next,' someone yelled. John and I lifted either end of the stretcher – joined immediately by two other Marines – and stumbled back towards the helicopter, now barely visible in the murk.

As we ran up the ramp, I looked down at the Marine we were carrying. He was unconscious, his head lolling from side to side, a bandage masking half his face. We laid him carefully on the floor of the fuselage and started back through the smoke. The next casualty was also unconscious. As we ran with him toward the helicopter, the rotor wash whipped back the poncho liner covering him, exposing a chest covered in blood-stained gauze. As we put him down, a Marine who had followed us up the ramp placed a stuffed toy beside his head, a gift perhaps, from a loved one, now intended as a symbol of comfort. That sounds like an improbably sentimental gesture for such an occasion, but it happened. People say and do things in combat that you wouldn't expect to see in fiction. I once heard a Marine, his leg shattered by an IED, exclaim: 'The bastards got me.'

If asked to describe Nasiriyah, or even the small portion that I saw, I would be at a loss. I have no congruent memory of the place, just a blur of confused images: the swirling smoke, the row of stretchers and shrouded figures, and the lung-searing run between the aid station and the helicopter – probably only three or four times, but memory suggests many more. One image though stands out sharply. As John and I ran back to the helicopter, the Marines who had carried the last casualty aboard jogged past us.

'Hey what happened?' John asked them. One of the Marines pointed back beyond the helicopter to a squat shape in the smog. As we mounted the ramp, we could see that it was an amphibious assault vehicle, ripped inside out like a ruptured soda can. We exchanged shocked looks as we took our seats and buckled ourselves in. The Frog reared back on its haunches, its engines climbing to a shrill crescendo, then lurched into the air and tilted forward, clawing for speed.

'ATGM,' John announced, once we had our headphones back on. We were closely packed together side by side, to make space for the row of stretchers on the floor. A couple of corpsmen had boarded with us and were now bent over their charges.

'Yeah, it must have been. Wow.'

It had indeed been an anti-tank guided missile that devastated the amtrac, killing several of its occupants and wounding the Marines who now lay in front of us – but not one fired by the enemy. First Battalion Second Marines lost a total of eighteen Marines in Nasiriyah that day, with another seventeen wounded. A subsequent investigation attributed as many as ten of these deaths and an unknown number of the wounded to a missile fired from a US Air Force A10 aircraft.

We did what we could to make the stretcher cases comfortable as the pilot set course low and fast towards division headquarters and a waiting surgical team.

# Chapter 12

On the flight back to regiment later that day we ran into a sand squall. It began as a dark line on the horizon then became a vast billowing cloud that engulfed the helicopter, buffeting it from side to side and plunging us into a brown twilight in which ground and sky became one. The pilots had no option but to land, inching cautiously downwards as all hands peered into the gloom in a vain search for reference points.

We knew that we were a few hundred yards away from the division line of march and thus close to a column of vehicles that stretched for miles but it felt as though we had landed on Middle Earth. We spent some twenty hours cocooned in our tiny world, while the wind hurled sand against the fuselage with a sound like a clothes dryer full of ball bearings. On the few occasions that I ventured out, I couldn't see more than a foot or two in front of me.

By the time the storm abated, it had inflicted more casualties on 1st Marine Division than the enemy to date. In the pitch darkness, an amtrac ran over Major Kevin Nave, the much-liked Executive Officer of 3rd Battalion 5th Marines (3/5), and four Marines drowned when their tank tumbled off a bridge into a canal; their loss going unnoticed for a whole day such was the confusion wrought by the storm.

While at Division we had learned that Task Force Tarawa had run into determined resistance from a paramilitary group known as the Fedayeen Saddam. The Fedayeen weren't well trained but had two things on their side: the courage of zealotry, and the ability to select the ground on which to fight.

Unaccustomed to combat as the Marines were, the Fedayeen had an effect out of proportion to their size. On one occasion a battalion of armored vehicles sent out on the division net a 'Slingshot' call, the code word to request immediate fire support from all available assets, to subdue a small group of lightly armed men.

The Fedayeen were able to use their tactics most effectively in the area north of the Euphrates where RCT-1's avenue of advance was marked by a string of small towns.

South of the river, the hapless Iraqi Army, facing a juggernaut of rolling steel and apocalyptic firepower, simply disappeared. For US troops primed for battle, it was difficult to understand that the much-vaunted foe had fled in the night.

This misunderstanding had, at times, tragic consequences. A day or two after the sandstorm, Jeff Eby and I found ourselves ahead of the lead battalion on Route One, a four-lane expressway south of the Euphrates. That wasn't as dangerous as it might sound; there was no real fighting taking place that day, and many civilians appeared to be going about their business as though their country was not being invaded. Nevertheless, we hadn't intended to get so far forward, so we pulled off the main road to let the lead units pass us.

We parked on a road parallel with Route One, just south of a crossroads, facing north: the direction of advance. From our position we had a good view down the road that intersected the cross roads from west to east, and which led on our right via a traffic circle to Route One. As we waited by our Humvee, a blue and white bus approached down this road from the west, our left. Jeff and I crouched behind our vehicle; we had seen civilians using the road all morning, but this was the first bus. It slowed as it approached us, and I could see children's faces pressed against the window.

'Kids – Jeff, looks like a school bus.' I waved it on. Jeff picked up the radio and passed to the lead unit, a scout platoon mounted on Humvees, a description of the bus along with the information that it was not a threat. Receiving an acknowledgment, he went on to give them a description of the roadway ahead. He was in mid-sentence when we heard the thudding of a heavy machine gun to our right. The bus slewed to a halt at the traffic circle, its windows shattered, its engine belching smoke.

'Cease fire!' Jeff yelled into the handset while I sprinted towards the bus, arriving as the passengers tumbled off.

Lying on the ground was a young girl, wearing a light blue dress the front of which was soaked with blood. Her father was holding her hand and begging me to do something. Her eyes were glassy, and, as I fumbled with the pressure bandage from my first aid kit, her other hand fell away from her stomach exposing a gaping rent. I tried to staunch the flow of blood but it soaked the bandage and my hands, pooling around my knuckles as I pressed them against the gauze.

Someone knelt by me, I glanced over, it was a corpsman – but I have no idea where he came from. 'She's done sir,' he said, and moved on to help someone else. I couldn't bring myself to remove the bandage – I stayed by her until she stopped breathing. Her father was sobbing, but I could do nothing to relieve his pain. I looked up to see that another corpsman had arrived and was bandaging a boy whose arm dangled uselessly by his side.

Jeff had driven over and was saying into the radio. 'You just fired up a civilian bus. We've got friendlies here at the traffic circle.' I picked up the other handset and called regiment for a helicopter to evacuate the wounded, looking over to the corpsmen to confirm how many – six, urgent. I felt detached, as though one part of me had shut down, while the other part was functioning as trained. I focused on the nine lines of the CASEVAC request and averted my eyes from the gruesome tableau in front of me.

Someone at the other end was saying that they didn't have the authority to launch a CASEVAC for civilian casualties. I started to argue with him, explaining that Americans had caused these casualties, but sensed that I wasn't going to get anywhere.

'Get the OpsO on the line,' I said.

I explained to Nick what had happened and asked for his support to launch the regiment's CASEVAC helicopters.

'OK Andy – got it. Will let you know when they're inbound.'

A single CH-46 arrived shortly afterwards, putting down in the center of the traffic circle, and we carried the injured children on board. I remember those fragments but few other details. I don't recall speaking to the family of the girl who died. I want to remember that I did; that I tried to help them – but feel certain that I was too preoccupied, or perhaps too afraid to face their grief.

As we drove to rejoin the regiment Jeff railed bitterly: 'I explained to everyone on the net about that bus, and they all rogered up.' He hit the steering wheel with the heel of his hand. 'Unfuckingbelievable.'

I was silent. I remembered waving the bus ahead. I had done nothing except watch the girl die while the corpsmen saved lives.

There were a number of such incidents during the early phases of the Iraq war. After seeing the heavy toll of civilian casualties during the battle for Nasiriyah, Bing West commented in his book:

In no previous American war had troops feared suicide bombings in cars. The embedded press was not strongly critical of shooting at moving vehicles, because they were at risk too. Despite a hundred rumors, however, actual suicide bombers in Iraq had been few, one for perhaps every ten thousand cars approaching US vehicles.

In war, unchecked rumors rapidly gain velocity. It's the role of commanders to strike a reasonable balance between self-defense and shooting the innocent. This isn't easy to do but there's more to the equation than a simple choice between whose lives you risk. For most people, and Marines are no exception, killing innocent people leaves an indelible stain on the conscience. In war there are moral as well as physical and psychological casualties.

I didn't think about the incident at the traffic circle again until Christmas Eve, some nine months later. I was attending midnight mass in an English church when the memory of the dying girl came back to me, along with all the feelings that I had suppressed to that point. I cried helplessly, hoping that those around me didn't notice. Over the years, others have joined her in my gallery of ghosts – but her face remains as clear as the day I last saw it.

# Chapter 13

On April 3, two weeks into the war, lead elements of the division reached a cross roads on Route 6 less than 20 miles south-east of Baghdad and ran into a Fedayeen ambush. Because at any given time, the entire division was confined to two or three parallel routes, a small band of determined men could bring all movement to a complete halt. The units in contact would invariably respond by using planes or artillery to clear the way but in these situations it takes time to mass fires at the desired point of impact. This was one of those occasions, and so on Route 6 that day a familiar sequence was playing out: thousands of men and hundreds of vehicles sat idle, while far forward, out of sight to most in the column, a small but desperate action took place.

RCT-5 had been in the lead for the previous few days with RCT-7 following behind, but now we anticipated getting the order to catch up so that both regiments would be in a position to attack Baghdad simultaneously. I was sent forward to coordinate this maneuver with RCT-5. Knowing that Route 6 had become a parking lot, I caught a ride on a forward-bound helicopter.

If there is a record for the most number of Marines ever packed into a single Huey then we must have come close that day. I counted myself lucky to be by the doorway, buffeted by the warm wind as we skimmed low above the procession of stationary vehicles, a great mass of dust-colored steel stretching to the horizon where black storm clouds merged with the dun earth.

As we neared the front of the column, the storm clouds resolved into plumes of dark smoke, an ominous backdrop to the scene unfolding below. I could see amtracs lining the road in a herringbone formation and a platoon of tanks in front of them, arrayed in line across the cross roads. We were almost above them now. Suddenly I was staring almost directly downward, blood flooding my face, safety belt clamping my stomach, as the pilot banked hard. One of the tanks was belching smoke, its sides glowing white hot, flames licking around its turret. *There's no way*, I thought, and leaned forward to get a better look, but lost sight of the tank as the Huey leveled, and began to drop. There was a flash of telephone wires and suddenly we were plummeting downwards, the ground rushing up beneath my feet. I gripped the edge of my seat with both hands and pushed my chin down onto my chest. We thumped down with enough force to jar my spine and throw the Marine next to me into my lap.

I wasn't sure if we had crashed or whether it was just a hard landing, but thought it best to assume the worst. I undid my seatbelt in a frenzy of fumbling, jumped to the ground, and sprinted for a nearby palm grove. One of the pilots got there before me.

'It was a landing,' he panted in answer to my question. 'But a section of Cobras reported taking RPG rounds just ahead of us, so I didn't want to waste time. And the bird was handling like a pig, what with the heat and the load.' No complaints from me, I assured him.

Later that day, Jeff arrived in his Humvee having driven off-road for most of the way. I told him about the tank that I had seen burning. The M1A1 Abrams is meant to be nigh indestructible. No one appeared to know for sure what had happened to this one. A friend of mine, a Cobra pilot who had been in the air at the time, was sure that he had seen an anti-tank missile launched at the tank.

'It was a Kornet,' he said, naming an advanced Russian anti-tank system with a distinctive appearance. Another eyewitness was certain that it had been an RPG. Whatever had caused the damage, the tank was still eking white smoke when Jeff and I went to inspect it that evening.

'Don't get close!' a Marine yelled as we approached. 'There's radioactive shit everywhere.'

I looked at the ground around the smoldering hulk and saw that it was covered in puddles of molten silver. Like every member of the coalition, both Jeff and I were wearing rubber over boots designed, supposedly, to protect our feet against chemical weapons. Mine now had splashes of silver on their sides, as did Jeff's.

Tank rounds are made of depleted uranium – the byproduct of a process that extracts the radioactive portion of the metal for use in the nuclear industry. When metal hits metal at five times the speed of sound, steel shatters like glass. Depleted uranium, on the other hand is twice as dense as lead, enabling it to punch through the front armor on most tanks, turning the inside of the vehicle into an inferno of white-hot gas and sparks. It's a poisonous heavy metal but, according to the Department of Defense, only slightly radioactive. Jeff and I were aware of these facts, but neither the terms 'poisonous' or 'slightly radioactive' are particularly comforting when you have the stuff splattered on you. We peeled off our over boots and jettisoned them with relief. *Maybe they were useful after all,* I thought.

The Fedayeen could not have harbored any hope of repulsing the invasion, but so far they'd done a pretty good job of delaying it – and they weren't done yet. Later that evening, I was squatting in a field answering the call of nature when I heard the distinctive hollow pop of a mortar firing in the mid-distance. I assumed that it was one of ours until a series of explosions on the road, some 50 meters away suggested that it wasn't.

My trousers were up before the echoes had died away, and I ran for a nearby ditch where I crouched waiting for the next volley. It arrived: three impacts on the road – and one in the field, very close to the spot where I'd just been.

I returned to our Humvee and laid out my bag for the night, regaling Jeff with the news of my close escape. Meanwhile, unbeknownst to me, a friend was raising the alarm that I was a casualty of the recent attack. I met Joe Corbett, a friend from Twenty-Nine Palms, earlier that day and had borrowed from him a roll of toilet paper – a highly prized commodity in any military operation. It was for me fortuitous timing because my stomach was cramping, the first bout of a fly-blown bug that was to decimate the division in a manner that would have exceeded the Fedayeen's wildest dreams. After seeing where the last mortar had landed, Joe ran into the field to check on me and, finding only charred remnants of his toilet roll and my discarded MOPP blouse, assumed the worst. He raised a search party, who woke me later that evening to confirm that I was indeed alive.

The next day, RCT-5 continued the advance, pushing past the contested crossroads with no further resistance. Several miles ahead lay the Diyala River, a tributary of the Tigris and the last natural barrier before Baghdad. Jeff and I would travel with RCT-5 before peeling off to assess the northern-most bridge across the Diyala as a potential crossing sight for 7th Marines.

We paused on the crossroads waiting for the lead units to move. We were in a drab commercial area. Warehouses, shuttered store-fronts and oil-smeared auto repair shops lined the four-lane highway which bore grim evidence of the previous day's fight. The tank was still smoldering, and along the side of the road lay the bodies of the Fedayeen who had fought to defend the crossroads, their bodies in the wax-dummy pose of sudden death: stiff limbs, gaping mouths, eyes half open. I was beyond ghoulish fascination, but something about them caught my eye. There was no doubt that they were combatants; they wore ammunition vests, and some still had weapons. But other than that, they were respectably dressed in collared shirts, slacks, leather belts and shoes. They looked more like teachers or doctors than Baathist zealots.

I was glad that they were no longer alive, but felt a sneaking sympathy for them all the same. They had fought bravely against overwhelming odds in the defense of their country, and died the sort of death that popular culture eulogizes. If they weren't the enemy, we'd have called them heroes.

# Chapter 14

I scanned the bridge. It was damaged but appeared still intact: a giant slab of concrete pockmarked by shell fire spanning the turbid water. About 100 yards in front of us two Humvees started to creep towards it, Marines walking on either side, their weapons at the ready, part of an engineer platoon, whose task was to assess whether the bridge had been rigged for explosives. Strewn along the road leading to the bridge were metal canisters, about the size and shape of dinner plates: mines that the retreating Iraqis laid down in a hurried attempt to slow down our advance. During our approach in darkness, Jeff and I had almost driven over one. They were undoubtedly still dangerous, but the engineers had simply moved them aside to make a path for their Humvees.

It was a gritty, gray day – made more so by pillars of smoke rising from the city that lay just below the horizon. We could hear our own artillery behind us, a constant angry rumble dulled by distance. Shells whooshed overhead with the sound of an underground train. Several rounds had fallen on our side of the river, kicking up geysers of dirt and concrete, close enough to make us duck, and every few minutes one or two would splash into the river by the bridge. Jeff had checked with regiment and was assured that these weren't ours. I don't know why that news reassured us.

Then RCT-7's radio intercept team reported that the Iraqis had at least one forward observer on the far side of the river, with eyes on the lead US units – which would be us.

A couple of kilometers to our south, 3/4 was approaching the one other bridge in our sector still standing. The plan was for the RCT-7 to funnel across both these bridges and establish a lodgment on the other side but 3/4 reported that their bridge was damaged and would not support vehicles. The regiment's bid to get into Baghdad rested on the northern bridge, the one now in front of us.

I picked up the handset. 'Ripper Three, the bridge looks intact. The engineers are checking it out now.' I had barely finished speaking when the last span of the bridge tumbled into the river with a sound like distant thunder.

'Goddammit,' Jeff's exclamation understated our feelings.

'So much for the Bridge at Remagen,' I added unhelpfully.

The radio net came alive with excited voices.

'Did you see that? Someone blew it.'

'Anyone hurt?'

'Nope – it dropped before we reached it.'

Ahead of us the engineers who had thrown themselves flat, got to their feet and started to edge forward again. The squad leader, a young sergeant with a strong Jamaican accent, came up on the net.

'Yep, last span is gone. It was blown alright – I can see wires.'

As is so often the case in war, it's still not clear what exactly happened to the northern bridge over the Diyala that day – even to those who were there. Jeff remains convinced that the bridge was destroyed by US bombs and that the last span fell from the cumulative effect of damage caused earlier. The engineers approaching the bridge are certain that the last span was dropped by an explosive charge, and years later in Mosul I met an Iraqi officer who corroborated that story with a description of the event that only an eyewitness could have given. Whatever the cause, the loss of the only remaining bridge capable of supporting vehicles appeared to scupper RCT-7's chances of reaching Baghdad before the Army's V Corps approaching from the west. Friction.

However, within a day, engineers had established a makeshift bridge capable of supporting vehicles; and RCT-7, led by 1st Tank battalion, crossed to establish a bridgehead on the other side.

We were now within striking distance of central Baghdad, and that night Division issued us the order to plan and execute raids – rapid strikes with a planned withdrawal – into the city. When Andrew Balding, Blade of the undersized shorts, returned from division headquarters with this news, Vuckovich convened a huddle.

'Division's concerned that Baghdad is going to be a tough nut.' Andrew's bald dome, adorned with a jagged scar made him look like the hitman for a motorcycle gang, but that impression couldn't be further from the truth. Blade was probably the most even-keeled and tolerant of us all, the only one who had not lost his temper at some point during the operation. He was not well liked at Division though for some faux pas whose exact nature we were never able to determine. As a result, Nick tried to avoid sending him there, but on this particular occasion both John and I had been otherwise occupied.

'The G-2 thinks that these Fedayeen cats are probably planning a last stand. Fortified positions, suicide bombers – the works, so the intent is to start prodding the hornet's nest with these raids.'

'When do we begin?'

'They want to get our concept of operations by 2400 hours'. Four hours away.

Nick pointed at John and me. 'OK – you two, come up with something by 2200, and we'll run it past the boss.'

That was Nick. No needless discussion or detailed instruction; just the expectation to come up with a solution without fuss or fanfare.

'You've seen Black Hawk Down right?' John asked me, as we poured over a map of the city laid out on a trestle table in the operations tent. 'I just don't think that it is going to be a good idea to send units into the city without the regiment's full weight behind them.'

I remembered the lessons of our exercise in Victorville where it had taken almost an entire battalion to secure a corridor into the city for a company-sized raid.

'You're right. We'd have to plan for their withdrawal which means keeping a route open, and the only way to do that is by sitting on it. We either take a huge risk that units will get cut off, or we give one or two battalions the mission of supporting the attacking unit by securing a withdrawal route. And if we are going to do that, why withdraw at all?'

'Well, we've got about ninety minutes to come up with something,' John reminded me, 'so let's get the regiment into Baghdad.'

RCT-7's assigned sector was in the south-eastern quadrant of the city, with the Euphrates River marking the boundary with the Army's V Corps. Rather than attempt a broad axis advance, moving block by block across our sector, we chose to designate specific objectives. The battalions would strike for these objectives in a free-flowing attack unhampered by the requirement to keep pace with each other. By attacking in this manner along multiple routes, the regiment's advance would gain, we hoped, irresistible momentum.

In planning any kind of military operation, one of the first steps is to identify what the military calls key terrain: ground that will give an advantage to whichever side occupies it. In a city, key terrain might comprise intersections, or buildings that are important because of their size, location or function. You want to control this terrain either by physically occupying it or by having a plan to hit it with fires – aircraft-delivered bombs and artillery – to deny its use to the enemy. If you can't do either, then you bypass or isolate it.

You always have to look at the map from the enemy's point of view: what's important to him becomes important to you. You want to target his ability to control his forces while attacking the seams between his units. But it is rare that you will have this quality of intelligence, especially in a city where buildings conceal movement and defy the most advanced collection techniques. Even in Fallujah, a relatively small city which US forces had months to study, the only way that we were able to find the enemy was by stumbling on him. And in Baghdad we had much less to go on.

We were pressed for time, which is why John and I resorted to the method described by Peter Maass in his excellent article for the *New Yorker* about the fall of Baghdad:

> They then divided central Baghdad into twenty-seven zones, with each battalion responsible for occupying four or five zones (several low-priority zones were unassigned). Schaar and Milburn had received from divisional headquarters a list of about thirty sensitive sites – a hodgepodge that comprised embassies, banks, detention centers, potential nuclear facilities, and hotels, including the Palestine. Schaar recently sent me a photograph of the twenty-seven-zone invasion map. The map has six thumbtacks marking key targets. One of them, in the central zones, was the Palestine Hotel. (The Toppling, *New Yorker*, Jan 10 2011).

The Palestine Hotel was key terrain because of its size and position overlooking the Euphrates. Because we knew it was being used by Western correspondents, we were careful to include instructions that approaching units weren't to shoot at it unless they were receiving fire. We were aware too that the enemy would likely take advantage of our predictable caution by using the hotel as a command post. The massive Ministry of Information dominated the entire area and so was also an objective – though we would have to figure out how to secure its imposing edifice without committing an entire battalion to the task. And we would have to seize the bridges across the Euphrates to block the enemy's ability to reinforce or counter-attack.

'A good plan executed now,' our instructors at Basic School would remind us 'is better than a perfect plan executed later.' Which is all well and good – but John and I had never had to put together so large an operation, in so little time, with so much at stake. The result was no operational masterpiece, but we believed, a sound, practical plan. After asking a few probing questions, Colonel Hummer agreed.

We issued the order later that night and found ourselves fielding a barrage of questions from the assembled battalion operations officers, until Nick interjected: 'Look – if any of you have better ideas then please share them with us. If not, we don't have time for any more "what–if–grandma–had–a–dick" questions. We're kicking off tomorrow morning.'

# Chapter 15

The next morning, Jeff and I linked up with a scout platoon from 3/7 who had been assigned the sector that included the Ministry of Information, one of our bigger concerns.

Soon after dawn, RCT-7 passed word for all battalions to cross the line of departure: the designated position on the ground behind which units prepare, beyond which they attack. The scout platoon uncoiled from the battalion's bivouac site by the Diyala River, and rolled into the outskirts of Baghdad.

Lying on the road by the river was the body of a young boy, maybe 5 or 6, staring at the sky with sightless eyes. He wore a bright orange T-shirt decorated with cartoon characters and blue pants. I couldn't help thinking of his mother helping him dress that morning, not knowing that it would be for the last time. I looked away – but he had already joined my gallery of ghosts.

The streets were deserted. There was an eerie silence broken only by the sound of our engines and staccato reports from the radio, as the platoon bounded forward, one vehicle covering another as they moved.

The narrow roads and squat dun-colored houses gradually gave way to wide boulevards, apartment blocks and government buildings. Our objective, the Ministry of Information, dominated the skyline, providing us with a handy aiming point as we pushed deeper into the city. We started to see people – a few at first gathered on street corners, many of them clutching white flags – but then more and more filling the sidewalks. It took a moment for me to realize that they were welcoming us: clapping and cheering, some even venturing onto the streets and reaching up to shake our hands. We grinned and waved back but stayed alert, the gunners scanning the upper stories of buildings as we passed, muzzles swiveling above the heads of the crowd.

As we drove, we could hear explosions and gunfire, muffled by distance, somewhere to our right. It is a common phenomenon in combat that while one unit may be fighting for its life, another immediately adjacent to it will find itself unopposed. So it was now as 3/7 cruised through the streets, while just a few blocks away the lead battalion of 5th Marines was fighting a determined group of Fedayeen.

For RCT-7 there were incidents of what journalists like to call scattered resistance, but none that came close to the scenarios that John and I had envisioned while drawing up the plan. Reports on the radio made things sound worse than they were, as reports often do, and it was by no means apparent at the time that the occupation of Baghdad was proving to be a cake walk.

As we approached the Ministry of Information, a series of shots raised spurts of dust in the road to our front, sending the crowd scrambling for cover and eliciting an ear-splitting clatter of return fire from every gun in the patrol. That was about it as far as resistance went. Aside from that, our biggest challenge was dealing with the increasing confidence of the crowds who surged forward to clasp our hands. 'Thank you!' they shouted, 'Welcome to Baghdad!' and, 'Bush, Bush, Buuuuuuush!'

Third Battalion, Seventh Marines occupied its designated area of the city and began to consolidate – companies and platoons setting up position in government buildings or in the open spaces in between. Jeff and I linked back up with RCT-7 as they set up bivouac in a park immediately adjacent to the Ministry of Information. It was a scene of organized chaos as Marines swarmed everywhere, parking vehicles, putting up tents, starting generators and carrying equipment in the now familiar drill of setting up camp.

As Jeff maneuvered our Humvee off the road and towards a gap in the hastily laid concertina wire circling the perimeter, a couple of bearded individuals in filthy camouflage utilities flagged us down. I climbed out and approached them cautiously – noting that they appeared to be Westerners. They carried weapons and one was wearing flip-flops.

'Hello mate, welcome to Baghdad.' I shook their outstretched hands. 'I'm Ivan – this is Tim, we're with a UK SOF det.'

'How long have you been here?' asked Jeff incredulously.

'A couple of days – you caught us up earlier than we expected.'

'It's lucky that we got to you before the Iraqis.'

'We were actually most worried about getting drilled by you guys.'

Tim chimed in. 'That's no joke – we pulled this side of the river because the army is firing up everything in their path.'

True by all accounts. Later that day Jeff and I assisted a distraught Spanish camera crew who had lost one of their team when a US tank fired on the Palestine hotel – despite widespread warnings about the presence there of Western media.

I led Ivan and Tim into the newly erected operations tent and introduced them to Nick who, wincing at the beards, flip-flops, and first name introductions, was uncharacteristically skeptical of their story. Ivan persisted politely, and when it became apparent that he and Tim had a better picture of Iraqi positions in the city than any of us, Nick's usual hospitable self returned and he invited them to bring the rest of their small detachment, six soldiers in all, into the 7th Marines' fold.

Later that afternoon, Jeff and I were in Firdos Square where we had linked up with the headquarters section of 3/4. Hundreds of Iraqis packed the square, swarming around the giant statue of Saddam at its center in scenes of riotous celebration. They engulfed the few dozen Marines present with displays of gratitude, bouncing up and down with joy. The crowd made a path for Marines to back a tank retriever up to the base of the statue, and helped them wrap a cable around Saddam's concrete torso. As the statue toppled, there were cries of warning, and the crowd parted just in time to allow the dictator's hapless effigy to crash to earth – bouncing upwards in fragments. An American flag appeared for a moment on Saddam's face, and then disappeared as someone remembered the prohibition on such displays of triumphalism and whipped it away. The crowd danced and bayed their delight. It was a moment of pure euphoria, the likes of which I had never seen before nor since.

It was, in a sense, the high-water mark of our relationship with the Iraqi people – from that time forward it would be in constant ebb. In the weeks that followed, encounters between the locals and the coalition were increasingly acrimonious.

'I am more worried about security now than I ever was about Saddam,' explained one Iraqi whom I met after a Marine patrol had almost shot him at an impromptu checkpoint he was manning to protect his neighborhood from looters. He was a doctor who had been educated in the UK; not the sort of person you expect to find brandishing an AK-47 in the street. He was also a Shi'ite whose brother had been imprisoned and tortured following the Shia rebellion of 1991, and thus had no love for Saddam's regime. But, he explained, even tyranny was preferable to an anarchy that threatened the safety of his immediate family.

During the three weeks we spent in Baghdad, I learned that this man's experience was a common one. US units lived inside hardened defensive enclaves from which they repelled even the most innocuous attempts by the locals to establish contact, and sometimes, driven by fear, they resorted to deadly force. Nervous sentries at checkpoints throughout the city dispatched several civilians a day; a practice that can only have fueled the burgeoning insurgency. Rather than dispel this fear, some commanders let it fester, thinking that it wasn't their responsibility to interact with the population.

This period marked the tipping point between liberation with all its possibilities, and the subsequent insurgency – the harbingers of which were already present as 7th Marines upped stakes and moved by convoy down to a staging area south of Baghdad.

We had no orders to put a stop to the widespread looting that began within days of Baghdad's fall, or to protect the local populace who, in the face of growing intracommunal violence, couldn't understand our apathy. The smiles and shouted welcomes soon gave way to sullen resentment, and petty acts of aggression: rock throwing and yelled insults. Our lack of contact with the population deprived us of the ability to understand what was going on, so we explained it away as lack of gratitude. The war was over; it was time to go home.

The incoming Coalition Provisional Authority reinforced this outlook with their supercilious 'we've got this now' approach to governing Baghdad. In June, the CPA passed the now-infamous Provisional Order Number One, making unemployable thousands of armed and trained young men, thus ensuring that the nascent insurgency would have no shortage of recruits.

Conventional wisdom has it that the euphoria of liberation was turned into an anger by the administration's failure to plan for an occupation, and by the CPA's ineptitude. I have no doubt too that our laissez-faire attitude to Iraqi life caused much of the resentment that fueled the subsequent insurgency.

The phrase 'No worst enemy, no better friend' gained considerable penchant and became the unofficial motto of the 1st Marine Division during this phase of the war. However, despite best intentions, it is probably the no worse enemy aspect that was most apparent to the Iraqis who crossed our path.

'We are very selective about cultural niceties,' Jeff commented to me some time later. 'We spent a lot of time learning about eating with your right hand, and not pointing your feet at people. But then we kill families because they don't understand when we yell stop at a roadblock.'

This wasn't due to any collective homicidal impulse, but rather to a lack of understanding. We were honed to expect a cauldron battle against a determined enemy and in such a fight it is inevitable that civilians sometimes get hurt. We use antiseptic phrases such as 'collateral damage', and 'military necessity' in acknowledgment of this fact, understanding that – while you can never resort to the simple moral expedient that the ends justify the means – there are circumstances during a military operation in which you cannot avoid spilling innocent blood.

But, as many of us were to learn, it's a really tough call to determine where the line of military necessity falls. As a commander, if you are inexperienced or morally lazy, it's hard to resist the impulse to look after your own people at the expense of those you don't know, and don't understand. Self-defense can be used as an argument to justify just about anything.

The problem is that commanders, even at the platoon level, are usually one step removed from the consequences of their actions; it's the junior Marines who are left with the moral trauma of killing innocents. And the 'military necessity' argument backfires when a civilian population seeks revenge against an occupying army that treats it with ruthless disdain.

Some of the theatrics attendant with the invasion also left me with a bad taste. In places, the Iraqis – notably the Fedayeen – put up real resistance to the invaders, but they were always vastly outgunned and I would guess that for most US participants the combat they experienced during the invasion paled in comparison to subsequent tours. The incidents I observed were often imbued with undeserved drama by over-excited reports, a result of inexperience rather than intentional deception. The embedded press for the most part lapped it up, partly because as guests of the military they were unwitting hostages to its narrative, and maybe too because they wanted to believe that this was a real fight. Their bosses, and indeed the American public expected it to be – and in so highly competitive a field, reputations, résumés and thus careers were linked to the story's dramatic value.

And so a series of broadcasts and articles suggested that US forces were battling their way to Baghdad against an implacable foe. It was a stark contrast to press coverage of the subsequent war in which US casualties rarely made front-page news.

Despite my uneasiness with some of what I had seen, it would be disingenuous for me to claim then a wisdom that was only conferred by subsequent experience. I was at the time happy to take the easy victory and call it combat, happy to accept the gratitude of welcoming crowds, happy to believe that the war had been a latter-day crusade to avenge 9/11 and prevent such an outrage from happening again.

# Chapter 16

Back in Quantico, I received less than a hero's welcome from Jolly Roger, and returned to my job at CSW, planning training missions in various countries around the world. Fitz needled me mercilessly about having escaped to go to war while leaving him to man a desk. Tony Marro, the other occupant of our den in the rear of a decrepit building, badgered me with questions about what combat had been like.

In truth, I didn't feel as though we had really seen combat. Despite some understandable posturing by the returning heroes of 1st Marine Division, the march on Baghdad had seemed to many of us a one-sided affair – a belief lent credibility by the relatively few coalition casualties. But Tony was genuinely interested in my recent adventure, and I was loath to disappoint him. A shaven-headed giant nick-named Bull after the character in the 1980s' comedy Night Court – Tony had begun his career as an infantry officer, before transferring to the Air Wing to fly helicopters.

A few years later he decided to return to the infantry – a decision that was probably not applauded by the manpower division of Headquarters Marine Corps who had overseen his selection to transition the other way. Nor, I am sure, was the aviation community overjoyed to see one of their own decide to return to the chrysalis of infantry life, having had the opportunity to soar as a butterfly. For exactly the same reason, infantry officers love to hear Tony's story.

Tony and Fitz exemplified traits that I have come across time and again among my fellow officers: supremely competent and driven, but unselfish to the core, always ready to drop whatever they were doing to help someone else. And beneath their professionalism bubbled an irreverent sense of humor that made even the slow times at CSW fun.

My relationship with Jessica had lasted eighteen months, and although we had been separated for much of that time (maybe because we had) was going well. Jess was now at San José University studying occupational therapy, and we managed to see each other for one or two weekends a month. I considered the opportunity to spend time together well worth the cost in plane tickets and, every time we said goodbye, found myself counting the days until our next meeting.

She was due to graduate in the summer of 2004, a year hence, and had decided to apply to join the army as an occupational therapist upon doing so. We were both excited when she was accepted from a wide field of applicants, though we knew that it would likely make it even tougher for us to stay together. People join the military for a variety of reasons, very rarely are these purely altruistic. But Jessica, in her own understated way, was a patriot in the noblest sense of the word, and despite being apprehensive about basic training, was determined to do her part.

Kaela and Siobhan came to stay with me that summer. We visited Washington DC together, the first time for both of them, went boating on Lake Lunga near Quantico, and played Frisbee football on the greensward in front of the base chapel. It was the first time that the two girls had spent more than a few days together at a time, and that vacation sparked a friendship that would lead to them becoming inseparable. It was an idyllic time for all of us.

Whenever you have three majors together with no Marines beneath them, you can assume that they will need close supervision. The lieutenant colonel given this unenviable task was Frank Topley. Frank was a diminutive, sharp-faced man whose meticulous approach to the job, and easy-going manner were often tested by our collective irreverence.

Frank did his best to shield me from the vengeful attention of Jolly Roger and others on the staff in Quantico to whom my string-pulling to get to the war smacked of disloyalty, a cardinal sin in the Marine Corps. If I had been a little more emotionally intelligent, I would have acted repentant – but I didn't, and this made Frank's job no easier.

Aside from the camaraderie, I enjoyed the work at CSW, which could be at times almost as hazardous as combat.

One such occasion arose during a trip to Ethiopia soon after my return. I was riding in a cab between two towns near the Somali border to link up with a US Army Special Forces team. All afternoon we bumped across a drought-blasted plain, and at dusk started to climb along a narrow winding road bounded on either side by vertiginous slopes, at the bottom of which lay a number of wrecked vehicles.

We were entering an area known locally as the 'Valley of the Penises' for its distinctive phallus shaped rock formations, when, upon rounding a bend, the driver slammed on his brakes, and we fishtailed to a halt on the hard-packed dirt. Through a cloud of dust, I could make out what appeared to be a makeshift roadblock and a crowd of armed men whose appearance reminded me of the incident in front of the Parliament Building.

The driver and I were hauled out of the cab at gunpoint, and there then followed a very uncomfortable few hours as we sat by the side of the road while our captors ransacked my belongings, and argued about our fate. One of them stood over us throughout, cradling his rifle and spitting quids of green Kat juice at our feet, all the time eyeing us malevolently. Rather disconcertingly, the cab driver wept continuously throughout.

Eventually, for what reason I do not know, we were allowed to go on our way. I even had my wallet returned, empty with the exception of my ID.

Incredibly, on the return trip a week later, the cab in which I was riding lost a wheel and I found myself again stranded in the Valley of the Penises as darkness fell. I flagged down the first vehicle to appear, and rode out of the valley sitting on a bundle of Kat. I have always thought that if I wrote a memoir, I'd consider the title 'Never Stop in the Valley of the Penises.'

On a trip to Colombia I almost met with disaster again. I mentioned that Fitz would drop anything to help someone, but this occasion proved to be an exception. I had embarked on a Columbian Navy patrol boat to ride south along the coast from Cartagena, the country's beautiful old colonial capital, to a nearby village, when – soon after departure – the boat's engines cut out, leaving us to drift steadily out to sea until the thin strip of green that marked landfall slipped below the horizon. The captain's repeated attempts to raise help on the radio were unsuccessful. The crew, visibly distressed, started arguing, and though their heated Spanish was delivered too quickly for me to understand much of what they were saying, I gathered that they were not optimistic about our chances of rescue. I had an iridium satellite phone with me – but, as anyone who has used these devices will tell you, their reception is less than perfect. I dialed a series of local numbers without getting a ringing signal, so I called Fitz.

'Fitz, it's Andy – I need you to get a message to the US Embassy in Bogota.'

'Andy – you're coming in broken. Did you say that you are calling from the US Embassy in Bogota?'

'Negative, I'm on a boat,' I glanced at the horizon, 'about 20 miles off Cartagena – drifting out to sea. The engine's broken.'

'Still can't make out what you are saying. You been drinking?'

It is an unfortunate aspect of the iridium that it distorts your voice so that it sounds as though you are slurring your words. I was not helped by the fact that Cartagena was a popular destination as a haven for hard partying.

'Goddamit Fitz, no.'

'OK, gotcha now, clear as a bell. Oh, and I believe you – now, what's up?'

I repeated my story, but to no avail. We had passed the right angle for reception, and my near desperate pleas for help were lost to the ether.

'Listen brother,' Fitz's voice was faint but discernible, which made his inability to understand me all the more frustrating. 'I'm running late for a date with Colleen, so gotta go. You stay out of trouble.' With that he hung up.

A short while later, just as dusk fell, the crew hailed a passing fishing boat, and we were towed back into port, mortified, but relieved. I like to remind Brian of this story even today. He is unrepentant, pointing out that I am still alive – and that he is now happily married to Colleen.

I had another awkward moment while attending a mess night held by the Argentine Marines. I had just finished leading an urban combat course for a cadre of their officers and senior NCOs – a two-week exercise that encapsulated the lessons that we had learned in Victorville. The US Marine Corps has a relationship with the Argentine Marines going back several decades and which includes the exchange of liaison officers. However, when the Argentinians invaded the Falklands (Los Malvinas to them), an operation in which their Marines played a prominent role, the US chose to side with the British by giving them valuable intelligence as to Argentine dispositions and allowing the task force to use Ascension Island, a US base, as a staging point. So it was with some consternation that I listened to the Argentine Marine Commandant raise a toast to loud applause: 'To taking back the Malvinas. I want to thank Major Milburn and his team for helping prepare us for this task.'

One trip ended in tragedy. It happened during a visit to Monrovia to assess the feasibility of a training program for the nascent Liberian Army. The team leader, Major Kris Stillings, was a friend of mine and I was grateful for his level-headed leadership as we found ourselves in a rapidly deteriorating situation.

Although the civil war had ended the previous year, Monrovia had a wild frontier feel. Gun-toting youths roamed the garbage-strewn streets and the atmosphere – beyond the ubiquitous reek of sewage – was tense.

Because there was no room in the US Embassy compound, our team was lodged in a hotel on the waterfront, a colonial-looking place with a Lebanese manager who while grateful for our custom, was concerned for our safety. It soon became apparent that he had good reason. Returning from viewing a training site, we found ourselves in the center of an increasingly hostile crowd. As we clambered into our vehicles, hands reached through the window grabbing Kris and me and ripping our shirts in an effort to pull us out.

That night a violent storm buffeted the hotel, causing me to get up and lock the shutters that opened onto my balcony. In the neighboring room was Jim, a civilian contractor and member of our team. In the morning, we found him lying in a pool of blood on the floor of his room, dead. Monrovia's one detective, also Lebanese, was assigned to the case and later explained to us what had happened. A gang of four or five individuals armed with clubs had climbed onto Kris's balcony and then mine, testing both doors. They had then tried Jim's door and, finding it open, had entered and beaten him to death before absconding with money and other valuables. The embassy found lodging for us that night on the compound, and we left for home the next day.

# Chapter 17

Towards the end of 2003, the Marine Corps was tasked with providing advisors to train the new Iraqi Army, and so it was that Frank Topley called me into his office one morning.

'As you are probably tracking, we are sending the first teams of advisors downrange in a couple of weeks, about thirty in all,' he said.

I was tracking, and knew a number of these lucky few. It's a strange but enduring phenomenon among Marines that we always regard with envy those of our colleagues heading for combat, under the assumption that they are profiting from an opportunity that will not be repeated.

'TECOM wants us to give them a course.' TECOM was the Marine Corps' Training and Education Command – CSW's higher headquarters.

'A course?'

'You heard me.'

Frank had probably voiced the same objections that were on the tip of my tongue: you don't put together a worthwhile course for so important a mission in a few days, and without resources. But that, evidently, is what we were being asked to do, and it made no sense to argue.

'You know, the Marine Corps has done this before – we ran an advisor program in Vietnam.' Frank continued, 'TECOM must have records of that training course buried somewhere in the archives. Of course, you are going to have to tweak whatever they have – you know, change Vietnamese to Arabic and so on.' Frank was not without a sense of humor. 'You've got Mark to help you.'

Mark Lombard was a reservist infantry officer assigned to CSW for a year under a wartime program that brought reservists onto active duty. He greeted my news with characteristic exuberance:

'Weapons-training, language and culture, foreign weapons familiarization, call-for-fire, advanced life-saving skills.'

He was spouting ideas faster than I could keep up on the whiteboard.

'Steady-on, brush fire. That will all work for subsequent courses, but we've only got a few days to put this first one together.'

A phone call to the action officer at TECOM narrowed our window even further:

'Well for this first go-round, you are going to have them for only two days, and it's got to be down in Tampa because that's where we're having them report. But bear in mind that we're dealing with Marines here,' he added, trying to be helpful. 'How much training do they need to advise a bunch of Iraqis?'

They were indeed Marines, which is perhaps why they put up with our initial pathetic attempt at a course without complaint. In the end we wasted two days that the fledgling advisors could have spent with their families, but they listened intently. They too had little idea of what lay ahead.

Upon my return from Tampa I called Bing West for help. Bing is a former Marine and best-selling author whose book about OIF 1, *The March Up*, first coined the phrase that Marines would thereafter use to refer to that phase of the war.

'Well – I can probably round up a handful of Vietnam advisors if that will work.' It certainly would, I told him; and a couple of weeks later we convened, in Quantico, a meeting of former Marine advisors to the South Vietnamese Army.

Their experiences spanned the full length of US involvement in Vietnam: from the early 1960s to 1973. And, predictably, they were a cast of characters. There was Major General Ray 'E-tool' Davis, so named because he once had to resort to an entrenching tool in close combat; Colonel John Ripley whose single-handed attempt to hold back the North Vietnamese advance in 1972 is a Marine Corps legend; and Lieutenant General Paul Van Riper, who served as one of the very first advisors before going on to a distinguished career.

Van Riper is well-known within the Corps as a determined champion of intellectual prowess (in the face, some might say, of entrenched anti-intellectualism). 'You need to cast your net wide,' he would tell my class at the School of Advanced Warfighting. 'If you just remain focused on your profession, you will miss something. Go to the ballet, learn about art, read the classics.' Tall, rail-thin and hatchet-faced, with round 'granny' glasses, Van Riper looked more like a venerable Oxford don than a man who once told a television presenter: 'I've had to kill men at less distance than now separates me from you.'

Now he and Bing drove the discussion, pulling the group back on topic when they appeared to be lost in reminiscence. At the end of the day, Mark and I had gleaned some useful nuggets about the selection and training of advisors.

We learned not to expect that all Marines will make good advisors. Courage and competence are indispensable but you also need to be patient and persistent, willing to make allowances based on cultural differences without taking your eyes off the mission. You have to be level-headed, mature and happy to be outside your comfort zone, physically and mentally.

In the months to come, I would have frequent cause to be reminded of this conclusion: living as one of two or three Americans in the company of Iraqi soldiers, amidst the devastation of Fallujah and in a besieged police station in downtown Mosul, facing an enemy who appeared to have the upper hand. Under such circumstances, you need someone who doesn't just endure, but relishes the separation from the security and creature comforts of a US Forward Operating Base. Although the Corps never came up with a formal selection process for advisors, it was my experience that Marines assigned to this difficult mission generally rose to the challenge and excelled.

Mark and I returned to the whiteboard and over the course of a day or two hammered out a three-week schedule we could run in Quantico. Mark, who sold medical equipment in civilian life, was in his element on the phone soliciting support from other units, while answering a litany of questions from inbound Marines.

We didn't have a budget, so the US Marine Corps' advisor training course began on a shoestring. We borrowed ranges and instructors from other units in Quantico to run courses – from basic combat marksmanship to foreign weapons familiarization, to how to call for fire support.

Working with TECOM's Center for Operational Culture, we brought in real Iraqis to teach language and culture. These were rudimentary courses. Just enough language training to teach a smattering of phrases and pique the interest of those who were serious about learning more; while culture covered a little bit of history and religion as well as the usual pointers of the 'don't-show-the soles-of-your-feet-don't-eat-with-your-left-hand' variety.

We press-ganged corpsmen from the hospital to teach advanced lifesaving procedures under the assumption that advisors would not always have access to the same rapid evacuation procedures that linked most US units with the nearest military surgical facility. Upon receiving reports about the difficulty of driving defensively in Iraqi traffic, we contracted with a civilian company to run a high-speed driving course on a nearby raceway. It's hard to quantify how useful this course was but it proved consistently to be the most popular. I went through it myself and could understand why: it was like three days of playing stuntman for the Dukes of Hazzard: high speed J-turns, roll-overs, threshold braking and 'pitting', which involved staging a side collision with another car at high speed.

And there was no shortage of volunteers. In January 2004, the First Marine Expeditionary Force, called I MEF, deployed to Iraq. With the situation there deteriorating, the advisor mission was a way for those Marines left behind to join the fight, and — typical of the breed – they were willing to suspend careers, family life and safety to get there.

That summer, I visited this first group of advisors to see how they were getting along. Morale was high but they were finding the mission frustrating. The Iraqi Army had not performed well in the first battle of Fallujah that April; the one battalion chosen to participate had deserted en masse before reaching the city.

Amidst great media fanfare, General Petraeus had just taken over the fetchingly titled Multi-National Security Transition Command, Iraq (MNSTC-I, or as it inevitably came to be known by the rank and file, *Manstinky*), with the overall mission of building the Iraqi Army. Within the organization there was a climate of forced optimism which, at times, conflated realism with defeatism – and the advisors' report of the Fallujah debacle was never circulated.

# Chapter 18

By the close of 2003, things were not going well for the coalition in Iraq. In Baghdad the CPA had earned the sobriquet 'Can't Plan Anything' for its ham-fisted approach to governance in passing a stream of policies that were either ineffectual or explicitly counter-productive.

In Anbar Province, home to the country's Sunni minority – newly disenfranchised by the downfall of Saddam – distrust of the nascent Shia-dominated government and resentment against the US Army's heavy-handed approach found explosive outlet in a growing number of attacks on the coalition.

Arriving back in Iraq in January of 2004, I MEF took over responsibility for Anbar Province from the army's 82nd Airborne – a move that Marines were fond of explaining, whether true or not, was based on the rationale that the toughest units should be assigned to the toughest areas. Every insurgency has a heartland, an area where terrain, demographics and history form an inflammable mix, awaiting only the right spark to fulminate. In Iraq, Anbar was this place. Stretching from the outskirts of Baghdad west to the Syrian border, Anbar is a desolate, hard scrabble expanse of desert interspersed with ugly, squat, concrete towns. Its inhabitants, struggling to make a living from the unyielding dirt, are sustained by tribal affiliations older and stronger than the reach of any government and are bound by those same affiliations to ancient mores of honor and vengeance.

Now Anbar was ground zero for the insurgency – the locale for an unlikely coalition of the disaffected: former Ba'athists, Islamists, foreign fighters, tribal warriors, and a pool of impoverished young men looking to vent their humiliation against the invader. It was a complicated, shifting mélange of ad hoc alliances forged by opportunism and anger against the US occupation, with no common goal beyond the shedding of apostate blood. In this they were largely successful. The majority of young Americans killed in Iraq began their long journey home in Anbar province.

Fallujah, the second largest city in Anbar, had a history of fostering violent insurrection even during Saddam's time. Now it had become the spiritual home of the insurgency, and the physical home to its leadership – namely one Abu Musab al-Zarqawi, who rejoiced in the title of 'Sheikh of the Slaughterers.' A Jordanian ne'er-do well, Zarqawi had left a life of drugs and petty crime to establish a brand of Jihad so violent that even Al Qaeda shied away from him. Just over a year previously, Zarqawi had been a little-known zealot, holed up with several hundred followers in a small camp in northern Iraq. He was on the run from Saddam's secret police who, according to CIA reports, were about to close the noose around his hideout when the US invasion kicked off.

Having inadvertently uncorked the bottle by toppling Saddam, the US subsequently nurtured this brutish but resourceful *jinn* (an evil genie in Arab mythology) by passing CPA Order Number One, banning all former Baath party members from official employment and thus supplying Zarqawi with a pool of well-connected recruits. Misstep by misstep, the US occupation provided the perfect incubator for Zarqawi's nihilistic movement, and his followers swelled into the thousands.

Bin Laden and his deputy, Zawahiri, watched the rise of this bête noir with mixed feelings. Zarqawi, uncouth and uneducated, was not one of them – the well-heeled and well-educated aristocracy of Jihad. But the rapid growth of his movement offered them a bid for relevance, so they pulled the Jordanian into the fold, publicly acclaiming the start-up of a new franchise: Al Qaeda in Iraq. It was a bargain that was to prove Faustian for the architects of 9/11.

In April 2003, soldiers of the 82nd Airborne fired into a crowd in downtown Fallujah, killing seventeen, and beginning a chafing cycle of provocation and response that led to the well-publicized slaughter and dismemberment of five American contractors a year later. In the aftermath of that outrage, I MEF launched an attack on Fallujah, only to be called off as its lead battalions fought their way into the outskirts of the city.

There followed an uneasy truce during which the insurgents consolidated their hold on Fallujah while a locally recruited Iraqi Brigade turned a blind eye. Over the course of several months the *Muj*, as Americans had christened their enemy, turned the city into a fortress: erecting barricades, digging fighting positions, and sowing reams of IEDs, to include street-long daisy-chains of explosive intended to incinerate entire units.

In the fall of 2004, the US high command decided to do Fallujah properly, once and for all.

To that end, I MEF arrayed two regiments in assembly areas outside the city, while appealing to the city's inhabitants to leave. In this they were largely successful – the vast majority of the Fallujah's population streamed out of the city in the weeks before the assault.

I arrived in Camp Fallujah in early November, intending to stay only long enough to meet with some of the graduates from our advisor course who were waiting to participate in the assault. Among their number was Mark Lombard, as relentlessly upbeat as ever. He was, he said, particularly happy to see me because, through a complicated chain of events which I have now forgotten, the contingent of Marine advisors found themselves one short. I didn't need much convincing.

On the night of November 8 the attack began, preceded by a pounding cacophony of fires that silhouetted the minarets of the city's numerous mosques against a backdrop of yellow and red flashes. Six battalions abreast surged into the city through three breach points in the surrounding berm, attacking southwards across a 3-mile front.

Just before dawn, I found myself bumping across the line of departure in the back of an amtrac, buffeted on either side by Iraqi soldiers whom I had yet to meet. Through the track's thin metal skin I could hear the crump of artillery fire preparing our way, and was reminded of a comment made by a British officer during the exercise in Victorville: 'Even the most high-tech campaign gets very primitive when the barrage lifts and the infantry goes in.'

Eventually we lurched to a halt and we rose unsteadily, facing to the rear and crouching in anticipation as the ramp lowered. One of the first Iraqi soldiers down the ramp was shot in the neck and died before we could drag him clear. As would prove commonplace, we never saw the shooter – he was long gone by the time that we cleared the building from which he had fired the shot.

Hugging the buildings we moved cautiously down the street. Streaks of tracer snaked overhead, and from all around came the flash and crump of explosions. In between the bursts of white light, the night was pitch black. Rain pelted our faces and whipped through the crannies in our body armor as though the enemy had marshalled the forces of nature against us.

I was less than conscientious at keeping up my journal during my first two weeks in Fallujah, but have no problem recalling, with all senses and startling clarity, certain events that took place during that time. But while the images are sharp, I remember them as disjointed fragments with no recollection of the order in which they occurred or what happened in between, like a series of unconnected video clips. It was a long two weeks.

I was the senior member of a two-man team assigned to an Iraqi company. My fellow advisor, a stocky master sergeant by the name of Andreas Elesky, was glad to have me. Our Iraqi protégés were not exactly pulling at the reins to get at the enemy, and my presence provided at least someone to share night-time watches and the danger of walking point. Without an American in front of them, the Iraqi soldiers would simply refuse to clear buildings.

I was less than conscientious at keeping up my journal during my first two weeks in Fallujah, but have no problem recalling, with all senses and startling clarity, certain events that took place during that time. But while the images are sharp, I remember them as disjointed fragments with no recollection of the order in which they occurred or what happened in between, like a series of unconnected video clips. It was a long two weeks.

In Fallujah, I learned that there are aspects of urban combat that no amount of training can prepare you for. The routine always began the same way, with two of us poised for long seconds on a doorstep, preparing to enter a house. At those times, I would find myself soundlessly repeating the same quote from *Hamlet*: 'Nothing is good or bad but thinking makes it so,' which, in retrospect, is not true. Standing in the doorway of a house occupied by medieval fanatics waiting to kill you is bad, whether you think about it or not. A more apt quote from the same play would have been: 'For conscience doth make cowards of us all'. It certainly does.

If the door was locked, you'd pound at the handle with a rifle butt – all the while waiting for the wood to splinter in a storm of outgoing fire. As soon as it swung open, you'd be moving with it, knowing that your life depended on getting your silhouette clear of the fatal funnel. Not running, because then you couldn't shoot, but moving as quickly as you could at a half crouch, peering into the gloom over the sights of your rifle, finger tense against the trigger.

And when shooting started it was absolute pandemonium. Usually it began with the ear-splitting stutter of an automatic weapon, flashes and smoke and dust shaken out of the ruptured walls turning the gloom into darkness. And you were firing – without conscious decision or thought – mind subject to impulse. Sometimes you could make out targets – crouched, furtive figures behind the muzzle flashes – but usually you were just shooting blindly. There were shouts, the harsh guttural sounds of Arabic – your men or the enemy it was never clear – and once a scream that froze the blood. And then it would be over. The air thick with cordite smoke, the sound of coughing, groans, urgent demands from those behind, and a loud hammering that you realized was your heart. And a back slap from the Marine behind you: 'You OK?'

Going upstairs was even worse because it meant feeling your way up the stairwell, upper body contorted so that you could cover the next floor with your rifle, at a clear disadvantage to anyone lurking on the landing with grenades in hand. On occasion, Elesky or I would glance back to find that no one was following us. And perhaps this was just as well. A day into the battle, one of our number was killed while clearing a stairwell. When the other Americans on his team recovered his body they discovered that he had been shot in the back of the head. From that moment on, Elesky and I took it in turns to sleep.

Everyone has his own priority of fear, and what scares one man witless may not worry another unduly, and vice versa. My own special antipathy was entering a darkened house knowing that there was a good chance that there were men inside waiting to kill you. Fallujah was one long procession of such incidents without respite. I would rather take my chances out in the open, dangerous though the streets might be. On the whole though I'd have preferred a pint of IPA.

Once I entered a room to find myself in locked gaze with two insurgents, their faces upturned in the dust-speckled shards of half-light, as though they were expecting me. In front of them was a table on which I could make out at least two grenades and several wrapped bundles. Blood thudding in my ears, front-sight tip dancing unsteadily, I paused for seconds that remain indelibly edged on my memory, aware, but at the same time oblivious, that my delay could prove fatal. A huge Iraqi NCO whom we'd christened Ogre was standing by me shoulder to shoulder. Now he broke the stand-off: shouting and gesturing with the muzzle of his weapon, but there was no response from the two *Muj*. Ogre yelled again, this time raising his weapon. I did the same, looking over my sights at the implacable faces, my finger on the trigger taking up the slack.

And then our interpreter Zaid pushed past both of us, his hands outstretched palms open – talking in a low calm voice. He was blocking my line of fire, so I stepped to the side, opening my mouth to tell him to get out of the way – but then noticed that both insurgents had raised their hands. I took a deep breath.

Ogre moved forward jabbing his muzzle at the *Muj*, gesturing for them to get on the floor. A few minutes later, he and another *jundi* pushed their captives, hands flexi-cuffed behind them, out the front door, as the rest of the squad started to search the house. They found a collection of weapons and bomb-making material to include enough plastic explosive to blow the place to pieces.

'An IED factory,' the Marine interrogation team leader announced, eyeing the pile of contraband that the *jundi* were piling on the sidewalk. He crouched to look into the blindfolded faces of the two insurgents who were squatting on the sidewalk. 'You're going to Abu Gharib, my friends.'

I sat on the curb. *Did I hesitate? Why didn't I shoot them?* My mind replayed the scene. Zaid appeared in front of me. 'You alright, sadi?'

I looked at him, wanting to ask why he had intervened.

'Yeah – I'm fine. Let's get all this shit turned over to the Marines and move on,' I said.

Mark Lombard was in charge of resupplying the Iraqi forward companies, assisted by Corporal Suo, a Marine reservist with a thick Bostonian accent, and frame so slight that his oversized flak jacket gave him the appearance of a 12-year old playing at being a Marine. But that impression couldn't have been further from the mark. Suo was wise beyond his years, and so unflappable that I couldn't decide whether he simply lacked fear or held it at bay with an understated black humor.

On one occasion, driving back into the city at night having delivered an Iraqi casualty to the field surgical hospital, there was an incandescent flash against the side of a building just yards ahead of us, the explosion buffeting our vehicle. Suo slammed on the brakes almost sending me through the windshield. We sat in silence for seconds, the negative imprint of the flash still floating in front of my eyes. Suo lifted his night vision goggles and stared into the darkness waiting for his sight to return.

'What the hell was that, Suo – an RPG?'

'I don't know, sir,' he said calmly. 'I don't really have anything to compare it to.'

On another occasion, Mark and I found ourselves in a track delivering supplies to forward units. As we rounded a corner, there was a deafening explosion close by, and the track's machine gun opened up with a sound like a pneumatic drill. The top hatch was open, giving us a grandstand view of the tracer fire scudding by, just feet above our heads. Then there was an almighty boom from next to us; a tank had pulled alongside and fired its main gun once then twice, with a noise so loud that after the second blast, all other sound, the shouting and crack of bullets, became muffled.

The tracer stopped, there were calls to cease fire, and then someone was banging on the back hatch of the track.

'Open up – we've got a casualty.'

The ramp lowered and two Marines struggled on carrying a limp figure between them. 'Make room.'

They laid him on the floor of the track; I could see that his head was bandaged and that he was unconscious. Dark, wet stains covered the front of his flak jacket like freshly spilt wine. An argument broke out between his carriers and a Marine dog handler, whose German shepherd sat quietly by him impervious to the commotion.

'That's the only thing that he'll eat – you can't toss it,' the dog handler was saying. In an effort to make room for their charge, one of the Marines had grabbed a plastic pail and made ready to throw it out of the back of the track. He put it down without argument, and turning back to the wounded Marine slipped a poncho under his head.

'He needs to get back to the FSH ASAP,' he told the track commander who had appeared on the ramp. The FSH was the field surgical hospital at Camp Fallujah, some 2 miles from the city.

Mark and I were trying to go forward not back to Camp Fallujah so we jumped off the track, finding ourselves standing by Anne Garrels from NPR whom, I think, we disappointed by appearing to be as ignorant about what had just happened as she.

One evening early on in the battle, Elesky and I issued orders for the company to billet down for the night. Elesky then beckoned me outside to the front porch of the house where we were staying with a conspiratorial whisper:

'I've got coffee," he said producing a handful of sachets. Sitting on the front steps, we lit a pile of hexamine tablets and brewed water in our canteens, adding his entire stash of instant coffee, and waiting impatiently for the contents to boil. I had barely taken my first sip when a deafening burst of gunfire erupted nearby. Across the street a squad of Marines, crouched or laying prone, were pouring fire into a house three doors down from ours. Elesky and I exchanged anguished looks and, clutching our canteen cups, moved as one for the protection of the perimeter wall, careful not to spill a drop. There we sat, drinking our coffee while the firefight raged just meters away until the Marines fired a rocket into the building silencing its defenders.

Another fragment: Marines dragged the bodies of eight insurgents into the yard of a house to be searched and photographed. A single rocket had killed them all, throwing them together in a contorted pile but leaving their bodies intact. I shuffled through the pile of belongings stacked by the corpses: photographs with families, letters, identification cards and a couple of passports, one Saudi and one Yemeni. The bodies were all bloated although they had died only an hour or two previously and all bore the now familiar trademarks of violent death, their skin waxy and gray, mouths contorted in rigid grins.

Two intelligence Marines posed for a photo, their arms draped around one another – grinning, as though this was just another holiday snap.

'None of these fuckers was an Iraqi,' commented another, prodding one of the corpses with his foot. 'They came a long way to die.'

'Leave them the fuck alone.' I said. They looked at me bewildered, and backed off. My anger surprised even me. I hated the enemy as much as anyone, but mocking their dead seemed to me obscene.

One night we billeted in a house recently occupied by the *Muj* and found a pile of CDs in the living room. Unable to sleep, I popped one into the laptop that Mark carried around with him, curious. I found myself watching what appeared to be a family going-away party for two young men. Women in colorful dresses danced to wailing music and placed wreaths of flowers around the young men's necks, an elderly man made a speech and kissed both of them on the cheek, then the camera cut back to the women again who were now crying.

'Suriye,' [Syria] said a voice behind me. I glanced up. Several *jundi* were gathered around watching.

The next CD showed a different group of people, but similar scenes – depicting what appeared to be a ritual for sending young men off to fight the American invader. In this one an elderly woman, dressed in an abaya, wept loudly as she hugged the departees. They were all dressed in Western-style clothes, their hair combed, beards neatly trimmed. I thought of the bloated corpses I had seen that morning dragged out in the yard.

The next CD was quite different, and more familiar. A masked man holding a knife stood behind a prisoner who, bound and blindfolded, sobbed soundlessly. Before the inevitable grisly dénouement, the executioner thrust something towards the camera – it was a small infrared strobe, the type that we called peanut lights, used to mark our position to aircraft.

'They found this thing on him,' one of the *jundi* explained, 'and call him a spy.'

The poor bastard probably just found it and now was going to die for his curiosity.

It was a perplexing glimpse of our enemy, a curious combination of domesticity and barbaric cruelty. Earlier that morning I had visited Jolan in the north-west quadrant of the city, and was shown round a *Muj* torture house by Major Todd Desgrosseilliers, XO of 3rd Battalion, 5th Marines whose area it was in. In the house filled with medieval contraptions for inflicting pain, the battalion found several corpses and one surviving prisoner whose legs had been amputated by his captors. The smell, impossible to describe, had us both gagging.

# Chapter 19

I can clearly associate some memories with a specific date. November 12 is one because I can tie particular incidents that occurred that day with the official history of the battle. It was an interminable, shocking day. We spent the morning as we spent all mornings in Fallujah, clearing houses. The *jundi* performed better than they had previously: moving with such momentum that they caught two insurgents heading out the back door of one house, and found an IED intended to cover their retreat. It was a small victory, but one that I trumpeted to the assembled company before we moved on.

We had just finished clearing one house and were moving on to the next, with Ogre in the lead, followed by Elesky and then me, staying tucked into the side of the buildings to avoid making ourselves a target. The streets were killing fields; I had learned that lesson in Victorville, and again for real here in Fallujah. Across the street the Marines from Bravo Company, 1/3 were moving systematically from house to house: as soon as one squad entered a courtyard another would leapfrog ahead to tackle the next one.

Most houses had a small forecourt surrounded by a concrete wall and an iron gate. The wall was typically 6 or more feet high and the gate a solid sheet of iron so that you couldn't see into the forecourt until you opened it or boosted someone up to look over the wall. We would do this whenever possible – but lifting someone up so that their head poked over the wall made them a target. Sometimes the gates were locked, in which case we would shoot the lock, or chain the gate to a vehicle and rip it off its hinges. You needed to have someone cover the second story as you dealt with the gate, but to do so they would have to step back into the street, signaling your intentions and making them a target. House clearing was all snakes and ladders.

I paused in front of our next house, waiting for the *jundi* to line up on either side of the courtyard wall, then stepped backwards into the street to get a view of the upper storys, glancing over my shoulder as I did so. A squad of Marines were preparing to clear the house directly behind me – two rows of grunts facing each other on either side of the gateway, crouched, leaning forwards, weapons at the ready. Greyhounds in the slips.

As I watched, two Marines staged themselves on either side of the gate and a third grasped the handle, while a fourth stood next to him sighting his rifle at the gate. They were maybe 10ft away from me when the one Marine tugged the gate open. A ripping burst of fire lifted him and the Marine beside him off their feet, hurling them into the street.

I have learned that memory plays tricks on you on such occasions – inserting details that you couldn't possibly have seen at the time. So it was that I have a vivid, but probably false, image of the bullets slamming into their flak jackets raising spouts of smoke as they drilled through the fabric and plates. I have since met several other Marines who were on the street that day, and none of us have exactly the same memory of what happened. In any case, I am a poor witness, because a split second later all hell broke loose, and I was lying on my stomach, hands over the back of my helmet, face pressed against the road as the air above me whistled and cracked. I opened my eyes long enough to see Marines up and down the road shooting into the courtyard, and then a pair of heavy machine guns started firing from the next intersection with a baritone hammering that I could feel in my chest.

One of the Marines later told that the *Muj* returned fire, tracers streaking across the street over my head, and scattering the Marines around the gun trucks, but I was trying to burrow into the concrete and saw nothing. Time often dulls the memory of fear, so that sometimes I can remember that I *was* scared without reliving the event. Other times, the memory alone brings back fear as real as the moment I felt it. This was one of those times. The bullets snapped overhead, so close that I seem to remember feeling the gusts of disturbed air in their path – which is probably also physically impossible, but a measure of my funk.

I don't know how long the firing lasted, probably only thirty seconds at the most but it seemed much longer. Then there was a thunderous explosion that caused the hard ground to vibrate beneath me, followed by a chorus of urgent voices: orders to cease fire, calls for a corpsman, and then a ringing silence. I raised my head and saw flames licking around the frame of an upper story window. Someone had fired a SMAW thermobaric rocket into the courtyard, quelling all resistance and setting the house alight. A SMAW is a shoulder-fired anti-tank weapon and the thermobaric round uses oxygen from the surrounding air to generate a high temperature explosion. It was proving to be a very useful weapon for urban warfare: the *deus ex machina* of house clearing.

I remember Marines walking past carrying their fallen comrades slung in ponchos, only the boots visible and the heat from the burning house. Then, herded by two Marines, a pair of prisoners appeared from a side street, blindfolded, hands tied behind their backs, wearing white dishdashas and sandals. Their escorts had them squat on the side of the street, their backs against the courtyard wall and, as I watched them – realizing that they had been caught fleeing the same house from which the two Marines were killed – the remnants of my fear congealed into intense anger. I wanted them dead.

The pall-bearers returned from loading their forlorn cargo into a Humvee, and one of them – a stocky redhead – looked at the prisoners.

'Motherfuckers.' He stepped towards them fists clenched.

A staff sergeant, one of the escorts, blocked his way, pushing lightly on his chest.

'That's enough, Erickson – turn around.'

'I got him, staff sergeant.' A Marine grabbed Erickson above the elbow and led him away.

The staff sergeant caught my gaze. 'Hey sir, you alright? Saw you out there alone and unafraid.'

'You're about 50 per cent correct there, staff sergeant.'

He laughed as though my comment was funnier than it was. 'And nice job,' I added, suddenly ashamed of my anger. I waved my finger capturing the scene: Erickson slouching away, his buddy's arm around his shoulders, and the prisoners squatting on the sidewalk.

'Oh yeah – thanks, sir,' he said, misunderstanding. 'I came down that side street just as these two fuckers were running out the back door. Right place right time, I guess.'

I walked back across the street where Pesh and Ogre were getting the *jundi* off the ground and back into line with their customary harsh cries of exhortation: 'Yallah, yallah!'

Elesky was talking to Zaid: 'Mutajim (interpreter) – tell 'em to hurry the fuck up. We're burning daylight.' He always passed word to Zaid, even when it didn't appear necessary, and Zaid always made the same exasperated gesture, hands upheld in an exaggerated shrug.

'You good Boss?' Elesky asked me.

I flashed him a thumbs-up as I joined him and Ali by the entrance gate to the next house.

'Giddy-up.' Ali pulled the gate open and the three of us ran for the front door.

The image of the two Marines falling backwards remained with me, the way the shadow of an object seen in the bright sun lingers on your retina when you close your eyes. It has never quite left.

Brian Medina was 20 years old, from Woodbridge, Virginia – his father Gregory said that no one had to tell him that he had been killed. At the time of son's death, he felt a sharp pain in his midsection and knew that Brian was gone. David Branning was 21, from Cokesville Maryland – he had plans after the Marine Corps to work as a chef in Europe. Three years later, while commanding the same battalion, their dog tags, along with fifty-nine others, hung on a memorial outside my office. Some evenings, I would find myself sifting through these tags, pausing when I came to theirs – running my thumb over their names. And that awful split second would return, as real as when it happened.

That evening I sat in Bravo Company's command post in the living room of a house that we had cleared that day, as Company Commander Jay Garcia gave instructions to his platoon commanders for the next day's operation. A Marine rifle company is a close-knit family – drawn together by bonds of mutual reliance forged over the course of months of shared hardship. In combat those bonds become all the more important, transcending the normal vicissitude of intra-personal relations. In combat only one question is important: can I rely on the Marine next to me? If the answer is yes – as it usually is – then personal likes and dislikes, differences in background, religion, politics, color and yes, gender become irrelevant. And the loss of just one member of the company becomes an event mourned throughout, even by those not in the same platoon, because it represents a tear in the fabric, a missing part of the whole.

Before the battle, Brian Medina had sent home an American flag signed by every member of Bravo Company. His death brought to eleven the number of signatories who had already died – a significant loss for a company of some 160 Marines. A visitor to the company that night, expecting perhaps to find a somber atmosphere, and finding instead one of upbeat good humor, albeit a little forced, might attribute this to callousness. Nothing could have been further from the truth. It was because the Marines felt the loss of their comrades so keenly, that the company's leadership had to make a determined effort to buoy morale. There was a job to be done: only a third of the city had been cleared, and Company B was tasked the next day with pushing down to Route Fran, the road that bisected the city from west to east.

Jay, his boyish face stubbled and worn with fatigue, launched into the next day's operation, tracing with his finger the company's route on a map nailed to the wall.

'We'll kick off with 1st platoon on the west side of the street and 2nd on the east, 3rd following in trace and back clearing. I'll be on the net with Alpha – making sure that we are moving more or less on line with them.'

He paused to answer a summons to the radio, returning with a message for me.

'Hey sir, the CO wants you and me at the battalion CP ASAP. I'll give you a ride.'

At the command post, another abandoned house, we joined a group of officers in the living room where the battalion commander and his operations officer were consulting a map on the wall. There was a roll call, a cursory intelligence brief, and then the operations officer began to talk about the next day's events; a single fluorescent bulb cast a halo of light about him, throwing shadows across the circle of faces. I found it hard to concentrate, my mind kept wandering back to the events of the day, and none of what he was discussing appeared to involve my company. I realized my mistake when the CO called my name, signaling me to step up to the map.

'I lost another three Marines today, Andy. I need your guys to show up tomorrow, and take their turn in the barrel.'

The CO's voice had a harsh edge to it, as he chopped the air between us with a knife-hand. The others gathered around the map turned my way. Their faces were half in shadow, but I sensed sympathy in their expressions; these outbursts were regular events, and I was not the first target that evening. Still I bristled. *All I've seen is the inside of the fucking barrel,* I thought.

And the *'your guys'* comment needled me. It wasn't that I was trying to dodge responsibility for the Iraqi soldiers, it was simply that I lacked any type of real authority over them. Much of what we got them to do was by dint of persuasion. It was, as Mark commented, like taking an unruly third grade class on a field trip. And a field trip wrought with such horror that Stephen King might have struggled to do it justice. We had some influence on the Iraqi officers but, in the end, they would do what they wanted to do and I had a feeling that their list of preferred activities would probably not include what the battalion commander was about to suggest.

'Roger, sir,' I said, reminding myself the battalion commander had lost twenty-four Marines already in a battle that wasn't a week old.

'This mosque is right on the corner between Fran and Michigan.' The CO pointed at the map. '1/8 reported taking fire from there today, so we need to make sure it's secure before I push Bravo down to Fran. I can't bypass it, and I don't want to blow it away unless we have to, so that's where your Iraqis come in.'

*I was right – they weren't going to go for this.*

If I had been a little more seasoned I would have asked why he couldn't blow it away. After all, US firepower had already lain waste to a number of mosques throughout the city on the basis that they harbored insurgents. It seemed arbitrary to deem this particular one a protected structure. On the other hand, I reasoned, here was a chance to make amends for the Iraqi Army's humiliating performance back in April. It made sense too that Muslim soldiers should be given first opportunity to enter a mosque ahead of their apostate comrades in arms.

But the real reason why I didn't speak up was that more than anything, I was afraid of appearing afraid.

'OK, sir – what do I get in support?'

'A couple of LAVs, a couple of tracks, plus a javelin section.'

'Any tanks?'

'Come on Andy, be serious. You know we don't have any to spare. I'm giving you a shitload of firepower.' His tone lightened as he clapped me on the shoulder. 'Just make sure that you don't use it unless you have to.'

I took a few minutes with the operations officer to coordinate next morning's link up with supporting units, and then trudged back in the rain towards the house where my Iraqi charges had holed up for the night. Bone-weary, filthy, with nerves stretched taut by repeated floods of adrenalin, my mood was at its lowest ebb. I knew that Elesky and I would have to lead the charge into the mosque, as we had done throughout the last two days, house after house, block by block. And now, given time to anticipate what lay ahead – the moment of breaking cover and running through the doorway – I was filled with dread. And I was alone. I had sent Elesky to the rear for a day to give him a badly needed break. He was due to return early the following morning but that all depended on the vagaries of our logistics system.

I paused, and slumped against a wall, taking a few deep breaths to recover. I was in an alleyway behind a row of houses that the battalion had just cleared that day. I could see an LAV parked on the corner; other than that there was no sign of life. It felt strange to be alone in Fallujah.

Courage is a quality much written about, but hard to define. For a small group of individuals it seems to be an inappropriate term because they act mechanically with no apparent signs of fear. I like to think that these people simply lack imagination. At the other end of the spectrum is an even smaller group who habitually succumb to terror: perhaps not refusing to advance, but hanging back, with a tendency to shelter at the first indication of danger. And then there are the majority of individuals who summon the will to face danger using a repertoire of internal bargaining and blandishment. A few quiet seconds to take a deep breath and gird the loins. For this group – among whom I count myself – it's the greater fear – that of letting others down, that propels us forward.

And for me courage has always seemed a fickle beast. There were times when I felt buoyed by a feeling of invincibility; and others when mere anticipation had the elephant kneeling on my chest. This was one of those times.

*If I tell the battalion commander the truth, that no power on earth will get the company moving, he'll do what he probably should do anyway: drop the building. That's the best course of action for everyone. No sense getting Elesky and me both killed to no end.*

Relieved to have decided on a path that made good sense I walked through the darkness to the house that was our home for the night. It was a three-story building, shuttered and dark, standing on the street that marked that day's limit of advance. On the other side of that street, which represented no man's land, I could make out the silhouettes of buildings, more houses like the ones that we had spent the last few days clearing. Lurking among them was the enemy – waiting for us.

The entry hallway was pitch black but I could make out a faint glow coming from the next room. I tripped over one supine body and then another with growing irritation, as I made my way towards the light to find Zaid our interpreter hunched over a candle and a bowl of noodles. He was a massive, bearded middle-aged man who had spent several years as a prisoner of the Iranians during the Iran-Iraq war. He was always grumbling and giving me unnecessary advice but I liked him. Among the jundi he had more authority than the lackluster captain who was nominally in command of the company.

'What's up Boss – what did they tell you?' Zaid's concern showed in his eyes, and probably wasn't allayed by my expression.

*Fuck it, no one forced me to be here.* A vaguely remembered fragment from Hemingway floated up from memory: '*You wanted combat for what? I don't know really why. Or really know why … But here it is.*'

'We've got to get everyone up. I'll explain what it's about when everyone's on the road,' I said. Zaid winced but rose and followed as I climbed the stairs, my flashlight throwing into sharp relief the pattern on the worn carpet. The second floor looked like a crime scene – a mass of bodies surrounded by items pilfered from the house: blankets, food and cutlery. Zaid shook the first figure he came across, and asked him where the captain was. The *jundi*, eyes hooded with sleep, pointed towards the master bedroom. There we found Captain Mohammed and his sergeant major, an equally unimpressive individual, curled up in bed together fully clothed. I let Zaid wake them.

'Tell him he needs to have everyone out on the road in a column facing south by—' I glanced at my watch. '0230, thirty minutes from now.' I knew that even wide awake the captain would have a tough time doing what I had asked, so I climbed the stairs to the roof looking for reinforcement.

I had been around the company long enough to know whom I would find there, and wasn't disappointed – three figures leaning against the balustrade staring into the darkness. Lieutenant Ali, the senior platoon commander was chatting with his two sergeants: the one I'd nicknamed Ogre for his intimidating appearance, and the other I called Pesh because he'd previously served in the Peshmerga, de facto army of the Kurdish enclave in Northern Iraq. These three men commanded respect out of proportion to their rank.

I repeated my instruction to Ali, who spoke excellent English; he looked at me quizzically and repeated, 'In thirty minutes.'

'Look – just get them down on the road as soon as you can.'

Ali was one of a handful of Iraqi officers who gave me hope for the future: he was bright, earnest and cared about the men. Now, he and his two cohorts waded into their sleeping comrades like Iraqi drill instructors; Ogre and the Kurd swinging their boots freely, eliciting muffled oaths and cries of protest. Gradually, the company came to life. They had few possessions beyond their weapons and body armor, and it wasn't far beyond thirty minutes when the last one stumbled onto the road. The night was chilly and a cold rain started to fall as the NCOs herded and prodded the *jundi* into two single file lines straddling the road. I walked to the head of the column and picked up the radio.

'Punisher, this is Pale Rider.' I have no idea who came up with our call sign, but it seemed appropriate at that moment.

'Pale Rider – you ready to move?' I recognized the voice of the battalion operations officer, impatient; his boss was probably leaning on him to get everyone underway. The further that we could move in darkness the better; the Americans had night vision goggles, the *Muj* did not. Neither did the Iraqi soldiers for that matter, but it would seem churlish to bring this up now in an effort to have the US battalion take the lead.

'Give me five. I've got to brief them up.'

There was frustrated exclamation over the handset. Like most Americans, he obviously wasn't familiar with the usual timelines for getting an Iraqi company on the move. It was a miracle that they were almost ready to go.

I briefed Ali and the other two platoon commanders. Their English wasn't as good as Ali's, so I had to pause after every sentence to allow Zaid to translate. I didn't tell them much – just that we were moving south and that we were going to clear a mosque at first light. There were no protests, but there wouldn't be at this stage. If they didn't want to do something, they would smile, nod their heads, and then just not do it.

'OK, as soon as I see you get back in line, I'm moving,' I said and turned to the radio.

'Stepping in two mikes.'

'Roger – we've got one company on the road but won't start moving until you give us the word that you've crossed the LD.'

Zaid standing close to me, tugged my sleeve like a carpet salesman in the bazaar.

'Sadi – this is not good.'

'What's not good?'

'They know that we are coming. We will all be killed.'

'Thank you, Zaid. I was a little worried about tonight but you've really helped put things in perspective.'

Zaid had an unusually dry sense of humor for an Iraqi, but it wasn't working for him now.

'Why did you agree to do this?' he asked accusingly. 'I tell you – I understand war – we are walking into an ambush.' He gestured behind him at the shambling rows of half-asleep *jundi*, some of whom were caped in blankets looted from the house we had just left.

'Look Zaid, we don't have a choice, so you need to cut this shit out,' I hissed. 'It's dark, they won't see us coming, as long as we keep the noise down.'

At that exact moment, and I swear that this is true, there was the most awful noise: amplified static followed by the whine of feedback – then a driving guitar line.

> *Please allow me to introduce myself*
> *I'm a man of wealth and taste*
> *I've been around for a long, long year*
> *Stole many a man's soul to waste.*

*This has to be a mistake,* I thought. Even now I can't hear *Sympathy for the Devil* without a tight feeling in the pit of my stomach, seeing again Zaid's expression and the *jundi* crouched in terror on either side of the road.

Zaid was beside himself – and I was beside both of them.

'What is that, what IS that?'

'Mick Jagger,' I replied, reaching for the radio.

'Lava 3, get hold of the PsyOp clowns and tell them to knock that shit off. We'll lose the element of surprise.'

'Are you kidding me? That's the whole point. It scares the shit out of the *Muj* – and the boss loves it. Told them specifically to play the Stones.'

I glanced at Zaid who was gesturing to the soldiers behind him – some had dropped their weapons and clamped hands to their ears. I shook my head and shrugged helplessly.

'You've got to be shitting me,' was all I could manage.

We got everyone moving again but not without enlisting the help of Ogre, the Kurd and even Zaid whose bulk and short temper intimidated the *jundi* more than the enemy.

We reached the intersection across from our objective as the sky began to turn gray, having – to my surprise – walked some five blocks without contact. Almost to a man, the *jundi* plopped to the ground and went to sleep but I was so relieved to have come thus far that I didn't care. A few minutes later, we were waking them up again to make way for four armored vehicles lumbering up the road towards us: two amtracs and two light armored vehicles known as LAVs. Their gun systems wouldn't penetrate the thick masonry of the mosque, now looming over us in the early morning gloom but their presence was nevertheless a fillip to my morale, and I found myself grinning as they came to a halt, ramps dropped and Marines jumped out of hatches.

A Humvee rolled into view, edged slowly around the armored vehicles, and stopped next to where I stood with Zaid. Mark Lombard emerged from the driver's seat.

'We went through all kinds of shit to get out here. Got stopped at every checkpoint.'

Elesky climbed out of the passenger seat, looking uncharacteristically happy.

'Heard you might need some help,' he greeted me.

'Well I'm glad to see you guys.' That was an understatement.

I gathered everyone together in the lee of a wall that hid us from the brooding outline of the mosque: Lieutenant Ali (Captain Mohammed had disappeared), Zaid, Mark, Elesky, the amtrac and LAV platoon commanders, and a British officer who had just shown up announcing that he was the UK liaison officer to 1st Marine Division.

I could just make out everyone's faces in the gray light. All were filthy, tired and unshaven; Zaid and Ali had cigarettes cupped in their hands and the Marines were digging grubby fingers into a can of Copenhagen that someone had passed around. The sound of gunfire and explosions provided a now familiar soundtrack to the tableau. All of them were looking at me expectantly.

# Chapter 20

Isquatted and using broken masonry built a crude model of the mosque and its surroundings – a fist-sized rock for the mosque itself, and a row of shattered tiles for the perimeter wall. The Marines around me got into the spirit, and soon we had a half-way decent representation of our objective area.

This wasn't going to be a doctrinal order, but I owed them the overall mission and their tasks. I had long since learned that it was better to talk through the draft plan with your subordinates than try to perfect it on your own.

'OK fellas, the mission is to secure that mosque.' I pointed at the rock. 'Which means, at some point, we,' I pointed to Elesky and myself, 'need to lead the company across that courtyard and into the building to clear it. I want to avoid the gate because that's where they expect us to enter. And I want to avoid bunching up, so we'll need two breach sites in the wall. I'm not allowed to use prep fires so I'm looking for your help in getting in there. Thoughts?'

The track platoon commander spoke up: 'We can breach the wall there and there.' He stabbed at the model with his finger. 'And we'll pop smoke to cover your movement. Then we'll move here and here.' He picked up two pieces of masonry and placed them inside the courtyard wall on either flank of the breach sites. 'So we can cover you with our guns.'

'Same here.' The LAV lieutenant joined the game, placing two more pieces of brick next to the tracks. 'I have my guys scanning the mosque now with their thermals. I'd like to let rip with my chain guns through the front door before you start moving – that will suppress anyone who's in there.' It probably would. The M252 Bushmaster cannon fires at a rate of 200 rounds a minute.

'Can't do that,' I said feeling like a killjoy, 'but I need you to be ready to shoot if needed. Watch your angles though because we're going to be moving fast.'

'Hey, sir' he said, looking at me intently. '1/8 reported seeing *Muj* in there overnight.' His face was haggard, the skin under his eyes puffy and bruised, making him look much older than his twenty-something years. 'I wouldn't go in there without prep fires.'

'My orders are to go in without them.' *I sound like an automaton.*

'Shit sir – when did we start caring about mosques in this city?' the track lieutenant agreed. 'It's just us here, no one's going to say that we weren't returning fire.' His argument had merit. Fallujah had more than its fair share of religious buildings, hence its Arabic nickname which means city of mosques – damaging this one wouldn't make much difference to the overall count.

A young sergeant had joined our group, and now spoke up with the earnest air of a high school football player making a suggestion to the coach.

'I can take down the top of the dome with a Jav.' At the top of the mosque's dome, just visible above the wall, was a small cupola ringed by a balcony. A Javelin anti-tank missile would make short work of its destruction.

'Any *Muj* up there will fuck you up as soon as you break cover. I wouldn't go in there without taking that out, Sir.'

When people ask me why I have remained a Marine for so long, what comes to mind is that scene in Fallujah: the hard knot in my stomach and the concerned voices offering help at a time when I could really use it. They were strangers, but were at that moment as close as family.

'Thanks fellas, all good suggestions, but we have to stick by the rules of engagement,' I said before continuing. 'OK, we're going to LD at 0700, thirty minutes from now – that means tracks and LAVs popping smoke.' I looked at Ali and Zaid. 'Line up the *jundi* behind the wall on either side of the tracks. Keep your eyes on me and Elesky. As soon as the tracks breach the wall, we're going through.'

We synchronized watches and the group dispersed to brief their men and get into position. I eased the radio off Elesky's back, and raised 1/3's command post on the net, asking for the battalion commander.' *How do I word this without sounding chickenshit? Maybe that's what's wrong,* I thought, *I am chickenshit.*

'Lava Six – Pale Rider, we're in front of the objective now. There's a good possibility that the enemy's in there. Request permission to use a Javelin to take out the tower.'

'An-dy'. The CO emphasized both syllables of my name, exasperation in his tone. 'You're not going to fire up a mosque – got it?' *I did have it, and so did everyone else listening on the net.* Looking back now, I am amazed how much that bothered me at the time. Minutes away from the possibility of death, I was worried about appearing overly cautious.

I glanced one last time at the baleful silhouette of the mosque, half hoping to see something that would allow me to open fire. We'd long since lost any element of surprise.

The *jundi* were lined up behind the wall: squatting or sitting on the ground, clouds of cigarette smoke wafting above their heads, as though signaling to any insurgents who might have slept through the earlier commotion that an attack was imminent. I took my position at the front of the line on the left, Elesky was opposite me on the right, between us we left enough room for the tracks to bash two holes in the wall.

'All vehicles in position,' the radio squawked.

'OK fellas, going to count down from five, pop smoke and breach at zero. '5-4-3 ...'

Ali and Zaid were yelling at the *jundi* to get to their feet.

'2-1 – Go!'

The tracks barreled through the wall with a roar of engines and a sound like a giant tenpin strike, then the pop of smoke canisters. I waited a few seconds until I could see tendrils of smoke swirl above the wall.

'OK – let's go.' I was up and running, a momentary feeling of cathartic release, through the newly hewn gap in the wall and into the smoke. I caught a glimpse of Elesky to my right and thought I could hear boots behind me, but couldn't tell above the rasping of my own breath. There was no time to look back. We were committed.

I was in a flat sprint but felt as though I was barely moving. Elesky pulled ahead of me, which was impressive given his size plus the weight of the radio. There were shots, but I couldn't tell how close. Then the brooding edifice of the mosque was towering over us.

Elesky and I clattered up the steps side by side, throwing ourselves against the outer wall, to the left of the gaping doorway. Gasping for breath, I turned in time to see Ali, Ogre and Pesh dash the last few yards and collapse beside me.

I scanned the courtyard behind them – it was empty.

'MU-THE-FUCK-ERR!' Elesky's exclamation, bearing all the fear, anger and frustration of the previous two days, reverberated off the masonry above us, echoing back and forth. A few nights earlier, we had heard the *Muj* chanting 'Allah Akbar' in an effort to psych themselves up, or perhaps to intimidate us. I wondered now what they made of this distinctively American battle cry.

I turned to Ali who was staring at the courtyard, perhaps hoping that his soldiers would magically appear.

'Ali, where is everyone?' *That's what you call a rhetorical question.*

Ali, crestfallen, raised his hands palms up.

'Top – give me the radio.' I keyed the handset and called the LAR lieutenant.

'Have you see our *jundi*?'

'Still back here, where you left them. They're done training.'

He must have realized how this flippant answer sounded to someone perched on the threshold of an enemy strongpoint with a single fire team, and added: '1/8 opened fire on a group of *Muj* running out of the back of the building as you approached. I'm going to move into position and scan what I can with thermals. Don't go in yet.'

'No fucking chance of that,' commented Elesky. I gestured at Ali who was talking into his hand-held radio, his voice quavering with anger.

'What's going on?' I asked him.

'My sergeants are trying to get them moving now.'

'Get Zaid on the radio.'

I heard the whine of engines, and an LAV moved into sight through the gap in the wall.

'Zaid here.'

'Hey Zaid, get everyone moving – now.'

Zaid started to protest.

'Now, Zaid.' *Poor Zaid – a year of fighting the Iranians, and two as their prisoner. If anyone deserved a break, it was him. But now wasn't the time.*

'Not picking up anything on the thermals,' this from the LAR lieutenant over the radio. 'Gonna move into the courtyard to get a wider scan inside the building.'

That made sense: the *Muj* couldn't launch an RPG from inside the building, and having the LAVs up front might inject some motivation into the *jundi*.

The tracks roared and clanked as they pummeled the perimeter wall into shards of masonry, and then all four vehicles lumbered over the rubble and onto the worn paving stones of the courtyard, their guns swiveling to cover the mosque. As the roar of diesel engines died to a subdued moan, the first squad of *jundi* appeared around the hull of one of the tracks, sprinting towards us, with Zaid, his ponderous bulk instantly recognizable, trotting in their wake. Ali stood up and, ignoring Elesky's advice to 'get-the-fuck-down', ran into the courtyard to beckon them on.

Within minutes we had a platoon staged on the steps of the mosque, ready to enter. Ali insisted on taking the lead, and I, happy to let him, joined the end of the line. I watched him giving the *jundi* last-minute instructions and wondered what made him tick. Ali pushed for responsibility in an army that distrusted initiative and consistently took risks when such behavior was an anomaly.

On my signal we burst through the doorway, the two lines of *jundi* streaming in opposite directions around the circumference of its cavernous, dark interior. There was plenty of evidence that the enemy had been there very recently: spent shell casings, blankets, bandages – some of them bloodstained – dishes bearing pieces of unidentifiable food and a smell that is hard to describe; but it was heavy and pungent and compounded of stale food, piss, sweat and … *Muj*.

We spent that night in the mosque; it was an eerie experience, every night in Fallujah was, but this one stands out in particular. I lay on the floor, only a thin carpet between me and the cold flagstones, exhausted but unable to sleep, running through the day's events in my mind. We had been lucky. The battalion commander's restriction on preparatory fires made no sense, and I should have ignored it. As Marines we are taught to obey orders; but being a leader means that sometimes you need to shield your subordinates from the effect of bad ones.

I remembered a quote from the elder Von Moltke to an officer who had justified a bad decision by claiming he was simply doing what he had been told: 'His Majesty made you a major because he believed you would know when not to follow orders.' This had been one of those times but I had not had the maturity to recognize it. I resolved not to make that mistake again.

Across the road a building was on fire, creating a dancing kaleidoscope of light and shadow on the ceiling far above. The noises outside were by now familiar: the muffled BRRRRRRRRRR of an AC-130 gunship shooting to our south, the distant crackle of small arms like dry sticks in a fire, and blaring through loudspeakers, a metallic voice intoning urgent sounding messages in Arabic interspersed by snatches of rock music: *Welcome to the Jungle*.

A shadow approached, proffering a pillow and blanket. 'Hey sir – wrap yourself in this.' It was Staff Sergeant Villa, one of the advisors with 3rd Company, who had linked up with us earlier to coordinate the next day's operations. 'I'm heading back to the company. Figured you could use some warmth.' This small act of camaraderie settled my tumbling thoughts and, cocooned in the musty blanket, I fell asleep.

# Chapter 21

I woke to bursts of automatic fire; urgent shouts in Arabic. It was still dark. I ran out onto the balcony that ringed the mosque's dome and ducked as a tracer streaked upwards from the street below. An alert sentry had seen figures approaching down one of the side streets and, upon challenging them, had been fired upon.

Others joined me on the balcony, a chorus of voices asking what was happening, but no one knew. The moon was up, and by its bright light we could see shadows running on all sides, hugging the walls of buildings which made it hard for us to get shots in. I filled a fresh magazine; the moonlight glinted dully off the brass of each round as I jammed them against the spring-loaded metal plate, and hooked them under the lip of the magazine with unsteady fingers. One slipped out of my grasp, bouncing on the ground with an accusing tinkle.

One of us, I can't remember who, raised 7th Marines on the net and called for air support. Within minutes an AC-130 gunship was overhead, checking in with us via the Fire Support Coordinator at RCT-7 since we lacked the radios to speak to the aircraft directly.

'Listen,' he explained, 'Basher can see the mosque, and he can see people in the streets but can't open fire until you can verify that you have all your people inside.' Basher was the call sign for the AC-130 gunship supporting 7th Marines.

We hunkered down on the floor of the main chamber, and listened to Basher shooting into the streets around us: the loud ripping sound of its 25mm Gatling gun, and the occasional crump from a 105mm artillery shell fired with uncanny precision. There was a loud clanging on the roof, and we all reached for our weapons before realizing that the noise was made by spent casings tumbling to earth.

The next morning, following a hasty meeting, we changed advisors between the teams to allow us to weight the forward-most company, while enabling one advisor a day to rotate back to Camp Fallujah for a brief R&R. No one had asked for a break, but everyone was tired, and we had all noticed a collective deterioration in mood. The previous night I had exploded at the Iraqi communications officer when I discovered that he had failed to bring any spare batteries for the battalion's radios.

I was now with 1st Company, paired with Major Paul Zambelli – a rangy New Jerseyan who looked like a taller Dustin Hoffman – and commanded by Captain Abbas, a veteran of Saddam's army, but a real leader nonetheless.

The next day was my turn for R&R on Camp Fallujah. I spent the morning pottering idly in the post exchange with its incongruous display of domestic comforts, and was on my way to the chow hall when I saw a group of Marines carrying casualties from a track into the field surgical hospital. I caught a glimpse of chocolate chip cammies which meant that they were *jundi* and then recognized one of them, an Iraqi lieutenant, one of 1st Company's platoon commanders. I had a hurried conversation with the lieutenant as he was helped into the FSH – he was able to walk having been wounded in the arm – five wounded, he told me, and, he thought, one missing.

Within an hour I was pulling up in front of the building where it had happened, easily recognizable as such because smoke was pouring from its windows. Two tracks were parked in the street, and Paul was sitting on the ramp of one, Abbas beside him.

Paul grinned at me – his face was filthy and he was smoking, which he didn't normally do.

'Where the fuck were you?'

'Don't make me feel worse than I already do.' I sat down beside him. 'What happened?'

Paul jerked a thumb at the house behind him.

'Lieutenant Taweel led the stack into that place, with me on the end – five of us in all. Some fucker was waiting for us at the foot of the stairwell, waited until we were all in, and then let us have it. Fucking chaos – *jundi* pushing past me to get to the door, and then Taweel who'd been clipped in the arm, yelling to me for help with a wounded *jundi*. We drag him out, get a head count and find we're missing one. So Abbas and I have to go in to get him.'

Paul took a deep drag on his cigarette.

'We close the door behind us – it's pitch black in there – and we're fumbling around trying to find this dude when Abbas just yells his name out loud. I could have killed him. Lucky he did, as it happens, because the *jundi* answers – he's crawled under the fucking stairs. And then – I swear to God – I hear a bolt go home, like Haji's clearing a jam, so both Abbas and I just start shooting. Got through an entire mag – no idea if I hit anything. Abbas reaches under the stairwell, grabs the *jundi* and just drags him out. I'm right on his ass – and we both fall down the steps like a pair of clowns.'

Paul pointed at the flames licking around the window frame of the house behind him.

'Got one of the 1/3 dudes to fire a SMAW into the place.'

Abbas wandered over and I congratulated him on his good luck – he just nodded, and asked if we were ready to move.

'Stay here, man,' I told Paul. 'No sense pushing your luck today.'

'Fuck that,' Paul said, reaching out for my hand and pulling himself to his feet. 'Yallah.'

That same day, one block over from us, Sergeant Rafael Peralta of Alpha Company 1/3 entered a building – his seventh of that day – as point man for his squad. He made it through the fatal funnel, and, with two other Marines close behind him, moved down the darkened hallway to a closed door near the back of the house. They kicked the door open and as they entered the room a burst of automatic fire knocked all three to the ground. The Marines behind them opened fire, shooting over their comrades' prone bodies. It was, like all such engagements, a hideous primal melee of blinding flashes and stupefying noise. Then an insurgent rolled a grenade across the floor and what happened next has been the source of controversy ever since. According to the Marines present, Peralta reached out and pulled the grenade under him, thus shielding his wounded comrades from the blast; a story corroborated to me later that day by the battalion XO who reported that the grenade fuse was embedded in his flak jacket.

A subsequent investigation found that Peralta's injuries would have killed him instantly thus rendering him incapable of such an act. For that reason, a board rejected the Marine Corps' recommendation that he receive the Medal of Honor, awarding him instead the Navy Cross. Then, in 2014, a *Washington Post* article quoted two Marines involved in the incident as claiming that they had concocted the story spurred by the belief that in the confusion of close combat they had shot Peralta, and hoping perhaps to assuage their guilt. Their story, poignant enough in itself, was denied by all the other Marines present.

To me, whichever story you believe, Peralta's courage is emblematic of all Marines who fought their way through that wretched city, regardless of the manner in which he died. Peralta didn't even have to be there that day – he was assigned to a different platoon and had volunteered to join an undermanned squad.

Peralta, who was born in Mexico, wrote to his younger brother Ricardo the night before his death, telling him to be prepared to be the man of the house.

'Be proud of me, bro' – and be proud to be an American.'

By November 17, a week into the battle, things were starting to get easier. As we pushed deeper into the city, the *Muj* were defending fewer houses, and the *jundi*, having shaken out the worst of their nerves, were gathering momentum. We must have been resupplied with grenades because I remember that we could afford now to roll one down the entry hall way of each house ahead of the lead man (you rolled it because thrown grenades had a tendency to bounce back). As the *Muj* learned to avoid this hazard by fighting from interior rooms vice the hallways, the Marines countered by using more grenades; 'every room with a boom' was the expression in vogue at the time.

We learned fast. In house fighting, as in most military operations, whoever holds the high ground has an advantage – so we carried planks of wood to bridge the gap between rooftops enabling us to clear from the top of each building down to the ground floor. If working with Marines, we would use their shotguns to breach doors, or rockets to blow a hole in the outer wall allowing us to avoid the fatal funnel altogether. It was never as tough as it had been, but it was still nerve-jangling, exhausting work.

A day or two later, a thin red-headed army staff sergeant joined us from another company. Staff Sergeant Calder was the sort of person for whom it is second nature to do things for others, quietly spoken but an expert soldier who made himself useful from the start. He was a dab hand with explosives and taught Paul and I how to make a satchel charge with just enough bang to clear a room without fragging yourself.

On the first night of the battle, Calder and his team leader Major Miller found themselves trapped midway up the stairwell of a house, pinned against the wall by automatic fire from insurgents on the next floor. They could neither go up or down, and the *Muj*, realizing their predicament, called to them mockingly in English between bursts of fire.

As far-fetched as though this may sound, I heard similar taunts from *Muj* positions at several points in the battle. Sometimes combat appears to replicate all the worst clichés of the war movie genre.

'Calder,' Miller had said. 'I need you to toss a grenade up the stairwell. That'll let me get a good shot at them. On three.'

'Not going to happen, sir. It'll roll right back on us.'

'Well, you've got a flash bang. Throw that.'

'Sir, they'll get me as soon as I step out.' It was typical of Calder to admit his own reluctance to expose himself to fire.

'OK,' Miller had conceded, 'I'll throw the flash bang – you shoot.'

Miller stepped forward and hurled the flash bang as rounds ripped through the floorboards by his feet. The bang sounded more like a muffled pop – but Calder stepped out anyway, firing on full automatic into the bannisters above their heads. That gave them both enough respite to hurl themselves down the stairs and out the front door. It took a tank main gun to clear that house – firing several high-explosive shells into the upper story until the roof collapsed.

Later that same night, on the rooftop of another house, one of Calder's friends was shot in the back of the head as he prepared to clear down a stairwell. Calder thought that it might have been an accident – the *jundi* fired their weapons accidentally with alarming frequency – but suspected that it was not.

'They were panicking. They thought that we were going to get them all killed – their lieutenant told us that much. So, I wouldn't be surprised if they fragged John to save themselves.'

He described the incident in a flat tone, but he smoked incessantly and I noticed that his hands shook when he lit a cigarette.

The first night he spent with us, we stayed up late planning for the next day. We had the support of an amtrac platoon this time, a rare luxury, and planned to use them to clamber onto the roofs of the houses we had to clear. From the roof, we'd usually be able to gain access through a metal door, but quite often these were locked. To prepare for this eventuality, we made a pile of satchel charges which Calder stacked in the corner of the bedroom that he and I shared that night. I fell into an exhausted sleep, but woke up a few hours later to find him by the window staring into the street below, pulling hungrily on a cigarette that he kept cupped in his hands.

'I've been watching dudes running down the street, and they aren't ours.'

It could well have been the case; one of the terrifying things about Fallujah was that nowhere was really secure: the *Muj* were adept at infiltrating back through our lines, even slipping into occupied buildings to kill Marines. So I sat on the edge of my bed, wide awake with my rifle across my knees, peering into the street below but could see little.

'How much longer do you have in-country?' I asked.

'Another month.' The words tumbled out of him in short bursts. 'Heading back to my civilian job. I'm a reservist – it was supposed to be a training mission, I wasn't expecting any of this shit.'

'What do you do in the world?'

'I organize events – conferences, conventions, stuff like that.' He laughed. 'I used to think that it was pretty boring. Man, I miss it now.'

In turn, I told him how I enlisted in the Marine Corps as a private after finishing law school in London.

'The recruiter is probably still chortling about that one. I drove a hard bargain though: guaranteed infantry.'

'Oh yeah – you rung him dry,' Calder laughed.

We talked until the sky outside turned gray, and the rattle of gunfire returned to the city. From the house below, we heard raucous cries as sentries rousted their sleeping comrades. Calder stood up abruptly, reaching for his flak jacket and rifle. 'Yallah,' he said.

# Chapter 22

'Sir, Major Lombard has been hit. He's OK – but took a round in the leg, and has been evac'ed to the FSH. He wants you to bring him his gear.'

Corporal Suo's voice, normally deadpan, sounded breathless over the radio. I heard later that he had driven Mark to the field surgical hospital on Camp Fallujah, which was quick thinking on his part, and undoubtedly the best course of action for a minor wound. All casualties had to be evacuated from the city by tracks, and there weren't always enough to keep pace. Mark told me later that Suo shed his customary façade to yell repeatedly: 'You're going to be OK, sir,' which made Mark think that his wound might be more serious than it appeared.

It was early afternoon and, after an uneventful day of clearing – the first such day – we had just got the company settled into a billet for the night. I grabbed Mark's backpack and went downstairs to get a vehicle and headed for Camp Fallujah with one of the *jundi* riding shotgun. The drive was only twenty minutes, but Camp Fallujah seemed like a different world. Marines without body armor strolled along the well-kept sidewalks clutching cups of coffee; there were traffic signs and trash cans and rows of portable toilets.

Mark was sitting up in bed when we entered his cubicle in the FSH. He greeted me with his usual enthusiasm and started chatting at the cyclic rate, fueled perhaps by adrenaline or painkillers or by just being Mark. He had been hit by a single heavy machine-gun bullet which must have been at the limit of its range, because it had just penetrated his leg, causing a good deal of bleeding but no serious damage. Mark was happy to have earned a Purple Heart at low cost, and was eager to rejoin the company.

'No chance of that,' commented a navy nurse. Her blonde hair appeared to hypnotize my *jundi* companion, and I had to squeeze his elbow sharply to avoid us embarrassment.

We appealed to a doctor, a harassed-looking lieutenant commander, who granted Mark's release along with a list of instructions about what he should and shouldn't do. As we drove towards the gate with Mark and the *jundi* squeezed together on the passenger seat, someone jumped in front of the vehicle and I slammed on the brakes, almost sending us through the windshield. A tall, thin, middle-aged Marine in regulation green PT attire walked around to my side of the truck, half leaning through the open window, eyes narrowed to slits, face taut with anger.

'How fast do you think you were going, major?'

I started to answer but he cut me off. 'Way above the speed limit – which is 15mph as you well know. You could have killed someone.'

He went on, his voice rising with the momentum of his indignation. The speed limit signs were everywhere; I couldn't possibly not have seen them; this was prime time for unit PT; I could have ploughed into a formation; I was an officer and should be setting the example; and why weren't my passengers wearing seatbelts?

I had just tumbled through the looking glass in reverse: from a world of chaos and sudden death to a familiar, orderly one governed by mundane rules. Marines gathered on the sidewalk to watch the tirade, with expressions suspended between humor and sympathy. My accuser paused, glaring at me.

'Where are you going?'

'Fallujah, sir.' I guessed that he out-ranked me.

'This is Fallujah, major.'

I pointed over his shoulder at the black plume of smoke that hung over the city.

'That's Fallujah, sir.'

He glanced over his shoulder and looked back at me, then took in the *jundi* sitting next to me.

'Well – go ahead then.' He took his hands off my door. 'But slow down.'

We drove out through the front gate and back towards home, each of us processing the incident in our own way. I was shaking with laughter, but Mark, incensed, was mouthing a stream of invective. The *jundi* sat bolt upright, eyes wide open and fixed on the road ahead, as though in shock.

'Welcome to the Marine Corps,' I said, patting him on the back.

We spent Thanksgiving night in a mosque just off Route Fran, the main thoroughfare that split Fallujah north from south. The Iraqi government had declared Fallujah secure by then, but the enemy hadn't received this news and nowhere in the city was yet safe. A MEF spokesman described the subsequent operation as 'mopping up.' But it's hard to appreciate that phrase when you're one of the ones holding the mop.

It was something of a reunion for the advisors. In addition to Paul, Mark, Elesky and Calder, there was Major Brian Mulvihill, an Irish-looking New Yorker with a dark sense of humor, Staff Sergeant Villa, who had given me his blanket, and a couple more whose names I cannot remember. We'd lost one killed and several wounded, but agreed that overall we had much to give thanks for.

Mark and Suo performed miracles by picking up a Thanksgiving dinner from the chow hall on Camp Fallujah and delivering it to us still hot. They had taken with them Pesh and Ogre who followed Mark back in an Iraqi truck filled with food for the *jundi*. We built a fire pit – the temperature outside was around freezing – and, after ensuring that sentries had been posted, ate until we were almost comatose. Then, reclining in the plastic chairs that furnished the mosque, we smoked cigars and listened to music: a CD of grunge that Brian had brought with him. It was one of the best Thanksgivings I've had.

The next day, we received orders to remain in place and prepare to repatriate the civilian population to their homes. The first busloads were due to arrive the following morning, and we came up with a simple plan to get them from the drop-off point outside the mosque to their homes. We designated what we called release points throughout the northern half of the city – the area south of Fran was still considered too volatile – at which we staged platoons of *jundi* to act as guides. The MEF would escort the returnees from their camps outside the city to our mosque and turn them over to us. We would record their names and addresses, issue them food and water, and separate them by neighborhood into groups before loading them onto trucks to deliver them to release points nearest their homes. Once there, it was the responsibility of the senior *jundi* to escort each man to his own home.

Early next morning, a convoy of trucks drew up outside the mosque, disgorging the first group of returnees. Mark and I stood in the courtyard as the *jundi* herded them into a column and led them into the mosque for processing. I couldn't help noticing that they were all young males, and wondered if the *Muj* weren't pulling a fast one on us with exquisite irony: using US assets for rest, resupply and transportation prior to re-infiltrating the city.

Despite our misgivings the repatriation continued without a hitch and, our task completed, we left Fallujah for an assembly area outside the city.

# Chapter 23

I have read reports that the fighting in Fallujah lasted only two weeks, but no one I know remembers it that way, because the enemy proved to be adept at infiltrating into areas that had already been cleared. Two days before Christmas, a full six weeks after the battle began, I was back in the city when three Marines were killed in a building adjacent to mine by insurgents who had entered an area thought to be secure.

I noticed a very different approach to this problem between battalions. Third Battalion, Fifth Marines, for instance, was very deliberate, using a well-coordinated combination of mortars, machine guns and tanks to soften enemy strongpoints in concert with the movement of dismounted infantry. Once an area was cleared, it was immediately fortified by engineers, and manned by a designated holding force: a unit given the mission of defending the captured buildings.

By contrast, the Marine battalion to which I was attached took a more laissez-faire approach: the battalion command group travelled around the battlefield, but made little attempt to coordinate the actions of subordinate units. This appeared to compound rather than alleviate the fog of war.

One Iraqi battalion participated in the battle, by that I mean fought inside Fallujah itself (others were involved in actions outside the city). I served with two of that battalion's four companies and so had a chance to observe its performance at close hand.

Overall what I saw was not encouraging. I said as much in the after-action report which I submitted to MNSTC-I within a week of leaving the city on Christmas Eve:

'Iraqi Army units are not ready for independent operations at any level,' I wrote. 'These (Iraqi) companies were, by necessity, led, not merely advised, by US personnel. These advisors had to run the company and conduct all external coordination such as requests for fire support, CASEVAC, and logistics support. [...] The 5th Battalion advisors were taxed to the limit of their mental and physical limits (sic) by the fact that none of them had within their companies a functioning chain of command.'

MNSTC-I buried my report; but Thomas Ricks resurrected it for his book *Fiasco*.

Soldierly qualities aside, I liked working with the *jundi*. They were unfailingly courteous: always ready with a smile and a polite greeting even in fraught moments before an attack; and hospitable to a degree that you rarely see among Westerners. While walking the lines, I would be greeted at every position by a cheery '*Shaku maku, sadi?*' (How's it going, sir?) followed by an invitation to join them for a meal or a smoke.

It was easy for Americans to pour scorn on Iraqi soldiers for their lack of enthusiasm but our tours were finite, and our culture nurtured the traits that made war fighting possible. They were always in danger, sometimes even more so at home than in combat. After Fallujah, we started to hear dark stories about soldiers on their way home for leave being intercepted at insurgent roadblocks and executed by the side of the road. Several officers told me that their profession condemned them to reclusion at home, afraid to even allow their children to play outside.

Not all our Iraqi charges were reluctant warriors. There were individual acts of great bravery, and men like Ali, Ogre and Pesh gave me hope for the future.

As for the enemy, many of us had developed a grudging respect for the insurgents who had made Fallujah so costly. Between November 8 and December 23 (when the battle officially came to an end), 95 US Marines and soldiers were killed and 560 were wounded. Bing West, author of '*No True Glory*', undoubtedly the definitive book about the battle, comments that it was probably as violent an engagement as the Battle for Hue during the Vietnam war, ascribing the lower casualty rate in Fallujah to improvements in body armor and medical technology. Most estimates of enemy casualties fall between 1,200 and 1,500 killed, with 1,500 captured.

My curiosity was piqued by the glimpses of the enemy I had seen. There were the two I had stumbled upon in that room, unhurried and unafraid in the face of death. The foreign fighters over whose corpses we had gloated, who had traveled hundreds of miles just to get the chance to fight us. And the small teams of infiltrators with enough courage and skill to slip back through our lines to kill and be killed. We had wrested a city from their hands, and killed hundreds of them, but many more, to include Zarqawi, had escaped, and we had done nothing to staunch the flow of fresh recruits to replace those who had been lost.

I always felt that there was more to the enemy than we were willing to admit. It was as though we sought to diminish the threat through contemptuous references and one-dimensional intelligence reports: they were religious zealots, suicidal, unsophisticated and evil; but we had little insight into their motivations or vulnerabilities. Like the prisoners in Plato's allegory of the cave, we could see only the shadows on the wall, and mistook them for reality.

On Christmas Eve, the *jundi* of 5th Battalion departed Fallujah for their home base in Taji. I had my first shower in weeks, and burned my utilities which stank of Fallujah. It was a deeply cloying stench of death and decay that I will never forget.

# Chapter 24

'ell the boss has you slated for this gig with the IIF,' Major
Matt McDivitt, the brigade advisor operations officer told me
over the phone. I had called him from Camp Fallujah to see
what plans they had for me. 'But that doesn't begin until January 4 or 5. So,
you've got two weeks off. You could come to Taji, if you don't mind spending
Christmas in a shithole.'

I laughed. 'Shithole' was a common expression used by everyone to
describe wherever they were in Iraq.

'What's the IIF?'

## ANBAR PROVINCE – 2004

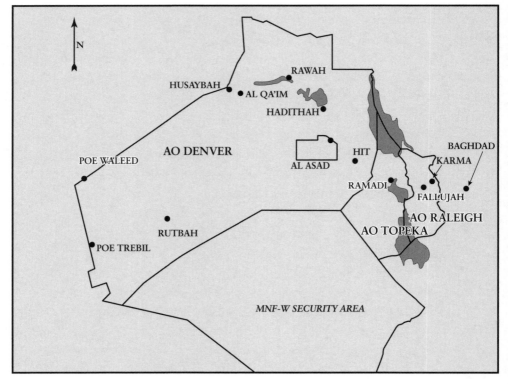

A US military map of Al Anbar province in 2004 showing its subdivision into areas of operation (AO), each of which
would be assigned to a tactical unit. The military code name given to the entire province was AO Atlanta. All of western
Anbar fell within AO Denver; Ramadi and environs were in AO Topeka; Fallujah and Karma were in AO Raleigh.

'The Iraqi Intervention Force, otherwise known as the Iraqi Army 6th Brigade. Petraeus got *Manstinky* to put together a unit made up of former Republican Guard and Special Ops cats, in the hope that there would be at least one unit in the Iraqi Army worth a shit. Anyway, the idea is that we form this super cool unit, and then set them loose up in Mosul to clean that place up.'

'OK – sign me up.'

'Oh, you're signed up, brother. And be careful what you wish for. Merry Christmas.'

I didn't relish the idea of going to Taji or hanging around Camp Fallujah for two weeks, but did have another option. Tony Marro was now the operations officer for First Battalion, Seventh Marines, a battalion that had just begun its tour in a place called Al Qaim in the north-western corner of Anbar Province.

'Come on out,' he'd said over the phone. 'We'll celebrate New Year together.'

I knew, of course, that he was making that part sound more fun than it would be. General Order Number One forbade most activities that Marines enjoy – drinking alcohol being one. But it would be good to see Tony again, so that night I headed down to the camp's helicopter landing zone to begin my journey to Al Qaim.

If there was a competition among locations in Iraq for the title of shithole, Al Qaim would at least make the semi-finals. The town itself was a collection of dun-colored cement dwellings surrounded by the featureless expanse of the Anbari desert. There was a railway station and a phosphate plant, both long since disused, and a border station that used to be the busiest waypoint for truck traffic with Syria but was now closed.

In addition to a heartland, every insurgency needs a porous border with a sympathetic state on the other side, providing a conduit of supply – men and material – and, when needed, a safe haven for its leadership. For the FLFN in Algeria, it was Tunisia and Morocco; for the Vietcong, Cambodia and Laos; for the Taliban, Pakistan – and for the *Muj* it was Syria.

Now Al Qaim was busy with another kind of cross-border traffic: it had become a staging point for the flow of young men from across the Arab world, come to Iraq to fight the American invader. The town was one link in a chain that extended from Damascus into Eastern Anbar and beyond. It was a well-designed chain, manned by small cells of insurgents who knew nothing about the next link, beyond what was needed to pass on their human cargo.

As Americans, we wanted our enemy to conform to the labels we gave them: they were the *Muj*, a lumpen homogeneous mass of religious zealots, anarchists, terrorists; the bad guys to our good. But our enemy included Iraqi patriots fighting from a sense of pride to oust the invader, forced by expedience to ally with those whom they had previously despised. In an unconscious mockery of our own inability to understand the depth of Iraq nationalism, we came up with the acronym AIF for Anti-Iraqi Forces to define anyone who launched an attack on the coalition. It was Orwellian in its absurdity. The war to avenge 9/11 and prevent Saddam from using weapons of mass destruction was now tinged by a dreadful irony. We had given our enemies common cause.

Whatever we wanted to call the insurgents, their leadership now represented an uneasy alliance of nationalists and Al Qaeda affiliates; while the foot soldiers were often poor, out of work young men or foreign volunteers driven by religious affiliation, and a sense of injustice fueled by the welter of internet propaganda depicting American occupation in a harsh light.

And you didn't have to be a zealot to find ample evidence of American heavy-handedness. The photographs from Abu Gharib had become public earlier that year, depicting a handful of West Virginia National Guardsmen amusing themselves at the expense of Iraqi prisoners. In the immediate aftermath of their publication there was a rise in the number of attacks throughout the province; a high price to pay for the sordid antics of a few soldiers who appeared typecast for the movie *Deliverance*. It didn't matter that across Anbar Marine battalions were struggling to protect the local populace – we were now all tarred with the same brush.

It was a downward spiral of action and counter-action that gathered momentum with tragic inevitability.

And as the insurgency spread, Marine units on the ground in Anbar learned some harsh lessons. In 2004, it was a fortunate battalion that reached the end of its tour with fewer than twenty Marines killed and five times that number injured. The battle for Fallujah where US forces and insurgents fought toe to toe, was an anomaly. Elsewhere in Iraq, the insurgency followed a more traditional pattern of asymmetric attacks: Improvised Explosive Devices or IEDs had become the insurgent's weapon of choice, enabling them to inflict casualties without offering the opportunity for set-piece confrontation.

We had trained to fight against an enemy who used the same weapons and tactics against us as we used against him. Although the vast majority of the world's population lives in cities, most Marine units typically spent only one or two weeks a year practicing urban combat. In mechanized operations, our drills focused on reacting to an enemy who stayed to fight. We were taught to put together intelligence estimates based on a conventional enemy, and learned to select key terrain based on physical avenues of approach. In the war that we found ourselves fighting, there was little use for this type of estimate with its overlays and cross hatch pen marks. Instead we learned that local demographics – a complicated mosaic of tribe and religion – were all important. People were the key terrain.

I MEF did its best to ensure that units deployed with training in the latest techniques and that all Marines were familiar with the principles of counter-insurgency. But understanding the principles was one thing; making them work in an atmosphere of fear and distrust, with a population that was sullen and uncommunicative, was quite another. And the truth is that there's no magic elixir to gaining the upper hand in a counter-insurgency. Every area is different when it comes to what works, and what doesn't. In Anbar province, battalions learned on the fly, by trial and error, reinforcing what worked and discarding what didn't, and best practices developed at the squad and platoon level were quickly adopted and disseminated.

In Ramadi, where I stopped for a few days en route to Al Qaim, every day was a movement to contact: a fight to open a route to the Government Center which had become a symbol to both sides of the government's ability to control the city. There I linked up with an old friend, Jeff Kenney, who commanded Golf Company, 2/5. Jeff had been one of the evaluators for our exercise at Victorville and had applied many of those lessons in Ramadi, a city that had become a byword for grinding attrition. Like the battalion before them and the battalion that would follow, 2/5 had already endured a steep cost – losing some sixteen Marines to include a popular company commander by the mid-point of their tour. It was an experience that would become all too familiar a pattern for battalions deploying to Anbar over the next few years: the loss of friends, the daily grind of danger and fatigue, the sense of isolation and a local population who appeared at best indifferent.

# Chapter 25

Tony had dark shadows under his eyes but was ebullient as ever, greeting me with a bear hug as I got off the helicopter.

'Yeah – it's been pretty rough out here,' he admitted as he took me to see the battalion commander. 'We've lost some good folks, fourteen so far to include three officers. You remember Alan Rowe? He was killed during the turnover. We get hit pretty much every time we leave the front gate.'

Lieutenant Colonel Chris Woodbridge, the battalion commander, added to Tony's last comment.

'Pushing out patrols simply to establish a presence achieves nothing, and makes us a target. We need to find another way to fight the enemy.'

Chris looked like a Russian power lifter but had one of the sharpest minds in the Marine Corps.

'When a patrol goes out now, it's for a specific mission, not simply trolling for trouble.'

Using a technique that was considered innovative back then, Chris used his signals intercept teams in combination with patrols to monitor enemy communications and pinpoint their location. He'd then use this intelligence to plan night raids, targeting specific individuals.

'I don't want to fight the *Muj* on the roads where he has the upper hand. I want to fight him at 0200 in his bedroom.'

These raids would net more intelligence, which would, in turn, drive more raids. In this way the battalion was making some headway but Woody was too realistic to believe that they could ever win over the local population.

'They're terrified of the *Muj*, and we've got nothing to offer them in return. We hand out soccer balls with tip line numbers, and the PsyOp team runs a radio station but we get nothing back. And we suck at information operations. The messages are controlled way too far up the chain, and by people who don't understand what's important to the locals. As for hearts and minds: we dig wells, and the *Muj* shits in them; we build schools and the *Muj* blows them up.'

Most of the battalion's casualties had been from IEDs which the *Muj* were making and emplacing with a sophistication that the battalion's EOD team was struggling to match.

'We never even see the fucking trigger man. We've bagged six or seven IED-layers during the four months that we have been here, but they're just poor out-of-work muldoons trying to earn some extra cash.'

'Other than that, most of our intel comes from interrogations. Our HET team is pretty good and playing these guys off one another. It's like the *Sopranos*. As for all that bullshit we learn about every Marine being a collector: the locals don't want anything to do with us, and who can blame them. Anyone who does gets capped. The *Muj* even killed our shit-sucker.'

'Your what?'

'The dude who vacuums the porta potties into a tanker truck. They killed him and dumped his body in the road, right in the middle of the town.'

At the stroke of midnight on New Year's Eve 2004, the *Muj* hit the FOB with a string of mortars, the explosions silencing the half-hearted cries of celebration emanating from around the camp.

The next morning, I jumped on a convoy to Camp Gannon, a combat outpost on the border. In a pattern that was commonplace throughout Anbar, keeping the road to Gannon open was a fight in itself. Most of the route was across open desert, but there were areas where the terrain converged to form predictable bottlenecks impossible to avoid. First Battalion, Seventh Marines picketed these areas with patrols but every convoy that left the front gate had a 50 per cent chance of hitting an IED.

I had some time to mull this statistic over as I waited in my assigned vehicle for the convoy to head out. Ahead of us was a fuel truck on the back of which was written in large red letters: DANGER OF EXPLOSION, INFLAMMABLE, KEEP CLEAR.

Sitting in the front passenger seat was Gunnery Sergeant Lehman, a tall laconic Minnesotan.

'Cooper, I don't suppose that you could have found any other position for us in the convoy,' he said to the driver who had been staring out the side window in an effort, perhaps, to avoid the sight in front of him.

'Sorry Gunny, those bastards in the motor pool made me fill out a bunch of paperwork, and by the time I drove up this was the only place left for us.'

'Well,' said Lehman, sighing. 'At least it will be quick.'

As luck would have it, it wasn't the fuel truck that hit an IED, but the truck in front of it: a 7-ton behemoth carrying half a dozen Marines in the back. It happened about half an hour after we left the FOB, as the long line of vehicles began to snake downhill into a defile between rocky outcrops. I had been enjoying the ride; it was a bright, crisp day – the sky a brilliant blue above the wide-open vista of desert mottled by the scudding shadows of clouds. It was an elixir after the dank streets of Fallujah, and I felt my spirits soar.

Then there was a crump, and the truck appeared to lift a few feet into the air before disappearing in a cloud of black smoke and sand. Without a word, we threw our doors open and ran towards it. The truck's back had been broken, the bed now canted at a sharp angle towards the rear. The Marines in the back were hurled against the tailgate in a tangle of limbs. I could see them moving, trying to extricate themselves as Lehman and I reached the vehicle – along with, so it seemed, every other Marine in the convoy. It was a phenomenon that I would see again and again following an IED strike: everyone in the vicinity rushing to help. Prior to deployment I had seen a video taken by insurgents of Marines running to a stricken track, only to be engulfed in flames by a second and larger IED placed to exploit this predictable reaction.

Several Marines and a corpsman had already climbed into the back, among them was a friend, Major Rich Bourgeois, who was using his knife to cut the trouser leg off one of the wounded Marines.

'Four WIA,' he yelled to me over the shattered tailgate. 'All four are going to need evac. Two urgent.'

*But all alive*, which seemed miraculous given the size of the explosion; but the 7-ton was a resilient beast and the Marines had been sitting atop sandbags which had helped cushion the blast. All four were conscious, though banged up severely enough to need litters. One had pulled himself into a sitting position and, surveying his bandaged legs, let loose a stream of profanity.

Everyone did what needed to be done with little direction. Lehman called battalion on our vehicle radio to launch the pair of helicopters designated to evacuate casualties. An EOD Marine cleared the area around the truck using a metal detector, while a second swept a path to the designated landing zone.

'Battalion's sending the QRF,' Lehman told me. 'I told them to follow our tracks.'

A few minutes later we heard the clatter of approaching Blackhawks. The helicopters flared, noses up, and we picked up the four stretchers and lumbered towards them, heads bent downwards against the blast of sand from the propeller wash.

The Blackhawks had just disappeared over the horizon when the QRF pulled into view, a row of Humvee gun trucks approaching at speed along the same route we had come, guns swiveling side to side, the gunners crouched in their turrets amidst swirling columns of dust. As they drew near, the lead Humvee took a left turn towards a ridgeline just beyond the landing zone. There was a resounding thump and a jet of smoke shot from under the vehicle, tossing it into the air in a blur of earth and metal parts.

The radio blared: 'Everyone stay put, convoy's moving.' As we started to roll after the fuel truck, I saw a group of Marines from the QRF converge on the twisted metal carcass.

I learned later that both IEDs had been made by stacking together two Italian-made VS-12 anti-tank mines, made of plastic thus eluding the EOD team's metal-detecting wands.

Tony was at the landing zone to meet the inbound casualties from the second strike. First to be carried off was Corporal O'Neal, the vehicle's driver. The blast had torn off both his legs and blinded him in one eye, but he gave Tony a grin and the thumbs-up sign as he was carried down the ramp.

The episode was one repeated countless times in countless places throughout Iraq.

Before leaving Al Qaim I listened to a brief by the battalion Intelligence Officer whose prognosis was anything but cheerful:

'We've seen an uptick in activity since Fallujah, and I hear that battalions across Anbar are experiencing the same. It's like a giant game of whack-a-mole.' *So much for Fallujah being a decisive battle.*

'Yep, we're just barely keeping the lid on.' Woody added, with another dispiriting metaphor. 'It's hard to see a happy ending to this.'

# Chapter 26

Many of the insurgents who fled Fallujah headed north to Mosul, where they ousted the local police and took de facto control of the city. The 101st Airborne Division had left the city earlier that year, replaced instead by a unit half its size, a single mechanized brigade that lacked the manpower to patrol the city effectively. In December, as the battle for Fallujah spluttered to a close, a suicide bomber dressed as an Iraqi soldier self-detonated on the main US base in Mosul, killing fifteen soldiers and wounding some eighty others – the highest toll from a single attack in the war to date. The blast undermined morale and destroyed any remaining vestige of trust between the US troops and their Iraqi counterparts. In its wake, Iraqi security forces in the city – police and National Guard – simply evaporated.

And so it was that in early January 2005, I found myself heading for Mosul with the newly formed Iraqi Intervention Force (IIF) which had the mission of helping wrest the city back from the hands of the insurgents.

Roughly two-thirds of the US advisor contingent to the IIF were Marines, with the remaining third composed of soldiers from an army reserve unit. As we moved by convoy up to Mosul, a twenty-hour ride interrupted on several occasions by IEDs and incoming fire, some of these soldiers voiced their unhappiness with the upcoming mission.

'Well, they didn't sign up for combat.' Captain Chuck Groen commented as we relieved ourselves by the side of the road just south of Bayji. It was our umpteenth break on the interminable voyage north from Baghdad. For the first few miles we had had Apache helicopters flying escort, as much to reassure the frightened *jundi* as to ward off ambush, but now we were on our own. 'It's not that they're chickenshit, but they're reservists, and most of them aren't infantry. They were told that they were going to be doing basic training, not fighting in downtown Mujville. Everyone knows that this is an important mission crying out for qualified guys, so why are they sending a bunch of bottle-washers and banjo-players? Goddamn army.'

His reference wasn't far off the truth. Among the soldiers travelling north that day was at least one cook, and a sergeant whose only military experience had been to play the trombone in the division band.

Chuck was an anomaly among the reservists: a former Ranger NCO and officer with some fifteen years of hard service under his belt before leaving active duty. His gregarious personality had not made a good first impression on the Marines who formed the majority of the brigade advisory team; but despite his flamboyant, chest-beating style, he was a shrewd leader and proficient soldier. And he understood the Iraqi soldier. He took the trouble to learn the rudiments of his language, shared his food, empathized with his plight, and could get him to do things that his own officers couldn't.

And the *jundi* loved him for it. Now, as he walked back towards his vehicle, exhorting the company to mount up in his own brand of pidgin Arabic, they leaned out of their trucks and yelled. 'Captain Chuck, *shaku maku?*'

Most of us agreed with Chuck's comment about the army assignment system. It was a mission as important as it was demanding; without proficient advisors there could be little hope of raising a credible Iraqi Army, and thus no foreseeable end to the US military's involvement in Iraq. Simply put, the advisory mission was the US military's exit strategy. Knowing this, it was hard to understand why the army didn't put more rigor into selecting advisor teams, or why it hadn't given the mission instead to its Special Forces who were ideally suited for the task.

The IIF moved into central Mosul by establishing battalion strongpoints throughout the city, with the brigade headquarters setting up shop in the grounds of Mosul University. The next two weeks were intended as a shaking out period for the three battalions and the best way to do this, we reasoned, would be for all advisors to accompany the first few patrols, encouraging the Iraqi battalion leadership to do the same. It sounded good in theory, but the plan depended on the willing participation of the IIF's battalion commanders; and here our assumptions proved to be overly optimistic, as Chuck and his team quickly found out.

Chuck was the advisor team leader assigned to the brigade's 1st Battalion. His team, all Marines, aside from him, had been together for several months, and were now eager to begin this mission. Chuck had misgivings about his battalion commander, Lieutenant Colonel Aziz, who seemed to want nothing more than to watch television in his office, but managed to get him to accompany the first patrol that day into central Mosul.

The patrol rounded a corner into a hail of fire, the bullets bouncing off the pavement and spinning one soldier to the ground. The column promptly disintegrated into chaos, with *jundi* firing in all directions out of sheer panic. Chuck and one other advisor ran for the downed *jundi*, pulling him out of the kill zone and into the shelter of a car, where the team medic started to work on him while the advisors returned fire. Seeing a pair of boots poking out from beneath the car, Chuck tugged on them and found himself looking into the distraught face of the Iraqi platoon commander. At least he had remained near the scene – several others, to include the battalion commander, simply ran back to base. At some point – it was difficult to tell when because of the volume of outgoing fire – the *Muj* broke contact, by which time only the advisor team remained at the ambush site. The wounded *jundi* was dead by the time the Americans loaded him in their Humvee.

Incensed, Chuck confronted Aziz upon his return, raising his voice in an uncustomary breach of cultural mores. The battalion commander was unrepentant and, Chuck was convinced, sought revenge by telling the *jundi* that the advisor team was responsible for the death of their comrade. Later that day, a group of angry Iraqi soldiers surrounded two of the advisors, jostling and spitting on them, shouting abuse. Such a raw display of violence was far outside the normal boundaries of *jundi* behavior, and there was no telling where the fracas might have ended had not Iraqi officers intervened.

The following day, Lieutenant Colonel Russ Jamison, the senior US advisor, convened a meeting with his counterpart, Colonel Abdul Amir, with Chuck and Aziz in attendance. Like school children being admonished after a playground scuffle, the two antagonists were prevailed upon to bury their differences and hug one another, which they did with obvious ill grace. The incident soured morale within 1st Battalion and left the rest of us with a feeling of ill portent. If one battalion commander was rotten, there were likely to be others. I wondered how much rigor MNSTC-I had put into recruiting the IIF's leadership.

Bad luck continued to dog 1st Battalion. During one of our weekly brigade advisor meetings a few weeks later Chuck announced that his battalion had come up against a sniper.

'Do you mean a man–with–a–gun?' asked the operations officer dismissively.

'No, I mean a fucking sniper. He's already wounded three *jundi* with tricky shots through gaps in their body armor. The *jundi* say that he's a Chechen, and that he's been offered a bounty for getting an advisor.'

This last comment elicited a barrage of jocular speculation about the relative value of those present; while Chuck sat silent, scowling. Two days later he was shot in the face at a range of several hundred meters, the bullet shattering his jaw into splinters. Two other advisors were also wounded in the head and neck in the same incident.

A week after arriving in Mosul, Russ Jamison called me into his office and offered me a cigar.

I took it, eyeing him curiously; they were Arturo Fuentes from Russ's private stash and usually didn't make an appearance unless there was a significant event to celebrate or bemoan. Cerebral and level-headed, Russ had the air of a university professor; a foil for the excitable Iraqis to whom he would listen with avuncular patience before offering advice.

Now he lit his cigar, puffing contentedly and squinting at me through the smoke.

'You're taking over the 3rd Battalion advisor team,' he said, handing me the lighter.

'OK, sir.' I hid a surge of excitement, focusing intently on lighting my cigar.

'But what happened to Dave Carlson?'

'He quit. He just called me and said that he was done with this bullshit, hadn't signed up with the reserves to get himself killed in some haji shithole.'

I was stunned. It was no secret that the 3rd Battalion team leader had been less than enthusiastic about the mission – he'd often voice his concerns querulously during brigade meetings – but I had never heard of an officer simply giving up.

The 3rd Battalion was housed in a building that we referred to as the Iraqi Police Academy or IPA, since that had been its previous function in the days when there was a police force, located in the Jadidah district of the city. Mosul was one of the most dangerous cities in Iraq at the time, and Jadidah had a well-earned reputation for being its most violent neighborhood. Carlson, unhappy with this assignment, had simply hunkered down and allowed the Iraqis to do the same.

'What's his team think about this?' Major Carlson was a soldier as were most of his team.

'I don't know, Andy, but you're going to find out for sure.'

I was aware that I was running to the end of my list of permissible questions; 'never explain, never complain' was an implicitly acknowledged ethos among Marine officers. Mission and intent are all you need to know; the rest is up to you to figure out.

'When do you want me down there?'

Russ looked at his watch. 'I'll have Gunny Gustavson out front with two hummers in thirty mikes to pick you up and bring Carlson back.'

'Great, that won't be awkward at all.'

I waited to see if Russ had any words of guidance or encouragement to give me before I left, but he just held out his hand.

'You'd better run and pack your shit. Good luck, brother.'

Then, as I turned to leave he called after me. 'Remember, we've got to provide security for the elections, less than three weeks from now.'

My thoughts were scrambling for traction as I climbed into the gunner's turret of Gustavson's vehicle (as an advisor you were either a driver or a gunner, we had no room for passengers).

Marines are bred to take charge. That statement may sound like hackneyed propaganda, but it's true; one of the Corps' hallowed tenets is that all Marines seek command, and I was no exception. But I was also aware that command under these circumstances might prove to be a poisoned chalice. Carlson was popular with his team. They shared a common history, and whatever his other shortcomings, he looked after them. They would see me as a usurper, a gung-ho Marine driven to pursue mission at expense of their survival. Commanding this team in the insurgent-held heart of Mosul, my position would be similar to that of a 7th Cavalry commander in charge of a mutinous garrison in the badlands of South Dakota.

A knife-edged wind lanced rain into my face as we drove through the deserted pitch-dark streets. It was late January, and the weather was as malevolent as the city. Iraqis sometimes refer to Mosul as Al Foyha, the Paradise, but I can't for a moment think why. To me, the drab concrete buildings and rubbish-strewn streets evoked none of the city's rich history as the site of the Assyrian capital of Nineveh.

By the time we pulled into the courtyard of the IPA, I was soaked and shivering uncontrollably.

I shouldered my rucksack and said good-bye to Gustavson.

'Take care, sir – be safe.' We both laughed at the absurdity of this stock phrase as I clasped his hand.

'Hey Gunny, you've come for me?' I turned around to see Carlson smiling amiably, his bags packed and ready to go. He grinned and slapped my shoulder, as he climbed into the Humvee.

'Good luck bro', you're gonna need it.'

I watched as they drove away. The metal gates were slammed shut by two miserable-looking *jundi*, both of whom I noticed had hands over the muzzles of their AK-47s, carrying them like walking sticks. Standing there in the sopping courtyard, I suddenly felt very alone.

Corporal Dropic on patrol in the Bermuda district of Mogadishu.

The platoon waits to go ashore in Mogadishu. This is a scene that any veteran, regardless of era, will recognize.

In order to provide security for the port, we had to push patrols out across the Green Line, the most volatile area of the city. It was an early lesson for me of how a commander must constantly balance mission against risk.

A tense confrontation on our first day in Mogadishu. This photograph has an interesting sequel. I was ordered to return the weapon to its owner who then used it to shoot a Swedish cameraman in the leg.

The boundary between Mogadishu's two most powerful warlords, the Green Line was the most volatile area of the city.

This boy, armed with a wooden gun, was a regular fixture on our patrols.

The mortar platoon enjoyed their reputation as the bad boys of the battalion, but when the chips were down, they performed magnificently. Here they celebrate their return from Somalia by throwing their platoon commander in the air.

My tour at MCRD was a painful one, but taught me some valuable lessons about leadership.

Walking point in Fallujah was always a nerve-wracking business.

When possible, we would use vehicles to tear open the padlocked metal gates. Then it was a desperate rush to get clear of the "fatal funnel".

Iraqi Army vehicles in Fallujah. The sheet metal offered scant protection against incoming rounds and none against IEDs.

Thanksgiving in the Al Sammari mosque, Fallujah. This was the only time in the battle that all the advisors were together. We'd lost one killed and several wounded, but agreed that overall we had much to give thanks for. From left: Mark Lombardo, Brian Mulvihill, Author, Paul Zambelli, Staff Sergeant Villa, Unidentified.

The jundi had an alarming tendency to bunch together under fire.

It would be several years before the US military would have a vehicle that provided adequate protection against IEDs. In the meantime, the 7-ton truck proved to be remarkably resilient.

A helicopter lands to pick up wounded Marines. A scene that was repeated countless times in countless places throughout Iraq.

Mosul; An Iraqi family on their way to vote in the country's first democratic elections, January 2005.

As Iraqis wait their turn to vote in the country's first free elections, a boy peers at us curiously.

01/30/2005

From left: Captain Zuher, Major Mohammed (no body armor), Author, Major Mohammed, the Battalion Operations Officer.

Major Aarmr checks that I am alright after a fire fight. Aarmr had served in the Iraqi Special Forces under Saddam and combined, in equal measure, graciousness and ferocity.

Peshmerga pray in an assembly area on the eve of an attack.

A Peshmerga soldier looks down on the lights of Mosul.

Incoming! The Islamic State were highly proficient in the use of rockets and mortars.

A Peshmerga sentry on the front line. Whatever army you are in, standing watch during the last hours of darkness on a cold morning is a miserable experience.

Training the Ninevah Strike Force.

Marine Raider and Peshmerga officer select targets.

Marine Raiders and Peshmerga on the front line outside Mosul.

With the family at a wedding in California, Summer 2017. From left: Marcus, Siobhan, me, Jessica, Sophia.

Kaela.

# Chapter 27

The first person I met as I entered the police station was Corporal Bill Smith, a Marine and the junior member of the team. He was sitting in the front office, feet propped on a desk, a green government-issue notebook on his lap.

'Hey sir!' he sprang to his feet. 'Here, let me give you a hand with your bags, I'll show you to your room.' I followed Smith down the hallway listening to his cheerful patter.

When you spend long enough with Marines you become accustomed to their sheer, sour prolonged bitching in adversity; but in every unit, there is also at least one Marine who remains genuinely upbeat no matter how awful the circumstances. I am sure that during the slog up Mount Surabachi some wag was commenting on the impressive view, and that amidst the retreat from the Chosin Reservoir, another was claiming to enjoy the cool weather. Smith was one of those Marines: you could drop him in pig shit and he would come up smiling. But I also had been around Marines long enough not to underestimate these optimists – their cheerfulness usually conceals iron-cast resolve. Despite his junior rank, Smith had a reputation among the advisors for initiative and rock-solid dependability, hence his assignment as a company advisor, a billet normally reserved for officers and senior NCOs.

Smith opened a door and gestured inside with a flourish. 'It's not exactly the Ritz, sir.' It was a small, windowless room in which the only furniture was three camp beds and a couple of plastic chairs.

'Better than being a pog at brigade, right sir?' Pog was the contemptuous term used by all Marines for those further from the fighting than they.

'That's right indeed, Corporal Smith. By the way, what were you working on when I came in?'

'Oh, that's a patrol schedule. Been trying to get the Iraqis out on patrol so we don't just sit here like bumps on a log waiting to get hit. Not much enthusiasm so far. I think that their commander agrees with me, but it's a tough sell for the *jundi*, especially since the other advisors don't seem too keen on it either, except for Captain Kajs of course. Speaking of which, let me grab him, he wanted to have a chance to chat before you met the team.'

He fetched Jay Kajs, another Marine, and the three of us sat down to talk in the front office where Smith and I had met. The air was fuggy with

cigarette smoke, cooking and the smell of unwashed bodies – but it was warm
– thanks to an ancient-looking kerosene heater spluttering in the corner.
Jay's greeting was cool, almost taciturn in contrast to Smith's enthusiasm;
and he waited for my cue before sitting down and starting to talk.

Stocky with red scrubby hair and the face of an English football hooligan,
Jay was a stranger to me, though I knew that he had a good reputation, which
is the coin of the realm among Marines.

Speaking in short terse sentences, he gave me a quick assessment of the
team, while Smith nodded and interjected from time to time. I listened
intently, only interrupting to ask the occasional question, and Jay began
to loosen up. His story echoed Chuck's observations during the ride up to
Mosul.

'It's not a bad team, sir, they want to do well, but most of them aren't cut
out to be trolling the streets. We've got an electrician, a generator mechanic,
an armorer and a musician.'

'The trombone player?'

'That's right, so you've heard about him. Well he's a hard charger, wants
to get out there with the *jundi*, and you don't need to stop him. He's good. As
for the others, they all want to contribute, and there is plenty of work back
here for them to do so.'

Kajs looked at me intently, and I realized that he was concerned that I
would sweep in and upset the tacit understanding that he had established
with the team. I balked at the thought of exposing some of them to greater
danger than others. On the other, I realized that the mission was going to be
tough enough without me putting inept soldiers in harm's way.

'What about the Iraqis?'

Jay shrugged. 'Well the *jundi*, are — *jundi*. The CO, Lieutenant Colonel
Falah is a pretty good dude, but he's tired. He was in Saddam's army and
has been up here before fighting the Kurds. I think that he just needs a push
to get going. Carlson didn't really mix with him, so I've been the one that
he talks to.

'The operations officer, Major Mohammed seems good, but a little quiet.
The intelligence officer, Captain Zuher is one of the best of the bunch. He's
bright and aggressive, and understands the need to collect intelligence to
drive operations. He seems to have contacts out in town, though he's been a
bit cagey about telling me who they are.

'The rest of the battalion staff and company commanders are a mixed bag.
I think that most want to do the right thing, they just need direction and,

frankly, they're scared. Watch out for the 2nd Company commander, Major Taleb. He's a shifty bastard, always giving us the evil eye.'

Jay paused and looked at Corporal Smith.

'You want to tell him about your company commander?'

Smith rolled his eyes and exhaled sharply. 'Captain Mehdi commands 1st Company, he's just heinous, sir – there's no other way to put it. Doesn't listen to me at all. He was the one who ordered his guys to open fire on a US patrol last week. Thank God his soldiers can't shoot. Apparently the Americans couldn't either, only a couple of *jundi* were wounded. I suspected Mehdi of being *Muj* too, but I've changed my mind. He's just balls-out incompetent.'

'He's connected though,' Jay added. 'When I bring his name up to the battalion commander, he tells me that he knows he's bad, but there's nothing he can do.'

Jay trailed off, as a *jundi* walked in with a tray of steaming glasses. 'This is Mahwan, sir – he's the CO's servant, but he looks after us too.' Mahwan, who looked about 16, smiled shyly as he served us tea. I sipped at the hot, sweet liquid, aware that the other two were looking at me expectantly.

'OK, thanks fellas. I'll talk to the team tomorrow morning – 0800. Just let me know where.' A thought occurred to me. 'How many patrols is the battalion running right now?'

Kajs and Smith exchanged glances.

'None,' Jay said. 'The companies ran a couple the first day, each with an advisor, but after two ambushes and a few wounded *jundi* they lost all motivation.'

*Well*, I thought, *at least I know where to start.* I followed Jay to meet Lieutenant Colonel Falah. Having seen the size of the building from outside, I was surprised to find that the warren of concrete corridors and offices had somehow absorbed 150 or so *jundi*. Iraqis are adept at making the best use of all available space; I later discovered that despite the cold weather, some twenty or so soldiers slept on the roof under an overhang.

We found Falah sitting in his office watching the news on an ancient television. He jumped to his feet and welcomed me with a few words of halting English, before beckoning us to sit on a battered sofa. All senior officers in the Iraqi Army, especially those who had served under Saddam, have a certain look to them. They invariably sport a heavy moustache, black well-groomed hair (seldom displaying signs of gray), a noticeable paunch, and a serious expression. Falah was no exception to this template, but I noticed also that he had voluminous bags under his eyes, and although friendly, appeared on edge. He offered us cigarettes; I demurred but Jay took one and they both lit up.

After the obligatory courtesies, I told Falah that I was taking over the advisor team and that I looked forward to working with him and his soldiers. He didn't ask what had happened to Carlson, just nodded and smiled. When I had finished talking, we all looked at the television where barely discernible images were battling a snowstorm induced by bad reception. Mahwan arrived with more tea and we chatted haltingly: small talk, families, how long we had been in the military, where we were from – anything but the business at hand. There would be plenty of time to do that; first I needed to build rapport.

As we rose to leave, Falah gestured at the couch upon which we were sitting. 'Please, this is your room too, you must sleep here.'

Later that night, while Falah snored contentedly on the other sofa, I listened to the rain lash against the windows and the intermittent crackle of distant gunfire, and thought about the task ahead.

In the brief time that I had to think about the mission, I had planned to handle one problem at a time: first the advisor team, then the battalion's leadership and lastly the enemy. Now I realized that I lacked the time for this leisurely approach; I would have to tackle all three at once – and on the very first day.

The battalion was arrayed in three combat outposts, or COPs, buildings thinly fortified with sandbags all within a few blocks of the IPA. As Marines we regard such locations not as defensive positions, but as launching points from which you sallied out to clobber the foe. By hunkering down in these outposts, the battalion had ceded the initiative to the enemy, allowing him freedom of movement and rendering themselves prisoners. The day before I arrived, an RPG had slammed into the side of the IPA, and a few hours later two mortars crashed into the inner courtyard, wounding two *jundi*. I had to get Falah to push patrols into the surrounding area, taking the fight to the enemy, or we would remain targets.

But I couldn't get the Iraqis to be more aggressive if my own team wasn't willing to accompany them, and that's what worried me most. It might make sense to allow those who felt better suited for indoor projects to avoid patrolling, but could I afford to do so? An advisor would have to accompany every patrol to provide a vital link to US units operating in the area, and to demonstrate common resolve by sharing the danger – an intangible benefit that no technology will ever replace.

What if the advisor team simply refused to go out on the streets? I knew the answer of course: inspire them to do the right thing by force of personality. That sounds like an easy solution when you are discussing these problems in a professional military education seminar, much harder to do when it's your force of personality pitted against the primal drive for self-preservation. I comforted myself with the thought that we had an immediate mission: the elections, giving me a clarion call for action.

# Chapter 28

The next morning, I addressed the team in the courtyard, the only place where we could find separation from the company of soldiers milling around the building. Eleven advisors, seven soldiers, three Marines and a navy corpsman stood in loose formation, hands in pockets, shoulders hunched against the cold, eyeing me with studied nonchalance. I cast aside any thought of trying to inspire them with a blast of once-more-into-the-breach-dear-friends. They didn't look like 'greyhounds standing in the slips' and, after a sleepless night, I wasn't feeling like King Henry on the eve of Agincourt. Nor, I sensed, was this an audience that would respond to an approach from the other end of the cultural spectrum: Gunny Hartman's 'because-I-am-hard-you-will-not-like-me' speech from Full Metal Jacket. Hard or not, I guessed that most of them already didn't like me.

So I played it without fanfare, in a level conversational tone: who I was and why I was there (being careful to avoid criticizing Carlson). I talked about the mission: to put the *Muj* on their back foot, securing the area and enabling the population to go about their business without fear of attack. I talked about the importance of the upcoming elections. I looked from face to face as I spoke. A couple were nodding, but most just stared back without expression.

'The first thing that we're going to do is get the Iraqis out on the streets. Each one of you is going to play a role in that because every patrol will have an advisor. I'm going to need your full support to do all the things we need to do,' I concluded. 'Are there any questions?'

Someone raised their hand – it was a Marine, a large, thickly muscled gunnery sergeant.

'Gunny Cook, sir – how are we going to do that?' he asked. 'By regs we can't leave the COP without another American, and an armored vehicle. We don't have enough people or vehicles to do that, to man the ops room and have a decent rotation that allows rest.'

'Well, we may only be able to sustain a handful of patrols a day but it's better than what we are doing now.' There were some nods, but most just continued to stare at me impassively. I tried another tack. 'And it may be that the Iraqis will begin to take some patrols by themselves.'

'They can't do that,' an army sergeant spoke up. 'We need to be with them all the time to avoid green on blue like what happened with 1st Company.'

*Exactly right, which is why I need your help,* I thought but shrugged. 'I don't think for a moment that this is going to be easy – but *we're* going to get them out there.'

Later that morning I met the battalion's operations and intelligence officers in an office that had been converted into an operations center by the addition of a few radios and a map of the city on the wall.

Major Mohammed, the operations officer, was tall and thin with a long mournful face and an air of quiet intensity; he gripped my hand firmly, but his tight smile never quite made it to his eyes, which were watery and sad, like those of a bloodhound.

By contrast, the intelligence officer, Captain Zuher was short and pudgy with the face of a mischievous cherub. A broad grin and eyes that glittered with amusement under gull-wing brows. Like Mohammed he spoke English but whereas Mohammed always appeared to be choosing his words, Zuher prattled away with abandon in a style that was unusual for a captain in the Iraqi Army. He had, I was to learn, a dry sense of humor that also broke cultural norms. Sometime during those first few days, he asked me why I spoke with an English accent – when I explained that I had grown up in England, but that my mother had been American, he looked perplexed. I thought that he might have misunderstood so I repeated my answer. He nodded 'Sadi – I understand. I'm just wondering how to explain to the others that you have a mother, I don't think that they will believe me.'

Over the course of time I came to recognize Zuher's irreverent sense of humor as a shield against the horrors that life had thrown his way. Like many of his peers, he'd had some tough experiences during the US invasion. His company was ordered to defend Baghdad Airport, and it was only after he had seen half his soldiers crushed or blown to smithereens by US tanks that his company commander passed the word that it was every man for himself. And now, like his comrades, he worried about his family in Baghdad, aware that his profession made them a target. Zuher's sense of humor could be annoying but it was his inner carapace, and I couldn't begrudge him that.

Zuher walked to the map and gave us an intelligence update, jabbing with his finger at various locations around our position. I was surprised how much he appeared to know about the insurgent groups arrayed against us, their background and areas of operation within the city, even their leadership. He explained that we were facing an alliance between former Ba'athists and a group known as Ansar Al Islam, an offshoot from Al Qaeda, led at one time by Zarqawi himself. I asked him where he was getting this intelligence, and he paused, glancing at Mohammed before replying.

'Because some of them were our friends. Not the Wahabis,' Zuher used the *jundi* term for Islamic extremists, 'but the guys who served in the old army. We talk on the phone. They warn us to stay away from certain areas. Sometimes they give us tips.' He shrugged and looked at me with a half-smile. 'I think that perhaps you don't believe me.'

As Americans we wanted things to be black and white; we weren't comfortable with nuance. But for the Iraqis success was survival, pragmatism trumped allegiance. We would only see glimpses of the relationship that the battalion's officers had with their former comrades, not because they wanted to hide these things from us, but because they knew that we wouldn't understand.

Falah agreed to start pushing patrols out beginning the next day. I figured that we could support up to sixteen patrols a day, at least through the elections. We would push the patrols out in a clover leaf pattern around the police station, each patrol overlapping others by time and route to reduce the threat of ambush. Satellite patrolling, it was called, a technique that I had learned from the British observers in Victorville.

I thought that it was a pretty good plan: it made tactical sense, and we could probably just manage it with two advisors per patrol. But it was my plan; I hadn't consulted Falah who owned the soldiers who would make it happen. He agreed to four patrols a day, at least for the first few days until we had a sense for how things were. He explained this with a smile in the manner that Iraqis do when they don't agree with you, but don't want to offend you. I wanted to point out that four patrols was a measly amount for 250 soldiers, that we had to impose a security bubble around our positions while establishing our presence in the Sunni neighborhoods that surrounded us, but I knew better than to argue. Falah had made a decision in front of subordinates; to push him would only entrench his position. In any case, I didn't know yet how many Americans I could count on to accompany the patrols, so I conceded with good grace.

'You've got five of us, sir.' Staff Sergeant Reyes was the senior Army NCO, a boyish-looking Chicagoan who appeared delighted to find himself in the middle of a war. I was secretly pleased that all but two of our army contingent had elected to participate in the patrol schedule. The remaining two were hopelessly unsuited to be walking the streets, and though it grated on my Marine psyche to give them a choice, I let them be. With five soldiers, four Marines (counting me) and a Navy corpsmen, we weren't in bad shape.

The corpsman, whose name was also Reyes, though we called him Doc to avoid confusion, was a bulky youngster with an eager-to-please disposition. The ability to provide on-the-spot care for the traumatically wounded depends on qualities beyond skill; even the well-trained can freeze with shock at the crucial moment. Doc Reyes, however, would prove to have that intangible gene that drove him to succor the wounded – American or Iraqi – regardless of risk to sensibility or self. At the time, I was simply impressed by his eagerness to go out on patrol.

The first patrol was going to be a leaders' reconnaissance, with Falah, Mohammed, Zuher and I visiting each of the two company outposts, beginning with 3rd Company who were billeted in a train station about a mile away from the IPA. That night I outlined the plan to Russ Jamison by radio, requesting a back-up QRF from his position at brigade should we need it. Russ agreed – and then added that he wanted to bring the Iraqi Brigade commander, General Shocker, along on the patrol.

'We've got to get them over this here-be-giants mentality. Having Shocker get out to see for himself, setting the example, is going to give them a boost,' he said. 'Shocker's been up here before, he knows the area – actually, I think this is where he lost his eye.' The brigadier had a glass eye, which he had the alarming habit of removing during meetings, setting it on the table as though to better observe his staff.

The day began well enough, with Brigadier Shocker and a small coterie from his headquarters linking up with us at the IPA, amidst the usual flurry of cheek-kissing and elaborate greetings. Falah showed the brigadier around the operations room, and they chatted excitedly in front of the map, which now depicted a network of planned patrol routes drawn up by Mohammed and Jay the night before. The brigadier seemed delighted by this, congratulating a beaming Falah on his aggressiveness and clapping him on the shoulder.

A little later we set off, a string of white Toyota pick-up trucks packed with *jundi*, wending our way through the barricades outside the police station and onto the main street that we called Route Nissan, a name that had become synonymous with reports of attacks on the US Brigade's tactical net. The 101st Airborne Division had named the city's major thoroughfares after cars, and their combat outposts after US cities. It made good sense from a military standpoint – it was much easier to track the progress of a convoy from Nissan to Porsche to Ford than it was to try to decipher Arabic names. I wondered too if it was also our way of trying to impose order on chaos, as though giving prosaic names to sinister places helped reduce their menace.

We entered the flow of traffic with much yelling and gesturing from the *jundi* in the back of each truck; the cars behind grinding to a halt to let us in, before following the last truck at a wary distance. By this stage of the war, Iraqi drivers were conditioned to stay away from military convoys by the proclivity for soldiers to ram and shoot anything that looked as though it might be a threat. In Mosul the threat was often real. On our first day in the city, I was on a patrol when a red Opel pulled up beside the lead vehicle and exploded (Opels were then ubiquitous on the streets of Mosul, and were used so frequently for attacks that they became the subject of a running joke among the advisors). Fortunately, the charge had not been wired correctly and only one of three artillery rounds detonated. The other two were hurled across the road intact along with pieces of the car and driver, splattering against the side of the Humvee but leaving its occupants unharmed.

Now each advisor rode in a separate pick-up truck – there was no sense risking more than one of us in the same vehicle. MNSTC-I directed that all US personnel were to ride in armored Humvees, but we only had one for the entire battalion. In any case, most of us had a problem with sheltering behind armor, while our Iraqi counterparts had only a pathetically thin strip of sheet metal to protect them from the savage blast of an IED.

Gunny Cook ran down the steps of the train station as we screeched to a halt out front.

'You need to run, gents, we've been taking accurate small-arms fire.'

On cue, there was a burst of gunfire and the *jundi* poured out of the trucks, scampering for cover. I jogged up the steps to the station, reaching the top as the next shots rang out. I turned to see a soldier spill down the steps, rifle clattering ahead of him, helmet rolling into the gutter. Almost instantly, two other soldiers grabbed him, one by the legs, the other under his arms, and hauled him back up the steps into the building with a speed fueled by adrenalin. Every *jundi* within sight started blazing away with a deafening racket.

Doc Reyes and an Iraqi medic were working on the casualty as Russ and I ran over.

'We need to get him to Maurez, sir. Gunshot wound, lower abdomen.' The *jundi* was unconscious, head lolling to one side in a comrade's cupped hands, his eyes half open showing only the whites. The brigadier was in a heated debate with Falah, Kajs was on the radio with brigade, and the *jundi* outside continued to fire away with reckless abandon.

Russ explained to the brigadier that we had to get the soldier to medical care right away, while I pulled Mohammed aside and told him to put a stop to the shooting. Mohammed gave me a quick nod, and ran down the steps, yelling for the NCOs. To my surprise, order was quickly restored and by the time that we had loaded the casualty onto a truck with Doc in attendance, the *jundi* were mounted up ready to go. I shook my head; sometimes it took forever to get the Iraqis to do the simplest things, while other times they made things happen faster than we would expect US troops to respond.

There was another burst of incoming fire as we pulled away from the train station, this time a concentrated barrage and I could hear the clunk of rounds hitting metal around us. I held on to the door handle as we gathered speed, careening around a traffic circle, the driver hammering the horn with the heel of his hand. The convoy split into two coming out of the roundabout: the brigade vehicles taking the first exit bound for Maurez, while we took the second, shooting out of the circle like a rock from a slingshot. Zuher, sitting behind me, yelled in my ear.

'The gunner's hit.' I swiveled around and caught a glimpse of boots, toes pointing skywards.

'I saw it – he was shot in the head.' Zuher gabbled. *Shit – can this be any more of a disaster.*

Back at the IPA, Zuher and I clambered out of the truck before it had stopped moving, and raced around to the tailgate. To our surprise the soldiers were still sitting in the back, laughing uproariously. In their midst sat the gunner holding his helmet in front of him – the bullet had torn a deep furrow along its side, shredding the Kevlar like cardboard but leaving him unharmed.

I grinned at the fortunate *jundi*, slapping his shoulder. '*Mubarek!*' Congratulations. In seconds he was mobbed by a crowd of soldiers, who lifted him from the truck and danced around him, hands raised above their heads, grinning from ear to ear. A procession of the battalion's officers made their way through the throng to hug and kiss the bulletproof soldier who was now standing by the tailgate, still holding his helmet in front of him like a birthday cake.

*Thank God for small mercies.* But the mission itself had been a complete bust: one wounded *jundi* and we had turned tail. It only reaffirmed the Iraqi's perception that the *Muj* owned the streets – or so I thought.

Falah called Kajs over to take a photo of the battalion's officers clustered around the charmed *jundi*. Zuher caught my eye and yelled above the din: '*Alhamdulillah*.' Thanks be to God. 'This is very good.'

Once again, I had failed to divine correctly the mood of my Iraqi partners. To me the *jundi*'s escape was an isolated incident of good luck in an otherwise luckless day but to them it was a symbol of new-found fortune, a portent of better things to come. The deflective properties of Kevlar had accomplished more than any appeal to duty. I signaled Jay and led Mohammed by the arm to the operations room to plan the following day's mission. Sometimes, as the saying goes, it's better to be lucky than good.

# Chapter 29

Over the next week, the advisor team began to pull together and the Iraqi battalion responded – gingerly at first but then with increasing confidence. There were fewer attacks on the IPA, though our patrols were often involved in firefights and we took a steady stream of casualties.

The advisors appeared pleased to have a clear mission, but I would have been insensitive not to notice an undercurrent of concern about the risks that we were taking: walking on the streets in our distinctively different uniforms and riding in unarmored vehicles, a single radio our only link to help. The nearest US unit was only a few miles away, but was in real terms much further. We would give them our patrol routes beforehand to avoid the risk of fratricide and to enable them to find us if we ran into trouble, but our routes often led us through areas that their vehicles – armored personnel carriers known as Strykers – couldn't easily reach, or were barred from entering without specific permission from the brigade commander.

As we pushed deeper into the Sunni areas, I noticed that the team had cohered into two schools of thought: those who thought that we were taking unjustifiable risks, and those who simply wanted to get on with it.

'What happens if both Americans are wounded, and unable to use the radio?' one advisor asked me after a patrol. The answer was that we'd have to rely on the Iraqis to call for help, which didn't satisfy everyone. I couldn't blame them. Of the three Iraqi company commanders, only one, Major Mohammed (not to be confused with Mohammed the operations officer) was competent; the others were so bad that we wondered if they were insurgents.

I had no frame of reference for what level of risk was acceptable, and it occurred to me more than once that I might be pushing the boundaries too far. It was an internal struggle between two instincts: the Marine ethos of mission first, men second; and a recognition that my responsibility as a leader was more complex than that. Sometimes you have to make sense of the mission by protecting your people. I had seen some commanders take that approach in Anbar. If the outcome was going to be the same, an area as hostile on the day your unit leaves as the day that it arrived, then shouldn't you concern yourself with lowering the cost? At what point do indecipherable or unobtainable goals shift the leaders' responsibility back to the led?

I wasn't sure how realistic our mission was, whether we would ever be able to reduce violence in our area, or even enlist the support of our Iraqi partners in trying to do so. 'They have to want it as much was we do, sir,' commented Corporal Smith after observing Captain Mehdi break into a house to escape an ambush, leaving his men on the street.

With a week to the elections, I pushed hard to increase the number of patrols, but as we stepped them up from three to six then twelve a day, I was aware that we were out on the edge. Some of these were vehicle patrols, but most were on foot, which made us less vulnerable, and enabled us to see more, while allowing the *jundi* to talk to the locals in an effort to elicit information and prompt them to vote. The locals were mostly terrified, but not openly hostile, and a few even started to welcome us as we passed by.

The enemy continued to hammer away at us with a vehemence that was so multi-vectored and unremitting that we were constantly off balance. A sniper fired on a patrol as they left their company outpost: two well-aimed shots leaving one badly wounded and one dead; three Iraqi National Guard soldiers were incinerated in front of the IPA by an IED made of jellied gasoline, their charred corpses welded into the bed of their pick-up truck like some grotesque sculpture; a shopkeeper who sold fruit to the soldiers was killed, his corpse dumped outside our front gate; insurgents strapped a suicide vest on a mentally disabled youth and directed him towards one of our patrols (mercifully the charge failed to detonate).

Most patrols came under attack. Sometimes it was a few scattered shots zipping between *jundi* or cracking overheard, close enough to send everyone scrambling for cover; other times it was a planned ambush. We would return fire, call for the QRF and deliver casualties to the US hospital on FOB Maurez. Sometimes US patrols were close enough to help us: their Strykers would plough into the middle of the firefight, machine guns hammering a cathartic tattoo, allowing us to escape the kill zone.

Despite the pressure, and whatever misgivings the team may have had, they responded like stalwarts. Kajs, Smith, Cook, Reyes, Doc and Bates (the trombone player) each led several patrols a day, and the advisors who didn't patrol manned radios in the operations room and otherwise made themselves useful. On the Iraqi side Mohammed and Zuher were running operations and collating intelligence with little guidance from us. Even Falah seemed energized after the incident at the train station and over our evening meals chatted happily with me about progress.

But at night I lay awake. I relished the mission and the freedom of action; it was so much more stimulating than being based on a FOB within the rigid hierarchy of the US military. But I wondered whether I wasn't urging the team too close to the precipice. I had no one to whom I could voice my concerns. Even if I had, I am not sure that I would have been able to articulate them.

I could order the team to hunker down or insist on getting more armored vehicles and just tell the Iraqis to push ahead by themselves; though there wasn't much chance of them doing that, I would remind myself. During the day I felt confident and energized and in charge, but at night I tied myself into knots with self-inquisition.

'You don't sleep well,' Falah said to me one morning over breakfast, as he stuffed a folded-up circle of flat bread into his mouth. The bread was really good, though the kitchen where the *jundi* made it would have sent Gordon Ramsey into fits. 'Are you having trouble at home?'

'No sadi, everything at home is fine.' I couldn't help smiling at the irony; it was a wonderful illustration of the gap between American and Iraqi culture. Outside the gates of the IPA was a world that Thomas Hobbes would have recognized: *no society; and which is worst of all, continual fear of violent death; and the life of man, solitary, poor, nasty, brutish and short.*

That knowledge alone would be enough to keep anyone awake, but Falah, who appeared fatalistic about his circumstances, assumed that my insomnia must be caused by problems at home.

The day before the elections, Jay and I toured our two polling stations, each one manned by an Iraqi company with an American advisor, located in schoolhouses that had been turned into fortresses: their walls bolstered by banks of sandbags and surrounded by reams of concertina wire.

'The Garrett wands are here,' announced Corporal Smith nodding at a group of *jundi* who were flourishing the hand-held metal detectors. We had fought hard to get these, and I was pleased to see that they had arrived. Even so, it was going to be a painstaking and dangerous business for the soldiers out front who would have to search every voter before allowing them entry to the building.

The prescribed way to search people in this type of situation was to have them lift their shirts while still at a safe distance. But suicide bombers, who tend to be determined people, are coached in methods to avoid exposing their explosive vests while rapidly closing the distance to a potential searcher.

Confronted with long lines and barriers that were close together, the *jundi* would have very little stand-off, and knowing that, would be quick to pull the trigger. After all, these weren't their people. Because of its Saddam-era heritage, the IIF comprised a higher percentage of Sunnis, roughly half the brigade, than the rest of the Iraqi Army which was 80 per cent Shia. But tribe matters even more than religious sect in Iraq, and our *jundi* were mostly from Bagdad and Eastern Anbar, a long way geographically and culturally from the Mosulites. Knowing this, we had prevailed on their officers to rotate the *jundi* searchers every half hour, a process that we knew would add to the delays.

Because Iraqis are by culture rank conscious, I had taken the liberty of promoting all Americans below the rank of captain to that temporary rank, hoping that this would give them enough authority – *wastah* was the Arabic term – to influence their counterparts. Corporal Smith now wore a pair of captains' bars as he showed us around the polling station while Captain Mehdi skulked in front of a television in the principal's office.

Sergeant First Class Bates greeted us at the next polling station, an unpainted two-story building housing a handful of dilapidated classrooms. Bates, a large blond Minnesotan, was a school teacher in civilian life, and had picked up playing the trombone as a hobby before making it the mainstay of his military career. I had been impressed from the start by his competence and maturity – and his willingness to do whatever the mission demanded. 'Hell, sir, I'm here now. Might as well make myself useful,' he'd told me in his characteristic measured way.

'First impressions are lasting impressions' is one of those catchy aphorisms that we in the military like to tell one another. I hope that most of us don't use it as a guide to action because people like Bates, who are more than they seem, would slip through the cracks.

The polling station was immaculate, not a trace of trash anywhere, the sandbags neatly piled, the soldiers standing post alert with their weapons pointed in the right direction, all indicators that were far from the norm in an Iraqi unit.

'Mohammed's done a great job as usual.' Bates told me when I commended him. Major Mohammed (Mohammed the Second, we called him to avoid confusion, the name being as common as Jones in a Welsh unit) shambled over from a corner of the roof where he had been pointing out something to a group of soldiers.

Among Iraqi officers, who are quite meticulous when it comes to personal grooming, Mohammed was an anomaly. He had shaggy unkempt hair, a straggly moustache that appeared as though it had been trimmed by a distracted barber, and graying stubble. Flip-flops, baggy camouflage pants and a field jacket, unzipped as always to expose the type of sleeveless vest that used to be called a wife-beater, completed the ensemble, giving him the appearance of a homeless wino. Mohammed was known to like the bottle, and had reportedly been relieved several times for drunken behavior, most recently for slapping Captain Mehdi in public which made him something of a hero among the advisors.

He had been reinstated each time because he was in many ways the best officer in the battalion: he took care of his soldiers, and ran a tight ship. He was also very brave, or foolhardy – I am never quite clear where the line lies between the two – refusing to wear body armor or helmet (although he insisted that his subordinates wear theirs) with an insouciance that endeared him further to his soldiers. 'Inshallah' he would say when questioned about this habit, entrusting his fate to the will of God. Mohammed and Bates couldn't have been more different, but they got along famously.

Jay and I said goodbye to this odd couple and drove off in search of a suitable location to lodge the QRF during the elections. Sometime later I learned that Bates and his wife started a collection in his home town for the school that housed his polling station. Several weeks after the elections, we responded to a call from the same school after students found a headless corpse in their playground. It was the only time that I saw Bates angry.

Later that night I sat with Zuher, talking to the owner of the hotel we had commandeered. We were in the hotel lobby, sitting around a table by the reception desk. Outside in the courtyard were staged three pick-up trucks, the QRF vehicles; we could hear the *jundi* shouting to one another as they unloaded their gear and traipsed into the building. The manager sat hunched over the table, staring at the floor, twisting a chain of prayer beads in his hand. He mumbled something to Zuher.

'He is very afraid,' Zuher explained. 'He says that the Wahabi will kill him when we leave. He begs us to go now.'

'Tell him that we will protect him,' I said, but the offer sounded hollow even to me.

The hotel had a generator, and the *jundi* stayed up late watching Lebanese soap operas until an RPG slammed into the second floor in a shower of glass and masonry, plunging us into darkness, and sending all but the sentries to bed.

In the morning, the manager was gone. I like to think that he left to seek refuge, but the memory of his fear remains with me even now – and I wonder.

# Chapter 30

The next morning the four of us sat in the lobby drinking sludgy coffee, smoking foul-tasting cigars, and staring at the radio that was our connection with the polling sites, like attendees at a séance sitting around a Ouija board.

From the crump of distant explosions and sound of gunfire throughout the city, we could tell that the *Muj* were making a determined effort to disrupt the elections; but Bates and Smith each reported no signs of trouble. Eventually I could no longer take the strain of waiting, and headed out to the polling stations.

As we drove onto the street that led to Bates' school, Jay exclaimed: 'Holy shit!'

There was a line of people so long that it doubled back on itself the entire length of the street. As we wended our way through the crowd, I noticed that it comprised not just young men but whole families and even women walking in pairs, dressed in abaya, the traditional Muslim robe that covers the whole body except face and hands.

One family caught my eye as we pulled to a stop. The father, dressed nattily in a sports coat and polished shoes, was carrying a young boy while his wife followed in tow, two little girls in bright dresses clinging to the edge of her abaya, peeking shyly at the *jundi* as they passed through the cordon.

I climbed out of the truck and stood for a while outside the wire, watching the crowd. There was a feeling of quiet determination to the orderly row of people shuffling steadily forward towards the school. A small boy broke away from the line to approach me, keeping a safe distance, but eyeing me curiously. He pulled himself to attention, and gave me a half-salute before running back to his parents.

Zuher punched me lightly on the shoulder. 'Hey sadi – not a good idea to wait outside. You may be British, but you look like an American in that uniform.' The US Brigade commander had passed word for all American personnel to keep a low profile on election day. I followed him into the building, wiping my eyes which must have been affected by the dust.

The *Muj* made only desultory attempts to interfere with voting in our area. Later in the morning Bates reported a string of mortar rounds impacting some 200 yards to his west, and sometime afterwards, Smith came on the net to say that a series of shots had scattered the crowd in front of his polling station but that no one was hurt. Neither incident interrupted the process for long, and the lines soon reformed.

It is a matter of record that there was a poor Sunni turnout for the national elections of January 2005, and that widespread violence disrupted voting in many areas of the country, to include Mosul. Nevertheless, I hold on to the memory of that patient shuffling line, whose message of proud defiance lent a sense of meaning, however temporary, to the months of bloodletting that preceded it.

The *Muj* went to ground after the elections and there were no attacks for several days. We could only guess why. They hadn't exactly suffered a defeat: the insurgent campaign of intimidation had deterred the vast majority of Iraq's Sunnis from voting, in Mosul as in the rest of the country. In Anbar, for instance, less than 1 per cent of the Sunni population showed up at the polls. Despite the hype, Iraq's first democratic election was the beginning of a slide towards Sunni disenfranchisement, a process that played into the hands of extremists on both sides.

Zuher, ever the optimist, opined that the *Muj* had simply been frightened into submission by the lionhearts of 3rd Battalion IIF.

Whatever the reason, there were no more attacks on the IPA, and our conditions there began to improve. The communal toilet with its intermittent water supply had long since become a chamber of horrors; it's a wonder that we didn't all succumb to cholera. Now we were delighted to get supplies of wood and four oil drums which enabled an ad hoc team of carpenters, Iraqi and American, to construct a field latrine by building a wooden frame with toilet seats under which half-drums containing diesel were positioned.

The next day, Jay and I heard a commotion in the courtyard and rushing outside were met by billowing smoke and a sheet of flame that shot into the air higher than the surrounding walls. Nonplussed because there had been no explosion, we watched the *jundi* throw bottles of water on the conflagration. As the fire burned itself down we were able to piece together what had happened.

The proximate cause was the order given by Jay to Captain Mehdi to 'burn the shitters.' This traditional command, when issued to Americans, leads to a simple process: the half drums of diesel and raw sewage are pulled clear of the wooden frame and their contents burned by means of a lighted match being dropped into each. As the order was translated into Arabic and passed from Mehdi to an NCO to the *jundi*, the part about first removing the drums was lost, and the entire latrine was engulfed in flame. Fortunately, we had sufficient materials to build it again.

Someone cleared debris from the water tank on the roof, and got the showers working, although the water was freezing cold. To complete our sense of new-found luxury, the advisors purchased two sheep which were duly slaughtered in the courtyard and turned into a feast for all; the *jundi* sitting on the ground outside, shoveling fistfuls of greasy mutton and rice into their mouths.

I had to visit Maurez to give the US battalion commander a report about the election, and took the opportunity to have my first real shower in a month. When I peeled off my filthy cammies and peered in the mirror, it seemed as though someone else was looking back. I had several days of stubble, but my head was completely bald, having shaved it like everyone else after rumors of lice among the *jundi*. I had purple bruises under my eyes and the skin on my face was gray and blotchy. I had lost weight; my ribs protruded, and my arms looked fragile.

I hung my dog tags carefully on a hook, they included my great uncle's identity disc which had been passed on to my grandmother after his death at Belleau Wood, and climbed in the shower. The hot water gave me goose bumps and I stayed in longer than the regulation three minutes.

Afterwards I labored over an email to Jessica. Over the course of the deployment, our relationship had become strained. We had been drawn to one another by a shared sense of humor, and conversation that volleyed back and forth effortlessly regardless of topic. But over the phone our voices sounded monotone and brittle; and our discussions slipped quickly into distracted small talk interspersed by ponderous silence.

Jess had just begun her internship at Walter Reed Hospital, which functioned as the first stateside waypoint for the most seriously wounded, arriving just as the flow of casualties climbed to new heights. The war was as much a part of her life as it was of mine. We had spoken only once since I had arrived at the IPA, and now I was ashamed to find a string of increasingly worried emails in my inbox. Not for the first time, I realized how much easier it was for me to be in these situations than it was for her to endure the torment of uncertainty.

I labored over a reply, writing a sentence or two and then deleting them, until Jay gave me the two-minute warning for our ride back, and I pressed send on a painfully inane missive.

# Chapter 31

We had only a few days of respite, and then the cycle began again as though the *Muj* had simply been taking a breather before the next bout. Chuck Groene's team was decimated by a single sniper; an advisor from another team was shot in the shoulder; and Gunny Gustavson, who had told me to stay safe as he dropped me at the police station, lost an eye to an IED.

Several of our *jundi* were wounded in ambushes, and then Joker was killed. Joker was an icon in the battalion: a young Iraqi soldier who earned his nickname from the advisor team for his happy disposition. He didn't speak a word of English but had befriended Reyes and the Doc who regularly played soccer with the *jundi* in the courtyard, amidst a raucous exchange of insults delivered in Arabic and English. Afterwards they would all sit on the steps, chatting in *Arabish* and smoking the disgusting cheroots that Joker had sent from home.

It happened as we pulled in front of the Mansoor power station that was home to the *battalion's* 2nd company. The sniper had been dormant for a week or more, and we assumed that he had been killed or moved elsewhere. But as we climbed out of the vehicles he opened up with three shots, one of which hit Joker just below his throat, ploughing downward into his chest. Reyes and a *jundi* grabbed him under the arms and pulled him under cover where Doc worked on him even after everyone told him to stop: that Joker was dead.

We lifted him into the back of one of the pick-up trucks for the trip to the morgue. As we pulled out of the power station, Reyes called me on the radio: 'We've got to stop at the IPA to tell his brother.' He knew, but none of us did, that Joker had a brother in the same company. At the IPA, we waited in the courtyard while Zuher and Reyes went into the building, emerging about ten minutes later with a red-eyed *jundi* in tow. Zuher tapped me on the shoulder as we pulled out of the IPA.

'Sadi, he needs to escort his brother's body home. It's a tradition when we have two brothers in the same unit.' Normally slain Iraqi soldiers would be flown from Maurez to Taji from whence the Iraqi Command would handle their repatriation. We had never encountered this situation before; but I knew that we had to deliver.

'OK, I'll see what I can do.'

The first stop on the trip home for all Iraqi and American soldiers killed in Mosul was the morgue at Camp Maurez, where mortuary affairs soldiers recorded various details while a doctor confirmed that they were indeed dead. Someone had to be present to identify the corpse, which was then packaged for travel: zipped into a heavy plastic body bag, and tagged with everything that the handlers would need to know en route. I had attended these events several times before and knew what to expect; so I took only the interpreter with me into the ice-cold hut, leaving the others outside.

I don't know the statistics but would guess that no other military occupation produces more psychological casualties than Mortuary Affairs. I had seen Marine morticians at work during Fallujah where, barely able to keep up with the flow of casualties, they dealt with a procession of bodies, many so badly mutilated that they would subsequently carry a tag that warned 'remains unviewable'. I can't imagine that anyone can do that repeatedly and remain unchanged.

Joker had not yet assumed the waxy gray tone of the dead. Someone had closed his eyes, and his face, with its signature beaky nose, narrow jaw and smooth cheeks, was untouched, peaceful as though he was simply asleep. Joker didn't look like a soldier; I remembered someone telling me that he wanted to be a computer programmer after the army.

I identified him, spelling his Arabic name to a female sergeant who wrote it on a clipboard. A nurse cut away the saturated bandage on his upper chest, and the doctor peered into his wound, using his gloved finger and a pencil to measure angles.

A PFC removed Joker's watch from his wrist, and held it up to his ear.

'Still ticking,' he said, placing it in the bag. Joker, whose life had been multifarious and complex and valuable, was gone; but his cheap watch continued to measure time.

They finished up: the doctor peeled off his gloves and nodded to me with a sad smile before leaving the room. I helped the sergeant and the PFC lift Joker into the body bag; he was very light so it wasn't difficult. Then the sergeant zipped the bag up, pushing Joker's head gently to one side so that the zip wouldn't catch on his nose.

Reyes intercepted me as I left the hut. 'Hey sir, you need to talk to the flight scheduler about getting Joker's brother on the plane. He's digging his heels in.'

The civilian contractor who handled flights out of Maurez was true to form: a pudgy, harassed looking man in a gray polo shirt displaying giant sweat stains. He wasn't going to budge; I knew before I had even started to speak.

'I want to help you major, but we need an authorization letter signed by a two-star general to get an Iraqi on the plane.' He meant a live Iraqi, dead ones were apparently no problem.

The plane was due to leave in thirty minutes; there was no way that we were going to find a two-star to sign the letter in that time. He knew it, but that wasn't his problem.

'Then the body can't go on this flight. He has to fly with his brother,' I explained.

'Nope, the body's going on this flight, it's already on the manifest. I'm not allowed to play around with bodies.'

I argued with him until, feeling an impulse to reach across the desk and push my thumbs into his meaty throat, I turned instead and left his office.

Joker's brother was sitting on a bench in the waiting area clutching a plastic bag and looking at his feet; he was alone, everyone else except Reyes was outside. I called Lieutenant Colonel Whitman, who had taken over from Jamison, and explained the situation. He understood immediately.

'OK Andy, hold the plane, I'll drive over to Maurez now.'

His response was typical of the man, but I couldn't hold the plane; mere majors didn't have the power to mess with flight schedules. I bought two cokes, and handed one to Joker's brother, he thanked me and put it in his plastic bag. Then I remembered Zuher telling me of a *jundi* custom to forgo food and drink for twenty-four hours after a comrade's death as a sign of respect.

The door opened and the contractor came out. He had a walkie-talkie in his hand and was fastening a yellow road vest around his expansive stomach. He paused and looked at Joker's brother.

'Is that him?'

'Yes, it is.'

Joker's brother continued to stare at the floor, impervious to all but his grief.

The contractor took a deep breath. 'OK. Give me his name for the manifest.'

We caught the sniper a week later. Anyone who has had to contend with a competent sniper knows how improbable this claim sounds; we were incredibly lucky.

On the other hand, as I made a point of emphasizing afterwards, our good luck was generated by sound tactical actions. We had adopted a practice whereby two or more patrols follow parallel routes that weave back and forth in an unpredictable manner, sometimes intersecting, sometimes diverging. The sniper fired at one patrol without hitting anyone, and as he made his escape, Dragonov rifle still warm in his hands, he ran slap-bang into the other patrol. Smith called me with the news; Zuher and I jumped in a truck and rushed to the power station.

The patrol traipsed through the gate, the spot where Joker had died, with their prisoner, blindfolded and hands-bound, stumbling in their midst. Chattering triumphantly, they gathered around our truck, and I eyed the captive sniper, curious to meet the man who had caused us so much angst. Dressed in shabby Western clothes: a checked shirt, dark blue trousers and cheap sneakers, he was short, skinny and harmless looking.

Zuher wanted to interrogate him, but I told him that we had to get him to brigade right away. One look at the *jundi* told me that we needed to take the prisoner off their hands.

They pushed and prodded him into a small room just inside the power station and made him kneel. One *jundi* cuffed him on the back of the head, another spat in his face.

'Cut it out,' I snapped. *'Imchi'*. Get out. They filed out reluctantly leaving Zuher and me in the room with the prisoner who was gasping for air like a landed fish.

'Zuher, I'm going to call brigade. Make sure nothing happens to him.'

'OK sadi.' Zuher was looking at the prisoner, not me.

'Zuher.'

'OK, I got it.'

Even a man as civilized and urbane as Zuher was not immune from the collective passion for vengeance. The problem was that I understood how they felt. There was something invidious about snipers: they invoke a special kind of fear, and the flipside desire for retribution, especially when you have seen your buddies drop lifeless or rolling in agony in front of you. Even as I sought to impose order, part of me too lurked in the same dark space of anger and self-justification where the normal rules of moral behavior lose traction. The man kneeling in front of me had doubtless relished his ability to kill with impunity. If he disappeared into the Iraqi court system he would likely be a free man in a matter of weeks, would find another weapon and get back to work. Killing him seemed the right thing to do. I could understand that belief, could feel it, despite all my advanced education in philosophy and law. But I already had seen enough to know that there's no end to vengeance.

Unless I pushed back, the dark space would expand and consume us all. So I called brigade to request that they take the captive off our hands.

I checked on the prisoner one more time before the convoy arrived to pick him up – he was squatting on the floor under the watchful eyes of two *jundi* whom Zuher deemed trustworthy. The convoy arrived, I exchanged a few words with the Marine advisor who accompanied it, watched as the prisoner was bundled into the back of one of the trucks, and started to walk back to the power station. I was halfway when a commotion broke out behind me. A crowd of *jundi* had formed around the convoy. Howling with anger, they were banging on the sides of the truck carrying the prisoner.

One of them tried to pull down the passenger window but was restrained by Zuher who had pushed himself to the front of the mob. Other officers joined him and gradually the din died down. The Marine advisor joined me on the edge of the crowd and explained what had happened.

'One of the brigade *jundi* handed the prisoner a bottle of water and a cigarette, and all hell broke loose. We're going to take off now before something else happens.'

Zuher was silent on the ride back, until we reached the gates of the IPA.

'He didn't deserve mercy because of the way he killed.'

I turned around to look at him but said nothing.

'But to the *jundi* from brigade, he was a guest, and deserved hospitality. This is just our way. It's you I don't understand. You are the one who pushed us to hunt the Wahabi, and now you are unhappy with the result.'

I shrugged, and turned back around.

'Do you know why our soldiers wear sunglasses?' Zuher went on. 'It's because Americans do, and the *jundi* want to look the same.'

'So?'

'So don't worry, my friend – eventually we will all be just like you.'

# Chapter 32

Major Taleb, the second company commander was worse than incompetent.

'Taleb is a Wahabi.' Zuher whispered to me once, early on during a battalion meeting, though when later I pressed him to tell me more, he denied having said anything. During my first week with the battalion, I visited Taleb's company who were billeted in the Mansoor power station and climbed up to the roof to get a view of their area of operations. As I peered over the balustrade Taleb loosed off a round into the sandbags beside me. He claimed that it was a negligent discharge, but there was no sign of shock or remorse on his saturnine features, and Jay, who had been standing behind him, told me that he had seen him push his safety catch off.

I was certain that the shot had been no accident but didn't pursue the matter. Distrust spreads like wildfire in these situations, and after working hard to build cohesion, I didn't want to stoke the tinder.

The other company commander who caused us problems was Captain Mehdi. Stocky with jet black hair and a Zapata moustache, Mehdi had a look of perpetual confusion that was probably not feigned. He distinguished himself on the first day in Mosul by opening fire on a US patrol – claiming that he mistook the Stryker-mounted soldiers for insurgents. He was fortunate to have picked a US platoon with good fire discipline for his target, and his error resulted in no more than a handful of wounded *jundi*, and no American casualties. We thought that that would be the end of Mehdi, but Falah gave him what the British call a bollocking and sent him back to his company.

What Mehdi lacked in intelligence he made up for with his unbridled instinct for self-preservation. It was he who tried to break into a house for shelter during a fire fight; and it was a relief to all when Mehdi decided thereafter that he would no longer go out on patrol.

There were rumors that Mehdi and Taleb were both well connected, but their retention in place marked a general trend: Iraqi officers were generally reluctant to relieve subordinates except in cases where their transgressions were well publicized. Realizing this, we became quite Machiavellian in devising schemes to skyline the most incompetent officers, thus forcing their relief.

Most of the neighborhoods in our sector were Sunni, their inhabitants not unfriendly but visibly cowed by the presence of insurgents in their midst. They appeared unresentful when we searched their homes, and often offered the searchers water or tea. In this we had a marked advantage over American troops whose incursions were met with stony silence.

We were insistent that the *jundi* conduct themselves properly during these searches, by replacing items and trying to engage the occupants in conversation. On one occasion we fired an interpreter for slapping a man while questioning him, but such incidents were rare.

The Sunni Arab neighborhoods were clustered together in the center of our sector, while around the periphery lived the Kurds, a fiercely independent ethnic group who share a common religion with their Arab neighbors, but little else. The contrast between their respective areas was startling. Kurdish women wore brightly colored dresses and headscarves instead of abaya and waved at us without embarrassment; the men gathered in clusters outside their homes drinking chai and smoking nargillah, the water pipes that are now fashionable in Western Europe; while the children ran unrestrained in noisy packs, the boys chasing soccer balls, the girls playing jump rope or a local version of hopscotch. Although violence was as much a factor of daily life for them as for the Arabs, and although the ramshackle, unpainted concrete buildings packed tightly together were evidence of their lowly status in the sectarian hierarchy, the Kurds were invariably cheerful, and welcomed us with shouted greetings and smiles.

It was hard to correlate this extrovert group with their grim history here in Northern Iraq where they had been the subject of a concerted pogrom by Saddam's regime. But they appeared to bear the Iraqi soldiers no ill-will and the *jundi* responded in kind, though many of their officers appeared to be suspicious of the Kurds, the depth of prejudice increasing with rank and length of service. Brigadier Shocker, a Kurd himself, was prone to making statements that sounded suspiciously nostalgic about how Saddam's troops used to deal with this troublesome minority.

It was my first introduction to the Kurds, a group that would some thirteen years hence play a prominent role as allies against an enemy even more vicious than the one we faced now. I enjoyed the patrols that took us through their neighborhoods. I made friends with a number of the children who would rush out to greet us, writing their names in my notebook alongside tactical observations and the names of wanted insurgents, so that I would remember them the next time I passed.

By late February, we had established a series of company outposts throughout the city, and were beginning to dominate the area with both mounted and dismounted patrols, averaging around twenty a day. Slowly, painfully, we were tipping the balance. There were now fewer enemy attacks in those areas of the city whose names once connoted intense violence: Mansoor, Jedeeda, Mohata, Bab al Beez.

But progress came at a fairly heavy cost; by early March, over fifty *jundi* had been killed or wounded, some 20 per cent of the battalion's total strength. American soldiers were often dismissive of the fighting qualities of Iraqi soldiers, but our *jundi* had persevered, despite a casualty rate that was staggeringly high for so short a period of time.

To add insult to injury, for reasons obscured within the Byzantine bureaucracy of the Iraqi's military pay system, soldiers of the battalion hadn't been paid during this time. We dispatched a US major from brigade to MNSTC-I with instructions to raise a fuss until this problem was sorted out, and a few weeks later it was, but only partially, and the *jundi* never received the back pay due to them.

About that time, I received a message from CSW directing me to Afghanistan where I was to link up with an advisor team for a thirty-day period. My replacement, a Major Rocco Barnes, was due to arrive a few days prior to my departure date. No one seemed to know much about him except that he was a reservist Special Forces soldier with a good reputation.

'They couldn't find a Marine?' I asked Russ with lamentable parochialism.

Russ delivered Rocco to the IPA a few days later. I sized him up as I shook his hand, aware that in a day or two I would be handing over to him something that had become part of me. He had sandy-red hair, a deeply lined ruddy face, and pale blue eyes that conveyed humor and intelligence. He was almost 50, ancient for a major, and had been in the army since the age of 18, interspersing his time on active duty with civilian jobs that spanned an eclectic spectrum from coal miner to Hollywood script writer to bodyguard for Arnold Schwarzenegger. I had to tease all this information out of him; Rocco wasn't one to give you his résumé up front.

As I walked him around, introducing him to everyone, he appeared friendly, but listened more than he spoke. Unreasonably, I bristled when he probed me about battalion procedures. They were all good questions and the truth was that Rocco was bringing up things that I had either overlooked or neglected; but after the experiences of the previous two months, I was hypersensitive, and not prepared to receive implicit criticism from a newcomer. Nevertheless, I couldn't help liking him and knew that the team was in good hands.

The morning of my departure, Rocco and I accompanied a patrol to COP Tampa. Tampa was a ravaged combat outpost, manned by a platoon of *jundi*. It occupied the key intersection between the two main thoroughfares through the middle of the city, and was a prime target for the *Muj*. A few weeks previously a dump truck packed with explosives had hurdled the surrounding concrete barriers and blown a hole in the side of the building, killing several US soldiers.

As we ran into the building a volley of shots rang out and a *jundi* dropped to the ground wounded in the head. We loaded him into the back of one of the trucks and sped towards the hospital at Maurez. As we pulled away, there was another rattle of automatic fire, a zip, zipping of rounds past the open window and loud pings as several tore into the sides of the truck. Our gunner dropped down into the cab without returning fire. 'You suck,' I counseled him, at a loss for the right phrase in Arabic.

There was a brief altercation at the gate when one of the US guards tried to deny us entry, whereupon Rocco threatened to shoot him (*point to Rocco*, I thought). The gate swung open.

Medics were waiting with a stretcher, and we carried the *jundi* into the small hospital where attendants, alerted by our call, had already prepared the operating room. He was in surgery within minutes of us arriving. It was a well-practiced procedure.

We wouldn't get any news on the soldier for an hour or so, and my flight was due to leave around the same time, so Rocco and I took Zuher and Mohammed (who had both accompanied the patrol) to the PX with us. While I poked around for a present to buy Jessica, Zuher bought a pair of aviator sunglasses (with a wink at me), and Mohammed bought an American flag to take home to his family. When we returned there was no real news on the status of our soldier. 'He's still circling the drain,' a nurse told me.

The four of us drove to the flight line – Zuher insisted on carrying my bags – and with hugs all round, and promises that I would be back, I boarded the plane. I learned later that the *jundi* died.

# Chapter 33

In Afghanistan I spent a few days with Chris Nicewarner in Pol-i-Charkhi outside Kabul, before heading south to Jalalabad. Over our morning ritual of coffee followed by a long run around the base, we shared notes from our recent experiences. It was a pleasant interlude, and I felt myself begin to unwind. Chris commanded one of the first Marine advisor teams in country and was tackling this challenging task with the same shrewd focus that he tackled everything. With my tendency to be, at times, impetuous, I have always envied Chris's ability to balance single-minded determination with the patience to step back when called for and take stock.

I stayed in Jalalabad for just under a month, as part of a Marine advisor team working with a company of Afghan commandos. Based on US intelligence, we executed a series of raids with our Afghan partners, who appeared to be better motivated and more self-sufficient than their Iraqi counterparts. On one memorable occasion, we flew into Nuristan where we met with local elders (the first time they had seen Americans) and patrolled through an emerald green valley ringed by towering mountains mantled with snow. It reminded me of the movie '*The Man Who Would be King*,' based on the Kipling short story of the same name.

When I returned to Mosul in early May, the battalion had moved across the Tigris River to the Palestine district of eastern Mosul, where it lived in a partially constructed building adjacent to a hospital.

'We are the fire brigade.' Mohammed told me with a rare smile as he and Rocco helped me carry my bags to the waiting trucks. 'We calmed central Mosul so it was time to move on.'

Rocco, Mohammed (now a lieutenant colonel) and two other advisors, whom I didn't know, met me at the airstrip. By incredible coincidence they had been on Maurez dropping off another Iraqi casualty at the hospital and told brigade that they would pick me up at the same time.

'Possession is 90 per cent of the law,' announced Rocco, aware that brigade expected me to join the staff there. It was an incredibly generous gesture on his part. Bringing another major on board, especially one who had previously led the team, was a move that would, under normal circumstances be guaranteed to cause friction. But Rocco seemed to have a confidence that we would make it work, and I was touched that he viewed commandeering me as a win for the team.

We headed through the gates of Maurez into a chaotic swarm of taxis, trucks and motorcycles, all jockeying for position in a brown haze of exhaust fumes, and across the Tigris, sluggish and chocolate colored in the late afternoon sun. My memories of Mosul, like those of Fallujah, were always overcast and gray, but now the city looked somehow less drab, more vibrant and alive, and I hoped that it was a sign of better times. I noticed some readily apparent signs of progress: all the *jundi* were indeed wearing sunglasses, and the Armed Forces Network now had a radio station in Mosul. As we pulled into traffic, the Iraqi driver turned the radio up and started to sing along to Fog Hat's *'Slow Ride'* as the gunner beat time on the roof of the cab until Mohammed yelled at them to knock it off.

As we drove, Rocco brought me up to date. 'Falah's still here. He's the brigade golden boy now because his staff,' he nodded at Mohammed, 'is kicking ass. They're running a daily cycle of patrols and raids which are netting us a ton of intel. We're tied in pretty closely with 1/5, 1st Battalion, 5th Infantry Regiment, same brigade as 1/24 who you worked with around the IPA. I've got them to put a liaison team in the hospital with us.

'Palestine is made up of Kurdish and Arab Sunni neighborhoods which blend into one another,' he continued. 'The bad guys, as before, are an alliance of old-school Baathists and Ansar Al Islam.'

Ansar Al Islam, once headed by Zarqawi, originated in Mosul and had been a small isolated group of crackpots until the US invasion removed its only predator, Saddam's army, and fed it a stream of new recruits. Now it was a formidable organization.

'We've got some pretty good leads into their leadership: either direct connections by cell phone, or via the Joint Coordination Center, the JCC, which is a joint Iraqi-US intelligence fusion cell. The Iraqis in the JCC pass us tips directly before sharing them with their US counterparts, which works well for us.

'The IED threat is through the roof. Much more command detonated stuff, very sophisticated, large enough to roll a Stryker and to absolutely vaporize these things.' Rocco slapped the side of the truck door. 'They know our tactics too – a lot of times the initial IED will be the bait to have us set up a cordon. They'll then detonate a daisy chain right under the cordon. They got some Joes from 1/24 that way a couple of weeks back.

'The EOD teams are so overworked they won't respond until an American, one of us, verifies the report of an IED.'

'How do we do that?'

'Therein lies the rub, my friend. We verify by getting eyes on the IED, which is of course absurdly risky. But if we start telling them that we can see the IEDs when we can't, EOD will just stop responding. It's the perfect Catch-22. I've got to remember that one for my book.' Rocco's plan was to write a book about our experiences that would make enough money for him to retire.

Two *jundi* swung open the gate to the hospital compound, we drove inside, past the hospital itself, a five-story building, quite modern looking by the standards of Mosul, and pulled up beside a half-constructed breeze-block building next door. I gathered my bags and looked around the hospital compound. It was about the size of four tennis courts, surrounded by 20ft walls and empty of cars except for our trucks and two ambulances. What caught my attention right away was the stream of people walking between the gate of the compound and the hospital: men, women and children, some hobbling on crutches or being pushed in wheelchairs, others outwardly healthy – it was as busy as a shopping mall. Rocco noticed my glance.

'Only decent functioning hospital in Mosul so it attracts quite a crowd. I would love to move us somewhere more secure, but the Iraqi leadership won't have it. Our presence here reassures the locals. And there's an upside to us being in the middle of Grand Central – we're getting more walk-in tips from patients and the hospital staff than we could hope for anywhere else. But we're a sitting target. We've been probed a couple of times, PKMs and mortars, and it's just a matter of time before we eat a VBIED. That's something we need to rehearse.'

Later that afternoon, we continued our conversation over cigars on the roof of our building, protected by a 4ft balustrade of concrete blocks that circumvented the edge, watching the sun set, a smoky orange ball glowing through the dusty pall that blanketed the city. It was a peaceful scene aside from the occasional rattle of distant gunfire and wail of sirens (another good sign, I reminded myself: the police were back.)

Jay Kajs and Corporal Smith had left two weeks previously. Reyes and the Doc were all that remained of the old team. I had met two of the newcomers already. Sergeant First Class Gene, hawk-faced and slight with prematurely gray hair, had been a platoon sergeant in the 82nd Airborne before transferring to the reserves, and exuded an air of quiet authority. Staff Sergeant Trevor Lefevre was a lumberjack from upper-state New York and looked the part: tall, broad shouldered with *Marvel*-comic features that reminded me of Ed Dropic.

'They're rock solid. Sergeant Reyes extended and is doing well but it's probably good that he's going home in June. This place wears on you pretty quick as you know. We've got one guy that I want you to watch out for though – his name is Graves, a staff sergeant, pretty old for the rank. He's keen but very inexperienced.'

Staff Sergeant Reyes appeared and gave me a bear-hug. He was as boisterous and positive as ever, launching into a 'you should have been there' exposition of events that had happened while I had been away. Just two weeks previously a raid on an IED factory had turned into a dramatic fire fight that culminated in the house being blown sky high, killing several insurgents but, miraculously, no friendlies. Reyes, who was a graphic artist in the civilian world, had captured it all on film, and described the incident with the same youthful enthusiasm as though it had been a paint-ball skirmish.

Sergeant First Class Gene joined us, and added in an undemonstrative way, his account of two soul-searing moments of tragedy. A boy, who sold flowers outside the hospital and played soccer with Lefevre and Reyes, was found dead outside the gate one morning. And just two days previously, a vehicle borne IED had detonated next to a group of children just two blocks from the hospital. The advisors had done what they could to triage and treat the wounded in the long moments before the ambulances arrived.

Rocco glanced at his watch. 'Andy, we've got a raid tonight. It's a capture kill – some Ansar shithead that Zuher's sources have tracked down. We're setting the cordon and doing the entry, no US involvement aside from QRF. I figured you'd want to come along.'

I had snatched only a few hours' sleep on the cold floor of a C-17 since leaving Afghanistan two days previously, and was shattered.

'Yes, of course,' I heard myself say. 'What time?'

'We take off at 0200, so reveille at 0030.' He stood up. 'Yallah!'

Rocco shook me awake several hours later and I struggled to the surface, foul-mouthed and drenched in sweat; the room I shared with Rocco was little bigger than a broom closet and sweltering hot. I took a gulp of cold coffee from the mug he handed me and groped in the darkness for my headlamp and boots – locating the latter by their distinctive smell.

I joined Rocco and Sergeant Gene on the ground floor of the building where we lived. There were no rooms, they had yet to be built, just a concrete floor and ceiling connected by breeze-block pillars. There were no walls either – the sides of the building were open to the hospital compound in which I could see a group of *jundi* milling around the pick-up trucks.

Rocco was talking to Captain Ali (no relation to Lieutenant Ali in Fallujah) who would be leading the raid, while Sergeant Gene tested the radio, and the Iraqi NCOs checked their people. It was all very businesslike and unhurried, quiet voices and shadowing figures, an occasional laugh among the mutter of orders, magazines being loaded, weapons being cocked and the light from a naked dangling bulb reflected on faces.

Our target that night looked like any other house in Mosul – a small, squat building set in a courtyard the size of a suburban driveway surrounded by a 6 ft wall. The squad assigned to the cordon peeled off from the column as we approached, and with a few whispered instructions, Ali directed two soldiers to climb the outer wall, which they did, carefully using their rifle butts to remove shards of broken glass embedded in the concrete at the top of the wall, and then helping each other shimmy over. One of them gave the signal that all was clear, and the rest of the squad followed, boosting each other up onto the wall and disappearing in quick succession into the darkness beyond. On previous raids, we'd have had at least one advisor enter the building with the first *jundi*, but now the Iraqis seemed to be running the show, another good sign – or so I thought.

Rocco and I followed, though somewhat less gracefully than the *jundi*, dropping heavily into the courtyard and pausing to get our bearings. As we checked our weapons and started to move towards the house there was a burst of firing: a brief stutter then the sound of several weapons on full automatic, amplified to an ear-splitting din in the close confines of the courtyard.

We sprinted across the compound and into a cluster of soldiers on the front steps of the house. The firing had stopped. Rocco and I hurled ourselves against the door which swung open, spilling us into a darkened hallway. I stepped quickly to one side, pulled out my flashlight, and swung the beam along the floor, revealing a dark puddle, and a smeared trail that led back into the darkness. Someone flicked on a light, and in the sudden harsh glare I saw that there was a body lying in the hallway face down.

A *jundi* advanced towards it, rolling it onto its back and kicking across the floor an AK–47 that had been lying under it. It was a middle-aged man, gray-haired and unshaven wearing a pajama top and baggy pants. His eyes were closed and his chest, a mass of blood and pulp, was still.

Rocco knelt over him to check the pulse on his neck, Gene and I pushed past them towards a light at the end of the hallway, our weapons at the ready. We stepped from the hallway into the kitchen and a sight that I will never shake loose. A middle-aged woman was sheltering under the table holding two children – a young girl and boy, probably around 3 and 5 years old. A third child, an older girl in her early teens, was standing behind the table staring at us with a mix of fear and hatred.

'It's OK,' I said. 'We're not going to hurt you,' suddenly realizing the awful import of what had just happened.

Before Gene or I could react, the girl darted past us into the hallway, and let out a piercing scream. Rocco returned her to the room, holding her shoulders with both hands and pushing her gently in front of him. He was saying 'It's alright, it's alright.' But it wasn't alright – she had just seen her father's corpse and was shrieking uncontrollably. The mother started to sob, her children staring at her open mouthed, uncomprehendingly.

We had an interpreter but there was little for us to say beyond the fact that we were very sorry and that we would send a vehicle the next morning to take them to the morgue where they could make funeral arrangements.

We still weren't sure what had happened, but I was beginning to fear that it had been a horrible mistake. Many families in Mosul kept a weapon for self-protection. The father must have heard the *jundi* banging on the door; maybe he saw the weapons, and assumed that they were *Muj*, or maybe he himself was really an insurgent. We had no way of knowing. In any case, he had opened fire, and they had shot him through the door.

I walked out the front door, two *jundi* followed me dragging the corpse, its head thudding down the steps.

'Pick him up for fuck's sake,' I yelled. And then, as they put him down, I saw his chest rise.

'Rocco – he's alive!'

We bent over him and Rocco reached for his pulse again but there was none.

'He's been shot in the heart, there's no way that we can bring him back. Those must have been some kind of post-mortem contractions.' Rocco said, rinsing his hands with a bottle of water. This faint hope now dashed, Gene, Rocco and I trailed the pall-bearers back to the convoy. On the drive back to the hospital no one spoke.

As soon as we came to a halt back in the compound, Gene dropped down from the turret, a stricken look on his face. 'We killed an innocent man.'

'Let's not jump to conclusions.' Rocco said. 'We need to talk about this.'

The three of us gathered in the room that Rocco and I shared, sitting on camp beds facing each other by the dim light of a flashlight suspended by cord from the ceiling.

'We will never know if he was really an insurgent or not,' Rocco began, 'you guys know how this works. We encourage them to collect intelligence and most of the time it's decent but sometimes it's not. It's all single source, and sometimes they make mistakes or someone with a grudge passes them false info. We do what we can to check that they're taking the right steps but that's not always possible, and in the end, we want it to be their war – right?'

We said nothing. I couldn't shake the images of the family from my mind. Rocco went on:

'If it's anyone's fault it's mine. But you know even if one of us had been up there with Ali it wouldn't have made a difference. Once that guy fired through the door, he was a dead man.'

'John?' Rocco looked at Gene.

'Yes sir. I feel better,' Gene said in a monotone.

'Get to bed, gents.'

After they had left, Rocco rubbed his hands over his face.

'I do believe that we are a force for good here, Andy,' he said – as much to himself as to me.

He climbed onto his rack and stared at the ceiling. 'But some of the shit that happens here is going to stay with me for a long time,' he said, and closed his eyes.

Despite my exhaustion, I lay awake reliving the events of that night, imagining that I had done something different leading to an alternate outcome. Despite Rocco's words, I was mired in guilt. Guilt for our callous entry into that family's lives, leaving them forever changed while ours went on as before. The daughter's scream continued to ring in my ears, until it was replaced by the muezzin's call to prayer as darkness gave way to the dusty gray dawn of another day.

# Chapter 34

I woke to a splash of cold water on my face. It was Zuher standing over me with a bottle poised above my head, an impish grin on his face.

'Wake up, sadi, we've been waiting for you.' He was a major now; all the Iraqi officers had been promoted as a reward for the battalion's success during that dark winter.

We caught up over breakfast, freshly baked flatbread and bitter coffee. We ate in the battalion operations room which, with its maps, radios and patrol schedule curated by attendant *jundis*, appeared very businesslike.

'Mehdi is gone!' Zuher announced – holding up his hand for a high-five. Apparently Mehdi's behavior had become so blatantly craven that the new brigade commander, Abdul Amir had fired him himself. Amir had previously been the brigade operations officer.

'He's very different,' Zuher said of Amir, picking his words carefully. 'He's professional, a real soldier but very— Shia.'

I had never heard Zuher mention religious denomination before, and my surprise must have shown.

'He doesn't like the Sunnis or the Kurds, says they're all Wahabi. He wants us to put our soldiers into the local neighborhoods, in disguise. What word do you use for that?'

'Undercover?' I offered.

'Yes – undercover. We send soldiers down to Taji to get special training, and when they come back we use them as spies.'

'Sounds pretty risky to me.'

In Iraq, religion, tribe and family conferred your identity. It wasn't something that you could simply adopt, no matter what they taught you in Taji.

'Yes,' Zuher agreed. 'Two soldiers from 2nd Battalion started doing this two weeks ago. One is missing and the other – we found his body in the street, without a head.'

I was to meet Abdul Amir a few times in the following weeks, and was impressed by his energy and intellect. Short and slight with piercing dark eyes, he came across as being somewhat haughty, supercilious, as though he was a couple of steps ahead of you and wanted you to know. Even then, it was clear that Amir was on the fast-track – he had that look and feel about him. Lieutenant Colonel Burke Whitman, who had replaced Russ Jamison as the senior US advisor, handled Amir with aplomb, and was able to talk him out of some of his more outlandish ventures while persuading him occasionally to do our bidding. At Burke's insistence Amir had the Mosul Police Chief fired after a string of incidents indicating that he was condoning widespread abuse.

By unspoken agreement I became Rocco's deputy, an arrangement that – somewhat to my surprise – we both settled into happily. Rocco had an affable personality with a direct approach to dealing with people that never shrunk from confrontation, but such was his easy-going manner, he seldom incurred rancor.

I had the feeling that he enjoyed being able to discuss decisions with a peer; something that I could well understand after my own feeling of isolation back in January. Burke Whitman accepted this arrangement with typical good grace but was fond of reminding me that he could pull me up to brigade at any time.

Although the Iraqis were proficient enough now to run their own patrols, we still had to accompany them as a link to the local US unit; and with only seven advisors on the team, our daily routine was an exhausting cycle of patrols as temperatures soared past the 100-degree mark. We still rode in the same vehicles as the *jundi*: white Toyota pick-up trucks with makeshift metal shields welded to the sides as scant protection against the ubiquitous threat of IEDs, though MNSTC-I promised that more armored Humvees were on their way.

Our living conditions were spartan: camp beds or bed rolls on the floor of a bare concrete building open to the air on either side. We ate the same food as the *jundi*, which was generally pretty good.

Because the Iraqi Army had no program to care for disabled soldiers, the battalion kept wounded soldiers on the rolls after their release from hospital. The building where we lived was home to a group of these invalids, some of them amputees, who shuffled around performing whatever tasks they could.

The *Muj* were still active, and the hospital compound was rocketed or mortared every few days. We had the *jundi* practice running to man prepared positions throughout the compound in defense against ground attack, an event that we constantly anticipated.

IEDs had become so ubiquitous that it was rare for a patrol not to encounter one, either by finding it or, the least preferred method, by setting it off. From the roof of the hospital, where the Iraqis maintained an observation post, we could trace the progress of US patrols around the city by the sound of explosions and plumes of smoke.

The battalion regularly received tips about the location of IEDs, but as Rocco had explained, the US EOD teams would not respond to an Iraqi report unless a US advisor had first confirmed its veracity. As much as we hated checking out IEDs there was a sound rationale for this. There were literally tons of ordnance lying around Mosul resulting in an incessant flow of reports, more than the EOD teams could possible keep up with. Our job was to confirm that the ordnance, usually artillery or mortar shells, looked as though it had been laid deliberately.

The presence of electric wiring was a good indicator, because wires are what is used to connect the explosive part of the IED to a detonator. The detonator in turn would be connected to a switch by more wires. The switch might be activated by someone applying pressure to it (stepping on it or driving over it) or by pulses from a remote control (a garage door opener or cell phone for instance). This would send an impulse down the wires to the detonator, sparking the explosion.

Sometimes you'd find just the explosives by themselves, already wired and awaiting the addition of a detonator. Sometimes it was the detonator hidden separately, awaiting the IED layer to connect it to the explosive package when the time was right. Sometimes it was the complete IED, waiting to blow.

One morning, a few days after my return, I witnessed first-hand what a dangerous game this was. I was leading a mounted patrol through the Sunni periphery of Palestine when Lieutenant Colonel Mohammed called me on the radio with an IED report. I scribbled down the grid and description, a gas station only a block away from where we were, and passed the hand set to Dhofar, the interpreter, so that Mohammed could pass him more details in Arabic.

'It's hidden in a paper bag by one of the pumps. The gas station's empty, someone must have told the people who work there. Mohammed says don't get too close.'

As soon as we rounded the corner and saw the gas station ahead of us, I already felt too close. I had the Iraqi platoon commander set up a cordon using our four vehicles, and then called 1/5 with a quick update.

'You want me to come with you,' asked Dhofar. He wore a balaclava helmet for disguise, which seemed a ridiculously uncomfortable precaution to take in this heat, especially since Dhofar was from Baghdad, and thus unlikely to be recognized. He was a rogue, but always game and his offer was genuine.

'Thanks Dhofar, no need, I'm good.' I felt anything but.

I got out of the vehicle and trudged towards the gas station. The sun beat down from a blue-slate sky, the heat bouncing off the tarmac like the blast from an open oven. Sweat stung my eyes, and I labored for breath as though jogging.

Moving to an angle from which I could see both pumps, I pulled out my binoculars and scanned the forecourt. The prospect of verifying the presence of an IED concealed somewhere in the indeterminate piles of refuse strewn around the pumps was patently absurd. I had to assume there were underground tanks full of gas, in which case it didn't make sense to get any closer. I paused, uncertain. A gust of wind whipped a cloud of dust into the air and rolled a soda bottle across the forecourt, with a jangling sound that did nothing for my nerves. Without conscious thought I started walking again, another 10 meters or so, and then stopped. My walkie-talkie crackled, it was Reyes.

'Hey sir, we're gonna call EOD anyway. Doesn't make sense for us to look for an IED in a fucking gas station for Christ sake. They can send in a robot.'

'Yep, thanks, was just coming to the same conclusion. We'll hold the cordon until they arrive but get an ETA.' We had learned from experience that the EOD teams could take forever to arrive. Half an hour was as long as I was prepared to wait; we were sitting ducks.

I turned and started back to my vehicle. Suddenly the road ahead erupted in a black cloud of asphalt and dirt. I ran through the smoke towards the truck, yelling at Dhofar to start the engine. Then gunfire behind me, the zip and crack of rounds whipping by. I dived behind the rear wheel, trying to burrow into the tarmac as another volley of shots skipped and whined off the road behind me. A second later Dhofar tumbled beside me, his hand clutching my forearm; I caught a glimpse of raw terror through the holes in his balaclava as he flattened himself on the ground.

Struggling to one knee, I pulled my weapon into my shoulder, sucked in a quick breath and popped around the wheel, exposing just the muzzle and right side of my face. There were two figures on the roof of the gas station. A split second to draw a bead, focus on the glowing red reticle, the shapes blurring into the background, finger tightening on the trigger and one, two, three, four shots, squeezing them off in rapid succession, aware that I was jerking the trigger on the last two but succumbing to the instinct to get them off before I became a target. I rolled back behind the wheel and glanced at Dhofar who had both hands over the back of his head. There was another burst of firing, and I heard the rounds *thunking* into the metal of the truck.

'Why isn't anyone returning fire?' I yelled at Dhofar somewhat rhetorically. As though on cue, the *jundi* started blazing away with a sound like the finale at a firework display. I peeked around the truck again – bullets were kicking up geysers of dust all over the side of the gas station – the figures were gone from the rooftop. The firing tapered off, replaced by the whine of approaching Strykers. I stood up, and walked around the truck as the ugly squat vehicles pulled into place in a rough line behind our cordon. A figure jumped down from the nearest one and strode over.

'Are you in charge of this goat-rope?'

Annoyed, I peered at this brash upstart. Contrary to popular perception, soldiers tend to look sharper than Marines in battle dress, and this one was a case in point: immaculate cammies, razor sunglasses, flight gloves, lightweight body armor with neatly arrayed magazine pouches, bloused boots and a weapon that looked brand new. I was filthy and disheveled and fuming.

'Who are you?' I spluttered.

The sartorial paragon laughed. 'Hey just giving you shit, man.' He held out his hand. 'Omar Jones, I'm the operations officer for 1/5. You must be Milburn right, Rocco told me about you.'

I shook his hand, suddenly at a loss for words. That didn't matter because Omar had enough for both of us.

'Brought our EOD dudes along – they'll take a look at the gas station, but I wouldn't be surprised if they don't find anything. That was the IED.'

Omar pointed to the hole in the road. 'The trigger man was on the roof, must have thought he had you, but clicked off too soon. Can't blame him, distance is hard to judge at that angle. Now he's pissed because you got away, so they pop off a few rounds, hoping to make good. One of those gents had a PKM – got a bolo out now for their vehicle, a black Opel.'

'Wow, you've got the Scooby Doo ending down pat.'

Omar cackled and slapped me on the shoulder 'Well, actually this works out well, Andy.'

'How's that?'

He gestured towards a group of four civilians standing by the ramp of his Stryker.

'Got the press today, and was worried we'd have nothing to show them. You know how it is, we get slammed every day, then a journo shows up and it's sleepy fucking hollow. This'll be a cool story, but we have to keep them away from the *jundi*. For some reason, we can't get the US media to say good things about the Iraqi Army, they always find the wrong cat who speaks English.' *Probably wise* I thought, looking at Dhofar.

Jones, I was to learn, was as competent as he was upbeat. He understood the importance of the advisor mission, and the challenges that we faced. It was he who had placed a liaison team in our headquarters to ensure that 1/5 was poised to bail us out of trouble when we needed it.

'Got to keep you guys alive,' he explained, 'because no one else wants your job.'

Rocco laughed when I told him the story during our customary bull session on the roof that evening. Usually it was just him and me, but that evening Rocco had invited the 1st Company commander, Mehdi's replacement, to join us. Major Aarmr had a ready smile, expressive brown eyes, and a fearsome reputation. A former Special Forces officer under Saddam, he now ran a network of sources that had enabled the battalion to roll up almost thirty mid-level insurgents in the previous month. When one of these sources had a change of heart and pulled a gun on him, Aarmr allegedly beat him senseless. Another story had him turning the tables on two *Muj* who tried to hit him in a drive-by shooting. As the story went, he jumped in his truck and gave chase, firing his pistol one handed out the window. He forced his attackers to crash their vehicle and, in the subsequent gun fight, killed one and wounded the other. Although probably exaggerated, the stories (about which he never commented) said much about his status in the eyes of the *jundi*.

'What did you do in the war, Aarmr?' I asked, as the three of us puffed on cigars, leaning against the parapet and looking out across the darkening city at a sky bruised vermillion by the last embers of the dying sun. A light breeze always picked up in the evening, cooling skin still hot from the day's punishing heat, and keeping at bay – for a precious hour or two – the hordes of mosquitos that came to replace the flies.

Aarmr demurred at first, but after Rocco and I insisted, told us his story. He had been in charge of a small group of Special Forces' soldiers tasked with delaying the Americans' approach on Baghdad.

'We linked up with a group of Fedayeen, and attacked the American column – they were Marines,' he said, nodding at me. 'We lost a group of Fedayeen but managed to destroy a tank. A few days later, one of my sergeants and I were tasked with blowing up a bridge across the Diyala River. We were hoping to wait until the first vehicles were crossing, but there was artillery fire and the sergeant blew it early.'

'You bastard!' I laughed, explaining that I had been on the other side when it happened.

He clasped my shoulder. 'Well *habibi*, now I'm glad that we didn't wait.'

After seeing all their vehicles destroyed by US aircraft, Aarmr had ordered the remainder of his men to don civilian clothes and disperse to fight another day. Some had joined the *Muj* and were still operating under his last instructions. Aarmr might have considered that line of work, but – fortunately for us – decided to join the IIF instead.

# Chapter 35

On Fridays, I accompanied Aarmr on patrol to various mosques throughout the city. He had started this routine to counter the pro-insurgent propaganda that, he claimed, many of the Imams were preaching. His soldiers would wait outside the gates of the chosen mosque and accost worshippers as they left after prayers. Their opening gambit, loosely translated, might sound something like this:

'*Y' ahkee*,' Hey brother, they would begin. 'Listen, we know what the Imam has been telling you guys, but you look too bright to believe that bullshit. We know all about this Imam and his Wahabi connections – he's probably going to end up in jail pretty soon. You don't want the same to happen to you right? Of course not. Who's going to look after your family? There are plenty of mosques in this city, why don't you find another one.'

The soldiers were also tasked with eliciting information, not by taking a blatant 'where-are-the-bad-guys?' approach, but by asking questions designed to give us a feel for what was going on in the area: the availability of work, food, water; their views of the coalition; and their concerns (security was invariably the answer). Occasionally the *jundi* would pick up what we called hard intelligence: names and locations of wanted individuals for instance, but such nuggets were uncommon. Most of the time it was simply a way to gain a better understanding of the area, more so than I could hope to glean by accompanying a US unit on a similar mission. I enjoyed Fridays. With Aarmr and his soldiers I saw parts of the city that few Americans would get to see.

Zuher often accompanied us on these junkets, glad to escape the dingy confines of the operations room. He would confer with Aarmr and his officers over the hood of one of our vehicles, scribbling in a large green ledger that he always carried with him, pausing every so often to translate the highlights to me. I would make notes, which became a report that we'd send to 1/5 entitled 'Prayer-time Atmospherics.'

The solders handed out leaflets that Zuher had made, depicting atrocities that the *Muj* had committed in Mosul against the local population. The leaflets included the number for a telephone tip line, manned in the JCC around the clock.

'The printing press is the greatest weapon in the armory of the modern commander,' T.E. Lawrence wrote, which is perhaps why US units were prohibited from distributing leaflets that had not been approved by a two-star general. We were authorized to kill people under the right circumstances, but using persuasive tactics to change their minds was considered too powerful a tool to leave in the hands of a battalion commander (though who better than he to understand the nuances of his area?) The Iraqi Army imposed no such restrictions and tactical commanders could use their imagination to influence the local population.

Because 3rd Battalion had earned a reputation for garnering good intelligence, we were not confined to Palestine, but were free to roam the city in search of problematic mosques. One of these was the Great Mosque of Al Nuri, which was nowhere near as grand-looking as its name suggested, but a plain sandstone building with one distinguishing feature: a leaning minaret which was referred to as Al Habna – the hunchback.

Zuher relayed to me the story from Sunni lore of how the minaret was blown askew by the wind of Mohammed's passage to heaven. When I pointed out the mosque was built 500 years after that event, he said that he should have known better than to waste his time explaining Islamic history to an infidel. Another officer, a Christian by the name of Major Talib (not to be confused with Taleb) told me that the minaret was bowing towards the Virgin Mary's tomb, which Iraqi Christians believe to be in Erbil.

Whatever its heritage, the Al Nuri mosque attracted a coterie of firebrand preachers whose amplified voices, guttural and threatening, we could hear from outside the courtyard walls; and when prayers ended, the worshippers would hurry past us with averted eyes. Nine years later, Abu Bakr al-Baghdadi, the leader of ISIS, would choose the Al Nuri mosque as the site from which to proclaim himself the Caliph of a new Muslim state whose army, he predicted, would conquer the entire Levant.

Towards the end of May I made a mistake that should by the laws of probability have resulted in my death, but led instead to the end of our role as IED hunters. It began while I was on patrol, with a call from Rocco, passing on the report of a nearby IED.

'This one looks legit,' Rocco said. 'It was spotted by a woman, who says that it's clearly visible.'

He gave me a description and the location, next to a school on a route we called Broadway (the previous US battalion had named everything in our area after places in New York).

We drove up Broadway and dismounted about 50 meters away from the location I had been given. Leaving the *jundi* in position around the vehicles, Staff Sergeant Graves and I approached the reported site: a shallow storm gutter that bisected the concrete median in the middle of the road. 'It's under a plastic bag,' Rocco had said. If we could verify the presence of a plastic bag in the gutter, that would be enough for EOD to respond.

We stopped about 20 meters away and looked up and down the gutter. There was nothing; we had found the only stretch of road in Iraq without a single discarded plastic bag.

Graves and I retraced our steps back to the vehicles, scanning the road from side to side. I spotted a burlap sack lying in the gutter and, without thinking, walked over and nudged it with my foot. The edge lifted, exposing two yellow wires now stretched across the side of my boot. We both saw it at the same time and froze.

'Run,' I yelled, and Graves took off at a flat sprint.

Recalling the incident afterwards, the strangest aspect (aside from my incredible stupidity) is that I cannot recall feeling fear, only the stark thought that I was about to disintegrate. By this stage in the war, most remotely detonated IEDs were also victim activated – hence my prediction.

By the book, I should have stayed exactly in that position until EOD arrived. Instead, as soon as I saw Graves reach the safety of a low wall just beyond our vehicles, I took off after him, boots pounding the tarmac, weapon bouncing against my legs, fists pumping, eyes fixed on the wall that now seemed distant. I rounded the vehicles, realizing numbly that I was still alive, and then pulled to a halt, not sure whether to be amused or incensed by what I saw. The *jundi* were crouching behind the wall, their fingers jammed in their ears like a scene from a Yosemite Sam.

EOD responded with unprecedented alacrity. The bomb disposal technician, a sergeant, was short and stocky and maintained a cheerful line of patter without actually looking cheerful. Only once did his tone and expression match when with a frown, he admonished me for my foolhardy move: 'Don't ever do that again, sir. Just fucking lie and say that you can see the IED. That's why I have this frigging robot, which my lovely assistant is now making ready.'

He leaned forward on the hood of his Humvee, using binoculars to peer at the burlap sack, which was all we could see of the IED some 50 meters away. Meanwhile, his assistant, a pasty-faced specialist with glasses so thick they made his eyes look enormous, unloaded the robot, which looked like a cluster of arm prosthetics mounted on a miniature tank chassis. He tested its motor using a control box and it moved back and forth with the sound of a kid's toy. Satisfied that it was functioning correctly, he placed it on the ground, and sat on a camp stool, the control box on his lap, peering at the screen.

The sergeant nudged the robot with his foot to point it in the right direction, and signaled to the specialist. We crouched together behind the Humvee, peering over the hood like mischievous kids setting up a prank. The robot churned across the stretch of wasteland that separated us from the IED, lumbering over garbage and tire ruts in the mud; then, midway towards its objective, it stopped, unresponsive to the specialist's desperate toggling.

'It's hot,' he explained, as though this were an unusual condition for Mosul in May. His glasses had misted over and sweat was dripping from his chin in an almost continuous stream. 'He doesn't like it when it's hot.'

'*It's* not a 'him'; *it's* an 'it'; *I'm* a 'him'. *I'm* the 'him' who has to do *its* work for it when *it* breaks down.'

It was as cogent an argument against personification as I have ever heard.

'Here, sir, give me a hand putting on my suit.' I helped him don the Kevlar outfit which resembled a green suit of armor. It was extraordinarily heavy, and we were both drenched by the time I lifted the deep-sea diver helmet onto his head.

I was feeling the familiar pressure in my throat: vicarious fear for the sergeant compounded by a sense of responsibility. He stalked out to where the robot had come to a halt, picking it up as though it was a recalcitrant dog refusing to come when called. The robot's tracks came to life and started churning. 'Turn it off!' the sergeant yelled at the specialist. He lumbered back to our position, retrieved a large bottle of drinking water and, with the specialist's assistance, fastened a small explosive charge to one end with deft moves of his hand. Returning to the robot, he clamped the bottle into one of its metal claws.

'I don't want to risk it breaking down again, so the recce's over. I'm going to use a water shot to disrupt the firing chain. We need to get under cover though because it could set the whole thing off.'

We checked to ensure that no one was nearer than 100 meters to the device, and moved the Humvee to a safe distance. A few minutes later with a pop and a spout of water that reminded me of the Coke and Mentos party game, the robot did its work. I helped the sergeant put on his helmet again and he walked out to examine the IED.

'It was dual primed – wired for remote detonation, but with an anti-handling device. Movement of the wires should have set off the switch,' he told me when he returned. 'Faulty connection probably, couldn't see anything else wrong, the detonator was attached so it should have gone off.'

The rounds were two 105mm artillery shells, enough to have turned Graves and me into manslaw.

'You were lucky,' he added unnecessarily.

Later that evening, after I had finished telling him the story, Rocco eyed me quietly for a few moments. 'I shouldn't have put us at risk looking for IEDs,' he said with characteristic humility. 'As for what happened today, Andy, a piece of advice from my own experience: when you stop feeling fear, it's time to go home.'

I wasn't sure that I had reached that stage yet, but I knew what he meant. Prolonged exposure to combat (and I realize that both prolonged and combat are relative terms) has an accordion effect on the nerves, which leads to a persistent state of heightened alert or its antithesis, complacency. And, as the signs at the exit to FOB Maurez warned us, complacency kills.

'Yeah, you're probably right,' I conceded, 'but I'm two weeks out from the Freedom Bird, so the end's in sight.'

'Don't tempt fate, brother.' But it was already too late.

# Chapter 36

In early June, we received a report that the news anchor from a local television station had been kidnapped. In the days that followed, Iraqi intelligence learned that Ansar Al Islam had abducted her, accusing her of pro-coalition bias. On the evening of June 7, Major Aarmr heard from one of his sources that she was being held in a specific neighborhood in Palestine, and that her kidnappers planned to move her two days hence.

Rocco and I sat down with Aarmr and Mohammed to plan a search of the neighborhood the following day.

'She is very famous here in Mosul,' Mohammed explained to us, 'it's important that we rescue her – not the Americans.' That made sense to me.

Falah agreed, and once he received permission from brigade to go ahead, I called Omar Jones, explained the situation, and requested a Stryker cordon around the neighborhood the following morning. Instead of giving him a specific time, I asked Omar to have the Strykers standing by – ready to launch with thirty minutes notice. To Americans, conditioned to plan these events in great detail covering all possible contingencies, this required a leap in faith. Omar didn't hesitate.

'You've got it, brother.'

In a US operation, the cordon would be in place before the search began, usually in the last hours of darkness. But it's near impossible to establish a cordon without alerting the entire neighborhood, and Aarmr was concerned that the kidnappers would move their prisoner as soon as they saw it moving into place. Aarmr, like most of his peers, had little faith in US cordons, and from what I had seen in Anbar and Mosul he was right – it was like trying to catch minnows in a volleyball net. So, we decided to send the searchers in first.

Before doing so, Aarmr wanted one more piece of information: a description of the hostage's location. That night, he got it; at least in Iraqi terms he did.

He blundered into our room like Kramer from Seinfeld. 'She's being held in a shop where they repair bicycles,' he said without preamble. He was clutching a piece of paper in his hand covered in handwriting; he raised it to the light and peered at it.

'Or a place where they make—' Aarmr mimed putting on a pair of glasses. 'An optician's.'

'Yes – an optician's,' he squinted at the paper again, 'or a place where women sell themselves.'

'A brothel?' I joined in the game of charades.

'Yes – where they sell themselves to men.'

'Well that narrows things down.'

'Do you know the exact location of this rather eclectic shop?' Rocco asked.

Aarmr shook his head. 'No, but I know the neighborhood.' He produced a map that we had given him: it was a large scale aerial photograph of Palestine upon which map grids had been superimposed. Aarmr had drawn a 500-meter diameter circle with felt tip pen around an area called Al Intisar, a Kurdish enclave in an otherwise Sunni neighborhood.

'There can't be more than one or two places like that in this area. Tomorrow morning early, I am going to take a patrol to find it. I have been given the name of a street where we can start.'

'Aren't you concerned about tipping them off?' I asked.

'No, it will be just the one patrol, and we go through that area all the time,' he replied.

It was one of a handful of times when we weren't exactly sure what was happening, but went along with the Iraqi plan because they would need us if something went wrong. It was better to be pulled along in their wake, than to be constantly prodding them to do things our way. 'Better the Arabs do it tolerably than that you do it perfectly,' T.E. Lawrence had written eighty years earlier.

The next morning, we gathered around Aarmr's truck to go over the plan before setting out: Rocco, me, Sergeant Reyes, Doc, Dhofar the interpreter and Lieutenant Hamid, one of Aarmr's platoon commanders. Aarmr briefed the route, dismount point and actions once we arrived at our destination. The intent was to locate the bicycle store-optician-brothel by questioning people who lived and worked in the same neighborhood, beginning in a specific street that Aarmr seemed to think was the best bet.

The previous day, Reyes had received a small video camera as a birthday present from his sister, which he now taped to his helmet. In the days before Go-Pro miniature cameras became commonplace, this was a novelty, and, as an aspiring filmmaker, Reyes was hoping to get footage that he might subsequently be able to use.

I decided to ride in the back of one of the trucks, and with delighted assistance from the *jundi*, clamored over the protective metal plate welded to the tailgate. It was a rocky ride, Mosul's streets were riddled with potholes and the Nissans lacked suspension. I clutched the top of the driver's window frame for balance, half listening to the news from Radio Freedom blaring from the cab. It was June 8 2005: there was a brief update of the Michael Jackson trial (a topic that had sparked a spirited debate among the advisors the night before with Gene of all people heatedly maintaining Jackson's innocence) and then a chirpy specialist came on to remind listeners to drink water: 'Mosul is hot this time of year,' she advised us.

We pulled into Al Intisar and slowed down. It was like any other neighborhood in Palestine: shops lined the narrow street, the shopkeepers sitting among their wares on the sidewalk haggling with passers-by; a group of men squatted together listlessly under the shade of a tree, drinking tea and smoking; two stray dogs rooted through a pile of garbage by the side of the road; children chased a soccer ball down the street; a squad of geese strutted past the truck as we dismounted. There were a few waves, a laconic exchange of greetings, but otherwise little reaction to our arrival.

The *jundi* ambled into patrol formation; Aarmr spoke to them sharply, then took the lead at a fast pace to a house some 100 meters down the road, and knocked on the door. A man opened it, disheveled and unshaven, blinking in the sun as though he had just been woken up. He and Aarmr stepped into the shadow of the front hallway and had a brief discussion, then Aarmr emerged, and, without a word, beckoned us to follow him.

At the next house, Aarmr disappeared around the back with a squad of soldiers, directing Hamid to approach the front. Rocco and I followed two *jundi* towards the front door, squeezing past a car parked in the narrow driveway. The first *jundi* rapped on the metal door, then – upon receiving no answer – he swung it open and entered. Inside the threshold was another door, glass paneled, a common configuration in Iraqi households. As the soldier reached to open it, the glass exploded in a sudden volley of gunfire and he dropped to the ground. The next burst caught the *jundi* behind him, striking him square in the chest, hurling him off the step and into the driveway on his back.

Rocco had stepped to the side of the doorway and so escaped the stream of bullets, but I was trapped between the car and the driveway wall, directly in the line of fire. The video from Reyes' helmet camera shows the wall by my head erupting in spurts of shattered masonry. I flinch and move my head instinctively to avoid the stream of bullets, looking for cover – but there is none. A panicked *jundi* pushes past me in a primal effort to escape. Reyes yells at me to fall back behind a stanchion that borders the entry of the driveway, and I manage to do so, as rounds kick up spouts of pulverized concrete around me.

The whole frenzied melee lasted less than thirty seconds, but if Reyes had told me that he timed it at twenty minutes, I would have believed him. I was in a state of mental extremis, reacting, but otherwise beyond conscious thought.

It was only when I found cover that conscious memory returns. At that moment, every soldier within earshot opened fire in unison, blazing away at the building from all directions, oblivious to my position in their line of fire.

'What are you shooting at?' I yelled. It was an absurd thing to ask, but it's captured on film so I can't deny it. 'Cease fire,' I added, with an anger born from fear. Reyes and the others picked up the call, and the shooting trailed off.

'Did anyone see the fucker?' I asked, referring to the shooter. Rocco bent down to check the *jundi* lying prone at his feet. He was not only alive but unharmed, having caught the full blast in the chest, squarely in the center of the protective Kevlar plate embedded in his body armor.

'Get up,' Rocco hissed unsympathetically; the soldier scrambled to his feet and scuttled out of the driveway.

'Is anyone hurt?' Doc yelled.

'I don't think so,' Reyes responded. But Rocco and I had seen the lead soldier go down. Without saying anything we both moved toward the doorway, strewn with broken glass. Rocco looked over his shoulder to check that I was with him, and stepped across the threshold reaching towards the inner door, which was slightly ajar. I don't know if I hesitated. Having seen two men shot in as many seconds on the same spot that we now stood, it is probable. Maybe just a moment to nerve myself, to gird the loins.

Rocco didn't hesitate, of that I am sure. For him it was reflexive: an automatic response to the realization that one of our soldiers was still inside. And once he moved, I was committed. I stepped behind him – weapon up, safety catch off, finger on the trigger – ready to shoot when the door opened. He reached out to seize the door handle and yanked it open.

The room, a square hallway, was dark and murky from cordite smoke. It was empty aside from the wounded *jundi* lying on his back in the middle of the floor, the blood pooling around his legs. Four rooms faced onto the hallway, all four doors partially open. The shooters (the volume of fire indicated more than one) must have withdrawn into one of those rooms and would have us in their sights if we ventured further into the hallway.

The *jundi* lifted his head and looked at us, eyes wide in a brute expression of pain and fear. Rocco put a finger to his lips, edged forward and whispered. '*Wen* Wahabi?' Where are the Wahabi?

Without taking his eyes off us, the soldier pointed towards a half-open door in the far-left corner of the hallway. Rocco pulled out a grenade and, signaling me to cover him, plucked off the pin, dropping it with a noise so loud it seemed to echo. Then, in a single smooth movement, he stepped forward and rolled the grenade underarm through the opening in the door. It was a good throw – if he had missed it would have bounced back on the *jundi*. We both crouched against the outside door frame covering our ears, I had forgotten to count, and was just thinking that the grenade must have been a dud when it exploded with a noise like a vault door being slammed.

As the echo of the explosion died away we both fired into the room, shooting blindly through the crack in the door, now purging smoke into the hallway. Then: Rocco covered me while I crossed the fatal funnel to grab the *jundi* by the arms and haul him towards the front door, leaving a trail of blood on the concrete floor. Surging with adrenalin, I shot backwards through the doorway into the arms of Reyes and the Doc. They took the wounded man from me and carried him down the driveway, yelling for a truck. I re-entered the house.

As I crept back across the hallway to rejoin Rocco, who was still covering the room, I caught a glimpse of movement out of the corner of my eye – there was someone in the room to my immediate left. Cautiously, I pushed open the door and there was a woman, diminutive in a brown abaya, and obviously terrified. Without ceremony, I took her by the arm and propelled her towards the front door. It didn't occur to me at that moment that she was the hostage – or even that we had stumbled on the exact place we had been looking for.

Only seconds had passed since the grenade explosion. Every moment we delayed clearing the room would give its occupants longer to recover. Without word or signal, Rocco and I popped around the door into the room together. It was empty. There was a pool of blood on the cement floor and a trail of crimson splashes that led across the room to an open window, swinging half off its hinges above a metal bed frame. I peered out the window – it overlooked an alley down which Aarmr was now walking, pushing a man in front of him.

'Got one,' he called, 'the other two got away, but they were both hurt, lots of blood.'

Rocco and I cleared the other rooms on the ground floor without incident though each showed signs of recent habitation: blankets on the floor, bowls of food and bottles of water. Hamid passed us in the hallway leading a line of *jundi* towards the concrete steps to clear the upper floor.

I walked out front; a gaggle of soldiers were standing around the kneeling prisoner, as Aarmr pushed a cell phone to his ear. Remembering the scene at the power station, I parted the *jundi* and stepped behind the detainee where Aarmr could see me.

'What's going on?' I asked. Aarmr held his finger up for me to be quiet, and whispered in my ear.

'He's calling his friends. Going to get them to meet up with him somewhere nearby.'

The first call was unsuccessful. Aarmr hung up and squatted in front of the detainee, staring into his face as he interrogated him.

The insurgent was wearing baggy trousers of the type that Kurdish men often wear, and a stained white T-shirt. He didn't seem afraid, as he answered Aarmr's rapid fire questions. Aarmr tried dialing again. This time someone answered at the other end, and the prisoner blurted out a few staccato sentences before Aarmr sent him reeling with a cuff across the back of the head. Aarmr, furious, grabbed the phone, raising his hand for another blow but caught my eye and lowered it.

At that moment Hamid called from the driveway. He and his soldiers had discovered a trove of insurgent material – explosives, weapons, ammunition and body armor – which they carried down the stairs and stacked in the driveway. Aarmr's mood changed, and he went to check on the former hostage who was now sitting in the cab of one of the trucks being waited upon by solicitous *jundi*. I couldn't raise 1/5 on the radio so I passed a quick summary of events to the battalion's liaison team back at the hospital, asking them to relay it directly to Jones.

The other two platoons from Aarmr's company arrived and began to search the neighborhood; I could see them down the street moving swiftly from house to house, clambering over walls and climbing onto rooftops. 'They're like fucking cats,' observed Rocco.

We started to walk down the street to watch the search.

'So here's a hot-wash for what happened,' Rocco said. 'We shambled up to that building like it was a soft hit, no cordon in place, QRF not pre-staged,' he shook his head in disgust. 'What a complete shit-show – we've all become complacent. And yet—. We rescued the hostage and captured at least one of the bad guys and a shit load of material. I've been on operations that were planned down to a gnat's ass that ended up worse than this one.'

I retraced the morning's events in my mind. We'd allowed ourselves to be pulled along in the slipstream of Aarmr's enthusiasm; but if we had done everything by the book, who knows what the outcome would have been? The *Muj* relied on extensive networks for their security and always got word of an impending operation before it started. But this time they had been as surprised as us; and we'd managed to gain the upper hand. It might have ended disastrously – but it did no good to dwell on these things. You count yourself lucky, learn from your mistakes, and move on.

We rounded a corner and Rocco pointed at a store front – there was a stack of bicycles out front in various states of disrepair.

'Let's check it out,' he laughed.

We were greeted like old friends by the proprietor, a jovial chubby man who ushered us to a table in front of the store. It was indeed a bicycle repair shop but also a grocery store and a tea shop. No sign of spectacles though, or of hookers for that matter.

Rocco and I bought Cokes and a box of Rich Tea biscuits, a brand that I remembered from my childhood in England, and chatted with the owner in pidgin Arabic. The Coke, icy cold and tangy sweet, cascaded down my parched throat. Even the stale biscuits tasted good.

Maybe five minutes later, we heard the distinctive high-pitched drone of diesel engines, and a column of Strykers came to a halt in the middle of the street; a familiar figure leaped down from the lead vehicle and strode towards us.

Rocco waved.

'Omar – what a surprise. Come and join us.'

Jones stepped onto the sidewalk and took it all in. Rocco and I both had our feet up on chairs, bottles of Coke in our hands; the packet of Rich Teas was almost empty and we were both covered in crumbs. I realized that it must look as though we had activated the QRF to provide security for our picnic, but was too tired to explain. Rocco was enjoying the spectacle of Omar Jones at a loss for words.

Zuher heard from his sources that one of the insurgents who had escaped out the window died later from his wounds; and that the other, seriously injured, was being treated in a safe house somewhere outside the city.

By the time we returned to base the event had become big news. Brigadier Amir and Falah appeared on Nineveh television with the hostage to tell the story of the rescue. Aarmr scoffed as we watched the show on the flickering set in the operations room, but Rocco scolded him. It was the kind of story that the Iraqi security forces needed in those dark days, and who were we to take that away from them.

Reyes's video appeared on television in the United States, which led to the History Channel covering the story as part of a series called '*Iraq's Most Wanted.*'

My tour came to an end in late June 2005. The night before I left, the Iraqi officers treated me to a farewell dinner, after which they presented me with mementoes: a ring from Zuher who told me that it had been blessed by an Imam in his native Baghdad, a knife from Aarmr, and a leather wall hanging depicting the Virgin Mary from Talib the Christian officer with an inscription on the back: 'I pray that God will return you safe to your family, from your friend Talib.' I was touched, and knowing that their war had no foreseeable end, I struggled for the right words.

As I was writing this book, Zuher contacted me to let me know that he had just been promoted to general; a milestone that augurs well for the future of the Iraqi Army.

Rocco, Reyes, Doc, Gene and Lefevre drove me to Maurez in the two Humvees that we had recently acquired. Burke Whitman ordered Rocco to ensure that I rode in an armored vehicle 'He's run out of lives,' was his comment – and I had to agree that he might be right. 'See you back in the World, brother,' Rocco said as we hugged. I was sorry to say good bye. In the military, I have met lots of like-minded people whose company I enjoy, it's one of the reasons that I have remained in uniform so long, but Rocco had become one of a small circle of close friends.

An hour later, sitting in the back of a Hercules C-130 heading for Kuwait, the Air Force crew chief leant down to yell in my ear. 'Hey sir, we just got word to put down in Balad to pick up some KIA. Your call whether you want to continue on this flight. The other two guys have decided to get off and catch another one.'

'I'll stay.'

It was dark by the time that we touched down in Balad to collect our grim cargo: four body bags loaded aboard with reverence but none of the ceremonial trappings that would later characterize such events. Once we were airborne, the crew chief and loadmasters disappeared up front, leaving me to share the darkness with the bodies of four young Americans who, unlike me, would never see home again.

When we landed in Kuwait, I boarded a United Airlines flight to Washington DC and slept the entire way, awaking only as we touched down in Dulles airport. Later that evening, unable to sleep, I walked from my apartment to a nearby bar in Old Town, Alexandria. There, surrounded by a boisterous crowd singing along with a mock-Irish band, I felt utterly alone, unreasonably resentful that life for those around me appeared so untouched by the war.

# Chapter 37

Jessica moved into my apartment a day or two after my return, along with two Jack Russell terriers, a cat, and a potted Ficus tree – an instant family. I was due to begin as a student at the Marine Corps' School of Advanced Warfighting in July a month hence, and in the meantime returned to work at CSW in Quantico. In my absence, the advisor course had been run by a Major Warren 'Lefty' Wright, improving by leaps and bounds from its primitive early days, and my role at CSW during those few weeks was undemanding. I was happy to be back, content to have one of those rare occasions in the Marine Corps when you aren't running full tilt, enjoying the time with Jessica and my new-found domestic routine. But you wouldn't have known it from the way that I was acting.

'Andy, I think that you need to get help,' Jess said to me one day soon after my return, as I stumbled bleary-eyed into the kitchen in search of coffee. We had gone into Old Town the previous day for brunch, which was the last thing I remembered. Apparently I had ordered a series of martinis with the buffet, and when it came time to leave, was barely able to stand up. Poor Jessica had had to help me downstairs into a cab in front of a crowd of midday diners.

'I'm OK, just haven't developed a tolerance for alcohol yet, I guess.'

I didn't feel as though I had a problem, of course. I wasn't an angry drunk, I didn't cause scenes, I just drank until I fell asleep. I would get into work early enough to get in a rigorous workout session, sweating out the previous night's excesses, but Lefty had noticed, and was too good a friend to let it go unpassed.

'You can't keep doing this, bro',' he said to me kindly. 'If I notice, so will others; you'll end your career. And, more importantly, you owe it to Jess to get your shit together.' I had just confided in Lefty, who was a decade older than me, that Jess and I intended to get married. He was right, and so I stopped drinking – well, reduced drastically – a decision that was reaffirmed when, a month or so later (*after* we were married), we found out that Jessica was pregnant.

Neither of us was in a state of mind to plan an elaborate wedding, so on June 30 2005, we married in the chapel at Quantico, with a small handful of friends in attendance, and Brian Fitzgibbons as my best man. We hosted a reception afterwards in our tiny apartment, serving take-out sushi and pizza. Despite almost forgetting our marriage license before the ceremony, and then failing to hire a photographer, two oversights of which Jessica reminds me from time to time, it was a blissfully happy occasion.

By now, Jessica, a newly minted second lieutenant, was halfway through her internship as an occupational therapist – an experience that had been in some ways more grueling than mine. The first half of 2005 had seen a steady rise in the number of serious casualties returning from Iraq. The first stop for nearly all was Walter Reed, and Jessica, along with her fellow interns, found themselves dealing with injuries that surpassed, in spate and scale, the medical staff's previous experience.

In Iraq, ten soldiers were wounded for every one that died, a higher ratio of injury to death than in any previous war. Body armor, rapid evacuation times, and improved medical equipment and techniques all played a part in saving lives that would previously have been lost. Jess and her colleagues were treating men and women who had suffered horrific burns, debilitating brain injury and multiple amputations, while trying to find their feet as fledgling occupational therapists amidst the hustle of a hospital at war. Two of Jess's patients had been wounded in Mosul: one shot in the head by a sniper and rendered permanently non-compos mentis, the other blinded in a VBIED attack. Knowing that I was in the same city must have added to her concerns.

For those in combat losing a comrade is upsetting; but once the casualty helicopter takes off, they are gone from sight, if not from mind. Jessica witnessed the prolonged tragic aftermath of combat, the devastation it wrought on the loved ones of those who returned changed forever. For most casualties, medical advances enabled them to achieve a level of mobility that would have been inconceivable for previous generations. But for the seriously brain-injured, deprived of any imaginable quality of life, and for whom no amount of support could ease the long term emotional burden born by their loved ones, I could not help but wonder to what end their lives were saved.

'It's not my role to play God,' a surgeon explained to me after I had visited one of my former Marines, his patient, who was horrifically burned, brain-damaged and without legs. He was right, of course. But that didn't make it any easier to bear.

In many ways, the sustained courage that Jess and her colleagues in the medical profession showed day after day was more impressive than all the adrenalin-fueled moments of battlefield bravery that I had witnessed over the previous seven months.

In early July 2005, I began the school year as a student at the Marine Corps' School of Advanced Warfighting, a course designed to teach a small group of selected majors the art of planning operations. I say 'art' because the Marine Corps' approach was not to teach a formulaic course heavy on technique, but rather to encourage a way of thinking that would enable planners to tackle complex problems (a counter-insurgency for instance) without resorting to checklists. My peers, including officers from Australia, Holland, Canada and Italy in addition to sixteen US Marines, were intimidatingly bright and fun company. I learned as much – perhaps more – from them as I did from the curriculum. Fresh from combat, thrown together with like-minded individuals, and responsible only for ourselves, we made the most of it, with a social schedule almost as demanding as the course itself.

In making selections for SAW, the Marine Corps appears to have found the right alchemy: nearly every one of the sixteen Marines who attended the course that year was subsequently selected for command. One, Mario Carazo a Cobra pilot, was killed in Afghanistan.

At SAW we studied the battles of Napoleon and the great wars of the twentieth century. We traipsed through the woods and fields of Virginia, Maryland and Pennsylvania tracing the footsteps of the armies of Northern Virginia and the Potomac. It was a long way away from Fallujah or Mosul – and I found it therapeutic. But none of us could really escape the war; we were tied to it by our recent experiences and the prospect of our return. I doubt that anyone of us consciously wanted to escape. It was something that we shared with one another but with few others among our countrymen.

'Fourteen Marines killed yesterday, but you'd have to search on the internet to find out what happened,' commented Dave Nathanson to me one day. Dave, who occupied the next carrell to mine in the student common room, had served with me in 7th Marines. His tone was more incredulous, than angry or bitter.

'Is this a country at war? It doesn't feel that way,' our Canadian officer Carl Michaud commented during an out-of-class discussion (we seldom talked about the war in class).

And when, during a visit to Congress, a senator whom we were scheduled to meet, stood us up, Trent Scott, an Australian, was more outraged then any of us.

'He couldn't even be bothered to poke his head around the door to say "thank you for your service." That should tell you how important your war is to these people.'

In any case, none of us wanted to waste time in useless introspection, this was our chance to enjoy time with our families and let off some steam. In fact, as the class president, I was one of the few with any responsibility, which was to keep track of my classmates. In this, I failed dismally. During our trip to visit the battlefields of Europe, I lost track of the number of times when I would give the thumbs-up to Colonel Jerry Driscoll, the long-suffering school director, indicating that we had everyone, only to look out the back of the bus window as we started off to see a student stumbling half-naked after us. In the end I resorted to assigning everyone a buddy to look after; but with Marine field-grade officers, even this foolproof technique didn't always work.

Despite this insight into my own leadership failings, SAW was probably the most enjoyable year of my career. And for those Marines to whom this may appear to be a blasphemic repudiation of the joy of command, I offer that command is invariably a rewarding experience, but not necessarily fun.

As mentioned, soon after we were married, Jessica discovered that she was pregnant, and as she neared the end of her internship, we both managed to get orders for Hawaii thus ensuring that we would be together – which was by no means a guarantee for cross-service couples.

In February 2006, I travelled to the UK to be with my father who had been admitted into hospital seriously ill with pneumonia. Dad, then 90, was a driven individual, not always easy to get along with, impatient, occasionally overbearing but always devoted to his family. His father had been killed in the First World War, leaving his mother and two small children to fend for themselves. With memories of his own impoverished childhood he determined that my two sisters and I would have a better start in life. He'd also had a rough war. One of my abiding memories from childhood was waking at night to hear him yelling in his sleep, his voice booming through the wall that separated my parents' room from mine. 'It's just your father having bad dreams again,' my mother would shrug, 'lots of people have them from the war.'

Now, as I sat by his bedside watching him draw bubbling breaths through a plastic mask, I wished that I had reached out to thank him for all that he had done for me. Now that it was too late, I was left confronted by my own selfishness.

My father died a day after I arrived, but not before opening his eyes and grasping my hand in a brief moment of recognition. I was thrilled and devastated at the same time.

Three weeks later I was sitting by another hospital bed several thousand miles away. I had received a call from Jessica's gynecologist at Tripler Army hospital in Honolulu to say that the baby had stopped growing and would have to be rescued by Cesarean operation. By the time I arrived in Hawaii ten hours later, Marcus had been born and was lying in an incubator in the natal intensive care unit – a tiny birdlike figure at the center of a web of tubes.

In such situations it is probably common to try to bargain with God. I did, promising anything in return for a healthy child. In my darkest moments I wondered if this was not some kind of payback for my failure to prevent a father's death that night in Mosul.

Jessica took it all with an equanimity that I found inspiring. The only time that I saw her upset was when we walked in to the natal intensive care unit one morning to find that Marcus had a feeding tube in his head, the only part of him that had not yet been needled. Her expression alone had the attending staff raise their hands as though to ward off a blow.

Slowly, over the course of a few weeks, Marcus gained enough weight for the hospital to release him into our care. Taking him home for the first time was a euphoric feeling for both of us. He was still so small that he appeared to disappear in his bassinet, and it was not easy leaving him to return to Quantico for the last few months of SAW.

# Chapter 38

Upon graduation from SAW I headed to Hawaii to begin my new job in the war plans division of Marine Forces Pacific (MARFORPAC) at Camp Smith, just up the road from where Jessica was working at Tripler Army Hospital. Marcus now three months old, still under-sized and somewhat sickly, attended day care in the same hospital which allowed Jess to check on him throughout the day.

My initial task at MARFORPAC was to rewrite the Marine Corp's plan for the next Korean War. The scale of such a war beggared imagination, and I always felt that it would be such an all-consuming conflagration as to render my plan irrelevant. 'It will pretty much be a come-as-you-are party,' was how my predecessor described it. Nevertheless, I gave it my very best effort, spending long hours studying maps and photographs of the designated Marine area of operations and visiting Korea some dozen or so times.

My assignment to the plans division of a headquarters was intended to be my payback tour for having attended SAW. It turned out to be a lot of fun, thanks largely to the group of officers who shared my section of the salt mine at MARFORPAC. Colonel Chris Blanchard, the plans division chief, was recovering from a serious heart condition that had prevented him from taking command, but bore his frustrations with grace. He kept a light but steady hand on the helm, while protecting his planners from the random predations of a highly eccentric commanding general. My fellow planners, Mark Hashimoto, Thad Trapp and John Sappenfield, were all cut from the same cloth: highly intelligent and competent, but with an irrepressible sense of fun. Thad would later command a battalion in the adjacent sector to mine in Iraq.

Jess and I had bought a house that fronted onto a golf course in Waikele, a scenic neighborhood overlooking Pearl Harbor. Everything seemed to be going well. But I was stumbling again over thoughts that wouldn't go away. I felt constantly on edge such that even minor frustrations angered me and left me feeling helpless. Jess and I had got into the habit of arguing about ridiculous things.

Marcus suffered from frequent bouts of asthma, a probable legacy, the doctor explained, of his difficult birth. During one of these periods I was sitting by his bedside in hospital when his little supine figure became that of the boy whom I had seen dead in a Baghdad street.

On another occasion, a flight attendant woke me to say that I had been yelling in my sleep. Over her shoulder, I was embarrassingly aware of the other passengers peering at me down the aisle. In an effort to stem disruptive thoughts, I threw myself into an intensive physical training program: early morning cross fit work-outs, interval training up and down the steep hill upon which Camp Smith perched, and lunchtime sessions with MARFORPAC's fight club.

That summer when the Marine Corps released the list of selectees for battalion command, I was on it. There are only twenty-four infantry battalions in the Marine Corps and several hundred Marine infantry lieutenant colonels, so I was genuinely in awe at having been given this opportunity. Chris Woodbridge summed up in one pithy phrase the right way to respond to this honor, 'Now earn it.' I have always suffered to some extent from imposter syndrome, believing that I have been selected for advancement simply because those making the decision have made a mistake. My greatest fear now was that someone would notice that something was wrong with me and reverse the board's decision. The more I worried about it, the nearer I came to making it a reality. On one occasion while at a conference in Quantico, a three-star general asked a small group of us a question about the war. Someone deflected the question to me, and I found myself stuttering hopelessly, unable to complete a coherent sentence. Lieutenant General Van Riper came to my rescue. 'Let me help Andy out,' he began, going on to give an answer that I wished I could have delivered myself. The conversation continued but I noticed Van Riper eyeing me curiously throughout.

Whatever the party line about combat stress – that it is an understandable condition, not something to be ashamed of – the truth was, and remains, that any such diagnosis jars with the Marine ethos. It wasn't something that I was prepared to admit even to myself. And my background reinforced the belief that conflated symptoms of stress with weakness. I remembered evenings in Hong Kong as a child, listening to my father and his friends regale each other with war stories, all of them apparently funny, over bottomless glasses of gin and tonic. Maybe that's what his generation did for therapy. They had been through far worse than I and handled it without fuss. I remembered Rocco's comment about seeing things that would stay with us a long time. *That's all it will take*, I thought, *time*.

In November of 2007, I took command of 1st Battalion, 3rd Marines; the Lava Dogs, the same battalion to which I had been attached in Fallujah.

Rocco came to Hawaii for my change of command and stayed with us for a week. At the reception I found him sitting at a table with the battalion's junior officers, not holding forth in the sententious manner one might expect from a seasoned field grade officer, but involved instead in an earnest two-way discussion about counter-insurgency tactics. That was Rocco.

Like any new commander, I was brimming with ideas, which I bounced off him during long runs and after-dinner discussions on the back porch. After a year in Iraq, I thought that he'd be eager to resume his life as a script writer in Los Angeles, but, of course, I was wrong.

'Your lieutenants tell me that 3rd Marine Division is deploying advisor teams to Afghanistan,' he said, as we made inroads into the bottle of vintage Jameson's that he'd given me.

'Can you get me on to one of them? I know how parochial you Marines can be, so I'll need someone to go to bat for me.'

'I don't know, man. Can you hang with a bunch of Marines?'

Rocco had a greater concern. 'My only reservation is that Afghanistan has been so quiet. It might be less exciting than a deployment to New Jersey.'

'We took our eye off the ball in Afghanistan, but the Taliban haven't gone anywhere. I'm pretty sure that they'll soon bring the level of violence up to your expectations.' I didn't need to ask him why he wanted to go. We'd spent enough time together for questions like that to be redundant.

'I've always felt that Afghanistan made more sense than Iraq,' Rocco said, staring across the moonlit golf course that extended from our back patio. 'As a question of policy, I mean. When you talk about inspiration and funding, one country holds the smoking gun for 9/11, and it isn't Iraq. But we invaded Iraq because we just couldn't bring ourselves to go up against Saudi Arabia.'

It was quite a statement coming from someone who had invested so much in the war but, like many of us, Rocco didn't allow himself to ponder for too long the dissonance between the war's nebulous origins and his desire to be part of it.

The next day I called Lieutenant Colonel Jay Senter, the 3rd Marine Division personnel officer to get Rocco on the rolls of a Marine advisor team bound for Afghanistan. Jay, as was his wont, made it easy: 'If you say he's a good guy, your word's good enough for us.' And with that, he made it happen. That was Jay: quietly competent without fuss or fanfare.

I broke the news to a delighted Rocco. 'Be careful what you wish for,' I joked as we clanked tumblers.

In the face of a burgeoning civil war in Iraq, the President had decided to double down on the US troop commitment by increasing the number of units deployed there, a move that became known as the Surge. It now appeared that this strategy might be succeeding, as indicated by a downward turn in the number of attacks (such statistics, invariably displayed in *PowerPoint*, were the military's coin of the realm in Iraq).

Even in Anbar there were signs that the tribal sheikhs, tired of Al Qaeda's indiscriminate brutality, were amenable to collaborating with the Marines (but not with the Government of Iraq, which one later described to me as being a 'nest of Shia vipers'.)

This Sunni shift became known as the Anbar awakening, but there was one area of Anbar that remained shrouded in the darkest of nights. East of Fallujah, on the very edge of the province, lay a town called, with unwitting irony, Karma. A succession of Marine battalions had been badly mauled there over the years with little to show in return. Karma was a dark place, its sullen population and unlit streets redolent with menace.

First Battalion Third Marines was scheduled to deploy to Karma the following summer.

# Chapter 39

A few days after taking command, I gathered my company commanders together in my office.

The battalion had just received a cohort of some 600 Marines fresh from the school of infantry, and it was going to be a challenge to get them ready to deploy in six months, even more so to keep them out of trouble amidst the temptations of downtown Honolulu.

I drew three circles on a whiteboard, labelling them *competence, cohesion* and *mindset*. With so little time available, I explained, all activity must contribute to one of these three areas. If it didn't we simply wouldn't do it.

Under *competence*, we came up with a catalogue of areas on which to focus: urban patrolling, counter-IED, tactical questioning, convoy operations, reaction to ambush, cordon and search – the list seemed endless. We needed to master all of them; but I recognized that these tactical actions would not, by themselves, enable us to make headway against the insurgency. To do that we would need to use our knowledge of the local area to get one step ahead of the enemy. We had to figure out, for instance, an approach to intelligence collection and dissemination that was immediately useful at company level and below. And not just information focused on the enemy, but also the nuances of community and tribe that were all important in Iraq.

To that end, my commanders and staff developed the concept of forming intelligence cells at the company level, manned by infantrymen we had cross-trained as intelligence specialists, plus one or two Marines who were the genuine article. Marines on patrol should be primed to collect intelligence instead of simply trolling along trying not to get blown up. But in order to make this method work, they needed to be given specific things to look for. That was the job of the intelligence cell, who would brief every patrol before it departed, and debrief it upon its return.

*Mindset* encompassed morale but also much more. Combat stress had already been identified as being a significant problem by this stage in the war, and we looked for ways to use training to bolster the resilience of our young charges: to develop in them a bulletproof mind, was the analogy we used.

*Mindset* also captured our responsibility as Marines to adhere to the rules of warfare whatever the provocation. 'We fight with the values that we represent – we don't adopt those of your enemy,' I would tell the Marines, remembering my own brushes with the urge for vengeance.

In November 2005, after losing one of their comrades to an IED, a squad of Marines was involved in the unlawful killing of 24 Iraqi civilians in the town of Haditha. When the news broke, I overheard my boss, a Marine colonel, assure his wife, "Well, of course they didn't do it." Part of me envied his cheerful naïveté, but I had witnessed firsthand the corrosive effect that sustained exposure to violence and fear can have on previously held moral convictions. I knew that under the right circumstances, almost anyone is capable of committing a war crime. Those circumstances had come together for me on a fire-swept street in Fallujah, when I found myself balling my fists as two detainees were led past the bodies of the two Marines whom I had just seen them kill. I wanted those Iraqis dead. I learned then firsthand how combat can make good people do bad things, which is exactly why it's so important to reinforce the message that it's not okay to do so.

In the aftermath of Haditha, the commander of the unit involved was relieved of his duties. A year later, I listened with a group of fellow battalion commanders as then Lieutenant General James Mattis explained to us why he had made that decision. "As a leader, you can't be a gray man," Mattis said. "Those of you who are introverts need to change or find another profession, because if you aren't aggressive about establishing ethical standards, someone else will fill that vacuum. Our Marine hymn reminds us to keep our honor clean. And the consequences of failing to do so, for our cause and for the young men and women involved, will be profound and irreversible."

I wrote his words down at the time, and with the benefit of experience remain convinced of their truth. When a leader, through his actions or inaction, grants his subordinates unrestricted license to kill, he neglects his responsibility for their welfare and undermines the cause for which they are risking their lives. Moral injury can be every bit as disabling as physical or other, psychological wounds.

And the 'all's fair in war' argument backfires when a civilian population seeks revenge against an occupying army that treats it with ruthless disdain. Being subjected to brutality tends to strengthen a person's resolve and nurture a desire for revenge. The Haditha killings were widely covered by the Arab media and became a rallying cry for our enemies.

Encouraging Marines to adhere to the rules of war has to involve more than simply giving them lectures on morality and classes on the law of armed conflict. In Iraq, a war as vicious as any, it was common for units to be imbued with a hatred for the enemy. In so highly charged an atmosphere only the uncompromising values of a strong leader will prevent the collective moral safety net from rotting away.

Your moral resolve sags under the experience of combat in a place like Iraq: fatigue from lack of sleep and the enervating effort of lugging body armor, weapons, and equipment in breathless heat; persistent exposure to a culture that appeared to exalt brutality; and, usually the catalyst, the frontal-lobe numbing effect of fear, grief, and white-hot anger. I had experienced it myself, despite having two decades on my Marines, and degrees in philosophy and law to boot. How do you take an 18-year-old and build up enough credit in his moral account that he can suffer a sudden debit and still remain solvent? There are no silver bullets, so you do everything you can. By bolstering the moral aspect of his adopted culture as a United States Marine; by explaining that his decisions will have consequences; and by exposing him beforehand, as much as is possible, to the pressures of combat.

We designed decision games; scenarios that platoon commanders would discuss with their Marines, encouraging them to think through these dilemmas before having to do so in the heat of the moment. Then we armed them with chalk ammunition, which hurts just enough without causing injury, and put them through training exercises with real Iraqis playing the civilians, and experienced Marines the enemy, repeatedly throwing them into tough situations, forcing them to think on their feet.

*Cohesion* meant developing that universal belief in collective identity, without which any unit will fall apart. Hard training and shared experience build cohesion, giving Marines the stories that they can tell about themselves, but these take time. We needed to draw our Marines into the fold as soon as they arrived. A Marine will graduate Boot Camp with all the right attributes and beliefs, but these tend to atrophy once he joins his unit and is exposed to external distractions or the negative influence of miscreants among his peers. To prevent this happening, I challenged the platoon commanders to get their Marines involved in productive activities during their off-time, while helping them assimilate to the battalion.

The young lieutenants rose to the challenge, and within a week we had a wide selection of clubs that ranged from kite-boarding to scuba diving, and motorcycle riding. The battalion had remarkably few disciplinary incidents during our work-up (only three DUIs, an astonishingly low figure for some 1,000 young men preparing for war), which was an indicator of involved leadership at platoon level.

On previous deployments, I observed how a dependence on interpreters does little to bridge the gap with the local population, and was convinced that we needed to have Marines who spoke enough Arabic to be able to conduct at least rudimentary conversations with the locals. Arabic being a difficult language to learn, the prevailing opinion among experts was that six months would be too short a period to teach Marines enough to be useful, especially in the face of competing training requirements. I reasoned we should at least try. After selecting a cadre of Marines based on their enthusiasm and language aptitude scores, we placed them in the hands of contracted language instructors, with the stipulation that they were henceforth to regard language as being their assigned weapon. Even the instructors were surprised at how quickly their students learned, and by the time we deployed every platoon had at least one Marine who was conversant in Arabic.

Six months seemed very little time to prepare a battalion for combat. During peacetime there had been so much more time to develop subordinates; and without the prospect of lives at stake there wasn't the same imperative to make a timely decision about someone who appeared either incapable or unwilling to do his job. I was very much aware that I had been allowed the latitude to make mistakes, and intended to do the same for my subordinates; but knew also that I couldn't afford to carry along someone who would likely let us down when it mattered most. As the pace of training revealed weak links, I had to make some hard decisions; and the battalion deployed with three lieutenants in positions normally filled by captains, after the incumbents proved not up to the job.

# Chapter 40

Mattis' guidance about not being a gray man was an interesting counter-point to the advice that young officers are often given, to just be themselves. In the right circumstances and for the right reasons a leader has to be prepared to put on an act: to disguise fear, to mask grief or to overcome reticence. I sometimes find that aspect of leadership exhausting.

And command *is* lonely. It's all very well when everything is running smoothly, when the unit is humming along enthused with the energy of common purpose. Then you have time to enjoy the profound sense of satisfaction that comes from stewardship of a good unit. But when your decisions make sense only to you, when plans unravel, and when bad things happen, your sense of isolation can be almost overwhelming.

In Iraq, each battalion was given an area of operations, a county-sized swathe of territory inhabited by thousands of people, and a broad mission: defeat the insurgents, protect the population and enable the Iraqi security forces to do their job. You were expected to figure out the rest. It was the kind of challenge that most Marine officers relish, but the responsibility was literally awesome. Your nearest peer would be dozens of miles away, so you nurtured those relationships before you deployed; sharing lessons learned, trying to keep each other out of trouble.

My two brother battalion commanders, Max Galleai and Nate Nastase, were both senior to me. Their battalions were ahead of mine in the deployment cycle so I probably benefited from this relationship more than they, and was grateful for it. I had known Nate, who commanded 3rd Battalion, 3rd Marines, since we were lieutenants together in 5th Marines. He was the senior among us three, a role that he filled with unstinting generosity, offering valuable advice in areas that ranged from training to the eternal quest to prevent 18 year olds from behaving as 18 year olds will.

I ran into Nate about a week or so after he returned from Karma, having handed over responsibility there to Max and his battalion. It was after a memorial service for the Marines from his battalion who had died during the deployment, and Nate was in a somber mood.

'It was a good deployment,' he said as though to convince himself. 'We started to see some improvement towards the end.'

It was a mantra that I would hear time and again, and would repeat myself. You had to believe that the months of grinding effort, of spilt blood, had achieved something, so you looked for some sign of progress at the end of your tour – like the false indications of a thaw in the depths of winter.

We were sitting at the bar in the Kaneohe Bay officers' club overlooking a golf course dotted with swaying clusters of palm trees, and in the distance, an impossibly blue ocean streaked with lines of white foam. I sometimes wondered if the Marine Corps had given us Karma to compensate for having previously placed us in so beautiful a location. We drank our beer and talked of other things, laughing at memories of our wild shenanigans as lieutenants living in San Clemente, California at a time when war seemed a remote prospect.

Max was also tired when I next saw him several weeks later in Iraq. 'There's so much here that you just can't train for. You are going to have to make decisions based solely on your gut,' he advised me. 'And trust your instincts. They've got you to this point and you'll find that most of the time they'll take you in the right direction, even if your guys are telling you to go in another.'

I had travelled to Iraq with my company commanders and staff to visit 2/3 and get the lay of the land before our own deployment a month hence. Max was optimistic that an upcoming meeting of the local sheikhs, which he had helped broker, would reduce the level of violence. Both he and Nate had devoted much effort to nurturing the most powerful tribal leader in the Karma region, one Sheikh Mishan, an enigmatic character who had recently returned from self-imposed exile in Jordan. It was Mishan who had offered to bring the tribal heads together to discuss cooperation with the Americans, and Max had given him his full support.

'Why don't you come along?' Max offered. 'It'll set the scene nicely for your deployment.'

I wanted to. Max had seemed preoccupied as though something was on his mind that week, but the prospect of this meeting had lifted the veil, offering hope of progress as his deployment drew to an end. But 1/3 was at Twenty-Nine Palms preparing for Mojave Viper, the battalion's final pre-deployment evaluation, and I needed to get back before the exercise began.

'Hurry back, brother, you're our way out of this shithole,' Max joked as we exchanged hugs at the landing zone.

The meeting was held in Karma's town hall, a square single-story concrete building set in a large courtyard. An hour or so before it was due to begin, the first sheikhs started to arrive. Dressed for the occasion in white flowing dishdashas and colored keffiyehs, they passed through the police checkpoint at the front gate and into the courtyard, moving with languid dignity in the stifling heat. The tribal dynamics of Karma were often rife with tension, but the atmosphere that morning was convivial, with the tribal elders cheerfully exchanging their elaborate greetings and mixing easily together in the courtyard.

It was true that a few prominent sheikhs had yet to show up, among them Mishan, but it wasn't unusual for the upper strata of tribal leaders to emphasize their exalted position by being late. Max and a contingent of about twenty Marines arrived, and made their way slowly through the throng towards a dais in the center of the courtyard, stopping every few paces to exchange greetings. As was customary during these events, the Marines had removed all their protective outerwear – helmets, glasses, gloves and body armor – as a display of trust.

A loose cordon of policemen lined the outside of the compound fence, and manned the gate, searching anyone who passed through them on their way to the meeting. Afterwards, various eyewitnesses recalled seeing a young policeman, unremarkable in every respect, approaching the group of Marines and sheikhs about to take their seats on the dais. Almost nothing is known about him except that he had spent the previous night in an insurgent safe house in Karma where he was outfitted with a police uniform and a vest containing 20lbs of home-made explosives packed with ball bearings. He was only a few feet from Max when he detonated.

One of Max's company commanders, Philip Dykeman, a much-liked officer who had impressed me during our recent visit, and a young corporal, Marcus Preudhomme, as well as the mayor of Karma and sixteen sheikhs were killed along with Max. Dozens were seriously wounded in the blast including the Battalion Sergeant Major, Patrick Wilkinson, who lost a leg.

Several days later a group calling itself the Islamic State of Iraq, an offshoot of Al Qaeda in Iraq, took responsibility for the bombing. Its leader, a man known as Haji Hammadi, was killed by US troops in Baghdad a few months after the blast, leaving room for the rapid promotion of his deputy in Karma. Less than five years later this former deputy, Abu Bakr al-Baghdadi, would announce the transformation of the Islamic State of Iraq into the Islamic State of Iraq and Al Sham (the Levant), soon to be known to the world as ISIS. As the pieces to this dark puzzle came together, they were to overlap my life again with what seemed like fateful symmetry.

Jess and I attended Max's memorial service a week before I was due to depart. His family – parents, brothers, sisters and in-laws – had flown in from Samoa and filled the first few rows of the theater at Kaneohe Bay. His wife Evelyn sat up front with their four children, the oldest girl comforting the others with a quiet dignity that I found all the more heartbreaking.

Major General Neller, our division commander (later Commandant of the Marine Corps) paused halfway through his address, looking downwards and it was a moment before I realized that he was struggling as hard as Nate and I to keep his emotions in check.

At the reception afterwards, one of Max's male relatives pulled me aside 'I don't understand why a lieutenant colonel was in the front line, exposed to danger like that.' I tried to explain that there wasn't a front line in this war, and that commanders were sometimes at more risk than their subordinates because their role called for them to attend high visibility events.

'I just don't know what we are doing over there,' he said. I could only nod, unable to think of an answer that would assuage his grief.

'How's Jess holding up,' Nate asked me, gripping my arm above the bicep and squeezing in a gesture that had always been peculiar to him.

'She's OK,' I said, blithely not considering the implications of his question.

A few days later, Jess and I sat in the car by the Kaneohe Bay airstrip, sharing our last few minutes together before I boarded the plane. In the backseat Marcus slurped happily on a sippy cup oblivious to the tension, while next to him, swaddled in diapers and a puffy pink dress, slept Sophia, the newest addition to our family, now barely 4 months.

That morning I had said good bye to Kaela and Siobhan at the airport as both girls returned home for school after a two-week visit. I had timed their visit to coincide with my pre-deployment leave, and we had made the most of it with a schedule that included a spectacular helicopter tour of the island the day before they left. At the airport, Kaela told me that the trip had been 'life changing', which, coming from a teenage girl, meant more to me than any professional kudos.

Now, all around us, Marines were saying their goodbyes: clutching wives and children in those miserable few moments before separation when any attempt to comfort sounds trite.

Jess, who has always been stoic at these occasions, started to cry. It hadn't occurred to me until that point that Max's death must have seemed to her an awful omen. I held on to her, feeling hopelessly inadequate. It's much easier to be the one worried about than the one doing the worrying.

# Chapter 41

The battalion's new home, Camp Baharia, had been an Iraqi Army headquarters under Saddam, and was still quite scenic, with a lake in its center skirted by a path lined with scraggly trees.

I had sent my executive officer Chris Lauer out to Iraq early to assist 2/3 in the aftermath of Max's death, and after dumping our bags, the company commanders and I gathered together in my office to hear his assessment. Studious looking, rail-thin, and soft spoken, Chris relished the kind of detail that I was happy to delegate, and would habitually play devil's advocate with me, a practice that I might not always appreciate at the time, but recognized as an indispensable function of the XO. Now he spoke carefully, as though to excise emotion from a situation that was so highly charged.

'We need to get in the saddle as quickly as we can,' he began. 'Not surprisingly morale's in the shitter, and we're going to have our work cut out for us to get things moving here again.'

Second battalion, Third Marines was still reeling from its loss, and, explained Chris, there were undercurrents of tension within the battalion that compounded the effects of the tragedy: a feeling of resentment against some members of the staff whom, it was felt, had been disloyal to Max in the final weeks prior to his death. The sooner we took the helm the better.

It normally takes a few weeks for one battalion to replace another in combat, to allow each incoming company time on the ground to learn the ropes from their outgoing counterparts. We were still in mid-turnover, with each inbound planeload of 1/3 Marines releasing the same number from 2/3 for the trip home. While I couldn't change the schedule of aircraft, I could take responsibility for running operations before all of 1/3 was on the ground.

After Chris, my operations officer Jason Borovies gave us an update on what still needed to be done before we could assume responsibility. Jason, whom we called Spock because of his uncanny resemblance to the *Star Trek* character, was universally acclaimed by all who knew him to be a genius and, to my great good fortune, another master of detail.

Jason would be running operations from a large room adjacent to my office which we referred to as the TOC for Tactical Operations Center.

From here, he would communicate via radio and classified internet-chat with the companies, tracking the location of all subordinate units on a large electronic map. During our pre-deployment exercises I would poke my head in the TOC first thing in the morning, but otherwise spent very little time there, a pattern that I intended to continue. Jason was eager to take control of operations from his counterpart in 2/3.

First Lieutenant Gary Keefer was my intelligence officer. A battalion's proficiency in combat is dependent on its ability to get intelligence into the hands of those who need it, in time for it to be useful. To do this right takes someone with extraordinary energy and focus, able to sift through reams of information to identify the nuggets.

Tall, skinny and ascetic looking with a tendency to pause before speaking as though listening to a translation, Gary looked like the quintessential intelligence officer, and played the role perfectly. I had given him a list of questions, priority intelligence requirements we called them, chief among which was to find out what we could about Max's killers. He now passed these to the company commanders along with the latest intelligence reports about our area.

'It's circumstantial at this stage, but Mishan's actions look pretty suspicious; he was the one who called the meeting, and then didn't attend. The police are reporting that they caught one of the gang who planned the attack, but it turns out that the police officer who made this report is Mishan's brother, so we don't know what to make of it.'

After Gary came my company commanders. An infantry battalion has three rifle companies, a weapons company and a headquarters company, each commanded by a captain. My headquarters company was commanded by Captain Rich Maidens who looked impossibly disheveled for a Marine officer, but was in fact a level-headed leader and perfect for the job (another good example of why you can't rely on first impressions). His company would be responsible for all the battalion's support functions, in some ways the most challenging mission of all, and would be positioned with his headquarters on Baharia.

Each of the other four companies would manage an area the size of a small town in the United States: protecting the local population, keeping the sheikhs on side, the local militias paid and the police out on the streets. Knowing this, I had focused on building my relationship with the company commanders during the previous six months, and knew that they were as strong a group as any battalion commander could hope to have. Now in turn they gave me a quick update on their areas and projected schedule of turnover; Chris Dellow for Alpha company, Mike Mayne for Bravo, Paul Stubbs for Charlie, and Dan Rhodes for Weapons. They too were keen to take the reins.

As a commander you try to focus on those things that only you can do, chief among which is to visit your Marines. There is simply no other way to get a real feel for what's going on in your unit than to see and hear for yourself. It's a balance of course; you can't take it to the point that you are getting in the way. 'They're happy to see you arrive, and happy to see you go,' my sergeant major would remind me. To enable me to do this, I had a small mobile platoon, which we referred to as the Jump Command Post.

It also helps to have other trusted agents who can be your eyes and ears. With the battalion spread out over a wide area, I couldn't be everywhere, and even if I could, Marines might not be comfortable telling me things that they would tell others. I had also learned that two people can visit the same location and see different things; there were a number of times when I would walk away from a company with one impression, while my sergeant major had quite another. There's nothing underhand in wanting to learn what is happening beneath the surface in your unit; if you're not, then you probably aren't commanding very effectively.

In the headquarters of 1/3, I had an extraordinary group of individuals who enjoyed being around Marines, were perceptive, and cared about nothing more than making the battalion more effective, even if it meant confronting me from time to time with situations that demanded tough decisions.

Rich Lewallen, my sergeant major, was one of the best that I have seen. Level-headed and involved, he had a doctorate-level mastery in the complex field known as Marine psychology. Chief Warrant Officer Craig Marshall, whom I had first met in Al Qaim, was the battalion gunner. A master of the infanteer's craft, Craig also understood how to tailor the techniques of counter-insurgency to the unique demands of a particular area. And, like all gunners, Craig had hit all the 'Stations of the Cross' in an infantry company before becoming an officer, and knew what made Marines tick. Lieutenant Brandon Harding, US Navy, was the battalion chaplain; a role that he executed with such aplomb that he has made the job tougher for every chaplain with whom I have served since. He knew an astonishing number of the battalion's Marines by name, family and background, had their trust and was adept at solving their problems.

Together with Lauer and Borovies, I used this group not just for advice, but also as a directed telescope, having them travel around our area of operations to see things for themselves. We formed a second Jump just for this purpose, which some wag christened the LDART for Lava Dog Assessment and Reaction Team. Under Gunner Marshall's tutelage, the LDART was manned by second-chance Marines, those who had run into trouble of some sort in the companies. Known as the 'Dirty Dozen', they repaid his trust by running the LDART with such proficiency that it doubled as a battalion QRF.

Most of the sheikhs who survived the blast had since disappeared in the pervasive atmosphere of mistrust that ensued, and would need to be located and nurtured once again. Their militias, comprising otherwise unemployed men many of whom were former insurgents, were in a state of turmoil, doubtless trying to figure out whether the $150 a month that we paid them was worth the risk. The local police, whose performance to date had been at best lackluster, now sensed a decisive shift in the balance of power, and were in an enhanced state of intimidation. With the local population likely seeing things the same way, it would be hard to imagine a tougher start to the deployment.

We completed our turnover with 2/3 and, the next day I paid a visit to Mishan. A year earlier, the commander of all Marine forces in Iraq had induced Mishan, the Sheikh of Sheikhs as he liked to be known, to return to Anbar from Jordan, in the hope that he would exert a positive influence on the troublesome tribes around Karma. It's hard to say how much effort Mishan put into this task, but what is certain is that he required much care and feeding from both Nate and Max who were never really sure where he stood. In one bizarre incident, one of his bodyguards had fired on Nate's Humvee, fortunately without causing injury. Mishan claimed that it was an accident, but the incident followed a tense conversation between the two, and Nate thought it more likely to have been a thinly veiled warning.

Now Mishan greeted me like an old friend in the living room of his palatial home, and introduced me to his policeman brother, a large, brooding thug of a man, with the demeanor of a malevolent nightclub bouncer. Mishan too appeared typecast: a hatchet, heavily lined face with graying beard pulled into a point under the chin, and hooded eyes. He wore a red and white checkered keffiyeh, and a black dishdasha, the color signifying his status as a sheikh of higher standing.

At my direction, our four-man delegation did not remove body armor, and I refused the tea that was brought out. It wasn't my intention to make a childish gesture, but I couldn't bring myself to accept hospitality from someone I believed to be connected to Max's death.

'We are in a hurry today, I'm afraid Sheikh Mishan.'

Mishan nodded, the smile frozen on his face, and gestured to his brother.

'I understand, and I am so sorry for the terrible tragedy. Colonel Galleai was a good friend of mine. But I have good news for you: my brother Omar has caught the man who ordered the killing.'

Mishan looked at his brother, but Omar appeared to have missed his cue and was digging in one nostril with a sausage-shaped finger.

'He has already admitted his guilt, and now a judge will send him to jail.'

I knew this to be a lie. According to reports that Gary had received, the man had been severely beaten in custody, so badly apparently that he had lost a testicle, and would thus be unlikely to appear before a judge anytime soon. The man who had reportedly administered this beating sat before us picking his nose.

I changed tack: 'Sheikh Mishan, why weren't you at the meeting?'

Mishan was visibly shaken. He shifted in his chair and tugged at his robe above the knee.

'I had something I had to do,' he said. *Surely you can do better than that*, I thought. It was as though he really didn't anticipate being asked this question. I remained silent for a few moments, letting the implicit accusation hang heavy between us. Mishan's brother stared back blankly and started on the other nostril.

'Well,' I said eventually. 'It just seems— strange.' I got to my feet, a sign for everyone to follow suit. Without offering to shake hands, I turned my back, and headed for the door. *Maybe it was a mistake coming here*, I thought, *maybe Max's death has skewed my judgment*.

By the time that I returned to my office, there was a message waiting from a friend on the MEF staff. I called him.

'Andy, Mishan just called up here asking to speak to the commanding general. I told him that the CG is on the road and offered to take a message. He sounded pissed and just said that he wanted to make a complaint, so I figured that I'd let you handle it first.'

'Well actually, it's me he wants to complain about.'

There was a pause.

'OK brother, I'm sure you know what you're doing, but be careful. Mishan's a big cheese, I heard General Allen flew to Jordan personally to persuade him to join the Awakening. Might not be worth your time to fuck with him, especially since it's your first day on the job.'

'Well I'm pretty sure he knew about the attack on Max before it happened, even if he wasn't involved.'

'I wouldn't be surprised, but good luck trying to prove that. These guys are way too savvy to get caught with a direct link to AQ. I can imagine how you feel, but I'd drop this one.'

I knew that he was right: we'd never prove a connection between Mishan and Max's death. And I'd only divert our energies trying to do so.

So that was it, as far as Mishan was concerned. A week or so later he disappeared, back to Jordan we heard, but were unable to confirm. The alleged suspect also disappeared, either murdered or released. We never found out which.

There was one sequel. One morning in early November I received a classified email from an unfamiliar address. 'Hello Andy, this one's for Max. One fight,' was all it said. I clicked the attachment and the face of a dead man sprang into view: ruptured forehead, beard and hair matted with congealed blood, eyes staring open. It was the man who sheltered, armed and directed the suicide bomber: the Al-Qaeda Emir for Karma, one Haji Hammadi. It was some consolation for never being able to divine Mishan's culpability.

# Chapter 42

On September 1 2008, the MEF was scheduled to turn Anbar over to provincial Iraqi control, as part of the overall plan to place responsibility for security in the hands of the Iraqi government. No one was sure yet what this would mean. The MEF's goal, which seemed increasingly aspirational as the date approached, was for the Iraqi police to take the lead in patrolling the streets, relegating the Marines to a supporting role. Seeing the way things were going in Karma, I watched the date approach with a sense of foreboding.

With the help of the sheikhs, Marine units throughout Anbar employed a local militia which we referred to as the Sons of Iraq. Many of these young men had at one time been insurgents, but switched their allegiance in return for a salary of $150 a month. Although some might think this a cynical ploy on our part, it made good economic sense; the cost of maintaining a thousand sons of Iraq for six months was less than the financial cost of one dead Marine. Now this program was under threat. The Iraqi government appeared reluctant to continue to pay these men after the transition, and it was unclear for how long US units would be authorized to do so. The prospect of thousands of Sons of Iraq disgruntled at no longer getting paid, disappearing with the weapons that we had given them, was not an encouraging one. Should this happen, we had to ensure that the police were prepared to fill the vacuum.

We had embedded squads in each police station in a move that was both practical and symbolic. It enabled us to train and mentor the Iraqi police while forming a relationship based on persistent proximity and trust. But it was proving to be an uphill struggle to get the police, or *shurta* in Arabic, to drop their live-and-let-live attitude towards the insurgents, and go after them with determination. Although it was my job to persuade them to do so, I could understand their reluctance. They shared with their enemy the same neighborhood, often the same tribe, and they knew that we wouldn't be there much longer; both our government and theirs trumpeted our imminent departure. I did have a powerful ally on my side. Brigadier General Sadoun, the commander of an Iraqi Army brigade based some 20 miles north of Karma, joined forces with 1/3 in a concerted effort to get the police out on the streets.

In Karma, the transition date passed without any real change. Marines still led most of the patrols, but now our ability to act on our own intelligence was inhibited by Iraqi law, which stipulated that all arrests had to be based on a warrant issued by an Iraqi judge. I formed a cell headed by the battalion's lawyer whose purpose was to train the Iraqi police how to collate sufficient evidence for a warrant, and then to arrest the suspect.

We aimed first to go after lower-ranking insurgents whom we could link with a specific act, laying an IED for instance; confidence targets we called them. In the weeks following transition we led the local police chiefs through a series of such arrests. Marines would collect the evidence, present it to the police and then provide the outer cordon. The Iraqi police would surround the suspect's house, usually in the early hours of the morning, and knock on the door, announcing to the house's occupants via loud hailer that it would be best to come quietly. There were a few gunfights, but for the most part these procedures netted the culprit without a shot being fired, boosting the confidence of the local police and their standing in the community.

In the process, we also strengthened the bonds between the police and us. Marines and *shurta* continued to live cheek-by-jowl in the Iraqi police stations, facing danger together on Karma's bleak streets. My company commanders and I spent many hours with the station chiefs, eating greasy mutton with our hands, discussing topics that ranged from geo-politics to who was behind the spate of IEDs on Route Chicago.

Then, just as we seemed to be gathering momentum, the enemy struck back. Their first victim was Colonel Salam, the commander of the Shahadi police station west of Karma, in the sector controlled by my weapons company. Salam had been the most aggressive of police chiefs, the first to start rolling up insurgents on the basis of his own intelligence, and so it wasn't a complete surprise when the weapons company commander, Dan Rhodes, called me to report that he had been injured by a bomb. Dan was already at the hospital with a small group of Marines from the squad embedded in Shahadi, among whom Salam was immensely popular. Salam, with both legs in casts and shrouded in bandages, squeezed my hand and thanked me in a barely audible voice for coming to visit him, then announced his intention of killing the Wahabi who did this to him. It was one of those moments that a script writer might reject as being just too clichéd, but he meant it.

A few days later Chris Dellow, who commanded Company A, called me with more bad news. This time the victim had been Lieutenant Colonel Ibrahim and his second in command, both of whom had been riding in

Ibrahim's car when it was seen to explode in the center of Karma. Ibrahim was a very different personality than Salam. Shy, almost timid, he spoke in halting English and seldom made eye contact, staring instead at his feet when he talked. Chris and I used to tease him that he was admiring his shoes, which were an incongruously fine pair of Italian brogues, highly polished with distinctively pointed toes. After weeks of prodding, Ibrahim had, just two days previously, broken an IED cell using intelligence gathered by his own policemen. That night, Chris and I had shared a celebratory dinner with him, a giant fish that he claimed to have caught in one of the many canals that crisscrossed the area surrounding Karma. I almost choked on a fishbone and accused Ibrahim of trying to kill me; and he, thinking that I was serious, became uncharacteristically animated in defending himself.

Chris had no news yet of whether Ibrahim had survived the blast, and launched a patrol to the scene in an area of central Karma we called the Lollipop after the shape of a prominent sign displaying a Koranic message. As soon as I arrived I knew that Ibrahim was dead. His car, a red Opel, had disintegrated, leaving only part of the chassis, twisted and charred, propped against the side of the Lollipop.

Dellow's Marines had cordoned off the area, and were helping a handful of Iraqi policeman search through the debris, plastic bags in their hands. As I walked towards the wreck something in the gutter caught my eye. It was one of the brogues that we had given Ibrahim so much grief for wearing, meticulously shined with the laces still tied. I was suddenly flooded with an anger so overwhelming that it left me rooted to the spot, unable to take my eyes off that forlorn shoe and all it symbolized.

The attacks continued with relentless savagery. Two policemen disappeared from a checkpoint opposite the cement factory that once provided Karma's main source of employment. We thought at first that they had simply deserted their post, it wouldn't be the first time that police had walked away from the job, but then someone (probably the kidnappers, we surmised) called the tip line reporting that both had been taken captive. A day later we found their bodies, dumped alongside the main road that ran through Karma. Both had been tortured, one castrated, news that spread rapidly through the *shurta* ranks. A few days later two Sons of Iraq were also found dead near their checkpoint, their bodies similarly mutilated.

The Karma police chief convened a meeting of local commanders, and I drove there with the Jump to attend. To a man they assured their boss that they were doing everything they could to track down the killers, there were some vague references to leads, but nothing substantial. Kiefer had obtained additional support from the MEF intelligence cell, but so far this had yielded little.

As we left the central police station where the meeting had been held there occurred an incident which, though relatively minor in itself, amplified my feeling that we were losing ground.

By this stage of the war, we all rode in large armored vehicles known as MRAPs – for Mine Resistant Ambush Protected. The MRAP in which I rode was usually at the front of the Jump convoy, but as we left the station, for reasons that now escape me, another vehicle led the way – straight into an IED. The MRAP is a remarkable vehicle: its V-shaped hull and thick armored plates protect its occupants from injury against all but the most powerful IEDs. Fortunately, this was not one of those.

There was a crump, and a spout of dirt and black smoke shot skywards from the passenger side of the cab. The front of the vehicle lifted slightly and then came to rest, the front wheels splayed, tires shredded. Everyone within sight converged on the stricken vehicle, the first Marines to reach it yanked at the vertical lever that secured the passenger compartment, and pulled out those inside. Aside from minor injuries the vehicle's eight occupants were unharmed.

The incident was troubling nonetheless. Whoever had laid the IED had done so while we were in the meeting, right in the driveway of the police station within direct view of a watchtower. It was a singularly bold move, and likely planned by someone who paid close attention to our movements and wasn't worried about the police seeing him.

A few days later Sadoun pulled me aside with a warning:

'You are in danger,' he said.

This might seem like a fatuous thing for one soldier to tell another in a combat zone, but Sadoun wasn't one to talk for the sake of it, and I knew that he had an extensive network of intelligence sources in the area.

'Do not trust anyone, especially the sheikhs.' He continued, 'They pretend to be your friends, just as they pretended to be Colonel Galleai's friend, but secretly they want you dead.'

I had to deal directly with the sheikhs and the police chiefs and the local dignitaries; I couldn't simply hunker down on Baharia without abandoning the mission. Nevertheless, the warning left me uneasy. It's one thing to face an amorphous, general threat, to have people want to kill you because you are an American; it's quite another when they're after you. Karma had become personal.

# Chapter 43

Two days later one of our Marines standing guard at Baharia was shot off the perimeter wall; he survived but was seriously wounded. The assailant had taken his shot from a spot almost 300 yards away, not the work of an opportunist. The following week an insurgent infiltrated the FOB and killed a Marine from another battalion before being killed himself.

Then three Marines from Company B were wounded in a drive-by shooting.

Gary Keefer was up all night with his team trying to find a lead. The next morning, he walked into my office with a strange look on his face. After admonishing him for not getting enough sleep I asked him what was up.

'Hey sir, remember Abu Duwud and the 1920 Revolutionary Brigade?'

I did. Abu Duwud had been on the wanted list of all battalions rotating through eastern Anbar for some time. He was the leader of a nationalist insurgent movement, formed mostly from former Baathists, who had allied themselves with Al Qaeda.

'Is he behind what's been happening?'

'I don't know, but he's asked to see you.'

'Really?' It wasn't common for an insurgent to request an audience with a US battalion commander.

Gary explained that he had received this message from a contact in another US government organization, who had offered to broker the meeting. If I agreed, it was to take place two days hence, in a layby off the dirt road that led to the gates of Baharia. I would travel in a white pick-up truck with Gary, an interpreter and two Marines as escorts, I would wear my body armor and carry a rifle but no pistol.

On the day, we disembarked our vehicle in the designated layby, and met two American civilians who had arrived just before us. A few minutes later a black Opel pulled up in a cloud of dust, and out sprang two men. Reflexively, my hand closed around the pistol grip of my rifle. They were young, wearing leather jackets, Western-style pants and sneakers, their hands were empty, but if looks could kill, Gary and I would be face down in the dirt. As our two civilian companions walked over to their vehicle, a third man got out, and they lead him over to meet us.

'Well, look who it is,' Gary muttered.

When seeing his grainy mugshot during an intelligence brief several weeks earlier, I had joked that he looked like an Iraqi Al Pacino. Not a bad description, I thought now, sizing him up as he was introduced – the stubbly beard and suit jacket reinforced the resemblance. He didn't smile as we shook hands. Nor did I; knowing that the hand in my grasp had undoubtedly taken American lives.

We walked together to the berm at one end of the layby. The two Marines and Duwud's bodyguards remained by their vehicles as we had arranged, eyeing each other with more curiosity now than hostility. Abu Duwud spoke first, pausing at the end of every sentence to allow my interpreter Khaled to translate.

'He wants to thank you for agreeing to meet him.' Khaled, normally a cheerful youth, appeared nervous. I nodded, and Duwud continued, his eyes flitting back and forth between Khaled and me.

'He wants you to know that he is not responsible for these killings. The police may try to blame him, but it is not him.' Duwud waited for me to nod again before continuing.

'Two of his own family have been murdered.' I wondered if these were the two Sons of Iraq.

'Does he know who is doing this?'

I understood Abu Duwud's answer without Khaled's translation: the Islamic State of Iraq, Al Qaeda – Abu Duwud's former allies.

'Can he give us any names?' I was pretty sure that I knew the answer to that but asked the question anyway.

'La, la'. No. But when Abu Duwud continued, Khaled's translation took me by surprise.

'He will find the killers and make them pay for hurting his family.'

Abu Duwud looked at me intently.

'OK,' I said. 'What does he want from us?' Iraqis are pragmatists. Abu Duwud was taking a risk by meeting me, so he must want something in return.

Duwud shook his head, and spoke briefly. 'Nothing,' said Khaled. 'He wants nothing, just for you to know that he has not been doing these attacks.' Duwud spoke again. 'And he did not kill Colonel Galleai.'

Duwud glanced over his shoulder at his bodyguards: it was time to go. We shook hands.

'It was good to meet you,' he said in passable English.

'Yes,' I said awkwardly, but was unsure how to follow that up; none of the usual pleasantries seemed appropriate. Duwud strode back towards his car, one of his bodyguards jumped in the driver's seat while the other held upon the back door. He got in without looking back, the driver executed a gear-grinding three-point turn and, with a rasp of tires, sped back the way they came. We thanked the civilians and they took off towards Baharia.

Gary shook his head, a rueful smile on his face. 'That was pretty fucking surreal.'

'It was. Do you believe him?'

'I think he is telling the truth,' Khaled said.

'If he was behind the killings, why meet with us?' agreed Gary. 'He's got plenty of *wastah* around here and if AQ hurt his family, he can't let that go. If he ends up doing our work for us, all the better. The enemy of my enemy and all that.'

Looking back now at the series of events that led to the meeting with Abu Duwud, I wonder if we weren't seeing the beginnings of the Islamic State at work. Abu Bakr al-Baghdadi had just assumed responsibility for operations in the Karma region, and was under pressure to prove himself a worthy successor to Haji Hammad. Certainly, the ferocity of the attacks bore the hallmarks of the organization that would make him famous.

In any case, after our meeting with Abu Duwud, the attacks tapered off though we never learned why. It might have been because Abu Duwud launched a vendetta against his former allies, or because the local population had had enough, or because the efforts of the Marines were finally gaining traction.

Each of the four companies had made a concerted effort in their respective sectors to tie in with the local population, setting up mobile clinics, and projects to support schools, local agriculture, and businesses. Weapons Company had even enlisted the help of a local female entrepreneur to run a successful venture that enabled women to set up their own businesses.

None of these projects were my idea, they were planned at company level and brought to life by my Air Officer, Patrick 'Elvis' Costello, an F-18 pilot who approached the task of finding money to buy school books or build an irrigation system with the same gusto formerly devoted to flying inverted loops at Mach 2.

And we started to get tips, a rare event in Karma, not via the telephone tip line, but in person from locals who no longer appeared intimidated by the prospect of retribution. Although very few of these offered intelligence specific enough to lead to an arrest, it was an indication that the enemy no longer had an inviolate refuge among the local population.

Meanwhile, our Marines had become adept at finding IEDs, uncovering a staggering number every week, which must have been disheartening for those who risked their lives emplacing them. And with memories of Mosul in mind, I was pleased to see that our supporting EOD units responded with alacrity.

As for our partnership with the sheikhs, we reinforced the *wastah* of those who had proven themselves to be allies by funneling money towards projects in their districts, while weaning from our patronage those whom we suspected of being opposed to our cause. For the reliable sheikhs, we worked hard to enroll their Sons of Iraq in a nascent Iraqi-government program integrating them into an Anbar security force.

After the transition of provincial control, the US military implemented a program to release all prisoners currently held in Camp Bucca, a massive US detention facility near the Kuwaiti border, designed to accommodate up to 20,000 prisoners. I was alarmed, but not surprised to learn that a disproportionate number of these prisoners hailed originally from Karma, and that they were scheduled to return by the busload over the course of two days. My commanders and I sat down with the police chiefs and sheikhs to come up with a plan to assimilate these men back into their communities, knowing that if we failed to so they had every potential of dragging Karma back to the bad days. Bucca was infamous for being a finishing school for insurgents, a place that seemed designed to harden their resolve while teaching them new techniques. Several of ISIS's prominent leaders were Bucca alumni, among them Abu Bakr himself, and his top five lieutenants.

When the first bus arrived, the prisoners shuffled off and into the central police station where they were welcomed by the police chief, tribal leaders and me, and presented with a starter kit of food and clothes, before being escorted to their homes. In Anbar, family and tribe are everything. We emphasized that tribal leaders were responsible for finding these returnees jobs and for checking on them daily, reporting their progress to the local police. It was a system that worked well, and we had no problems with any of the released detainees; at least not during the remainder of our tour.

When attacks did occur, they appeared to be poorly planned, as though last-ditch efforts. In one instance, a young man walked up behind one of our patrols and attempted to shoot the rear-most Marine in the head. His pistol jammed and the Marine, a shy somewhat awkward radioman, shot and killed him. It transpired that the shooter, a youth of 17 who had seen his father killed by Marines, had been armed and primed for vengeance by the local AQ cell. Before the attack, a witness reported seeing him in tears, apparently terrified by the prospect of what he planned to do.

# Chapter 44

'Lava Six, just received a CASREP from Charlie. One KIA. Grid to follow.'

The words sent a cold chill running through me. I glanced at Corporal Estrada my driver; he had heard, and was peering at the blue-force tracker, an electronic device that depicted the location of all the battalion's units, ready to key in the grid.

'Send it,' I said, resisting the temptation to blurt the stream of questions running through my mind. Somewhere out there in the darkness, my Marines were dealing with the shock of sudden death.

Borovies read the grid, then added. 'Just had the one report, no more details. QRF's on the way.'

I looked over Estrada's shoulder as he programed the tracker; it was an intersection in central Karma, only a couple of kilometers away; we'd be there before the QRF.

'We're heading there now.'

It was drizzling as we drove through the empty streets. As we approached the intersection, we could see the darkened shapes of Marines crouching on the sidewalk. One of them stepped into the road and walked ahead of us, beckoning us to follow through a roadblock formed by two parked Humvees, then turning to face us, raised his clenched fist above his head in a signal to halt. Through rivulets of water streaking the windshield, I could see a third Humvee standing alone in the middle of the intersection.

'What happened?' I asked our guide, a young staff sergeant whom I recognized as the patrol leader.

'An RPG I think, sir – hit that hummer. He's in there, the KIA I mean.' The stilted phrases, blanched face and brittle voice should have told me that he was in shock. I didn't know yet what he had just seen.

I looked at the Humvee confused – it appeared undamaged. But then I noticed a blackened hole in the armor behind the rear passenger window nearest to us. It didn't look like an RPG, I glanced back at the staff sergeant. 'He's still in there?'

'Yes sir. The others were wounded, we had to get them out.' He gestured to a litter being carried towards the Jump. 'They're gonna be OK, just a little shrapnel, but we lost the one.' *Strange*, I thought, *that he's not using the Marine's name*.

'We tried to get him out, but—' He tapered off.

'Hey you did what you could.' I patted him on the shoulder. 'I'm going to take a look.'

I walked towards the Humvee, realizing that none of the Marines around me were looking at it. A Marine rifle squad in combat is a tightly knit family, especially so when its members have been together since recruit training.

Steeling myself, I yanked open the rear passenger door. The inside of the vehicle was a mess. *At least it was quick.*

I found his ID in the top left-hand pocket of his cammie blouse, just where he'd been told to keep it. I looked at the picture, and recognized a Marine with whom I had joked while visiting Company C the week before. No one grins when they are having their photo taken for a military ID, but Lance Corporal Thomas J. Reilly, 19 years old, had clearly found it impossible to keep a straight face. It was, I would learn, an expression typical of TJ as he was known, whose irrepressible humor and open heart made him a much-liked character in his platoon.

I turned to Sergeant Major Rich Lewallen who had followed me to the vehicle. 'Grab a couple of our Marines from the Jump and bring over a stretcher.'

I removed TJ's body armor, then lifted him onto the litter; he was surprisingly light.

'We're going to have to send him back in a hummer, sir – we sent the third MRAP back with the wounded,' Lewallen said. 'We need to keep the other two here to cover the squad until they can extract.'

'OK – give me one of the Jump Marines to drive.'

I was breaking my own rules by travelling in a single Humvee, but I wanted to get Reilly away from his buddies as quickly as I could, and I didn't want to direct someone else to do it. He was my responsibility. He was dead because of my orders. That may sound self-flagellating, overly emotional – but it was true in a very real sense. It had been two months since the transition, and I was still having the companies conduct patrols to augment the fledgling efforts of the local police. I understood our mandate to push the Iraqis into the lead, but believed that we needed to be aggressive in order to nurture the transition. In Karma, security was a fragile thing; faced with another bout of attacks, it would evaporate overnight.

It's not that anyone had argued with me, telling me that this wasn't our job anymore, that it was our mission now to take a back seat. No one needed to, I questioned myself all the time. Losing a Marine didn't make me wrong, but if I had given different guidance he would still be alive.

I called in a situation report to the battalion, asking Borovies to relay it to the regimental commander, then Lewallen and I lifted TJ off the stretcher and into the Humvee. The driver and I hardly spoke a word on the way back except for a few terse directions to the morgue. The doctor and two mortuary affairs Marines were waiting for us as we pulled up.

After the forensic analysis we were able to piece together what had happened. TJ was killed by an RKG-3, a type of grenade designed to penetrate armor using a shaped charge, a molten metal plug propelled with supersonic momentum by the focused blast of the grenade's explosion. The charge had punched through the Humvee, killing TJ and peppering the others with shrapnel. It was a remarkably sophisticated weapon, not one likely to have been entrusted to a run-of-the-mill insurgent. We were never able to catch the person who did it.

Sadly, as is so often the case when in command, I would learn much more about TJ in death than I had known when he was alive. He was from London County, Kentucky, and had been brought up by his mother Georgina. He was devoted to her, dutiful in a way that few teenagers are, calling and writing to her regularly, trying to reassure her that things weren't as bad as they seemed in Iraq. It was she who had sparked his interest in cooking at an early age and his dream after the Marine Corps was to become a chef. Now he was on his way back to her in a casket marked 'Remains Unviewable'.

We said good bye to Lance Corporal T.J. Reilly in a ceremony at Camp Baharia, and later in Kaneohe Bay at a service attended by his mother and his sister. He was the thousandth Marine to die in Iraq.

In January 2009, the battalion supported the Iraqi police in providing security for the elections. By then the police really were taking the lead, and we just stood overwatch at a discreet distance, prepared to respond in the event we were needed. We weren't. There wasn't a single attack throughout the greater Karma area, and by the end of February we were able to stroll unhurriedly through the market in the center of town, pausing to chat with locals (General Petraeus did so without body armor, although we were prohibited from following suit).

The MEF commanding general commented that the battalion turned Karma from the most violent place in Anbar to one in which there was hope of lasting peace. My regimental commander wrote that we had done what no battalion had managed before. As proud as I am of 1/3's accomplishments, the truth is that our success was a result of the hard work and sacrifice of all the battalions that had preceded us. And I believe that we were able to bring about tangible improvement only because the tribal leaders were fed up with Al Qaeda's brand of nihilistic violence. As for lasting peace, well, we did believe it at the time. And when, amidst a mighty cheer, our plane took off from Taqqadum for the long trip home, I really did think that I was never coming back.

# Chapter 45

Two months after returning home, it was time for me to relinquish command. For two years the battalion had played a greater role in my life than my family, becoming part of me – which is why it was time to leave. Command holds a hallowed place in Marine culture, but in the end, it's a period of stewardship, not part of your identity. Someone else takes your place, and the waters close in your wake leaving barely a ripple. Whatever legacy you think that you have left will soon be forgotten, unless you were the type of tinpot tyrant who uses his position to give free rein to eccentricity, in which case you will remembered for a while.

As a reminder of this truth, I have always thought that Shelley's poem *Ozymandias* should be read out loud at every change of command ceremony:

> '*My name is* Ozymandias, *King of Kings;*
> *Look on my Works, ye Mighty, and despair!*
> *Nothing beside remains. Round the decay*
> *Of that colossal Wreck, boundless and bare*
> *The lone and level sands stretch far away.*'

I can't remember if I was pondering the fate of *Ozymandias* as I sat in my office on the eve of the change of command, or simply thinking through the events of the next day so that I wouldn't screw anything up. There was a knock on the door, and in came Matt Baker who was my designated replacement. We chatted for a while, about the battalion and the next day's ceremony, and he rose to leave. Then, as his hand was on the door knob, he remembered something.

'Hey, did you hear the division advisor team lost someone in Afghanistan last night?'

'No, I didn't.'

'One of their guys was killed in an MRAP rollover. Strange thing is that he was an army officer. Don't know what he was doing on a Marine team.' Matt glanced at his note book; my throat was in a vice. 'A Major Rocco Barnes.'

Usually, I would look forward to the evening drive off Kaneohe Bay – the road climbs into the sunset, up the side of a vertiginous mountain, lush with thick vegetation and waterfalls; it's a stunning sight. But that evening, blind with tears, I didn't even see it.

Two days later I spoke to Major Mike Buckley, who had been Rocco's deputy in Afghanistan.

'Hey sir, I wanted to check in with you because I know that you and Rocco were close. He talked about you a lot.'

'Thanks Mike.'

'I'm going through his stuff, and there's a couple of things that I know he would want you to have. Notes, thumb drives and a booklet that he wrote, all about your tour in Iraq. I'm sending it to you.' I could hear Mike catch his breath. 'I just wish that he'd been killed in combat instead of in an accident.'

'It probably wouldn't make a difference to him.' Rocco didn't need a cause for validation. He went to Afghanistan without really thinking that we were doing much good there anymore. 'We're still in Afghanistan, because Pakistan, which is the real problem, is just too tough to handle,' he'd said on our last night together. For him, doing something worthwhile didn't have anything to do with policy or end state – it had everything to do with looking after the people around him, and he had a gift for that.

We hung up and I reached for the bottle of Jameson's that Rocco had left me, remembering a passage from Hemingway's '*Farewell to Arms*' that remained lodged in my mind over the years: 'The world breaks everyone and afterward many are strong at the broken places. But those that will not break, it kills. It kills the very good and the very gentle and the very brave impartially.'

Rocco's mother Grace turned out to be a reflection of her son: gracious and kind and solicitous in the midst of her sorrow. From the moment we met before the funeral, she and Rocco's sister Therese treated me as an old family friend. I wasn't scheduled to speak at the funeral, but as a National Guard general delivered the eulogy, Grace reached over the back of her pew to grip my arm. 'I want you to talk to everyone about Rocco.' I was barely holding it together as it was, but wasn't going to say no to Rocco's mother.

The church was packed, Rocco's friends from the very different segments of his life, Hollywood and the military, brought together by his death. As I walked up the aisle I searched for words that would resonate with them all.

I talked about how the military teaches you a list of leadership traits, but how in practice you really only learn what makes a good leader by observing the ones you meet. Rocco was an exceptional leader, but he had something more, something that you couldn't quite capture until things started to go wrong, and you saw how others turned instinctively to him. It was more than character—an aura almost – that enabled him to instill confidence and infuse calm at times when it was most needed.

On a lighter note, I talked about Rocco's ability to capture contradiction: the man who had once been a coal miner and then Arnold Schwarzenegger's bodyguard was also a closet intellectual, probably the best-read military officer that I have met. He was one of the very few people I have known who could argue, with equal coherence and enthusiasm, either side of any political discussion. And he delighted in doing so, which at times caused outrage to his reflexively conservative comrades in arms. But no one could stay angry at Rocco for long. He could talk about any topic under the sun, and I remembered in particular that he had an encyclopedic knowledge of every great movie ever made.

I finished by saying that Rocco died doing what he loved. That wasn't a trite cliché – he loved soldiering, and he brought to that brutal business a sense of virtue that made us all feel as though we were doing the right thing, regardless of cause.

The National Guard general shook my hand, and in a flash I remembered Rocco saying that he had not been in this man's good graces. 'So, you're the reason why he ended up in Afghanistan,' he sniffed. I had been trying to suppress this thought since hearing of Rocco's death, now it floated to the surface. Grace hugged me, thanking me profusely, which made me feel all the worse. She later wrote me a note; it's among my most prized possessions.

Rocco was laid to rest in Holy Cross Cemetery, just outside Cleveland. It was a beautiful setting: the afternoon sun shimmering through the trees surrounding the burial site, dappling the well-kept lawn with the dancing shadows of their leaves. With hoarse commands, the carrying detail executed their stiff ceremony flawlessly. Grace accepted the flag with a wan smile, clutching it tightly to her chest. The honor guard fired their salute; the sound of shots, harsh and incongruous, sending birds chattering into the sky. The mournful notes of the Last Post died away leaving in its wake the sound of someone sobbing. The priest intoned final prayers and the crowd filed by Rocco's coffin. When it came my turn, I removed my gloves and rested my hands lightly against the smooth wood. *Goodbye my friend.*

That evening I met Kaela in Ashland where she lived, about an hour's drive away. She wanted to show off her new car, a black convertible beater that she had just bought, and took me for a drive to the dairy stand where she worked part-time that summer. We hurtled along the country lanes,

Kaela clamping her foot on the gas during the straight ways, braking sharply before each curve, clearly trying to elicit a reaction from her terrified father, who was equally determined not to say anything. Until we almost spun off a curve and I could take it no longer.

'Kaela, stop driving like a demon!' I yelled. She grinned happily and slowed down.

We sat on benches outside the store, slurping our chocolate blizzards. It was one of those idyllic summer evenings in the country: a golden hazy light, wisps of cool mist gathering along the hedgerows, the buzz of crickets, and smell of fresh-cut grass. It reminded me of childhood in England, of a time when the prospect of returning to school at the end of summer was the darkest shadow on my horizon.

'I'm sorry about your friend, Dad. What was he like?'

'He was like you.' It was true. The same open-hearted honesty, composure, selflessness, and love for life.

'You must be very sad.'

'I am sad. But happy at the same time. Rocco would understand.'

# Chapter 46

After battalion command, I attended the Marine Corps War College in Quantico Virginia. It is by far the smallest of the service war colleges with a class of only twenty-four students, less than a tenth of the size of its army and navy counterparts. I was happy to be in a more personal, less formal setting and enjoyed being back in Quantico, a place that had fond memories for Jessica and me. But despite having more time with my family, a relaxed schedule and few responsibilities, it was a difficult year.

While in command and deployed, I was able to keep my dark moods at bay, but with the move to Quantico, it felt as though my life slipped out of focus once again. The broiling thoughts returned, with renewed energy and additional outlets. At the War College I found myself getting unreasonably angry at my fellow students during class discussions about current events. It was very much a new phenomenon for me; I had always prided myself on being able to argue even contentious issues dispassionately. But I now seemed to have lost perspective; everything seemed personal. I must have been an absolute pain, and it is a credit to the character of my fellow students that they remain friends today.

And I was experiencing crashing bouts of melancholy that would bring me to the verge of tears, which in turn would lead to self-recrimination for being so weak. *I was a Marine officer, what the hell was wrong with me?*

While at the War College, I wrote for my thesis a paper called *'Breaking Ranks – Dissent and the Military Professional,'* whose central argument was that under certain circumstances, a military officer is obligated to disobey orders – even legal ones. My point was that the military officer is not an automaton; he has an obligation to the nation, derived from his oath to defend the constitution, and to his subordinates, implicit in the extraordinary position of authority he has over them, to exercise some degree of moral autonomy in the gap between receipt of order and execution.

I went on to say that this dual responsibility gives the military officer not just the prerogative to question orders, but, under certain circumstances, the obligation to do so. I point out that in the military, enlisted personnel (those below the rank of officer) take an oath to obey all orders given to them by those of higher rank. Officers, however, do not, which confers on them the responsibility of ensuring that those orders serve a purpose.

The higher an officer climbs in rank, the closer he comes to the nexus between policy and military strategy, and the weightier that obligation becomes. 'Best military advice' is the well-worn phrase used to describe the responsibility that a military officer has towards his political masters; but it falls short in capturing the full extent of that responsibility. The tendency of Congress not to exercise rigorous oversight of the nation's wars emphasizes the importance of this obligation to speak up. 'Best military advice' doesn't shelter an officer from the consequences of disastrous policy, allowing him without question to prosecute wars that drag on without purpose and at great cost.

The article was published in the Joint Forces Quarterly, a scholarly Pentagon quarterly, igniting a heated discussion that rapidly became ad hominem. I was vilified by academics, policy wonks and columnists alike, who appeared to view me as a dangerous subversive, hell-bent to undermine civilian control of the military. Some even called for my resignation, which I took as a compliment. I was gratified that throughout the fracas, I received messages of support from senior officers in the Marine Corps, active duty and retired, to include my former MEU commander Lieutenant General Newbold, who had resigned over the decision to go to war in Iraq.

Within a few months I would find myself inadvertently following the direction of my own article. And my critics very nearly had the last laugh.

Upon graduating from the War College, the family moved to Stuttgart Germany where I began my new job at Special Operations Command Europe, known as SOCEUR. In March 2011, with the rebellion against the Libyan dictator Muammar Gaddafi in full swing, I flew to Malta tasked with coordinating the evacuation of US citizens from Tripoli.

In military parlance, this type of operation is called a Non-Combatant Evacuation which, of course, has an acronym: NEO. US involvement in this NEO was going to be very low key: no military ships or planes – nothing, for instance, like the large operation orchestrated to evacuate civilians from Beirut five years previously. It was basically just me and Sergeant Beltran, an extraordinarily versatile and talented signals sergeant from SOCEUR. We were going to have our work cut out for us, because the US Embassy staff had already left Tripoli, and no one seemed to know many US citizens remained.

The British military had set up a NEO coordination center in Malta and were leading the operation with participants from nine different countries.

'So, the Yanks show up late to the party, empty-handed asking for us Europeans to bail them out,' was the greeting I received from the head of the

British team, a ruthlessly efficient lieutenant colonel by the name of Craig Sutherland. I assured him that I was there to help.

'Well dive in mate, there's plenty to be done.'

Craig was grappling with how best to organize the combined evacuation from a city that was becoming more hazardous every day. I sat down with him to plan a process that would get foreign nationals trying to escape from Tripoli through the airport and out to waiting planes, a task more complicated that it sounds. The airport was deluged by thousands of Egyptian foreign workers trying to get home, and the Libyan security forces were proving less than cooperative in assisting would-be evacuees. To make matters more complicated, a group of pro-Gaddafi militiamen were tearing around the runway in technical vehicles like a scene from Mogadishu.

That afternoon we briefed the twenty or so members of the NEO cell, as we had come to call the international group of officers whose task it was to plan the evacuation of citizens from their respective countries. The cell would provide the link between inbound aircraft, guides in the airport, and the evacuees.

Armed with a laptop computer, a BGAN satellite modem and a cell phone, Sergeant Beltran and I set to work. I contacted the US State Department's Libya desk to obtain a list of contacts from a hotline they maintained for US citizens trying to escape Tripoli. Then, as conditions in the city worsened, we started to receive direct calls from Americans desperate to leave.

My instructions to these would-be evacuees sounded like an excerpt from a Jason Bourne movie:

'Head to the airport,' I would tell them, 'when you reach the Libyan security cordon, show them your passports and ditch your car. Once inside the terminal, go to the Air Malta desk where you will find a Romanian diplomat. He will get you out to the plane.'

'We need a description of your guy in the airport,' Craig asked the Romanian contingent, 'I don't suppose you can get him to wear a carnation or something?'

On the second day we were frustrated to hear that our aircraft were taking off from Tripoli empty, even though we knew that there were scores of foreign nationals waiting at the airport. It turned out that the problem was that the Libyans were no longer allowing the Romanian to lead evacuees from the terminal to the plane.

'We're going to need people with enough diplomatic muscle to gain access to the terminal and escort evacuees the last 100 yards,' Craig decided. The call went out to various embassies in Malta, and soon we had a pool of diplomats from various countries on stand-by to fly into Tripoli to perform this task. We called them our expeditors.

The NEO cell occupied a large conference room in a rented building by the harbor in downtown Valetta. Military officers from the various nations involved sat around a large table on which were arrayed the radios and telephones that allowed us to talk directly to evacuees, expeditors and aircrew. At one end of the room was a map of Tripoli airport, at the other a large whiteboard on which was displayed the tail numbers of inbound aircraft along with the number of people awaiting evacuation.

By the standards of a modern military operation, it was very low-tech process, with officers yelling numbers back and forth like brokers on the floor of an old-style stock exchange. Because it was so simple, we were able to handle, quite effectively I thought, the large amount of friction thrown our way.

Every morning a British sergeant would write that day's aircraft schedule on the whiteboard. As soon as he had done so it would be rendered obsolete, and Craig would prod everyone for a running tally, raising his voice above the babble of cell phones and radios in the manner of an auctioneer:

'OK everyone,' Craig would say. 'Who's got the next inbound aircraft?'

'We have a C-130, he just left Rome,' the Italian officer, a full colonel as befitted his country's robust contribution to the operation, would reply. 'Scheduled to arrive Tripoli at 1030 hours.'

'1030,' Craig would offer, 'anything earlier than 1030?'

'Yes, I have the prime minister's plane, due to land at 1015,' would announce Darragh, the Irish Special Forces captain who headed his country's contingent. The prime minister of Ireland had provided his own executive jet to support the NEO. In a much-celebrated incident the plane had recently landed on a strip of road outside Tripoli to rescue a French family.

'What's the capacity?' Craig would ask, tossing the Irishman a marker for the whiteboard.

'Fucked if I know. No wait, what did they carry last time? Fifteen – that's if we have one fella sit on the toilet again to make room.'

'How many do we have waiting?'

'Forty-three on the tarmac.'

'I'm tracking four Swedish nationals, just arriving at the airport now.'

'OK, forty-seven total. Darragh, tell your crew to grab fifteen and turn around sharpish. Rudi,' this to the Italian, 'you take the remainder, plus anyone else who shows up in the meantime. Plan for fifty.'

The airport was a chaotic scrum, and it could take two or more hours for an evacuee to make it to the tarmac. The voices on my cell phone became increasingly distraught.

'Just keep pushing through,' I would say, aware that this was advice easier to give than follow.

As conditions in the city became more dangerous, a growing number of embassies removed their diplomats from the pool of expeditors, until by the fourth day only four countries were still in play. No Americans were allowed to participate, military or civilian. During my initial visit to the US Embassy in Valetta, the senior defense attaché, a navy captain, had made this very clear.

'Our instructions couldn't be clearer: US personnel are not permitted to set foot in Libya.' Her tone became stern. 'That means whatever the circumstances, Andy. Do you understand?'

'Yes ma'am,' I had replied in good faith.

But friction leads to circumstances not covered by the phrase *whatever the circumstances*. On the fifth day of the evacuation, I was in contact with two American families making their way to the airport, and watched with concern as the pool of expeditors was whittled down to a handful of Irish and British diplomats. The situation on the ground had become too risky for most participating nations, and that morning there were reports of a militia group threatening to shoot down foreign planes.

An Italian C-130 aircraft took off from Rome, bound for Malta where the plan was for it to pick up two Irish diplomats before proceeding to Tripoli. But as it touched down in Valetta, the diplomats, who were in the NEO operations room with us, received a call from their embassy barring them from participating.

Craig looked around the room. 'Well, that's it then. I have one British diplomat available, but he can't go alone. We'll have to hold the plane here until we can make up the numbers.' That would leave the two American families, whom I had urged to reach the airport, stranded.

An hour later I was on the aircraft bound for Tripoli, wearing a vest labeled 'British Embassy' – more worried about the prospect of ending my career than I was of running afoul of the Libyans.

# Chapter 47

The plane descended sharply over the blue waters of the Mediterranean and touched down on the tarmac of Tripoli airport. The ramp lowered, and I walked down it with the genuine British diplomat, pausing for a moment in the bright sunlight to get my bearings. Some 300 yards ahead of us was the terminal, an aging edifice of concrete and glass, in front of which stood a loose cordon of Libyan security men in blue uniforms. Around us on the tarmac circled a procession of pick-up trucks, packed to the gunnels with wild-looking men in green fatigues waving Libyan flags. It was part political rally, part *Mad Max*: the men chanting and yelling, banging on the sides of their trucks, drivers honking. As we started to walk, a jeep peeled away from the parade and pulled to a halt in front of us. There were three men inside, dressed in olive green fatigues and carrying AK-47s.

'Are you British?' asked the driver in good English. He was in his twenties, unshaven, wearing aviator-style sun glasses.

'Yes,' we both replied in unison.

'You,' he gestured to me. 'Where you from?'

'London.' *Why is he picking on me, don't I look British?* Thinking back, I wonder if it was the Marine haircut that made him suspicious.

'Ah London!' he made a gesture with his fingers to his lips. 'My favorite city. Where in London?'

'Kensington.' This was easy, I had lived there for ten years.

'Nearest tube station?'

'Gloucester Road.'

He appeared satisfied. 'OK English – go.' He pointed at the row of Libyan airport security officials a couple of hundred yards behind him. 'But only as far as them. Do not go into the terminal. Your people will come out and meet you here.'

This was a new development, but I wasn't too concerned, the Romanian diplomat was still in the terminal and would know to find us.

We stopped a few feet short of the cordon and waited. The security officials eyed us silently but without obvious hostility. Eventually a short, chubby man appeared through the glass doors behind them, leading a row of frightened looking people.

'Constantin Bibescu – Romanian Embassy,' he said, proffering his hand.

'Andy Milburn, British diplomat,' I replied. We were having to shout above the noise of the jamboree behind us.

'Do you have any Americans?' I asked.

'Yes, I have two families.' *Thank God.*

I found them as they trailed the Romanian through the cordon towards the plane. There was only time for a quick introduction, the briefest glimpse of harried-looking parents clutching bawling children, then, at a signal from the British diplomat, I turned and started to follow the gaggle of evacuees towards the plane. I had taken only a few steps when the same jeep pulled in front of me.

'Hey English,' the driver called, his swarthy face now furrowed in a scowl behind the Ray-Bans. Over his shoulder I could see the line of evacuees walking up the ramp of the C-130 like a trail of ducklings.

'You are coming with us,' the driver said, gesturing towards the back of the jeep. 'You are an American, I heard you say so.' I hadn't, of course. He must have overheard me questioning the Romanian.

Ray-Bans reached out to grab me. I dodged the outstretched arm and took off running, around the front of the jeep and towards the gaping tail of the waiting plane, dimly aware of shouts and the sound of a revving engine behind me.

The British diplomat had reached the aircraft, and glanced over his shoulder as I sprinted towards him, the air rasping hot in my lungs.

'Get on the plane,' I gasped. He was midway up the ramp when I tore past him and into the shadowed sanctuary of the hold.

The evacuees had filled the plane from front to back, but there were still a number of vacant seats nearest the ramp. I selected one against the bulkhead hidden, I hoped, from outside view, and buckled my seat belt, shackling myself to safe haven.

Still heaving for breath, I leaned forward and peered outside. There was already a small crowd of militiamen clustered at the foot of the ramp, like a pack of hounds on the scent of a trapped fox.

The pilot, a tall Italian Air Force major, walked past me and down the ramp, donning his uniform cap as he did so, perhaps hoping that this symbol would elicit some degree of respect.

'Who is in charge here,' he called in English and then, upon receiving a response from Ray-Bans, he asked. 'Do you speak Italian?' He did. *He's quite the Renaissance man*, I thought.

I was happy not to understand the subsequent conversation which consisted of strident demands from Ray-Bans and responses from the pilot whose tone, calm to begin with, soon became edged with frustration. It seemed incongruous to hear Italian, with its lilting tones, and memories of lazy brunches by the harbor in Trieste, used as the language by which my life was now being negotiated. As the discussion dragged on, I stared straight ahead at the empty seat opposite me, trying to cast my thoughts elsewhere.

Eventually the voices stopped and the pilot plopped with a sigh onto the seat in front of me, his lips pursed with irritation.

'They want you off the aircraft,' he said. 'They've surrounded the plane and won't let us take off. These people.' He paused, and raised his hands in front of him, palm upwards as though appealing to God. 'They don't listen to reason.'

'Well thank you for trying to argue with them.' I paused, about to tell him that I wasn't getting off the plane. The passengers would be inconvenienced, but their lives were no longer in danger; mine most definitely was. Fortunately, I didn't have to give voice to this craven thought.

'You must stay on the plane.' He made it sound like an order, and I thanked him silently for doing so.

Darkness had fallen, and the Libyans drove their pick-up trucks to the foot of the ramp, their headlights illuminating in stark relief the rows of frightened passengers who turned their blanched faces from the glare. The militiamen were turning it into a party, their shadows dancing on the ramp and across the bulkhead in a scene that reminded me of childhood nightmares. One of them had a loudhailer in hand and every few minutes would broadcast in tortured English an unenticing invitation.

'We know you are there, Americee. Come out now.' *Not by the hair of your chinny-chin chin*, I thought, having passed beyond the initial surge of fear to a state of exhausted resignation.

Only once previously had I felt so helpless. While travelling through Iran as a student, I had been arrested by the Iranian Revolutionary Guard and questioned overnight. But even then, I had the feeling that certain rules were at play; that I was dealing with people who could be reasoned with. That was not the case now; the men outside were baying for blood.

The pilot returned to the cockpit, leaving me to grapple with my thoughts. It was one thing to face danger while armed and accompanied by others; quite another when you are alone and completely helpless. Then my phone rang.

'Andy, you alright?' It was Craig.

'I've been better.'

'Yeah, we got a call from the Swedish Embassy saying that the Libs were holding a plane on the tarmac until someone on board gave themselves up. We figured that it was probably you.'

I craned my neck to peer out the back of the plane, shielding my eyes against the glare. The shouting had subsided, but the sinister figures were still there.

'OK mate.' Craig was trying to sound reassuring but there was obvious concern in his voice. 'Stay put. Whatever you do, don't get off the plane.'

'Don't worry, there's no chance of that happening.'

'Alright mate, cheers for now. Call me if you need anything.'

'I need you to fucking beam me up Scotty.' But he had already hung up.

Sometime later the pilot returned.

'I have been talking to my command in Rome,' He began, and for an awful moment I thought that he was about to tell me that he had orders to turn me over.

'Now I am on my way to the terminal to talk to someone.'

'You think that's wise?'

He shrugged. 'They aren't going to interfere with me. The Italian government is Gaddafi's only remaining friend. Besides, I have something to offer, some money.' I noticed that he was carrying a small backpack; I wondered how much I was worth.

He continued down the ramp, calling to the Libyans who were evidently expecting him – a jeep pulled up and he got in.

'They need the money more than they need you,' said the man next to me, a middle-aged European, with a reassuring smile. I hoped that he was right, but every moment of waiting was heavy with ill-portent.

Eventually the jeep returned, the pilot disembarked and strode up the ramp.

'OK,' he said to me with a wink as he rushed past. My heart started to pound.

Then the engines came to life with a loud whine and the ramp started to rise. I leaned forward and watched it inch upwards, screening from view the lights and trucks and threatening figures – like a drawbridge raised in the face of an invader.

Everything was happening in slow motion. The plane lurched, stopped, lurched again, and then, with a roar of engines, started to move. A few minutes later we came to a halt. 'Oh, sweet Jesus.' I exclaimed. The propellers changed pitch again, this time downshifting from a roar to a hum as the plane settled back on its haunches. *What was happening?* The brief glimpse of hope rendered the prospect of its demise impossible to bear.

Then we were moving again, slowly at first, then with a deafening burst of acceleration that lifted the plane's nose at a sharp angle, bending me sideways into the adjacent seat.

We rose in a steep climb, clawing for height. An alarm started to shrill. I remembered the threat from militia anti-aircraft missiles but dismissed the thought. No one wants their death to be tinged with irony.

The plane banked hard, pushing me forward in the shoulder straps, pumping blood into my face. I craned my neck to peer out of the nearest porthole but saw only blackness. We continued a much shallower climb out over the ocean, and then there was a tap on my knee. It was one of the aircrew bending forward to shout in my ear; despite the noise and his accent, the message was gloriously clear:

'We are out of Libyan airspace.'

I realized that I had been gripping the metal bar at the edge of my seat so tightly that my knuckles hurt.

Sometime later the pilot returned, after I had thanked him he said, 'It is too late for us to stop in Malta now. I must go straight to Rome. We have alerted all the embassies, so there should be someone there to meet you.'

'I'll take care of myself, thanks.' I guessed that the US Embassy in Malta had already learned about the incident, and I wasn't ready yet to deal with the fall-out. I had my wallet, and credit card – and my life. The recent prospect of languishing in a Libyan jail expunged any concern about having ended my career. *Every rank beyond corporal has been a bonus anyway,* I told myself with genuine feeling.

We landed at a military airport outside Rome, and I bid an almost emotional farewell to the air crew. There was a large welcome party waiting for the evacuees: representatives from each of their embassies and a host of Italian officials. I peeled off the side of the ramp as we disembarked, and lurked in the shadows by the wing until most of the crowd had dispersed. As I walked towards the terminal, I was hailed by a well-dressed woman with a British accent.

'Are you Lieutenant Colonel Milburn?'

'I am.'

'I'm with the British Embassy. We received a request to make sure that you were taken care of tonight. Do you need a ride?'

I did indeed. 'Lieutenant Colonel Sutherland would like you to give him a call.' The diplomat told me as we drove from the airfield to a hotel in central Rome where the British Embassy had made me a reservation.

Later in my room, I called Craig.

'Glad you're OK mate, we were worried.'

'You're such an old woman.'

'Listen, mate, our Foreign Office is trying to figure out how much fuss to make over the incident today. It's a little awkward for us because you aren't actually one of us.' He sounded as though this was revelation. 'But they are prepared to contact the US State Department at the highest levels to give them a full account.'

'Let's not do that, Craig.'

'Got it, Andy. The cat's out of the bag about you being on the ground, but we won't volunteer information.'

'Thanks Craig, I'll make a beeline for the NEO center when I get in.'

'Night, mate, I'd have a couple of beers if I was you.'

*Good idea*, I thought, intending to head down to the hotel bar. Instead, I fell asleep in the bath.

My flight touched down in Valetta around noon the next day, and an hour later I arrived at the NEO center, wearing the expensive Italian shirt and trousers that I had purchased at the airport to replace my filthy clothes from the previous day.

If I had been expecting a hero's welcome, I would have been disappointed:

'What time do you call this?'

'Nice togs, mate – you just rolling in from a night on the piss?'

I had barely sat down, when the US Defense Attaché walked into the room and beckoned me outside. She came straight to the point:

'Andy, were you on the ground in Tripoli yesterday?'

'Yes, I was.'

She took a deep breath and fixed me with a look that reminded me of boarding school.

'Did I not make it clear that US personnel were not allowed to set foot in Libya.'

'You did.' This wasn't the time to claim extenuating circumstances. She shook her head, apparently nonplussed.

'Well I have a message from the Ambassador.' Here it comes, I thought, Persona Non Grata and a bad-boy note to my command.

'He wants me to thank you,' she was smiling now. 'The Maltese government told him yesterday that the Libyans were holding an American serviceman in Tripoli airport, and he asked me if I knew anything about it. I told him I didn't, but then called over here to make sure. Your Brit friends said that you must have finished your shift for the day.

'Then this morning he gets a call from an American who thanks him for sending someone to help him and his family get out of Tripoli. Then a call from the Sierra Leonean Ambassador to Libya, saying that he and his staff were denied permission to board a Romanian plane but that an individual, who identified himself to the crew as an American, interceded on their behalf.'

I remembered the incident. A man in ceremonial West African garb had asked for my assistance as I stood outside the terminal waiting for the Romanian diplomat. I never worked out what the issue was, probably just a question of two different nationalities trying to communicate under duress in heavily accented English. In any case, once I had identified myself to the Romanian pilot the matter was quickly resolved.

'So, then he calls me back in and asks me if I am sure that no military personnel were on the ground. This time I tell him that I don't know, but will check that you didn't lose your mind. And he just says: 'I don't want him to get in trouble, Jane, I just want to make sure that he's OK – and please thank him for me.'

'Just stay out of trouble the rest of your time here in Malta.' She shook my hand, turned to leave, and then remembered something. 'Oh, and the Ambassador said that he would like to meet you in person, so be prepared for a short notice summons.'

Tripoli airport shut down the next day, and my small team packed up and took a cab for the airport and our plane back to Stuttgart. The Ambassador's call came while I was on the way to the airport, and I was unable to meet him. My command at SOCEUR had received word of my disobedience, but there were no repercussions.

The first line of the Marine Hymn ends with the words *To the Shores of Tripoli*, a reference to the exploits of Lieutenant Presley O'Bannon whose landing near that city in 1805 is part of Marine legend. Now whenever I hear those words sung, I think back to those long hours at the mercy of Gaddafi's goons – a fate that I faced with considerably less resolve than O'Bannon showed against the Barbary pirates all those years ago.

*Part III*

# Reckoning

*'The spark has been lit here in Iraq, and its heat will intensify until it burns the Crusader Armies in Dabiq'*

Abu Musab al-Zarqawi (Founder, Al Qaeda in Iraq),
September, 2004

# Chapter 48

I took command of the Marine Special Operations Regiment in December 2012. The regiment is the centerpiece of the Marine Special Operations Command (MARSOC), and parent unit of all Special Operations Marines. As such, a fast-paced, challenging command; particularly so at the time that I assumed the helm.

The war in Afghanistan dominated much of my time at MARSOC: training Marines for deployment, while dealing with the war's effects on returning Marines and their families. I made multiple trips to the country during my time in command, and couldn't help feeling that the US war effort appeared to be making little headway. Just as in Iraq, the war was being fought as a series of unit deployments, each one beginning where the previous one had also begun.

Though the overall security situation had not improved significantly in Afghanistan by the time the last MARSOC unit returned in early 2014, the regiment's Marines did make progress in training Afghan special operations forces. Afghan SOF remains the country's most reliable security force, as the United States begins its eighteenth year of involvement in that country.

Measured objectively by standard tests of physical and mental capability, MARSOC comprises some of the highest quality Marines in the Corps. Nevertheless, we had our share of the issues that are the inevitable legacy of years at war: PTSD, prescription drug dependence, alcohol abuse and broken marriages. And, of course, casualties, not all of them the direct cause of combat. In one awful sequence of events, we lost one Marine to suicide and then another, when the private plane he was piloting crashed as he traveled to the funeral.

Despite these setbacks, my tour at MARSOC was immensely rewarding, due in no small part to the impressive team that I had there to assist me.

In an organization such as the Marine Corps that places so much emphasis on command, it takes both character and talent to play an effective role as second fiddle. The billet of executive officer, or second-in-command requires someone with the ability to read his boss, give him advice even when he seems loath to take it, cover his blind spots, execute his intent, and free him from all the necessary but tiresome chores that might otherwise distract him from doing those things that only he can do. Even working for the best commander in the world, it's a demanding assignment, requiring someone with enough emotional intelligence to subordinate their ego and personal feelings to the task of enforcing someone else's will. And when, as the commanding officer is a tin-pot tyrant, the role of executive officer becomes all the more difficult, and necessary. In such cases he will find himself having to shield the unit from the impact of the commander's worst instincts – and, in extremis – make the decision to report the commander's behavior when it has stepped out of bounds. Where those bounds lie though is not always clear, as Herman Wouk lays out masterfully in the Caine Mutiny – a book that I had all my lieutenants read when, as a company commander, I heard them complaining that our battalion commander was certifiable. While I like to think that I was nowhere near the extreme represented by Wouk's Captain Queeg, I am aware that my XOs had no easy task, and thus was fortunate at MARSOC to have three superb ones in a row. Ben Chapman, Mike Butler and John Rochford were all, in their different ways, a perfect foil to my personality and kept both me and the regiment on course during a somewhat turbulent time.

I was fortunate too in having in one Pete Acosta, an extraordinarily talented sergeant major. Diminutive and feisty, Pete was a reconnaissance Marine by background and ethos, that is to say, that he was uncompromising when it came to standards of physical fitness, marksmanship, appearance, discipline, work ethic, and resilience -- pretty much every quality that, in his opinion, defined a Marine. Although in his late 40s, he very much lived by the standards of his own creed, departing every lunch time for a ten mile run, even in the punishing heat of a Carolina summer, and subsisting – as far as I could make out – on a diet of sunflower seeds, Coca-Cola and Copenhagen chewing tobacco. But there was much more to Pete than the hard-bitten, demanding sergeant major portrayed time and again in books and movies about the Corps. He cared deeply about his Marines, regardless of rank, gender or occupational specialty, and was known as someone who would go to any length to help them solve their problems. There was always a line of Marines outside his office, and he always had time for him.

In time, I learned of another interesting, and revealing, aspect to Pete's life. He and his wife had turned their home into a sanctuary for pit bulls rescued from the barbaric sport of dog-fighting that still flourishes in some benighted areas of the South. There were even rumors, never confirmed, that Pete and a small coterie of his former recon buddies broke into dog-fighting dens at night to free the caged animals and find them better homes.

In Scott Conway and Craig Wolfenbarger I was blessed to have two strong operations officers at a time when we were working to develop within the Regiment some unique capabilities that would enable MARSOC to establish its own identity in the special operations community. In this effort we were to receive assistance from an unexpected source: ISIS.

In December 2013, Iraqi Prime Minister Maliki sent security forces into Ramadi and Fallujah to put down Sunni demonstrations. The event didn't receive much coverage in the US media, but it caught my attention because I recognized the name of the most influential tribe in Anbar, the Dulaimis, who started the protests after a string of incidents that put them on collision course with the central government.

After the last US troops left Iraq in 2011, Maliki, at the head of the hardline Shia Dawa party, embarked on an agenda that was blatantly sectarian: disbanding the Sons of Iraq, arresting tribal leaders without reason, and edging Sunni politicians out of power. Those of us who had served in Anbar and witnessed at first-hand the distrust that the province's Sunni population had for the government in Baghdad, weren't surprised to see Anbari resentment turn to violence.

As Iraqi security forces arrived in Fallujah to put down the protests, they found themselves involved in street battles with tribal fighters. A few days later, a convoy of jihadists arrived to join forces with the Dulaimis, quickly routing the army and police; and in January 2014 the victors raised their distinctive black flags over the town, announcing that they belonged to a group called the Islamic State of Iraq and Al Sham (the Levant) – or ISIS as it came to be known. Ten years after the hard-won Marine victory, Fallujah was back in the hands of jihadists.

I was stunned, both by the dreadful futility that this news symbolized, and by the lack of US response. It received barely a mention on US television, and I searched intelligence reports for clues as to how it had happened.

Abu Bakr al-Baghdadi, the man who had been a high-ranking member of Al Qaeda in Karma at the time that Max was killed, had formed ISIS in the spring of 2013 in a merger between Al Qaeda in Iraq (AQ-I) – also known as the Islamic State of Iraq (ISI) — and the Al Nusrah Front, a jihadi group spawned by the Syrian civil war. Al Qaeda had lost ground in Iraq, but Syria offered the group new opportunities. Assad's vicious reaction to the Arab Spring, and Western reluctance to get involved, enabled the jihadis to use resistance to the Syrian regime as their cause célèbre. During 2013, thousands of young Muslims from around the world travelled to Syria in answer to Baghdadi's siren song, swelling the ranks of his nascent organization.

Raqqah fell in the summer of 2013, and after that there was nothing to stop ISIS from pouring across the Anbar border to reinforce their Sunni brothers. Although Baghdadi was the overall mastermind, it was an Anbari, by the name of Abu Wahid who spearheaded the recapture of Fallujah. A strutting thug from the Dulaimi tribe, with a penchant for social media snuff videos, Abu Wahid represented a disturbing trend: the link between ISIS and the tribes of Anbar. The Awakening was well and truly over, and in its place was an alliance rooted by ties of kinship rather than mere expedience.

Karma had fallen as well – someone showed me a photograph of the central police station now adorned with black flags. I combed the reports to find out what had happened to the sheikhs that I knew. A few had been killed, some had fled, others disappeared, but most had sided with ISIS. They didn't really have a choice: the Maliki government had pushed them into a corner and ISIS offered them a way out. And those who refused the Islamic State's offer had a habit of disappearing.

A few months later Mosul fell. In four days, a force of some 1,500 fighters wrested control of the city from 10,000 Iraqi troops, who ditched their uniforms and fled using whatever transport they could find. Several hundred Iraqi soldiers fell into ISIS hands and were publicly executed, an event that was filmed and posted on social media with the slick production that had already become one of the group's hallmarks.

On July 4 2014, Baghdadi climbed the minbar [pulpit] of the Al Nuri mosque, the same mosque that we had visited on Fridays, to announce the birth of a new caliphate, an Islamic empire encompassing a third of Iraq and Syria, an area larger than Israel and Lebanon combined. The time for conquest was now, Baghdadi announced, the caliphate was real, no longer an aspirational concept, as had been espoused by Al Qaeda's more cautious doctrine. But in order to survive, it must grow. No true Muslim could ignore the call to arms – each Sunni was now presented with a simple choice: swear allegiance to the caliphate or be declared an apostate, an unbeliever.

It was over that Independence Day weekend 2014, that the US media really started to pay attention. Each night, after the rest of the family had gone to bed, I stayed up late, watching the news, brooding, hoping for some indication that the US government was planning to intervene. The stream of Islamic State conquests was a gut-wrenching litany of places whose names evoked for so many Marines and soldiers memories of bloodshed and suffering: Tal Afar, Mosul, Al Qaim, Haditha, Fallujah, Karma.

Siobhan and Kaela were staying with us for the week, and I'm afraid that I must have been morose company though I tried to put a cheerful face on it. To this day, I feel awful about snapping at them over something ridiculous while we were out kayaking.

I managed to contact Zuher who was now the intelligence officer for a division based in Taji, a town that was one of the last bulwarks standing between the Islamic State and Baghdad. He reported that Lieutenant Colonel Mohammed had been fired from his position as battalion commander after the debacle of Mosul; Falah was a division commander, while Abdul Amir was a three-star general, and the operations officer for the entire Iraqi Army.

In the fall of 2014, with ISIS just 30 miles from Baghdad, the President authorized the US military to conduct air strikes in support of Iraqi and Kurdish security forces, and to deploy to Baghdad a Special Operations Task Force. This enabled the Iraqis to save Baghdad from falling, but wasn't enough to prevent ISIS from consolidating its hold on Anbar province with the capture of the provincial capital Ramadi, a city in which hundreds of Marines had been killed or maimed.

At this point I need to apologize to the reader for introducing another acronym, but there is just no way around it. In military parlance, the term 'Combined' connotes participation by non-US forces whereas the term 'Joint' means that more than one service is involved. So, the addition of these two elements to a Special Operations Task Force, turns its manageable moniker SOTF (pronounced SO – TuF) into a tongue-twisting CJSOTF (pronounced C-J-SO-TuF).

One CJSOTF was assigned to command all US and coalition special operations forces in Iraq. The plan was to replace this CJSOTF every six months in a rotation that would be led alternately by the Naval Special Warfare Command (headquarters of the SEALs) and MARSOC. In December 2014, I learned that I would command the first MARSOC rotation of this task force scheduled to deploy a year hence.

A year seemed like a long time, but the knowledge that I would at least play a role in striking back helped relieve my angst. In the meantime, Iraqi and Kurdish security forces backed by the weight of coalition air power had, for the time being, halted ISIS's inexorable advance.

The prospect of having MARSOC personnel lead a CJSOTF caused no small amount of angst in the special operations community, to which MARSOC, having been formed in 2006, was a latecomer. From the outset, we were under pressure to prove that we were up to the task.

MARSOC is a small organization: comprising less than 3 per cent of the United States Special Operations Command's total manpower; it's a fifth the size of the Naval Special Warfare Command and less than a twelfth that of the US Army's Special Operations Command. Because of this, our challenge was to figure out how to man a CJSOTF without closing shop at Camp Lejeune; and the only way we could do this was to form an ad hoc unit comprising Marines drawn from across the organization and the wider Marine Corps. The six months that we had available for pre-deployment training shrank to five when we accounted for leave and public holidays; not a lot of time in which to train so disparate a group for a mission so complex.

In meeting this challenge, I was fortunate to have as the CJSOTF Operations Officer Lieutenant Colonel Jeff Buffa, a hard-bitten mustang, the term Marines use for an officer who comes up through the ranks, with almost twenty years of operational experience. Jeff was, in the words of one of his many admirers, a Marines' Marine; unleashed on a mission, he had the tenacity of a pit bull, which was just what I needed.

I recruited him from his job at the MARSOC schoolhouse thanks to the unstinting generosity of his boss Colonel Neil Scheuele.

'He's the guy you need,' Neil agreed. 'But be warned. Jeff's a diamond in the rough.'

It was true that Jeff could be irascible with those whom he regarded as being obstructive; but although he was to meet an astonishing number of people in this category during our deployment, he never gave me cause for regret.

Jeff would run the operations directorate from the Joint Operations Center (JOC), a large auditorium-style room, bedecked with computers, phones and giant screens. If the operations directorate was the CJSOTF's central nervous system, the JOC was its brain, home to the various sections that comprised the directorate: the Fire Support Section, responsible for delivering bombs and artillery onto the right target at the right time; the Future Plans Section whose members would translate my broad guidance into workable plans; and the Current Operations Section who would then turn those plans into orders for subordinate units and monitor their execution.

'Intelligence drives operations' is an axiom commonly used, but seldom executed well. Since inception, MARSOC had focused much effort on developing a stable of Marines highly trained in exquisite collection skills, from the more traditional use of people as sources (known as human intelligence or HUMINT) to various technical methods that had become highly advanced in the seven years since I had commanded a battalion. The CJSOTF would need an intelligence section with the training and experience to direct collection by all these means; then to fuse the results – that is to bring together, analyze and interpret them – into information that could be integrated into operations.

It's not enough to know who the enemy is and what he's doing; good intelligence must lead to specific options for going after him, by attacking those components of his organization that will have the greatest effect. This is where intelligence meets operations in a process called targeting.

With its love of euphemism, the military packages targeting under two headings: kinetic, the use of bombs and missiles to cause physical destruction – and non-kinetic, the use of information or mis-information to influence the enemy or the local population. We would have to be expert at both.

The CJSOTF was most vulnerable in the support function of logistics. It's a difficult function to perform well at the best of times, made all the more complex in the support of special operations, when logistic support entails delivering small packets of rapidly consumed items to multiple austere locations across great distances, using aviation as your only means of doing so. We would need a logistics team who could anticipate demands and make this process, from request through delivery, work with deceptive ease. We had, scattered throughout MARSOC, very few logisticians who had this kind of experience and I set out to recruit them.

And, of course, we wouldn't be able do anything unless we could talk. With the CJSOTF conducting multiple operations simultaneously over hundreds of miles, this would be no simple task, and was made all the more difficult by the polyglot nature of the task force, which comprised units from eight different countries, none of whom used the same communications systems that we did. We also had to communicate with our Iraqi partners so that we could support them with responsive and accurate fires. Then there was the matter of classification, we needed systems on which we could pass intelligence to these units without violating rules that were developed with only US units in mind.

As an infantry officer, I had always learned only what I needed to know about communications, regarding its intricacies with the same superstitious awe that ancient tribes viewed the local witch doctor. So I was delighted to find a virtuoso for the billet of communications officer: Major Steve Hurley who had just finished a tour at the Joint Special Operations Command, and was well-steeped in the black art. I can pay him no greater compliment than to comment that I never once had to worry about losing the ability to communicate with our units.

As Jeff and I tackled the task of putting together the CJSOTF, it occurred to us that something was missing. The C in CJSOTF stands for Combined, which infers the inclusion of non-US personnel; but though we had several subordinate task forces from other countries, the headquarters was still all-American. To fix this we contacted the respective special operations commands of the UK, Australia, Italy and Spain to solicit personnel contributions. Given the opportunity to participate in the only coalition Special Forces (SF) headquarters in Iraq, each country sent their best, and I was able to fill several key billets with foreign officers.

I wanted also to include at least a smattering of soldiers from the army's Special Forces. I had a couple of motives for doing this. Green Berets pride themselves on their ability to train and advise foreign soldiers, it's what they call their core competency (remember the movie *The Green Berets* with John Wayne). Of course, MARSOC Marines think that they can do the same thing just as well. I wanted to give SF the opportunity to plant a couple of trusted moles inside our organization, thus dispelling, I hoped, any traces of skepticism. At the same time, when it comes to running a by-the-book training command, which is what we wanted to establish for Iraqi SOF, no one does it better than the army; and I knew that I would get experts in this field. I wasn't disappointed; in response to my request, we received a small cadre of top-notch Green Beret officers and NCOs.

# Chapter 49

As we started to put together the headquarters, I was able to spend some time with one of the CJSOTF's subordinate units, a MARSOC company, who were scheduled to deploy at the same time as us. I was pleased but not surprised to see how enthusiastic they were about this particular mission – 'At last, one that makes complete sense,' one of the Marines commented – as they threw themselves headlong into a demanding training schedule.

Then tragedy struck. The news came, as it always does, in the early hours of the morning. I groped for the phone as Jessica groaned with the weary anticipation of a wife who has endured many late-night calls. But this one was different.

'Sir, Team 8231 took off in a helo last night, and didn't return.' It was John Rochford, my unperturbable XO. 'Hurlburt's got personnel out looking for them. I'll have the company commander call you with the latest, but wanted to give you a heads up.'

John was giving me all he knew in his customary succinct manner, so there was no point hounding him with more questions and thus wasting time. I knew the team well, having spent a good amount of time with them over the previous few weeks, including a brutal PT session just prior to their departure for Hurlburt field on Florida's panhandle.

Less than twenty minutes later, while I was in my car on the way to work, John called again. 'Sir they've just found wreckage in the Santa Rosa Sound off Destin. Looks like the helo but no sign yet of the fuselage or bodies.'

I caught the first flight to Destin and while changing planes in Atlanta watched with dismay as news of the crash appeared on television. The Department of Defense had not yet released information about the missing helicopter because, until that point, it was still possible that the pilot might have made the decision to land somewhere until the weather improved. But now the families of our seven missing Marines would see news of the crash, and assume the worst before we had had the chance to notify them. Although I didn't know it at the time, that's exactly what had happened. A group of wives and girlfriends associated the story on television with unanswered texts from their loved ones, and gathered together in one of their homes on

Camp Lejeune to await news. My responsibility was clear: I had to find out what had happened to our Marines, and ensure their families knew.

The helicopter had indeed crashed, hitting the water with such force that wreckage was thrown over a wide area. All inside were killed instantly. Over the course of the next two days the search teams recovered seven bodies in the sound, and confirmed that two more, the pilots, were still trapped in the cockpit which was buried nose first in the seabed under 30ft of water. But even this information wasn't enough for us to inform the families that their loved ones were no longer missing but confirmed dead. The bodies would have to be identified in a formal process which would take time. Fortunately, someone at the right level in DOD made the decision that I could identify the bodies, and that this would be enough to permit official notification.

I knew all seven members of the team, but because of the impact of the crash would need information about tattoos and other distinguishing features to identify them. These were sent to me, and I entered the morgue on Hurlburt to perform my grisly task. I was accompanied by the senior military surgeon on site and, for the sake of ensuring that we did this correctly, I talked him through the process by which I was able to identify each corpse.

It was a gut-wrenching business, but I was driven by the determination to allow the waiting families to escape limbo. We had just begun when my phone rang; it was a doctor in Nicaragua, where my daughter was participating in a college trip, calling to inform me that she had been in a traffic accident. I elicited the information that she was being treated for neck injuries but was expected to be OK, before returning to the task at hand.

For the next few weeks, I travelled around the country visiting the families and attending funerals. As a commander, trying to comfort the bereaved loved ones of my Marines, I felt totally helpless and, illogical though it may seem, ridden by guilt. Guilt because they had been my responsibility and because I would never be able to step inside the tight circle of grief experienced by those who had loved them. That the wives, girlfriends and parents were all incredibly gracious made it all the worse. Most seemed to derive some comfort by knowing that their loved one died instantly, among friends, doing something that they believed to be important.

My trip to visit each of them was a tour through America's diverse spiritual heartland: from an upscale neighborhood in Connecticut to a trailer park in New Mexico – the only common thread being a connection with the Marine Corps. With every visit, I absorbed a little more ambient grief, until one morning, outside a small town in Louisiana, I felt suddenly overwhelmed, and pulled into a lay-by to recover. I was resting my head on the steering wheel, taking deep breaths, waiting for the feeling to pass when someone knocked on the window. It was a state-trooper, wondering what a Marine in full dress blues was doing slumped over his dashboard, in the back of beyond.

We reconstituted Team 8231 by transferring six Marines and a corpsman from elsewhere in the battalion. A Marine Special Operations Team, or MSOT, has fourteen members, so the loss of seven from one team was bound to have a devastating impact on the survivors; but the pre-deployment training schedule left little time for mourning, and they were soon back in the thick of it. As I was to learn myself, having to focus on the task at hand doesn't overcome grief, it just postpones having to deal with it.

Kaela recovered from her injuries, which included a potentially serious blow to the neck, and returned to her job working in a home for the severely mentally disabled in one of the poorer sections of Managua. I took a few days off to visit her there, and was struck by how well she handled even the most unruly patients, earning the respect of her Nicaraguan co-workers who were unaccustomed to seeing American college students roll up their sleeves with so little inhibition. She and Siobhan graduated from college that summer, after which both girls chose vocations dedicated to serving others: Siobhan moved to California to work with special needs children, while Kaela joined a group in Colorado dedicated to helping the homeless. Not for the first time, I wondered how I had ended up with daughters who were so genuinely altruistic.

Meanwhile, I turned over command of the regiment and dived headlong into the task of preparing the CJSOTF for deployment. Master Gunnery Sergeant Jay Root had now joined the team as my senior enlisted advisor – a welcome addition since, as any commander knows, you can't command effectively unless you have a means to keep a finger on the pulse of your unit, a conduit to the enlisted personnel who are the ones most impacted by your decisions. And Jay, a bullet-headed Hawaiian, tough as nails, was just the man to do that.

I was also to be getting a SEAL as my executive officer to round out the team. A recent graduate of Harvard's JFK School of Governance, Commander Andy F. had some seventeen years of experience in the special operations community, and was a level-headed officer with a penchant for thorny problems; just what I needed in an XO.

I had concerns with one member of my primary staff: the CJSOTF logistics officer who was vastly out of his depth. I found out later that he had been bounced from unit to unit before ending up under my command; evidently someone thought that the fight against ISIS was the perfect place to put an officer struggling to perform. I worked with him, hoping that he would start to gain traction, but with just two months left prior to deployment, it was clear that I simply couldn't afford to take him with us. We found a replacement, and I made the decision to move him back to his unit rather than fire him, what is known in the Marine Corps as a soft relief. It was a tough call, he was a newly promoted major confronted with an extraordinarily demanding job, but I should probably have sacked him instead of passing the problem on to someone else. These decisions are never easy.

The convergence of strong personalities serving together for the first time, and under the gun to perform, created no small amount of friction; and I found myself playing a variety of roles from counselor to coach to disciplinarian in an effort to maintain cohesion as the date for the final pre-deployment evaluation approached. But for the most part things were coming together, and I was pleased with progress.

Then my world shattered. It began again with a late-night phone call – this time I could barely make out the voice at the other end, just enough to learn that Kaela had been knocked off her bike by a truck and was undergoing surgery in hospital. Then, as I rushed to the airport for the first available flight to Denver, my phone rang again. It was the surgeon who had been working on Kaela now for several hours.

'Mr Milburn, I have done all that I can, but I'm afraid that it doesn't look good for Kaela. She has sustained massive injuries to her pelvis and has lost a lot of blood. I recommend that you get out here as soon as you can.'

I called Siobhan who was in California and booked her a ticket to Denver. As I drove to the airport, I was tormented by memories of all the times when I had been too busy to visit Kaela; if she would only live, I promised, I would never make that mistake again.

Throughout the interminable flight, I could only stare at the seat in front of me, desperate for news. Upon landing, there were fifteen voicemails waiting for me; I returned the latest call – it was her doctor. 'She's alive, and appears to be responding,' was all I heard. 'She can move her legs, so we're hopeful.'

I told Siobhan the good news when she landed about twenty minutes after me, and we hugged in blissful relief amidst the crowd disembarking her plane. Kaela was conscious when we got to the hospital; unable to speak because of her oxygen mask, she clutched our hands and cried softly before drifting off to sleep. The truck had rolled over her lower body, the surgeon told us later that morning, causing the worst pelvic injuries he had ever seen. Poor Kaela – but at least she was going to live, I told myself. Even if that meant being in a wheelchair for the rest of her life, it was still a miracle.

But I didn't get to make that decision. Kaela's mother Nancy and grandmother Jeanine joined Siobhan and I later that day, and together we kept vigil by her bedside six days. The room filled up with cards and stuffed animals, and the nurse braided Kaela's hair and Nancy sang to her – but she never recovered consciousness. An MRI revealed massive brain damage – although it took a day for the hospital to tell us. The medical team skirted Nancy and me, eyes averted. No one came to talk to us, but I caught them looking back at us from the end of the corridor and knew that they had bad news. I fought the sense of mounting dread that clamped my insides in a vice; I felt frozen, rooted to the spot by fear, unable to bring myself to ask the question that would confirm what I already knew. She was only 23.

Afterwards, after they had taken Kaela off the machine, and she had taken her last breath, Siobhan and I clung to each other, not knowing where to go or what to do.

I remember Kaela's grandmother clutching my arm and saying: 'Thank you for being such a good father.' Which meant the world to me, but couldn't wash away the burden of guilt for all the times that I hadn't been there for her. And for not being able to protect her; that's what fathers are supposed to do.

In the end, what kept me going during the hours and days that followed was the strength of others: Nancy, Siobhan and Kaela's grandparents, Chuck and Jeanine who had already lost a son, and now a much-beloved granddaughter. Nancy and Siobhan were the ones who took the cards down and gathered up the stuffed animals with Kaela lying still in the hospital bed. I lacked their strength, and instead walked the streets for hours, wishing that I could take Kaela's place.

A few days later, I rejoined the CJSOTF for our final evaluation exercise in Fort Bragg. The unit emerged with flying colors; I am told that I performed well but have no recollection of the exercise. General Votel visited us on the final day and, taking me aside, offered me the option of handing the CJSOTF over to someone else. I told him truthfully that I wanted to continue. Kaela had been excited about the prospect of our mission, and was incensed by media reports of ISIS atrocities, in particular the rape and murder of Kayla

Mueller, an American humanitarian volunteer. For my part, I knew that if I didn't deploy, I would not know how to deal with my grief.

Before losing Kaela, I couldn't have imagined reaching the nadir of despair that I felt during that time and to which I returned for a period after my return from Iraq. The experience taught me much about resilience, about having to grasp for an inner core of strength when swamped with grief. I knew that I would be forever changed, and decided then that it would have to be for the better. I haven't always lived up to this promise, but when I find myself lagging, the memory of Kaela remains an inspiration.

# Chapter 50

After surging through Mosul in the summer of 2014, the Islamic State foundered against the breakwater of Kurdish defenses that surrounded the city on three sides. In the eighteen months since, both sides manned opposing trench lines only a few hundred meters apart in a scene reminiscent of the First World War.

The attack on December 16 2015 was intended to shatter this impasse by punching a hole in the front line, big enough to allow thousands of fighters

### IRAQ – JAN 2016

Map Of Iraq, January 2016 showing area controlled by ISIS.

to stream through. For this breakthrough, Daesh chose an area north-east of Mosul, where the rugged terrain with its numerous draws and dried river beds offered ample concealment for an attacking force.

The only disadvantage from the point of view of the Islamic State was that this sector was manned by a particularly good Kurdish unit: the Zeravani Brigade, who were partnered with a seventy-man Canadian Special Forces detachment. This may have been why the Daesh commanders decided to attack in the late afternoon, rather than at dawn, as was their custom. They would have learned from surveillance that this was the time when the Peshmerga conducted a shift change, and would thus be distracted. And during late afternoon, the setting sun would be directly in the defenders' eyes, while the incipient cold of early evening would bring with it shrouds of mist that gathered in the draws and hollows of no man's land.

The night before the attack, a freezing fog rolled off the surrounding hills, perfect cover for the hundreds of Daesh fighters moving silently into their attack positions. Some of them wore explosive vests with the mission of running into the Kurdish front line bunkers before detonating. Suicide vehicle-bombs were guided to their launch positions along carefully reconnoitered tracks, out of sight from the Kurdish positions. ISIS field commanders scanned the Peshmerga lines alert to signs that they had been spotted, but there were none.

The attackers lay still under dun-colored ponchos lined with foil, which concealed their body heat from the Canadians' thermal night sights. At 1600hrs on the dot, a chorus of whistle blasts signaled the attack.

'They came from five directions,' one Peshmerga commander commented later. The vehicle-bombs led the way, detonating in earth-shaking explosions that sliced the air for hundreds of yards around them with shards of jagged metal. An armored bulldozer drove through the Peshmerga lines, flattening concertina wire, crushing trenches and bunkers. And right behind them came Daesh's assault troops: wide-eyed berserkers yelling jihadi war-cries.

By the time the Canadians heard about the attack it was dark. They dispatched a team to Zeravani headquarters where General Khorshed, Brigade Commander, requested their help. And so it was that the plan to throw Daesh back across the line was put together in short order by a Canadian sergeant and his team.

The attack reached its culmination point at nightfall. The Daesh fighters halted to secure the positions they had seized with plans to continue the next day, giving the defenders a temporary respite. The Canadians launched a drone to determine the enemy's location while coordinating with the US headquarters in Erbil to line up aircraft for the counter-attack. Then they moved with several hundred Kurdish fighters to Tal Aswad, a small village several miles from the front line, their designated line of departure. They had no way of telling that Daesh was already in the village, occupying houses within a stone's throw of the school house which the Canadians had chosen as their command post.

The next morning was foggy and visibility was poor. 'We could not even see our hands in front of us,' Khorshed said later. Nevertheless, the counter-attack stepped off on time. The Kurds ran into the enemy right away, and the Canadians found themselves supporting a close-quarters fight to clear Tal Aswad, firing over the heads of the Peshmerga to kill the Daesh fighters who swarmed towards them.

The fog cleared rapidly, laying bare the Daesh positions to dozens of aircraft waiting to attack. The Canadians continued to run the fight, no easy task for a small unit having to control strikes in close proximity to friendly forces while in a direct fire fight with the enemy. Meanwhile, Canadian medics were tending the wounded at a nearby aid station, treating over a hundred casualties, blast injuries, gunshot wounds and traumatic amputations. By late morning, the Peshmerga had moved back into their positions on the line now strewn with Daesh bodies; some 250 according to their subsequent count.

There are few text book examples in combat – but the attack and its aftermath illustrate some distinctive aspects of the special operations fight against ISIS. The way in which the attack was planned and executed highlighted the quality of ISIS's field commanders, who had perfected their techniques during four years of combat in Syria. It was their expertise coupled with a steady flow of eager recruits that made ISIS so formidable a fighting organization.

The special operations mission in Iraq was to help our partners, the Iraqis and Kurds, without becoming directly engaged with the enemy *wherever possible*. This incident, and many others that were to follow, taught us that this wasn't always possible. That fighting a campaign against a vicious enemy might occasionally involve contact with that enemy probably won't come as a surprise to the reader but it was the cause of much consternation to my chain of command. In the weeks ahead I would find myself repeatedly having to justify why units under my command had engaged ISIS in direct combat.

The Canadian response to the attack was a perfect illustration of how Special Operations Forces can deliver effect out of proportion to their strength in numbers but the incident also provided an interesting lesson in the philosophy of command. The sergeant on the spot knew that he had the backing of his task force commander, who knew in turn, without the need for consultation, that his chain of command back in Canada would not quibble with his decision to engage the enemy.

The Canadians were operating under the principle of mission command: the theory that when you give someone a mission, you explain your criteria for success, provide resources and support where needed, but otherwise stay out of the way. In turn, the subordinate commander owns the mission and any risk that he incurs. He is responsible for the results – good and bad. The manner in which the Canadian Task Force handled this situation illustrates the value of a mission command as a doctrine, and perhaps – because of the level of trust required – why the US military finds it so hard to adopt.

I have oversimplified this discussion for the sake of brevity, and opened myself to criticism that in an environment like Iraq where tactical actions are likely to have strategic affect, the topic of risk management is more complicated than I have allowed. All true, but I'll continue with the story of the campaign against ISIS, from my admittedly biased perspective, and let the reader decide whether the US method of conducting war with its emphasis on centralized control doesn't lead overall to greater risk.

# Chapter 51

The Task Force deployed on New Year's Day 2016, tasked with degrading, dismantling and defeating ISIS – a mission that had a pleasing alliterative ring to it. This would be a countrywide campaign designed to undermine the enemy's leadership and morale, while systematically killing his foot soldiers, and wresting back key terrain. Our ultimate goal was Mosul.

However well prepared you believe your unit is, and in spite of your peoples' instinct to tug at the leash, once on the ground you have to plan time for assessment. War prompts rapid change, and the conditions upon which you based your plan may no longer be valid. Assessment is not something that we in the military typically do well. It involves much more than making *PowerPoint* charts that show easily measurable data with no necessary correlation to success (estimates of enemy casualties and equipment destroyed are a great example of this). It's a continuous process, and the commander has to be personally involved, venturing out to all units under his command.

I realized, even before deploying, that unless I brought in another task force, I would have problems with my span of control. There's no substitute for being able to see things for yourself – I had learned that as a battalion

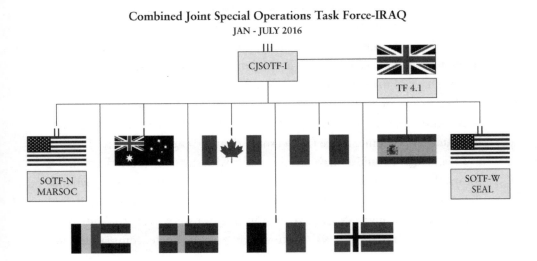

**Combined Joint Special Operations Task Force-IRAQ**
JAN - JULY 2016

commander – but with a unit spread over hundreds of miles, I couldn't visit every single team with enough frequency to get a real feel for what was going on. I needed enough subordinate commanders to be doing the same, assisting me to command and assess throughout our area of operations. This was something that I lacked.

As CJSOTF commander I commanded eight task forces, but only one of these – a Special Operations Task Force (SOTF), composed of SEALs – was large enough to conduct independent operations. The problem was that this SOTF had too many units spread over too wide an area to be able to manage them all effectively. Its geographical span of control, ranged from Anbar Province in Western Iraq to the Kurdish sector in the north. These were two distinct fights; the Iraqi and the Kurdish commanders fought the war against ISIS separately, as though they belonged to different countries, which in a real sense they did. It was too much to ask of a single SOTF commander – with his limited resources – to focus on two such disparate areas of operation. I would need a second task force. So I put in a request for a MARSOC task force to lead the campaign in the north – a request that stirred up no small amount of angst among cynics in the special operations enterprise who saw this as being a parochial bid on my part to get more Marines into the fight.

As for my relationship with those above me, all indications were that I was in for a tough time. Special Operations Forces were leading the campaign in Iraq in the sense that only SOF had the authorities and training to do what needed to be done. But as CJSOTF commander, I was subordinate to a conventional army division headquarters, heavy with generals and determined to make a name for itself in combat. The division had twice as many personnel on its headquarters staff alone as we had in the entire CJSOTF. It was only half in jest that I would modify a famous Churchillian quote to apply to this top-heavy arrangement: 'Never in the field of human conflict have so many invested so much, to lead so few.'

I had to joke to maintain my sanity. Although it's a time-honored tradition in the military to complain about the next level up, it's not often that higher headquarters becomes more troublesome than the enemy.

In contrast, I couldn't have been happier with the task forces that worked for me, from the larger Canadian and Australian contributions to the smaller detachments from Holland, Norway, Belgium, France, Sweden, Italy and Spain – each brought distinctive capabilities and were eager to contribute. I never once ran into a situation where a subordinate commander felt compelled to pull a red card on me, indicating a conflict between my orders and his national chain of command. At times I was not beyond using their national authorities to circumvent the burdensome restrictions placed on US units.

Similarly, we had a close relationship with the Iraqi counter-terrorism service, known as CTS or ISOF, and the famed Kurdish Peshmerga. We were also tasked with training and deploying some 10,000 Sunni tribesmen against ISIS in Anbar province, which was going to be a delicate task, given the less-than-symbiotic relationship between Anbari tribes and the Iraqi government. Fortunately, Maliki was no longer prime minister, having been replaced the previous summer by Haider al-Abadi, a pragmatist who realized that in order to win Anbar back he would need the support of the country's Sunni population.

Then, there was the enemy. The Islamic State had steadily gained territory over the course of the previous year, and now, with over a third of the country under its control, was only 30 miles from Baghdad. As we arrived, CTS was leading an attack to reclaim Ramadi in a block-by-block slugging match that dragged on for almost three months. Even with Ramadi back in government hands, ISIS still held the vast majority of Anbar Province and had the benefit of fighting closer to the Iraqi capital than to its own.

While the Iraqi security forces were focused on the fight in Anbar, I wanted ISIS to feel pressure closer to home. We would continue to support CTS as they fought toe to toe with the enemy, but to have strategic effect (which should always be the objective of special operations forces) we needed to focus our efforts on the enemy's center of gravity. We could kill Baghdadi's foot soldiers all day and it would make no difference as long as he continued to draw recruits from across the Muslim diaspora. And at the rate that the Iraqi security forces were clawing back territory it would take two more bloody years to reach Mosul.

It was Mosul, from whence Baghdadi issued his call to arms, which symbolized the Islamic State, it was the magnet that drew followers to the black flag. Mosul was Daesh's center of gravity, the source of its moral strength. And in war, as Napoleon famously said, the moral is to the physical as ten is to one. Mosul was where we were going to use that principle to even the score.

All of this was easy to say, but much harder to make a reality. Fortunately, I had the right team: a brainy cabal of junior officers: Marines, Green Berets, SEALs, Australians and Brits, who put together in short order an ingenious but simple plan. In its essence it involved loosening Daesh's grip on Mosul simultaneously from inside and out, in a manner designed to elicit an atavistic reaction from Daesh's leadership, while offering to Mosul's long-suffering inhabitants the message that help was on its way.

We called this Operation Emerald Bounty. The origin of this name was like the clue to a crossword puzzle. Emerald City was our term for Mosul (I coined the phrase to signify Mosul's value to both sides, though I couldn't help thinking that it was a wholly inappropriate description of the shoddy city whose forbidding streets I had patrolled several years previously), and Bounty was a play on the word's actual meaning as a prize, and its connection with the term mutiny as in Mutiny on the Bounty. Inciting mutiny – or more accurately, revolt – would be one method by which we proposed to win Mosul back.

Marine Corps doctrine directs you to find the enemy's critical vulnerability, the chink in his armor that will tip him off-balance and bring him down. In practice, it's not so clear cut; if the enemy does have a critical vulnerability it's seldom apparent. So, you look for a range of vulnerabilities and work on them all simultaneously, ready to exploit success. That's what our campaign was designed to do. I didn't think for a moment that any one of our initiatives under Emerald Bounty would be the silver bullet to bring the Islamic State to its knees, but in their aggregate, I was confident that they would have an effect, enabling the Iraqis to take Mosul earlier and at less cost than would otherwise be the case.

Looking for vulnerabilities inside Mosul would mean working with disaffected members of the local population, of which there were many. The Islamic State's failure to deliver on the basic obligations of civil government while imposing their medieval version of the rule of law, had alienated the city's population. The question was whether they had been cowed into submission – or were angry enough to take action.

I can't disclose how we went about enlisting the help of allies within Mosul; but this would make a captivating story in itself. It takes extraordinarily talented people to persuade others, whom they have never met, to rebel against an occupying force at the risk of their lives. And it takes a good understanding of group psychology: that it's best to start with small acts of defiance, graffiti or minor vandalism for instance, even if their contribution to your objectives may appear insignificant. Once someone takes that initial step it becomes easier to persuade them to do more. In this we were enabled by ISIS, who punished all acts of defiance in the same draconian manner, bringing to mind the old English proverb 'You might as well be hanged for a sheep as for a lamb.'

Our inside approach also included using advanced targeting methods to identify and take out the Islamic State's mid-level managers. Killing the top people of an organization like ISIS or Al Qaeda, while satisfying, achieves little in the long run – and can even make things worse than before. The greatest period of bloodletting in Iraq occurred after Zarqawi's death. Baghdadi was third in line after Zarqawi, the two intervening leaders having been killed by US strikes. We were fighting the Hydra; every head we lopped off would quickly be replaced. On the other hand, if we could take out of play the people whose expertise Daesh depended on, the men who really ran the organization and commanded its units in the field, then – so we reasoned – we had a better chance of causing real damage.

To exert pressure from outside the city, we needed to find a group of Sunnis to conduct raids into the Mosul's outskirts. The majority of Mosul's population were more fearful of a vengeful Shia liberation than they were of ISIS. We needed to show them that their fellow Sunnis were taking action, however symbolic, to challenge the Islamic State's grip on the city. ISIS had only been partially effective in eliminating use of the internet in Mosul, and we knew that such news would travel fast.

We weren't looking for a relief force – just a group of fighters who could strike and then withdraw. 'Sunni dudes with balls who are willing to cross the front line and shoot their weapons at the enemy,' was how Jeff Buffa summarized our requirements. But where to find people with these qualifications?

Enter one Atheel al-Nujaifi, former governor of Mosul until the city's fall to ISIS. Nujaifi, a Sunni, was a controversial figure. Maliki's government had issued a warrant for his arrest on a variety of charges from spying for the Turks to collaborating with the Islamic State. Our own reports suggested that he had ties with a shadowy organization called the Naqshbandi Army, a Baathist insurgent group. The Naqshbandi was now reported to be allied with the Islamic State, while also negotiating with the Iraqi government on a plan to raise a counter-ISIS force. I had spent enough time in Iraq to believe all of the above.

Nujaifi would be our man. War makes for strange bedfellows, the enemy of my enemy is my friend, I reasoned. I had a chain of command, however, who were understandably concerned that such a relationship might result in bad publicity. I would have to tread carefully, keeping them informed of everything that I did to avoid playing to their expectation that SOF could not be trusted.

# Chapter 52

For my initial meeting with Nujaifi, I took with me Brandon Griffin, a Green Beret lieutenant colonel whom I planned to put in charge of the northern task force until I could get a Marine headquarters in place. Stocky with dark almost saturnine features, Brandon had three qualities that I regard as being indispensable in a leader: a penchant for solving complex problems, a genuine interest in people, and a keen sense of humor. We got along famously, and I was not surprised to learn on the drive to meet Nujaifi, that we also shared an eclectic taste in music.

The meeting took place in Camp Zurkhan, an old Iraqi army base in the hills some 15 miles north-east of Mosul. We were met at the gate by Nujaifi himself, accompanied by an escort of his militia, smart-looking soldiers in dark green camouflage who greeted us with great fanfare – British-style open-palm salutes, accompanied by much stamping of feet and yelled commands. Nujaifi, who looked in his mid-sixties with heavy jowls and a Saddam moustache, was full of charm, smiling broadly as he hugged us like old friends.

We brought two escorts with us, Marines from the MARSOC company in Erbil, whom I had tasked with poking around while we were in the meeting, taking photographs of the camp, and finding out what they could about the militia. We parked inside the gate, and followed Nujaifi into a single-story building with a flag pole outside, clearly a headquarters of some sort. Inside, he led us to a conference room in the midst of which was a large terrain model depicting Mosul and its environs. Standing around the model were Nujaifi's commanders: grizzled, hard-looking men without the paunches customary among Iraqi officers.

Once introductions had been made, Nujaifi had his intelligence officer give us a brief. Using a pointer he walked us through the terrain model, pointing out Daesh's defensive positions and order of battle – down to the name and exact location of each unit. I was impressed.

Nujaifi's operations officer then pointed to a town called Bashiqa, on the north-east outskirts of Mosul. I knew it well since I had spent a night with the Canadians on the front line overlooking this town. Bashiqa was in ISIS hands, and Nujaifi wanted to take it back. When he explained why, I thought that his words must have been mistranslated.

'I used to own a ranch near this town with many horses. When ISIS came they let all my horses go. I thought I had lost them, but now we have seen some of them in Bashiqa. I want to capture the town and get my horses back.' I paused before replying – a motive's a motive, but I was hoping for something less quixotic from the former Governor of Mosul.

'That's a great plan, Governor, and we can help you do that. Our goal is to create the conditions to take back Mosul, and raiding Bashiqa is a good start.' I was careful to substitute the word raid for capture. A raid meant a planned withdrawal – we didn't want to get stuck in no man's land holding on to useless terrain, and vulnerable to counter-attack. 'We want to message the local population what we are doing, that it is their own people conducting these attacks.'

At this point Nujaifi grew quite excited, and beckoned to his intelligence officer.

In fluent English, the intelligence officer launched into a description of conditions inside Mosul: the shortages of food and fresh water and the increasingly harsh measures that ISIS was taking to control the population.

'Every day there are executions – hangings, crucifixions, burning people alive.'

'This is against our religion,' Nujaifi interrupted. 'Only God can punish by fire.'

'Just yesterday, Daesh shut thirty people in a cage and drowned them in a swimming pool,' the intelligence officer continued. 'The people have had enough.'

I was intrigued. 'Where do you get all your intelligence?'

'Directly from people in the city. We speak to many of them every day – that is how we know so much about Daesh.'

ISIS had pulled down most of the city's cell phone towers, but Nujaifi's contacts were still able to find places where they could get a signal. I took the name of his intelligence officer – we needed to stay in contact with him.

Nujaifi then got to the point. 'We need your help – your training, and support for this attack.'

There was great opportunity here, but I had to be careful not to promise him anything – rule number one when negotiating with Arabs unless you knew 100 per cent that you could deliver. I didn't think that we would be allowed to support a force that was associated with Nujaifi, and I had noticed something else during the meeting that gave me cause for concern. In the back of the room stood a Turkish soldier taking notes. Nujaifi made no secret of his links with this soldier's parent unit who occupied an adjacent camp, but they had entered Iraq uninvited, and I was forbidden to deal with them.

Rather than beat about the bush, I explained all of this to Nujaifi, ending with a proposal.

'If you were to allow us to take, say, 200 of your men,' – he claimed to have 1,000 – 'under the command of your best commander, then we can do this. But we need to separate them from the rest of your force, and,' I nodded to the Turkish observer, 'from them.'

Nujaifi nodded slowly, and then launched into a diatribe about the government. 'Daesh didn't capture Mosul; it was handed to them by Maliki. He ignored all my warnings and allowed the army commander to go on leave days before the attack. He doesn't care about the city because it is Sunni.' It was a story that I had heard before, but I listened patiently knowing that it was de rigueur for any Sunni leader to complain about Baghdad. When he was done, Nujaifi took a sip of tea and then turned back to me.

'OK, I agree. I have the commander for you. Let's go meet him.' He stood up and I glanced at Griff who winked. On the way out of the room I made a beeline for the Turkish soldier.

'Hello, how are you?' I said in Turkish, the limit of my repertoire in that language. Flummoxed, he fumbled his notebook into a pocket and took my outstretched hand.

'Good afternoon, sir,' he said in English, courtesy overcoming surprise. I glanced at his uniform: a colonel. We smiled at each other briefly, before I turned to leave.

Nujaifi led the way out of the headquarters – Griff and I in tow followed by a gaggle of his officers – to the parade deck where a formation of soldiers was marching back and forth.

'Where do they get their weapons and uniforms?' I asked him, noticing the smart turnout and new looking AK-47s.

'The Turks provided the uniforms. I paid for the weapons.' The soldiers were marching in a style that was part-British, part-Third Reich, with a precision that was about on par with a platoon of Marine third-phase recruits. I wondered if this was Nujaifi's show team. My suspicions were confirmed when the formation came to a perfect halt several paces from where I stood, and the officer in charge reported to Nujaifi with the ceremonial aplomb of a Grenadier Guard.

Nujaifi stood the soldiers at ease and introduced me to the officer in front of him.

'This is Major Ibrahim.' The first thing that I noticed was the moustache. It was a flamboyant handlebar that sprouted out on either side of Ibrahim's face, giving him the appearance of a character in one of those vintage British war movies. Above the moustache were a pair of intense eyes that bored into mine as we shook hands.

'I think I've seen this cat on wanted posters,' Griff whispered. I wouldn't have been surprised. Ibrahim's look wasn't quite hostile but it seemed to say: 'I don't normally shake hands with Americans, but will make an exception now for the boss.'

'He's your man,' Nujaifi said, and then spoke to Ibrahim in rapid Arabic. Ibrahim looked straight ahead like an academy plebe, saying '*naam sadi*' (yes sir) several times during the monologue. When Nujaifi had finished, Ibrahim saluted and stamped, turned on his heel, and jogged back to his men without a glance at me.

We ate lunch with Nujaifi and his commanders back in the headquarters' conference room. It was a sumptuous affair with several courses: heaped plates of saffron rice, vegetables fried in olive oil, and greasy chunks of lamb and sheep. Everyone ate with their fingers and chatted freely; Nujaifi seemed relaxed and even Ibrahim smiled from time to time.

Afterwards we exchanged phone numbers, with Griff making plans to link up with Ibrahim and his men a week hence at a location far enough away from the Turks. Griff would bring with him a team of SEALs to conduct an assessment of Ibrahim's men. It was February, and we agreed that we should launch the first raid in mid-April, but didn't commit to a specific target. Emerald Bounty was underway.

But Daesh too had plans.

# Chapter 53

Two weeks after our meeting with Nujaifi I was woken by Jeff in the early hours of the morning.

'Sir, we've got a TIC in Sector Seven.' TIC was the acronym for Troops in Contact, and Sector Seven was one of eight sectors that comprised the Kurdish area of operations.

Awake instantly, I pulled on my boots and followed Jeff. The JOC was shaped like a theater, with rows of seats and computer monitors descending from the back of the room to the front wall upon which were fixed several large screens. The middle one was an electronic map, displaying the position of every unit throughout the CJSOTF, while the screens on either side showed live video streamed directly from cameras aboard drones. At any given time, these screens would be playing several drone videos depicting different operations or different aspects of the same one. Now, all eyes in the JOC were fixed to one of these screens. I watched, but couldn't interpret what I was seeing, just columns of smoke, and shadowy figures moving across the ground.

'Sir, we have a Trident in contact with a larger force of Daesh, Sector Seven, just north of Tisha junction. Looks like Daesh breached the front line to the west sometime during the night and launched an attack.'

Trident was the call sign used for our SEAL task units, each of which was roughly equivalent in size to an MSOT, about 14–16 personnel.

'Do they have air?'

'Not yet. Ceiling was too low, but it's on the way now.'

'Other units in the vicinity?'

'The Pesh have linked up with them, but it's still a pretty small force. TF 4.1 have pushed a team into overwatch about 300 yards north of Trident.' Task Force 4.1 was a British SOF unit.

Major Morgan Ritter, the officer who ran the JOC pointed to the electronic map.

'And we have the MSOT from Sector Eight on the way.'

'OK – get hold of the MSOT and tell them to find a place in overwatch, go firm, and coordinate with Trident to link up there. Tell them not to attempt link up at Trident's current pause.'

If we simply threw the MSOT into the fight we would likely end up with two teams in trouble instead of one, and would risk fratricide. Better to get them into a secure location and then have the Trident fall back – if they could.

'Sir,' it was one of the JTACs – a Joint Tactical Air Controller, the formal designator for personnel trained to direct aircraft on to targets in close proximity to ground troops. 'VBIED moving on the team from south-west.' Vehicle-borne IEDs, or VBIEDs in the labored lexicon of the military, were typically makeshift armored cars packed with explosives, a weapon that ISIS employed time and again with devastating effect. A few seconds later, an outlandish looking black vehicle came into focus on the screen. It was lumbering slowly but inexorably towards the gap in the berm, looking from drone's eye view like a giant beetle. It was maybe 500 yards away from the team at the most.

'Air on station,' called Major Mike Proctor, the strike cell leader who was monitoring the fires net. We weren't in a position to help the team by providing fire support – that was the responsibility of the target engagement authority or TEA, a one-star army general who sat in the Division JOC in Erbil, and had control over the use of all coalition planes and artillery. His job now was clear cut: to push all available aircraft to the team on the ground, allowing them to strike targets. It's a hallowed operational tenet that when you have a unit in trouble, you give them what they need.

'Hey sir,' Proctor again, phone in hand. 'TEA's refusing to push air support to the team. Says that he has the best situational awareness.'

I grabbed the phone. It was a direct line to the TEA but he had one of his deputies manning it now. 'Milburn here at the CJSOTF, I need to speak to the general.'

'He's busy, sir—'

'Does he realize that they've got a VBIED closing in on them?'

'He doesn't think it's a VBIED.'

'What the fuck does he think it is – a school bus? Listen, I need to speak to him now. He's got to push air to the team.'

'He's not coming to the phone, sir. He's aware of the situation but has concerns about the team's qualifications.' I thought that I had misheard.

'What qualifications?'

'JTAC qualifications.'

Another hallowed operational tenet is that *in extremis* anyone can jump on the radio to direct close air support. And it didn't get much more *in extremis* than this.

The vehicle continued to advance. This must have convinced the general that it was indeed a bomb, but he still refused to allow the team to speak to the aircraft. We watched as he controlled the strike himself, using the JTACs sitting in his command post with him. A plume of smoke appeared on the screen – the beetle crawled on unscathed.

There were howls of frustration in the JOC. There's nothing worse than watching men for whom you are responsible face imminent danger without being able to do a thing to help them.

The vehicle was heading for a low ridgeline where the Trident had linked up with a group of Peshmerga. It would hit them from the flank in a matter of minutes.

The second strike missed too, the plume of dirt erupting just behind the vehicle. Then, a second or two later, the beetle detonated in an expanding cloud of black smoke and flame. Everyone cheered. We assumed a fragment from the bomb had caused it to explode, and only later were able to piece together what had really happened.

Earlier that morning, before first light, the Trident had linked up with their partnered Peshmerga unit to set up an observation post on the front line. As the combined patrol moved to their designated position in the gray twilight of pre-dawn, they noticed shapes moving in the mist just in front of them.

'We thought it was sheep,' the team leader laughed when relating the incident to me later. After the attack had been repulsed, the team found dozens of ghillie suits, camouflage coveralls discarded by the attackers, designed to disguise their human shape and make them blend into the background.

'Then we saw that it was Daesh pouring through a hole in the berm. We opened fire and fell back to a ridge line behind our OP. We couldn't see any Pesh, aside from the handful who were with us.

'We called for air but were told that there was none available. At first, I thought we had things under control – we could see them trying to flank us, but they fell back when we lit them up. Then we saw that VBIED. That's when it got crazy with the TEA refusing to pass control to Trey our JTAC – asking us how we could be sure that it was a VBIED.' He shook his head and laughed incredulously.

I had met the general a couple of times and, in truth, wasn't that surprised. Tight lipped and supercilious, he reminded me of one of my boarding school teachers.

'He's a one-star JTAC,' one of his own officers told me. 'He gets really focused on the strike – what angle to bring the jets in from, type of bomb to use, the whole shebang – he loves it.' Every conversation that I had had with him had consisted of him lecturing me – about the Kurds, about ISIS, about how I needed to keep a tighter grip on my people. I knew, and he knew that I knew, that I couldn't afford to get into a confrontation with the US army division. They were looking for a chance to label the CJSOTF as cowboys – unreliable hip-shooters who didn't understand how to run an Air-Land battle. So I endured his criticism without argument.

'Anyway,' the team leader went on. 'When that first bomb missed the VBIED, we started to take shots at it ourselves: two AT-4s and a Carl Gustav.' These were shoulder-fired anti-tank weapons that packed considerable punch. 'I know we had at least one hit – I saw it bounce off – but the VBIED kept rolling. Then, one of the Pesh cats nailed it with a Milan.' The Milan was a French-made, wire-guided missile that had proven to be one of the few direct fire weapons capable of stopping a vehicle bomb. Whoever had supplied them to the Kurds was responsible for saving many lives.

'After the VBIED blew, more Pesh arrived and started to pour it on. Pretty soon there were no Daesh left alive on our side of the line.'

I stewed over the incident as I lay in bed that night. The next day I sent the CJSOTF lawyer, a Marine captain, up to Erbil to take statements. Division sent him back to us, and I was advised by my SOF chain of command not to pursue this course of action. I complied – because in the end no one had been killed, and because I knew my role was to support the division, not the other way around.

I understood why fires had to be controlled through a TEA: we were operating in a sovereign country and the host nation needed assurance that we wouldn't go hog-wild with strikes. However, as soon as we had our own people on the ground in danger, this rationale disappeared. How could a US officer, a general no less, not understand this?

In my mind his actions bordered on criminal negligence, but I let it die for fear of undermining the mission – wondering if I had simply sold out.

# Chapter 54

In Anbar, my SEAL task force was planning an ambitious operation to recapture a town called Rutbah in the remote western part of the province. This would involve bringing together a number of disparate Iraqi units, to include Shia police and Sunni Tribal fighters, in a combined attack supported by US aircraft.

The final planning meeting for the Rutbah operation was held at Taqqadum, a base in south-eastern Anbar that I remembered well from my previous tours. There were some larger than life personalities at the meeting, and if I hadn't worked with Iraqis before, I would have considered it a disaster.

General Rasheed, who headed the 10.000-man tribal militia force in Anbar was a huge posturing bear of a man. So eager was he to impress, that it would be easy to dismiss him as being an ineffectual buffoon – but there was more to Rasheed than met the eye. Somewhat surprisingly for a Shia, he had strong connections with tribal leaders throughout Anbar, and thus was able to bridge the gap between them and government forces. The CJSOTF had a clear mandate to bolster the Iraqi Sunni minority, but our efforts to mobilize, train and equip the tribes made the Iraqi government uneasy. We were always walking a fine line – and Rasheed, with his credentials and connections enabled us to do so.

He had enough *wastah* to pull together dozens of sheikhs, many of whom hated each other. And he coordinated the distribution of American weapons and equipment, not to mention the Iraqi government-provided salaries for these fighters, with only a moderate amount of corruption. All in all, Rasheed was a valuable asset. But despite his managerial skills, he was a disaster as a tactician, and one of my goals for this meeting was to persuade him to delegate tactical command of all tribal units to one of his deputies, Sheikh Shaker.

Shaker, the younger son of one of Anbar's most influential sheikhs, was a fast-talking wide boy with slicked back hair, heavily ringed fingers and a taste for double-breasted, shiny suits. You never knew what to believe with Shaker: he was prone to dramatic declarations and treated every conversation like an audition. I couldn't bring my customary interpreter, a woman, to the meeting because Shaker would try again to persuade her to marry him with unabashed declarations of undying love. The meeting was bound to have distractions aplenty as it was.

And it certainly did. The cast of characters bellowed and postured and bragged with such gusto that at one point Ryan S., the SOTF commander, and I thought that we might have a fight on our hands. In the end, though, we got what we needed: an agreement among the tactical commanders as to who was responsible for doing what, and when.

It was now down to the SOTF, in the days prior to the attack, to remove from play the key Daesh commanders. This they did, with a surgical skill that made it look easy. And, despite a last-minute fracas in the assembly area during which Shaker accused another sheikh of breaking into his house and stealing his furniture, the attack went according to plan; Rutbah fell at the cost of very few casualties.

David Ignatius commented on the operation in his weekly column for the *Washington Post*:

> The battle showed how the campaign against the Islamic State [...] is supposed to work: This month, a US drone attack on a nearby highway killed Shaker Wahib, the terrorists 'military emir' in Anbar, shaking morale. The day before the battle the United States dropped two huge bombs on minefields and berms surrounding the town.
>
> Then came the attack from a combined force of Iraqi Army troops and hundreds of recently recruited tribal fighters who had been trained by US Special Operations Forces. When they moved in, only thirty Islamic State fighters stayed to fight.

The loss of Wahib (the Dulaimi who led Daesh's attack on Fallujah) did indeed undermine the morale of Islamic State fighters in the province, validating our approach to go after the mid-level tactical commanders. Morale is an interesting thing. In the case of the ISIS rank and file there was no straight-line correlation between morale and expectation of survival. Again and again, we saw Islamic State units fight with a happy heart though all hands faced almost certain death. But there was a connection between morale and leadership: the presence of a commander, whose proficiency and charisma lent meaning to their sacrifice, was all important. Remove that – take away the calm voice on the radio – and even foreign fighters, typically more fanatical than their home-grown comrades, were likely to evaporate in the face of determined attack.

Ignatius's article was well informed, but only scratched the surface in describing how well planned the operation was. By carefully mapping key nodes in the enemy's tactical communication network, the SOTF was able to take out almost every one of the Islamic State's leaders in Rutbah on the eve of the attack, undermining both the enemy's will and his ability to fight. It was a virtuoso piece of targeting, bringing together all the intelligence disciplines in support of an operation with devastating effect, a method that the CJSOTF would repeat in every subsequent operation.

By now we were getting good intelligence on the enemy: his leadership, his order of battle and his intentions. But what really fascinated me were insights into the psyche of the Daesh foot soldier: what made him tick. In order to undermine his will to fight, we needed to understand what motivated him.

It would be easy to paint our enemy in simple tones of savagery; there were daily reports aplenty of ISIS atrocities. But if you looked closer, you could find evidence that the Islamic State's soldiers shared with our own some common motives: confidence in their leaders, camaraderie, and a sense that they were fighting for a common cause, a greater good than themselves. Most recruits were drawn to ISIS by its stand against the brutality of the Assad regime, and would justify their decision in moral terms.

Our teams would often use hand-held radios, set to the same frequencies used by ISIS, to listen to the fighters talk to one another. I am not talking here about the high end technical aspect of signals intelligence, the type that allowed us to target so effectively, but simple monitoring of unencrypted nets. Their conversations gave us a feel for the enemy's morale and would sometimes warn us of impending attack.

In one case I was on the front line with one of the Canadian teams listening to radio traffic between Islamic State fighters who occupied a village less than half a mile from our position. With me was a Canadian officer, Lebanese by birth and a fluent Arabic speaker, who translated what we were hearing:

'They are asking each other how much they get paid. Apparently, the fighters from some countries get paid more than others, and these guys are complaining.'

That sounded very much like a group of Marine lance corporals. And so it continued in the same vein: complaints about the length of their shifts on the front line, questions as to when they were getting relieved and in what order. And the Canadian officer made an interesting comment about the way that they spoke to one another:

'They treat each other with great respect – they're really tight.'

On another occasion Jeff came to my office.

'Hey, sir, come to the JOC – you have to see this.'

We were supporting CTS in their attack on Fallujah (a fight that I found almost unbearable to watch). It had so far been a much easier battle than Ramadi, and two weeks after the initial attack, the city was almost completely back in Iraqi government hands; only a small segment of the north-eastern part of the city, and Karma of course, still belonged to ISIS.

We had a drone over this part of the city now, and everyone on the JOC floor was watching the live footage displayed on the big screen. It was a volleyball game. A group of ISIS fighters were battling it out on a makeshift court, their weapons stacked neatly to one side, cheered on by a small crowd of their comrades. We watched transfixed, and, with no sense of irony, became lost in the game, cheering points and groaning at near misses. As the ball bounded out of play the strike cell leader turned to me:

'Sir, do you want to take them out.' The drone was carrying Hellfire missiles. Jeff and I looked at one another and shook our heads simultaneously. 'No, let them finish the game.'

On another occasion I was given a captured cell phone by our Italian contingent commander, who worked with an Iraqi SOF unit called the Emergency Response Division or ERD (a unit whom US SOF were prohibited from supporting because of the commander's extremist Shia affiliations).

'Sir, take a look at this. It belonged to one of your countrymen, no longer on this earth.'

By countrymen, Luigi meant a Brit – the fact that a Marine colonel spoke with a British accent fascinated him. The Italians had unlocked the phone, and I skimmed through the photos: pictures of a young man with an engaging smile striking various poses with his comrades; the type of mock-warrior goofy pictures that young soldiers everywhere love to take. But it was the photos of the dead man's home and family that caught my attention: pictures of a chubby teenager, only just recognizable as the ISIS fighter, with his sisters and parents. In one shot, the boy was standing in the drive way of a council house somewhere in the UK with his arms draped around his parents' shoulders. It was a happy domestic scene, a world away from the brutality of his ultimate destination. We turned the camera over to British military who, I understand, then passed it to their police to do the forensics on the council house photo and thus identify the boy and inform the family that he was dead.

# Chapter 55

Meanwhile Griff was giving me regular reports on the Nineveh Strike Force, as we had christened the contingent of fighters given to us by Nujaifi. Most of them had some prior military training, and the unit was really coming together. Ibrahim was turning out to be a natural field commander, and although his methods of exerting discipline through liberal application of corporal punishment appeared draconian by our standards, he had the loyalty and confidence of his men, something that fear alone couldn't buy.

We had already written the order for the raid. It wasn't going to be Bashiqa – the town offered little of value (aside from runaway horses) and was riddled with IEDs – but another village nearby that ISIS used as a strongpoint for its defense in sector.

Now we had to get approval for the plan, or CONOP for Concept of Operations as military jargon dubbed the templated *PowerPoint* slides by which we fought wars. CONOPs were given a numerical category of risk, the higher the number, the higher the risk, and the higher up the chain of command it would have to go for approval. This one had to go to the division commander himself, and I personally shepherded it every step of the way to explain why the risk was worth it. The bigger a staff you have, and the division staff was huge, the greater the chance that a CONOP will languish on the desk of some well-meaning but officious staff officer eager to find flaws. Emerald Bounty wasn't just another CONOP – it was our plan to grab the caliphate by the nether regions and give them a hearty squeeze. I wanted to ensure that everyone understood that. It was approved, but with a warning:

'This can't fail, Andy. If we end up with a bunch of dead Sunni tribesman there will be hell to pay.'

Risk was a topic that came up in every conversation with the division staff. Although we had an excellent relationship with the TEA in Baghdad, a Marine one-star general, we still had continuous problems with his army counterpart in Erbil who guarded jealously his control of fires even when friendly lives were at stake. Whenever any of our teams felt compelled to use their own weapons against ISIS (instead of calling for air support), I was called to account. The area between the front and Mosul itself, where these engagements occurred, had been largely cleared of civilians, and ISIS was, in the terms used by US rules of engagement, a declared hostile force, so it was hard to understand the general's lack of trust. It became so acute a problem that I would routinely accompany operations so that I could take personal responsibility for the use of our own weapons.

In one such operation, a MARSOC team was working with the Peshmerga to take back a town called Basheer, just across the front line from Kirkuk. We had identified Basheer as being an important hub in the enemy's defensive line; its capture would enable us to sever the route by which the Islamic State transported men and material north to Mosul.

The Iraqi Kurds are not a homogenous political group. They are split into two main political parties: the Kurdish Democratic Party (KDP) and the Patriotic Union of Kurdistan (PUK) which, at times in recent history, have fought against one another. The KDP were now in power as the ruling party of the Kurdish region, collaborating, albeit uneasily, with the Iraqi government. Both the KDP and the Iraqi government were deeply suspicious of the PUK, who had a history of fierce, sometimes violent, campaigning for the cause of Kurdish independence.

The Basheer operation was to be fought by the PUK branch of the Peshmerga, under the command of one Wastah Rasul, an iconic commander with a long history of fighting Saddam's army, and at times the KDP. Because of this, it had been a struggle to get the Basheer plan approved.

As an example of the disproportionately influential role played by special operations forces in Iraq, Wastah Rasul's most trusted US confidant was a MARSOC captain, one Scott Holub, and it was Scott's team who were responsible for supporting the Basheer operation. The night before the attack he woke me for a call from the TEA.

'Andy, I need you to confirm that there are no Shia militia involved in this attack, or it's off.'

The Islamic State was not our only enemy. The war had spawned a mosaic of Shia militias, many of which were Iranian-backed zealots, openly hostile to Americans, and US forces were forbidden to have anything to do with them. But why I was being asked this question now was beyond me. As so often in my conversations with the TEA, I felt as though I'd slipped into an alternate world.

'Sir, I haven't seen any Shia militia. Where's this coming from?'

'General Amir. You know how he feels about the PUK, and now he's telling us that they are tied in with the Shia militia.' My old friend Abdul Amir was now the chief of staff for the entire Iraqi armed forces.

'Sir, there's no way.' I sounded more confident than I had a right to be. Who knew what units were on either side of us in the dark? But the PUK had recently clashed with Shia militia in a nearby town, and it just didn't make sense that they would now turn to them for help.

'OK Andy, I am holding you responsible for ensuring that we don't end up supporting anyone other than the Kurds. Got it?' I told him I did, although I had frankly lost track of everything that he held me responsible for.

But our problems weren't over. The next morning the attack launched on time; the Peshmerga used bulldozers to breach the berm that marked the front line, and soon vehicles and men were pouring through the gap. I stood on the berm and watched the cavalcade flow past, creating a reddish twilight of choking red dust. The attack had an almost festive air to it: the passing vehicles, trucks and jeeps, were packed to capacity with Kurdish soldiers, grinning, waving Peshmerga flags and flashing Churchillian V-signs. A tank rumbled by, a giant Peshmerga flag streaming from its turret – a cluster of soldiers clinging to its hull, shouting and punching the air, drunk with exhilaration.

As I drove back to our command post, which was positioned on a roof top about half a kilometer back from the front line, I noticed with some concern that the friendly side of the berm was a mass of stationary vehicles; in their hurry to get everyone through the breach, the Pesh had created a traffic jam. It was the worst possible time to get the news that Scott Holub passed to me when I arrived at the CP:

'Sir, there's been a delay. We've got no planes inbound for another hour.'

Just at that moment an F-15 roared over our heads. 'That looked like a plane to me.' I commented unhelpfully. We swiveled our heads to follow the gray shape, holding our hands up to shield our eyes from the sun.

'It's Iraqi,' Scott yelled. Sure enough, I could make out the Iraqi flag on the jet's tail fin as it banked then hurtled back towards us. We watched with horror as a dark shape detached from its underbelly. There was a flash, a gout of dirt and a dull boom, as the jet shrieked over our heads.

'That was right on top of the Swedes,' Scott yelled. Our Swedish SOF contingent was manning an observation post – known as an OP – on the front line. Scott jumped on the net to check on them; they were unhurt but shaken – the bomb had fallen less than 100 meters from their position, close enough to send shards of shrapnel singing over their heads. I raised the TEA on my radio.

'Sir, we're getting bombed by the Iraqi Air Force.'

'Are you sure?'

'Certain, unless ISIS now has an air force. They almost hit one of my teams.'

'OK Andy, got it. Will find out what's going on.'

At that moment a helicopter gunship clattered overhead; it too bore Iraqi markings. It banked over our heads, into a shallow dive towards the front line, and fired three rockets – yellow dots of flame streaking down towards the Peshmerga packed in the breach site. There was a flash and one of the Pesh bulldozers disappeared in a billowing black cloud as the crump of an explosion reached us. We discovered later that the driver, displaying cat-like reflexes, had jumped from the cab seconds before impact and survived.

'Mother fucker.' Someone yelled, articulating the phrase in four distinct syllables. Scott grabbed my sleeve. 'The Pesh are taking incoming in the breach.'

I followed Scott's outstretched finger and saw several columns of smoke shroud the mass of men and vehicles jamming the breach site. At first, I thought that it was from the rockets, but as I watched, two more plumes rose into the air: mortars.

'Sir, we've got the point of impact.' Scott, handset jammed to his ear, was talking to one of the OPs. He raised his team chief, Master Sergeant Craig Kalby on the radio. Kalby was manning the team's support position on the line, about a kilometer from the breach site.

'Got mortars ready to shoot in direct lay. Fifty cal too, and switchblade.' All MSOTs had a complement of machine guns, including the venerable .50 caliber M-2 known colloquially to generations of Marines as the Ma Deuce or fifty cal. From the oldest weapon in our inventory to the newest: Switchblade was a kamikaze drone that could be directed onto a point target with surgical precision, leaving its immediate surroundings untouched.

'OK, shoot.' I told him. We needed to get enough rounds downrange to distract the ISIS gunners from firing the next volley.

A few seconds later I heard the *thunk* of outgoing mortars, then the distinctive *thud-a-thud* of the fifty cal.

'Sir, it's the TEA' Scott called. *How did he find out so quickly?*

I took the handset, preparing myself for the argument to come.

'Andy, what the hell is going on. Are you firing mortars?'

'Yes. The Pesh are taking fire in the breach, and I have OPs only 300 meters away.'

'Are US personnel under fire.'

'Not yet.'

'Well you aren't authorized to make that decision.'

'Sir, our partners are in trouble, and it's a matter of one correction before our guys are too; I'm not prepared to wait.'

'That's not up to you, colonel, that's my decision – you need to cease fire now.' I could picture the scene in the JOC as everyone craned to hear the exchange without appearing to be listening.

'Sir, got to go.'

I was flabbergasted. We were under attack from ISIS *and* the Iraqi Air Force, with no supporting fires other than our own. Our partners were getting killed, there were no civilians in the area, and the enemy was clearly identifiable. And yet a US colonel wasn't authorized to give his men the order to open fire. I had fallen through the looking glass into a world so absurd that I decided to pretend it was a dream.

There were no more inbound mortars; the Peshmerga succeeded in capturing Basheer by the end of the day after a tough fight. I never heard any more about my decision to authorize the team to open fire at the enemy, and though I submitted a full report on the Iraqi Air Force's performance that day, I heard nothing on that count either. The general told me that it had been an error, and I assumed that he was correct – why would Iraqi pilots fire on their allies? But Wastah Rasul was convinced that it was no accident.

'They hate us more than ISIS,' he told me with a sad smile. I remembered how eleven years previously Amir had railed about the Kurds, and wondered if Rasul wasn't correct.

For the Kurds, Sunnis and Shia, the Islamic State was a temporary distraction. For them the real fight was yet to come.

Many of the Shia militias regarded the US as being the real enemy, and appeared to be waiting for the right time to take a crack at us. On more than one occasion this tension led to open confrontation. A week or so after Basheer, I was involved in one of these incidents.

It happened just outside our base in Baghdad, on the compound owned by the Iraqi Emergency Response Division, the unit partnered with our Italian SOF contingent. I had undertaken the task of training a battalion of border guards for the purpose of deploying them to man the Al Waleed border crossing between Anbar and Syria. One of Ryan S's teams was running them through their paces on a range owned by the ERD, and Jeff Buffa and I drove out to visit them.

Both the Border Guard Force and the ERD belonged to the Ministry of Interior, a bastion of Shia sectarianism. We were therefore not surprised to find a group of about fifty Shia militia gathered in a loose semicircle behind the firing line. They were watching the training, smoking and chatting among themselves, and parted easily at our interpreter's request to allow us through. Clad in blue camouflage fatigues with new-looking AK-47s slung on their shoulders, they eyed us coldly as we passed. About twenty minutes later we were standing on the firing line, watching Ryan's team run the first relay and listening to the senior chief in charge give us a run-down of the day so far, when one of the interpreters interrupted us.

'Gentlemen, we must leave now.' He nodded his head behind us and we turned. The militia men had clustered close behind us, several of them with weapons raised, at the ready. One of them, a man dressed in a uniform different from the others, was speaking to them in an urgent tone.

'What's going on?' the senior chief asked the interpreter uneasily.

'Sadi'. The interpreter addressed me directly. 'That man is telling them that you are the enemy.'

The SEALS on the firing line, noticing the tension, had joined us. They carried only pistols which were holstered. We exchanged glances; the militia had the drop on us; we were outnumbered, outgunned and postured to react crucial seconds behind our adversaries in a shoot-out. I clutched the pistol grip of my weapon, ready to raise it in an instant. I noticed Jeff doing the same.

At that moment, a commotion broke out. A group of ERD soldiers led by a major were pushing their way to the front of the crowd, yelling angrily, weapons raised at the militiamen. The major reached the front of the group and turned around to berate them, making a shooing gesture with his hands. Slowly the militiamen turned and walked back towards their vehicles which were parked by the ERD barracks.

'Shit, that was close,' said the senior chief. He glanced at the interpreter, who appeared terrified. 'Thanks for the heads up.'

The militiamen drove off, and I canceled training for the rest of the day, returning to our headquarters to report the incident. The next day I visited the ERD commander, Major General Thamer to thank him for his men's intervention. Knowing his background, I thought it would be churlish to ask him what the militia were doing outside his headquarters in the first place. We were all questioned by an intelligence team sent by Division. Reading their report, I was not surprised to learn that every one of us had assumed that we were on the verge of being shot when the ERD intervened.

# Chapter 56

The night before the NSF raid, Griff and I slept at the Trident's team house near the front. We were woken at 0230 by Mike the team leader who, ever chipper, handed me a cup of coffee and a baseball cap with his platoon's insignia.

'We'd like you to wear this today, sir – might bring good luck.' I was instantly awake and energized with excitement; it felt good to be up and moving with purpose at that hour. Since losing Kaela, nights had been especially difficult for me.

Cup in hand, I wandered into the team's TOC. Sitting behind computers were a group of operators to whom I had assigned a very specific and highly classified mission. I watched them at work, though to a casual observer they didn't appear to be at work at all, just a group of young men chatting with friends on Skype. But I knew that these friends were risking their lives by using social media at all, and were doing so at this hour to avoid detection. Not for the first time, I reflected on the wide range of skills that we expect from even our most junior ranks. These soldiers chatting away on Skype could walk outside the TOC and exchange places with the SEALS readying for a raid without missing a beat.

An hour later we were in position. Although it was mid-April, the mornings were still cold in northern Iraq, and Griff and I stood shivering, hands thrust in our pockets, watch caps pulled down over our ears. We could make out dim silhouettes in the trench line in front of us, Peshmerga sentries peering over the parapet into no man's land. It doesn't matter what army you're in; no one likes the graveyard watch on a cold morning, the last hours of darkness when spirits are at their lowest.

'Well this is it, sir,' Griff said, spitting a wad of Copenhagen on the ground and turning to me with a wry smile. 'If this goes south, we'll both be looking for new jobs.'

'Yep. And no one will want to try this again. Until the Iraqi Army slugs their way up north sometime next year – if they're lucky.'

Mike wandered over. 'Want to drop by to say hello to the Pesh commander? He'll be awake now.'

I did, it would have been an unpardonable sin not to thank him for his cooperation. Besides, we needed to coordinate the forward passage of lines, the military term for the movement of one unit through another while facing the enemy.

Griff and I followed Mike along the trench line, squeezing past sentries and trying to stay on the duckboards that lined the trench floor. Behind us our portly interpreter slid and splashed, blaspheming in tones that I feared must be audible to ISIS. To our right, the parapet rose in a black mass of sandbags and car tires against a velvet sky resplendent with stars. We turned left and descended a short flight of stairs into a dug out, a musty concrete bunker lit by a single fluorescent bulb suspended from its low ceiling. The commander was sitting on a plastic picnic chair against the far wall, sipping a glass of tea, a squat, barrel-chested man with a face whose deep lines bore testament to the Peshmerga's hard travails. He rose to his feet and beckoned us over, signaling to a soldier who stood by the door to bring us tea. We exchanged the customary greetings in Kurdish. Although all the Peshmerga officers spoke Arabic, they used it reluctantly.

'*Merhaba, choni?*' Hello, how are you?

We sipped our glasses of tea, sweet and piping hot, and discussed the upcoming operation.

'He says that his mortars will be ready to fire,' the interpreter said. 'And he is bringing up his one tank, in case you need it.'

Mike talked the commander through the link up plan with the Peshmerga guides, the soldiers who would lead the NSF to their attack position behind the front line. Then we thanked him, shook hands and filed out.

As we walked back to the OP, Mike's radio crackled.

'They're running late,' he grimaced, the nearest that I had seen him to looking less than cheerful. 'I just hope that we can get them moving before daylight.'

We emerged from the trench line to see an ancient T-55 clank past, belching clouds of exhaust smoke, guided along the track by a Peshmerga soldier holding a flashlight. Back on the OP, I peered through binoculars over the dark expanse of no man's land to Mosul beyond. Some trick of the atmosphere, probably caused by a conflux of warm and cold air, made the pinpricks of light glimmer and sparkle like stars giving the city an air of tranquility. *Well at least ISIS can keep the lights on*, I thought, *that's more than we could do back in 2005*. Rocco would have laughed at the irony: here was a city that had consumed us, taken from us so much, stamped us indelibly – and now we were trying to break back in.

'They're here,' Joe the team chief announced. With a large handlebar moustache and the mannerisms of a surfer, Joe was a steady hand, one of those people who never seems to get flustered no matter what the provocation. He had been on the patrol that had almost fallen victim to a vehicle-bomb, and I remembered his voice calm and level on the radio despite the general's refusal to relinquish control of the fires. He and Mike walked down the slope on the backside of the OP to find Ibrahim. I heard the low murmur of voices and looking to my right could just make out figures as the NSF traipsed past us and descended into the trench line, a long line of shadows bringing with them a feeling of anticipation. Although I wouldn't be climbing out of the trench with them, I felt a familiar flutter in the chest, a tightness at the back of the throat at the prospect of violent action.

'They're psyched,' Joe had told me a few days previously. 'They've all lost their homes because of ISIS – some of them much more.'

The first glimmers of dawn were lifting darkness from the horizon when we received the word that we had been waiting for.

'LD'ing now.' LD stood for the Line of Departure, the physical demarcation between preparation and the attack. For those crossing it, the LD marks also a psychological transition: the point when you stop wondering, take a deep breath and move out.

# Chapter 57

On my way back from the Turkish position, I stopped to watch the giant pall of black smoke billow into the air, accompanied by a crump that I felt as much as heard. *A vehicle-bomb.* The ground sloped upwards in front of me, obscuring the point of impact, but I knew that it must be close to Ibrahim's men. I started to run again, up the side of the OP towards the row of machine guns now hammering away in a deafening crescendo. I was relieved to see that the column of smoke rose from a point a good 200 meters or so beyond the NSF fighters who were running like ants into the buildings on the far edge of the town.

Griff was peering through binoculars, spotting for the guns.

'Gun two, you need to come left about 100 meters. Got troops in the open, heading for the town from the west.' He was having to yell, relaying his commands through the assistant gunners who lay on their sides by the men firing the guns.

You have to fire a machine gun in six to eight round bursts or you run the risk of melting the barrel. When you have more than one gun firing, the preferred technique is to stagger the timing of each gun's burst so that you have a continuous stream of bullets going downrange. The gunners were doing that now, the assistant gunners and Griff hollering to each other to ensure that they weren't all massing on the same targets. As they spotted a group of Daesh fighters converging on the town, they'd swivel the gun and open fire. The first burst was usually low, kicking up spouts of dirt in front of the running figures; the next was usually on target, knocking men off their feet, and sending the survivors diving for cover.

I didn't need binoculars to see the enemy. There were large groups of them, perhaps twenty to thirty fighters apiece, moving on the town from different directions. Several vehicles crawled towards us across the rolling terrain.

'Sir, need you to talk to the TEA,' yelled the JTAC, proffering his hand set.

'Andy, what's going on there? We aren't picking up good feed from ISR, and I can't get anyone there to paint me a picture.'

'Sir, we've got multiple Daesh, on foot and mounted, moving on the town.'

'Can you pull back?'

'No sir, we can't. Our tribal guys are still in the town.' *And even if we could pull back, why would we do so? This is our chance to catch the enemy in the open.*

'OK, well we've lost situational awareness, so I am going to push control to your JTACs. Think that they can handle it?'

'Yes sir.' *You bet.*

In minutes the JTACs had several planes overhead and were directing them onto the targets in front of us. It wasn't an easy task – the forward Daesh fighters were close enough to the NSF to make fratricide a real risk, and there was so much shooting going on that it was hard to mark targets using our machine guns. The JTACs were having to talk the aircraft onto the targets, a tricky procedure at the best of times, now made more difficult by the smoke and chaos in front of us.

'Hey Boss,' Joe called to Mike. 'We're getting low on ammo.'

The four of us conferred, yelling through cupped hands to be heard above the guns.

'We need to pull them back, while we can,' I said. The others nodded.

'We've got air stacked, so that shouldn't be a problem.'

'They've done what we wanted anyway – poked the nest.'

There was an almighty explosion, the shock waves pummeled my ears and a huge plume of black smoke rose into the air, amidst cheers from across the OP. Another direct strike on a car bomb – and this one was close, probably their party piece.

The interpreter got on the radio to tell Ibrahim to pull his men back.

The machine guns slowed their rate of fire to desultory bursts and then, at Mike's order, ceased altogether. There was nothing left to shoot at: the menacing figures had disappeared, and the few vehicles still visible were flaming wrecks. Ibrahim reported that a handful of Daesh fighters had reached the edge of the town only to be gunned down by the NSF. The lull might mean that the enemy had given up, or that he was preparing for another onslaught.

Griff and I helped carry ammo cans from the vehicles up to the OP, the last of the team's supply. The physical activity provided welcome relief from tension as Ibrahim rallied the NSF for their withdrawal.

'They're ready,' the interpreter shouted.

The gunners slammed feed-tray lids shut and peered over their sights. The JTACs were talking to a fresh set of pilots awaiting in the overhead, describing who was where in terms that could be understood by someone flying at supersonic speed 15,000ft above our heads.

'OK, tell him to go.'

We watched, breathless, as the NSF returned in clusters of three and four, crossing the open ground crouched almost double in a flat sprint. Then, at last, Pipe Hitter himself walked back, upright and nonchalant, flashing us a thumbs-up as he reached the berm.

'Looks as though Daesh shot his bolt for the day,' Griff said.

'Well, he lost a lot of dudes.'

He certainly had. The destruction was satisfying, but, we knew, meant little by itself, as long as the Islamic State had the means to replenish its losses. It was the enemy's reaction to the attack that pleased us. The buzz of communication between ISIS field commanders during and after the raid indicated that it had shaken them up for all the reasons that we intended. And in the following days, we amplified that message to the population of Mosul:

'These are your people. And Daesh is powerless to prevent these attacks.'

Walking with Griff down from the OP to our vehicles, I felt confident enough to paraphrase Winston Churchill:

'This isn't yet the end. It isn't even the beginning of the end. But it is the end of the beginning.'

Division headquarters may have agreed. That evening it released for wide dissemination a *PowerPoint* slide with photographs and a brief description of the raid. The storyboard was emblazoned with the division's insignia.

Aside from ISIS, the only person who appeared unhappy with the day's events was the TEA. A day or two later I ran into him at Erbil airport.

'Andy, let's talk about the other day,' he said, putting his arm around my shoulders in a typically condescending gesture. 'Your JTACs need some work. When I passed control to them they were taking forever to put together simple talk-ons. My team could have done it in much less time – might have saved you some problems.'

I could have explained that his team would never have the same awareness of the battlefield's geometry, the rapidly shifting positions of the enemy and our own people. And I might have added that things seem much simpler when you are sitting in a hermetically sealed room miles from the action. But I sensed that such explanation would have been futile.

# Chapter 58

The best time to launch a ground attack is usually around dawn. The innate human fear of darkness tends to instill alertness among soldiers standing watch at night, whereas dawn brings with it a sense that the worst is over; after hours of vigilance, the expectation of relief and thoughts of breakfast and bed. And in the crepuscular light that precedes sunrise, it is difficult to distinguish shapes, especially for eyes tired from staring into darkness.

Knowing this, the special operations units serving in Northern Iraq trained their Peshmerga partners to adopt a custom known in Western armies as Stand-To. During this time, which normally ran from an hour before dawn until an hour afterwards, every available soldier would man his battle station in full gear, weapon ready, staring into no man's land.

But the Peshmerga didn't have enough troops to man the entire length of the front in strength, and this rendered them vulnerable to penetration at a single point, a favored ISIS tactic.

Islamic State field commanders would identify those areas of the Peshmerga line that appeared most vulnerable and designate them as breach points. That's the smart thing to do when attacking a fortified position. You don't want to dissipate your energies in a widespread attack – images of the First World War come to mind with long lines of infantrymen plodding forward against the enemy front line. Instead you figure out where the enemy is weakest, this might be at the seam between two units, or where terrain affords the attacker covered movement, and you concentrate your force at those points. This principle hasn't changed since medieval times when a besieging force would use battering rams against the weakest part of a castle's defenses; but it's one that requires careful analysis, training and imagination to make work. And luck, you always need luck.

Instead of battering rams, ISIS used vehicles packed with explosives, so heavily armored that anti-tank projectiles routinely bounced off them like BB pellets off a charging rhino. It was a simple weapon, absurdly so by the standards of twenty-first-century warfare, but a devastating one all the same. The drivers of these vehicles were, by definition, expendable: jihad fodder – indoctrinated but otherwise untrained. It took skillful direction to ensure that they detonated in the right place at the right time, and that the exploitation force, the assault troops, were ready to pour through the gap.

Previous ISIS attacks had followed a predictable pattern, breaching a weak spot in Peshmerga lines to seize a redoubt, then inflicting casualties and chaos before being beaten back. But the attack on May 4 was intended to shatter the impasse in Northern Iraq by punching a hole in the line large enough to allow thousands of fighters to stream through and capture Erbil, the capital of the region that the Kurds called their own.

That morning, a unit of SEALs were on their way to Tal Askuf, a small town north-west of Mosul, 2 miles behind the line. It was a routine patrol; the team intended to link up with the commander of their partnered Peshmerga brigade to discuss upcoming operations. As they entered the town, an RPG slammed into the lead vehicle, tearing off the driver's door and crumpling the hood. The vehicle's occupants, four SEALs, bailed out and sprinted for a ditch by the side of the road as a second RPG tore past.

In the early hours of the morning, ISIS had breached the line and poured into Tak Askuf with over 100 fighters and some 20 armored vehicles. They now controlled the town, turning the road down which the SEALs had arrived into a kill zone.

Joe, the chief who had accompanied us on the NSF raid was the senior man.

'That road was like a bowling alley,' he told me later. 'There was no way we were getting out the way we came in.'

He ordered the team to make for the nearest house, dashing in buddy-pairs across the open terrain, while the others fired at the Islamic State fighters clearly visible just over 100 yards away. 'I figured that the only thing to do was to strongpoint that building and call for help. Our JTAC Trey called for air before we started moving, and we had F-15s overhead by the time we reached the house. I called the MSOC to get them to launch the QRF.' The Marine Special Operations Company based in Erbil was the team's next higher headquarters.

For once the TEA didn't quibble, and pushed inbound aircraft to Trey who directed them onto ISIS positions. Meanwhile the team took up firing positions around the house while Joe raised the QRF on the radio to guide them to their location.

They were in a precarious position. Daesh fighters occupied buildings on three sides, and were pouring fire into theirs. In such situations, it is difficult to use close air support without risking your own people. The QRF arrived and were quickly assimilated into the defense. One of their number, a 31-year-old SEAL named Charles Keating joined Trey and Joe on the roof.

'The Pesh were trying to regroup but they'd taken a pasting,' Joe continued. 'At one point, this one Pesh dude runs around the corner of our building straight at the Daesh positions, shooting from the hip and yelling. They drilled him in seconds, poor bastard.'

Trey was trying to direct aircraft onto an adjacent rooftop from which Islamic State fighters were firing at them.

'Those cats could shoot. I was willing to risk dropping danger close to take them out, but we were having problems getting control.'

Then Keating was hit. Trey felt for the wound which appeared to be in the gap between the ball of his shoulder and his chest, and staunched the bleeding using a field dressing. In the meantime, Joe called the JOC in Erbil to have them launch the two casualty evacuation helicopters standing ready on the airstrip for this purpose.

Meanwhile, US aircraft had shown up in force: drones, A-10s, even a B-52, and were pummeling ISIS positions in the town but were unable to hit the buildings closest to the team for fear of fratricide. Trey carried Keating downstairs, no easy feat since Keating was well built and over 6ft tall. Adrenalin can tap extraordinary reserves of strength.

Two members of the team ran to the nearest flat area outside the building, ready to signal the inbound helicopters, but in the confusion that attends all combat, the helicopters approached the landing zone on a course that brought them directly over ISIS positions. When you're riding in a helicopter it's usually hard to tell above the noise of the engines when someone is shooting at you; but for those aboard the CASEVAC birds there was no missing the flurry of incoming rounds. When they checked the helicopters after their return the maintenance crew counted over 100 bullet holes in each.

Keating's comrades carried him to the helicopter, handing him over to the medics on board, and within seconds it was airborne, flying low and fast towards Erbil. Sitting helpless in the CJSOTF JOC, I heard the next transmission clearly.

'We have a fallen angel.' Chuck Keating was dead.

The incident received close scrutiny from division, and I had to answer a myriad questions about why the Trident was there, why they didn't withdraw at first contact and so on. A subsequent investigation found no one at fault.

Both Chuck Keating and Trey were later awarded the Navy Cross, and we named the CJSOTF compound in Baghdad Camp Keating.

In mid-May, Lieutenant Colonel Craig Wolfenbarger arrived with the headquarters from 2nd Marine Raider Battalion, giving me the SOTF that I needed to command the fight up north.

'We've got the band back together,' he announced happily when I met him at the airport.

Wolf, as he was known, had been my operations officer in the regiment before taking over 2nd MRB, and was just the type of commander that I needed for the increasingly complex fight around Mosul. Since early January, when I had submitted my request for forces, he had been preparing his team for Emerald Bounty, and arrived with a plan ready to go.

MARSOC places great emphasis on integrating intelligence and operations at the lowest level. The military has, of course, an acronym for this process: F3EAD, which stands for Find, Fix, Finish, Exploit, Analyze, and Disseminate. The fix step involves limiting the enemy's ability to maneuver. This means restricting his movement by the use of fires or by surrounding him with friendly forces; or by non-physical means such as removing his ability to communicate or see.

Finish means removing the enemy as a threat by killing or capturing him. Despite its title, finish is not an end in itself. Every contact with the enemy brings with it opportunities for fresh intelligence through interrogation or the capture of material – this is the exploit phase that keeps the cycle moving.

By virtue of its makeup – highly trained personnel, and state of the art equipment – a Marine special operations team can conduct F3EAD by itself. The MSOT has a greater capacity to collect and analyze intelligence than I had as an infantry battalion commander. Partnered with indigenous soldiers, it can fix and finish the enemy using an impressive array of organic weapons plus support from external assets, planes and artillery, controlled by its JTACs.

This capability is amplified by the MSOT's peculiar demographic. Those Marines who are not operators – the intelligence specialists, the JTACs, the EOD technicians and the dog handlers – play such an integral role within the team that there is no room for tribal separation. It helps, of course, that every member of the team is a Marine, with the exception of the corpsmen who hold a treasured status in any Marine unit. It helps too that emotional maturity is considered an essential trait in the selection of Marine Special Operators. They recognize, for instance, when intelligence collection is the main effort, and will do everything that they can to support the collector.

That capability grows exponentially at every level: from MSOT to MSOC to the SOTF headquarters, which has at its disposal a wide range of options for finishing the enemy. That is why I had requested a Marine Raider Battalion as my second SOTF. Wolf and his team soon vindicated my stubborn insistence to get them to Iraq: in less than two weeks SOTF-North had divined the Islamic State's order of battle, and was wreaking havoc.

I would have them for only a month before it was time for the CJSOTF to return home, but that didn't matter. The next CJSOTF after ours would reap the benefits of their work, and that's really what it was about. One problem with the unit rotation system in Afghanistan and Iraq was that it led to a tendency among unit commanders to fight the war in six-month or one-year increments, rather than as a long-term campaign. If we were going to prove the worth of the Maritime CJSOTF, as the MARSOC/ SEAL task force had been dubbed, it wouldn't be during our deployment, but over the course of several rotations culminating in the fall of Mosul. Every one of MARSOC's operational battalions was now committed to the counter-ISIS fight: 2nd MSOB would be followed in rotation by its two sister battalions, until they were no longer needed.

In May, the Marine and Canadian task forces enabled the Kurds to launch their largest offensive yet in the war. Several brigades of Peshmerga surged over the berm across a 30-mile front, seizing hundreds of square miles of terrain and allowing the Iraqi security forces to push to the very edge of Mosul. Although hugely successful, the operation was not without pitfalls. A British SAS team was very nearly cut off by an Islamic State counter-attack using multiple suicide car-bombs, and it was only the quick reaction of the Canadian task force that enabled them to escape. Although rocked on their heels, the Islamic State commanders demonstrated again their ability to strike back: nearly all our OPs were pounded by rockets and mortars, and we suffered casualties, though none fatal.

Our tour came to an end in late June, and I turned over to my SEAL successor, Captain Keith Davids. Keith combined razor-sharp intellect with a keen sense of humor, and I knew that the SOF campaign in Iraq would be in good hands. His team subsequently enabled the Iraqi Security Forces to attack Mosul, and the city fell a few weeks after his departure.

As much as you may look forward to the end of a deployment, it's always a strange feeling to turn over responsibility to someone else. Command is all-consuming. Combat command especially so. I found leading the CJSOTF to be the most challenging, sometimes painful, experience of my career – but also the most rewarding. It was the one deployment that I returned from believing that we had accomplished something of lasting good.

My performance report covering the deployment comments that the CJSOTF had a 'devastating effect on the enemy'. Such reports are notoriously inflated, and no one takes their wording seriously; but I like to think that this one phrase was not hyperbole, though credit goes not to me, but to every member of the CJSOTF. By the time we turned over, the area of Iraq under control of the Islamic State had shrunk to less than half its size at the beginning of our deployment; and the Iraqi Security Forces had started to push towards the outskirts of Mosul. It was a combined effort; but the unique capabilities of SOF enabled the CJSOTF to make a contribution out of proportion to its size.

The campaign against ISIS brought to war fighting a new dimension: the use of the internet as a medium for psychological operations, intelligence collection and for recruiting surrogate forces from among the population in enemy territory. And for Western soldiers accustomed to enjoying air superiority a startling development: the threat of attack by drones.

After turning over to Keith, and with two days before my flight home, it seemed strange to be kicking around camp with nothing to do. My sister Susan had sent me packages of toys from the UK to hand out to children in Iraq, and now seemed a good time to do so. Through contacts in Erbil, I learned of an orphanage for children whose parents had been killed by ISIS. Most of them were Yazidis, an ethno-religious group indigenous to Northern Iraq, whom ISIS had made a determined effort to annihilate, killing thousands, and taking the women captive as sex slaves. After coordinating with the orphanage staff to make sure that what I planned to do was appropriate, I showed up in civilian clothes with my bag of toys. The kids were hesitant at first, but then rushed forward excitedly when they saw what I was handing out. I took photos to send to my sister, and we both treasure one in particular. In it a little boy walks away from the mob of children clutching a handful of toys, his face a picture of delight.

# Chapter 59

It was in the departure lounge of the Istanbul airport, that I realized with a pleasurable shock that I had no more responsibilities. My part of the fight against the Islamic State was over. There would be no more urgent requests for decisions or explanations. There was no chance I would be called to the JOC to handle a Troops-In-Contact – just a short flight to Adana and a comfortable hotel. I sat alone at a cafeteria table, clutching a cold bottle of Turkish Efes beer, happily anonymous amidst the polyglot murmur of bustling passengers and clatter of flight announcements.

On the second call for my flight, I shouldered my backpack, and threaded my way through the crowd towards the departure gate. As I approached, I could see a line of passengers waiting to board, among them three men whose appearance stopped me in my tracks.

Two, with thin angular faces framed by shoulder-length hair and wispy unkempt beards, were obviously of Middle Eastern origin. The third, was an anomaly: short, heavy set with ginger hair, wire framed glasses and a close-cropped chin-strap beard. There was no mistaking who they were or why they were heading to Adana, still a well-used crossing point for Islamic State recruits.

My contentment evaporated. My war might be over but the war itself was not. And here in front of me, against the incongruous backdrop of smiling flight attendants and billboard advertisements, was the reason.

Ginger-hair glanced in my direction, holding my stare for a moment before turning away with an insouciance that I found more unsettling than any expression of hatred.

I paused for a moment, and then stepped into line behind them. Together we filed onto the plane.

# Chapter 60

Upon my return from Iraq, the family and I spent a week at the beach on Camp Lejeune where, I'm afraid, I must have been poor company, spending much of the time asleep. Later that summer we moved down to Tampa where I joined Special Operations Command Central (SOCCENT), as the Chief of Staff. The next two years were overall a happy time, I enjoyed the mission and the chance to spend more time with my family than ever before.

While at SOCCENT, I've had a ringside view of US involvement across the Middle East, and one of the most intriguing aspects of the job has been the opportunity to visit SOF contingents in their far-flung outposts at the ragged edge of US foreign policy.

In the south-east corner of Syria, just a few miles from the borders with Iraq and Jordan, stands Al Tanf Garrison, an isolated US outpost surrounded by desert and little else. That description may conjure up in the reader's eye romantic images of a Beau Geste-style fort amidst a landscape of rolling sand dunes – but nothing could be further from the truth. The desert that extends from Anbar province in Iraq through central Syria is just hard packed sand strewn with rocks as far as the eye can see. And the garrison itself is as ugly as the war that spawned it: a collection of ramshackle wooden structures, metal shipping containers, sandbags, mortar tubes and concertina wire. It is, in the words of its inhabitants, a complete shit-hole.

Shit-hole it may be, but it is one with strategic importance, lying as it does near the border with both Iraq and Jordan, on the old Baghdad to Damascus highway, and athwart the territorial aspirations of all players in the Syrian conflict. The presence of a handful of US personnel in this desolate place has enabled the United States to establish a 30-mile exclusion zone around the garrison, thus barring access to all others. This line in the sand is a beautiful illustration of the American way of war: the troops are there not to defend the area (they couldn't hope to do so), but to provide a raison d'etre for the area's defense. Their presence has no tactical value; neither their patrols nor their engagements with local tribal fighters have achieved anything of great military significance. However, the fact that the Stars and Stripes flies over Al Tanf Garrison gives the US carte blanche for the use of force in its defense. Over the course of the last year the Syrian regime, and their proxies, Shia militia and Russian mercenaries, have tested US resolve by crossing designated boundaries, incurring hundreds of casualties from American planes and artillery as a result.

Which is why, as I write, the garrison is still there, and why recently I found myself on my way to visit it, bumping in a convoy of armored dune buggies across the desolate plain. Al Tanf is manned by part of an Army Special Forces Company, and a handful of support units. I had known some of them from my tour as CJSOTF commander, but even if I hadn't, would have felt at home from the time that I linked up with them on the Jordanian border. The team that picked me up could have been one of my own: the same upbeat personalities striking an easy balance between laconic humor and understated competence. And the same philosophic acceptance of their fate:

'We're a speed bump,' the team leader acknowledged. 'The regime could take Al Tanf tomorrow if they really wanted to. The question is whether they would be willing to pay the price.'

We pulled to a stop in a billowing cloud of dust, the four vehicles in a fan formation, gunners swinging their muzzles outboard. Ahead lay the Syrian border, just a waist-high berm for as far as the eye could see on either side, broken only by a single gap directly ahead of us, little wider than our vehicles. A soldier climbed out of one of the vehicles, and walked towards the gap holding a metal detector. I peered from side to side, expecting to see more soldiers disembark to provide security for the EOD tech, since this is what Marines invariably do in these situations, but everyone else stayed put. The team leader, sitting beside me behind the wheel, noticed my glance.

'No sense risking anyone else. That's why those EOD dudes get the extra pay,' he grinned. But his eyes never left the lone figure approaching the gap in the berm. He was right, of course. The Marines' cultural adherence to the buddy system sometimes transcends tactical sense.

The Islamic State had attacked the garrison repeatedly, including a cleverly planned assault from multiple sides that was repulsed only after a desperate melee inside the wire a few months previously. That evening, one of the soldiers who'd been there talked us through what had happened.

'First we knew of it was a series of explosions at the wire.'

Four of us were perched on the platform of a wooden guard post, from which we had a clear view of the cluster of tin-roofed buildings below us, the barbwire perimeter fence, and the bleak landscape beyond.

'They came right down that draw,' he gestured at a dry wadi that led into the camp. 'Must have scoped out the area beforehand. We only had two teams here at the time, so weren't doubled up on the guard towers, and they got inside the wire without anyone seeing them. Fortunately, at least one of them detonated early, and that got us up in a hurry. It was total confusion – everyone hollering, running for their posts. I came here, just me and one of our Syrian dudes, tried to get radio comms with the team, but couldn't raise shit on the net. We could hear them though – yelling to each other, they were that close.' He paused and gestured towards the front gate. 'That's when they hit us with the three VBIEDs. The first breached the gate when it went off, and the next two ploughed right inside the perimeter, heading for where we are standing now. They must have known that this was our TOC. That's when our own Audie Murphy stepped in to save the day'. A single Syrian tribal fighter, manning a heavy machine gun, had the courage and presence of mind to engage and detonate both car bombs before they reached their destination.

'Then our guys started to come up on the net – but it was hard to make out what was going on. Every time anyone keyed the mike all you could hear was gunfire. We were burning through ammo at the cyclic rate, breaking out more, but barely keeping up.

'Time passed – hard to tell how long, you know how it is during these things, but we gradually got a better picture of what was going on, and the news wasn't good. We'd killed the ones inside the compound, but there were more of them trying to get in, we could see them rushing into dead space just beyond the wire. We were spread thin because most of our militia dudes were on leave. They couldn't have timed it better.'

'What about air?' I asked.

'Well, headquarters was routing aircraft our way – but that takes time of course.

'Meanwhile, they managed to get back inside the wire again – couldn't tell how many but enough to set up a base of fire over there by the water tank, while another element started making their way building by building towards the TOC.

'By the time we had air on station everything was danger close. We had them drop that building there,' he pointed to a pile of concrete rubble, a football field away from where we were standing. 'That, and repeated strikes at their forming up points, seemed to do it.'

Gradually, the fracas ended as the ISIS fighters withdrew, leaving behind a carpet of corpses strewn like broken dolls around the perimeter.

That attack, well planned and coordinated though it was, appears to have been the last-ditch effort by the Islamic State in south-eastern Syria. Thereafter the organization focused on defending its last bastion, in the Middle Euphrates Valley dozens of miles to the north.

But the garrison's real significance now no longer has anything to do with ISIS. Its mere presence in this remote corner of Syria enables the US to block further movement by the regime (and their Russian and Iranian backers) towards the Jordanian and Iraqi borders. And so Americans continue to occupy Al Tanf.

'We are here because we are here,' one soldier commented to me, unconsciously echoing the words sung by First World War British soldiers to the tune of *Auld Lang Syne*. 'Any clue as to when we're gonna be done?' another asked me. But he was smiling because no one here wastes much time speculating about policy decisions.

The defenders of Al Tanf are well aware of their role as pawns in this great game, and also aware that their mission is not likely to result in any tangible outcome, that eventually, they will be withdrawn, returning the area to regime control. But this realization has not diminished their buoyant morale, or the determination with which they continue to tackle their thankless mission.

As I write, the President has just announced the withdrawal of US forces from Syria. One thing I know without having to check: the defenders of Al Tanf will execute this task with the same indomitable spirit.

A few days ago, US special operations forces, with help from Syrian Kurds, killed Abu Bakr al Baghdadi, head of the Islamic State. I'm pleased, of course, that his life has come to an end, but know that his passing marks merely the end of one chapter in the organization's existence: the physical manifestation of the Levant-based caliphate. Baghdadi is, of course, eminently replaceable, as will be his successor and the one after that. It's the message that continues, the ethos that is already enabling ISIS to reappear in other parts of the world: from Zamboanga in the Philippines, to the Congo to Libya and soon again, I fear, to parts of Europe. It's the same message that I saw in the unblinking gaze of the two insurgents in a room in Fallujah, and the eyes of the ginger-haired recruit in the departure lounge at Adana.

The Islamic State, or at least its manifestation as a physical caliphate, is near defeat, leaving in its place an absurdly complex spangle of warring factions that continue to make the region as unstable as ever.

The war in Syria and Iraq has been one primarily fought by special operations forces, whose partners: the Syrian Democratic Front (SDF), the

Peshmerga and the Iraqi Special Forces (ISF), were the principal architects of the Islamic State's defeat.

Back in 2014 when ISIS held a swath of Syria and Iraq the size of the United Kingdom, it was the Kurds –the SDF in Syria and the Peshmerga in Iraq – who offered the US administration its only realistic hope to stem the tide.

Now, in Northern Syria, the SDF is fighting for its life after a precipitous US military withdrawal left them vulnerable to a Turkish offensive aimed at creating a Kurd-free zone in the border region.

All partnerships have to come to an end sometime, but there was good reason for the US to end this particular one in a more deliberate manner. Despite lacking a coherent policy in Syria to guide it, the small US military presence there served a useful purpose — maintaining a fragile stability, while keeping the territorial ambitions of the various factions in check. It was a near perfect example of what special operations forces can achieve in a volatile and politically sensitive environment.

Perhaps most valuably, theirs was a grudgingly accepted presence that could be bargained away *for the right concessions from Turkey, Russia, and Syria.* In so doing we could have ended our partnership with the SDF in a manner that didn't throw them in the path of the Turkish Army. It's not naïve to expect our great nation to act with that kind of enlightened self-interest. Instead, the hasty US departure from a shaky but relatively calm status quo has squandered the gains made by troops on the ground and is likely to lead to greater volatility in the region. That should trouble even the most ardent proponents of isolationism. And, in an age of hybrid warfare, it is likely that US reliance on proxy forces will become more common. Turning our backs abruptly on the SDF sends a strong message about our reliability as a partner.

Assad remains in power – perhaps more firmly ensconced than he was at the outset of the war – beholden now to Iran, Russian, and Lebanese Hezbollah who enabled him to turn the tide against the opposition. Iranian proxies: the Shia militia in Iraq, and Hezbollah in Syria, have established a land bridge from Iran to Lebanon – and the borders of Israel. It would be hard to imagine a more volatile outcome. And one not helped by a US policy that is sometimes as hard to discern as proclamations from the Delphi Oracle.

In Iraq, the Peshmerga and Iraqi Army are involved in a tense stand-off over the autonomous region of Kurdistan. The Kurds believe that they purchased with their blood the right to call this land their own after the Iraqi Army fled Mosul. For their part, the government of Iraq will likely never agree to give up a region that contains under its fertile soil massive oil reserves. And beneath this territorial dispute courses a blood enmity as old as the country of Mesopotamia itself.

Elsewhere in that troubled land, chaotic events continue to unfold, as an Iraqi friend of mine commented sadly to me the other day by e mail:

> It has been more than 40 days and Iraqis continue demonstrating against their corrupt government. More than 300 of them have been killed, and 15,000 injured. The main power supporting the government is a political block led by Hadi Al-Amiri, the leader of the Badr organization and one of Iran's main allies. Everyone is asking what is the American stand on this? Is the US just going to watch this?

So many unintended consequences were unleashed that day when our armored columns sped across the border at Safwan opposed only by the forlorn barking of a stray dog. Hundreds of thousands of lives later it does appear, as my friend indicates, that Iran has been the only real winner. And as his plaintiff question illustrates, the US will never be able to meet the expectations of the few friends it has left in that country.

Yemen has become the scene for a proxy war between Saudi Arabia and Iran, with US SOF playing a delicately parsed role in the melee, focusing their efforts originally on the Al Qaeda threat, and now on the flow of Iranian sponsored lethal aid and expertise that is enabling the Houthis to drop ballistic missiles increasingly close to Riyadh. In the process, we have found ourselves allied with the Saudis – an ironic outcome in light of that country's murky involvement with Wahabi extremists from the architects of 9/11 to ISIS. 'We invaded Iraq because we couldn't bring ourselves to go against Saudi Arabia,' Rocco had commented during our last meeting.

Meanwhile, the seventeen-year war in Afghanistan shows little sign of abating; and US forces are surging to prepare for yet another Taliban spring offensive. Many of the soldiers involved would have been in diapers when the US involvement in Afghanistan began.

Despite this bleak outlook, morale in the two communities with which I am familiar – the US Marines and Special Operations – appears to be as high as ever. That is not to suggest for a moment that its members lack the sophistication to understand the significance of world events. Far from it.

It's simply that they realize that they have joined a profession that commits them to being instruments, but not architects, of national policy. That is the lot that they have chosen. 'Theirs is not to reason why; theirs is but to do and die', in the words of Victorian poet, Lord Alfred Tennyson. Today's volunteers would express this sentiment in much more prosaic and probably profane terms – but with the same intent.

# Epilogue

Long after my return from the Iraq deployment I continued to grapple with inner turmoil. Until, realizing at last that things weren't going to get better, I sought help in counseling – one of the best decisions that I have ever made. Only then did I realize what a strain it had been trying to tamp down the chaos inside, while pretending that nothing was wrong.

In writing this book, this aspect of my life presented me with a dilemma. How do you recount personal experiences of the emotional trauma that combat leaves in its wake without sounding self-piteous, self-indulgent or just dreadfully clichéd?

Whatever we may say otherwise, Marines find it hard to admit that for most, combat leaves an indelible stamp on the psyche. In a culture that by necessity values emotional toughness, how can visible cracks in the façade be seen as anything other than weakness? You show compassion for those who display them, but you don't want to see them in your leadership, and you definitely don't want to discover them in yourselves.

For this reason, the first two drafts of this book mentioned nothing of my sometimes erratic post-deployment behavior. In the end, a friend and fellow Marine reminded me that if you are going to write about yourself, you have to be completely honest. I am glad that he did, though doing so was not easy.

Combat was relatively easy to recover from compared to the loss of Kaela. As any parent who has suffered the loss of a child will tell you, you never get over it – nor would you want to. But by focusing on the family you have left, you find that you are able to tread water, and the waves that were swamping you gradually diminish in frequency and ferocity.

Kaela's legacy of helping others continues. Xavier University has established the Kaela Allton Wellness Leadership Award, which it gives each year to a student who, in the words of the university, 'embodies the qualities that Kaela exemplified.'

Jessica left the army when Marcus and Sophia were still small, and in the years since, like all service wives, has been somewhat of a hostage to my career. She has just begun to work again, as an occupational therapist for Hillsborough County schools here in Tampa, and it has given her a new lease on life.

In early September 2018, I traveled to Parris Island to see Kaela's younger brother Tyler graduate from Boot Camp. At the conclusion of the graduation parade, I watched with a feeling of vicarious pride as his mother Nancy, and grandmother Janine – both of whom had shown such courage after Kaela's death – rushed across the parade deck to congratulate their new Marine. It was a scene that I had seen countless times, and it never failed to lift my spirits: the beaming Marines, mobbed by loved ones, taking pride in their new-found identity as part of something greater than themselves.

This time though, I was surprised to feel a tinge of sadness that I couldn't simply dismiss as regret that my own time in the Corps was coming to an end. I had last visited Parris Island for my nephew's graduation in the company of Kaela, and my mood was probably partially attributable to memories of her, now embodied in a sense of responsibility for her younger brother. But I was also troubled by a darker concern: that all the pride and optimism and sense of purpose on display that day was so easily squandered by the careless ministrations of those in power. Since 9/11, so many young men and women who had drawn their first breath as Marines on this same parade deck, had drawn their last in places with no significance, and for a cause without rationale. Places whose names don't even register recognition among the vast majority of their countrymen.

These, of course, are personal observations likely to be challenged by the argument, which I do not dispute, that the average American holds the military in high regard and supports the man or woman in uniform. But there is a difference between the superficial trappings of this kind of support, the well-intended but glib *thank you for your service,* and the deeper sense of responsibility to ensure that their blood is shed for a coherent cause.

Perhaps some would tell me that I am being maudlin, that no one forced me or anyone of the youngsters in front of the reviewing stand to join the military, and that having made that choice we had no right to expect more.

'In modern war there is nothing sweet or fitting in your dying,' Ernest Hemingway commented in his essay *Notes on the Next War*, 'You will die like a dog for no reason.' His solution is an interesting one, though no longer practical in this day and age: 'No one man nor group of men incapable of fighting or exempt from fighting should in any way be given the power, no matter how gradually it is given them, to put this country or any country into war.'

I don't share Hemingway's cynicism, nor do I agree with his proposed solution; but do hope to see a more rigorous (and thus healthy) debate about the purpose of future wars.

These thoughts were enough on that day to cloud what should have been a happy occasion – and a reminder that it was time to move on.

And just over a month later, I did. When you retire people tell you that need to have a ceremony for the sake of your family; and they are absolutely correct. But it was also an opportunity to catch up with old friends, and – I realize now – the right way to bring to an end thirty-one years in uniform. And just as anyone at the bar in the local VFW will tell you, it has flown by. It does seem like just yesterday when I arrived in Parris Island wondering what I had gotten myself into.

Another cliché that turns out to be true, is that the Marine Corps is a family. Over the years, most career Marines experience the full gamut of emotions about the Corps, as with any family, but seldom indifference. And in the end, as mawkish though it may sound, it's being in the company of like-minded people, brothers and sisters, that causes us to remain Marines. Despite the irritations of service life, the long hours and time away from loved ones – or maybe because of them – the Corps becomes home, and as such was tougher to leave than I expected. I already miss it.